ANTISEMITISM IN FILM COMEDY IN NAZI GERMANY

Valerie Weinstein

INDIANA UNIVERSITY PRESS

This book is a publication of

Indiana University Press
Office of Scholarly Publishing
Herman B Wells Library 350
1320 East 10th Street
Bloomington, Indiana 47405 USA

iupress.indiana.edu

© 2019 by Valerie Weinstein

All rights reserved

No part of this book may be reproduced or utilized in any form or by any means, electronic or mechanical, including photocopying and recording, or by any information storage and retrieval system, without permission in writing from the publisher. The paper used in this publication meets the minimum requirements of the American National Standard for Information Sciences—Permanence of Paper for Printed Library Materials, ANSI Z39.48-1992.

Manufactured in the United States of America

Cataloging information is available from the Library of Congress.
ISBN 978-0-253-04070-1 (hardback)
ISBN 978-0-253-04071-8 (paperback)
ISBN 978-0-253-04073-2 (ebook)

1 2 3 4 5   24 23 22 21 20 19

ANTISEMITISM IN FILM COMEDY IN NAZI GERMANY

CONTENTS

Acknowledgments vii

Note on Translation xi

Introduction: Reconceiving Antisemitism in Third Reich Film Comedy 1

1. Overt and Inferential Antisemitism in Nazi Writings and the Film Trade Press 36

2. Overt Antisemitism, Jewish Difference, and Colonial Whiteness in Early Third Reich Film Comedy: *Nur nicht weich werden, Susanne!* and *Die Blume von Hawaii* 61

3. Comic *Ersatz*: *Viktor und Viktoria* and *Glückskinder* 97

4. *Wenn wir alle Engel wären* as the Model of a Racialized German Humor 127

5. Capitalism, Colonialism, and the White Jew in *April! April!* and *Donogoo Tonka* 154

6. Mistaken Identity and the Masked Jew in *Robert und Bertram* 184

7. Jewish Absence, Epistemic Murk, and the Aesthetics of Cremation in *Münchhausen* and *Die Feuerzangenbowle* 213

Conclusion 247

Works Cited 255

Index 275

ACKNOWLEDGMENTS

IN MY FANTASY OF AUTHORSHIP, I SQUIRREL MYSELF away in a tower, write madly and uninterruptedly, and emerge from my solitude with a brilliant book in hand. Of course, it doesn't work that way. If I had insisted on going it alone, I would still be locked in that tower, struggling to complete my project. I couldn't have written *Antisemitism in Film Comedy in Nazi Germany* without a strong professional and personal support network, and I offer my heartfelt thanks to the institutions and individuals who helped me write this book.

The generosity of various entities at my home institution, the University of Cincinnati, made *Antisemitism in Film Comedy in Nazi Germany* possible. I am especially grateful for the substantial support this project has received from the Charles Phelps Taft Research Center. Multiple travel grants to visit archives and attend conferences and a Collections Purchase Grant for Langsam Library to acquire microfilm reels of Third Reich film periodicals put essential resources in my hands. A Taft Center Fellowship gave me a year to think and write and an interdisciplinary community of fellows with whom I could exchange ideas. By inviting Eric Rentschler to campus as my interlocutor for the Taft Symposium, the Taft Center enabled a valuable conversation with him about an early draft of my manuscript. I am so grateful for his careful reading of my early drafts, his generous feedback, and our productive discussions about the project, and I am grateful to the Taft Center for facilitating this conversation. A Faculty Research Grant from the University Research Council also supported my work in its early stages. The Department of German Studies helped me along the way with a semester-long teaching release. The Department of Women's, Gender, and Sexuality Studies provided me a graduate research assistant to help prepare the final manuscript for submission.

Many of the librarians and archivists I encountered while doing my research deserve special thanks: Olga Hart and Mark Konecny at Langsam Library; Birgit Scholz and Peter Warnecke at Potsdam Filmmuseum; Ute Klawitter at the Bundesarchiv-Filmarchiv, Berlin; Regina Hoffmann, Lisa Roth, and Anett Sawall at Stiftung Deutsche Kinemathek/Berlin Filmmuseum; Renate Göthe and Annika Kaiser in Pressedokumentation at the

Hochschule für Film und Fernsehen Konrad Wolf, Potsdam; Alice Schumacher of the Naturhistorisches Museum, Wien; and Bettina Erlenkamp at the Deutsche Fotothek, Dresden. William Gillespie, of the Gillespie Collection in Sydney, Australia, has been an important scholarly resource for me ever since he sold me my first two hundred VHS tapes of Third Reich films almost two decades ago. On many occasions, Bill has helped me find rare sources, shared useful information, and scanned images for me from his world-class collection of Third Reich film posters and publications. I value his generous and ongoing professional help and support.

I am rich in friends and colleagues whose feedback has enhanced this project. First and foremost, I want to thank my dear friends Ashley Currier and Furaha Norton, who probably have pored over every page of this manuscript more times than they care to count, who have pushed me from the beginning toward more clarity and sophistication in my thinking and writing, and who have served as devoted mentors and cheerleaders throughout the entire process. My frequent collaborator and close friend, Barbara Hales, has been a constant scholarly interlocutor and professional support for many years. Barbara has been infinitely generous with her time and insights. She and I have had countless inspiring conversations, and she has given me valuable feedback on so many iterations of this project—conference presentations, articles, drafts, and the complete manuscript. Most hearty thanks go to Deb Meem, for her keen eye, and for her selfless gift of time and last-minute help with copy editing the manuscript. I am very grateful to my writing group, which is a source of wisdom, motivation, friendship, and joy, and to everybody who has read and responded to drafts of various parts of my manuscript, including Leslie Adelson, David Bathrick, Gergana Ivanova, Horst Lange, Biddy Martin, Michelle McGowan, Carolette Norwood, Andrés Pérez-Simón, Mihaela Petrescu, John Pettey, Michal Raucher, Eric Rentschler, Sunnie Rucker-Chang, Jeffrey Timberlake, Evan Torner, Jim Walker, and Rina Williams. My anonymous peer reviewers at Indiana University Press were much more generous in both their praise and their substantive suggestions than I ever could have anticipated. Their thoughtful and constructive feedback has enhanced the final product.

Maura Grady at Ashland University, Brechtje Beuker and Sam Spinner at UCLA, and David Weinstein at Wake Forest University all invited me to share my work on this project with audiences at their institutions, who gave me valuable feedback. I have also benefited from conversations with colleagues at professional meetings, particularly the German Studies

Association, the German-Jewish Studies Workshop, and the German Film Institute; also the Ohio German Studies Workshop, the Kentucky Foreign Language Conference, and the Popular Culture Association. At the risk of—and with advance apologies for—forgetting important scholarly interlocutors, a human failing that seems inevitable to me, I'd like to thank the following colleagues for productive conversations about this project at various stages of its development: Ofer Ashkenazi, Nick Baer, Maya Barzilai, Darcy Buerkle, Margarethe Eirenschmalz, Veronika Fuechtner, Mila Ganeva, Sabine Hake, Sara Hall, Anjeana Hans, Laura Heins, Dagmar Herzog, Todd Herzog, Ingeborg Majer O'Sickey, Alexander Maxwell, Rick McCormick, Mihaela Petrescu, Christian Rogowski, Lisa Silverman, Brett Van Hoesen, Cynthia Walk, Kerry Wallach, and Tamara Zwick. Phone calls with Tracey Patton and Jonathan Skolnik when I hit crucial theoretical sticking points helped greatly in moving things along.

Janice Frisch at Indiana University Press has been supportive and professional from our first moment of contact on. I am especially grateful for her outstanding selection of peer reviewers, whose complementary approaches enriched this project and expanded its interdisciplinary reach. Thank you also to Maya Bringe, Dave Hulsey, Darja Malcolm-Clarke, Steven Moore, and Kate Schramm, who all helped transform my manuscript into the book you have in your hands. Maggie Kane researched rights and permissions, captured images, formatted footnotes, and otherwise helped me prepare the manuscript for publication. West Bancroft stepped in with some last minute logistical and research assistance. Thank you also to Elizabeth Keith, Kent Meloy, and Emmanuel Wilson for help with acquiring screen grabs.

Finally, none of this would have been possible without family members' love and patience and their financial, logistical, and emotional support. Bennett and Marina Kottler and Alex and Naomi Weinstein have my deepest love and gratitude.

NOTE ON TRANSLATION

All English translations of German sources are my own, unless otherwise noted in the endnotes by a citation from a published translation. For readily available sources, I have not included the German here. For quotations from less-accessible sources and in which the original language is particularly salient to my argument, I have included the German in the endnotes, before my citations.

ANTISEMITISM IN FILM COMEDY IN NAZI GERMANY

INTRODUCTION
Reconceiving Antisemitism in Third Reich Film Comedy

EVERY WINTER HOLIDAY SEASON, THOUSANDS OF GERMAN FANS gather for cult screenings of *Die Feuerzangenbowle* (The Flaming Punch, Helmut Weiss, 1943/1944), with props and audience participation reminiscent of screenings of *The Rocky Horror Picture Show* (Jim Sharman, 1975) in the United States.[1] Audience members sound alarm clocks during the breakfast scene, shine flashlights when the protagonist sits in his geology and chemistry classes, and sing along with beloved songs.[2] Other Germans watch this comedy at home as part of their holiday traditions. *Die Feuerzangenbowle* and its star Heinz Rühmann exemplify the conventions and comedians made popular in the 1930s and 1940s. Rühmann's cohort and their style of petty bourgeois situation comedy dominated German film comedy in the 1950s, '60s, and '70s and still command a significant following. Fans wax nostalgic about these old comedies and treat them as innocent, old-fashioned fun. Yet Germany's "classic" film comedies were produced under the leadership of the Nazis' Reichsministerium für Volksaufklärung und Propaganda (Reich Ministry for Enlightenment and Propaganda, henceforth "Propaganda Ministry"), represent the bulk of Third Reich film production, and reflect that era's values.

Comedies were the main product of German studios in the years immediately before Adolf Hitler became chancellor in 1933 and throughout the Third Reich. More than 60 percent of German films made in 1931 and 1932 were comedies and operettas, humorous light operas that were the forerunners of musical comedy.[3] Between 1933 and 1945, 523 of 1094 German feature films (48 percent) were humorous, and in every year of this period except 1945 (in which only 12 films premiered), German studios released more comedies than any other type of film.[4] In 1934, 1935, 1940, 1943, and 1944, between 50 percent (1935) and 62 percent (1943) of films produced were comedies.[5] Despite comedy's dominance in Third Reich film studios and on Third Reich screens and these films' lingering appeal in the postwar era, scholarship has emphasized Nazi Germany's politically, artistically, and thematically more serious films. At the same time, many Germans remain nostalgic about Third Reich film comedies, viewing them as part of the Nazi era that was not tainted with antisemitism. In *Antisemitism in Film Comedy in Nazi Germany*, I argue that this widespread perception is mistaken. Antisemitism left an indelible mark on Nazi-era film comedy.

Most people think of antisemitism in Nazi film as the overt propagation of hateful stereotypes. I, however, conceive of antisemitism as a subtle process of defining and excluding the Jewish. *Antisemitism in Film Comedy in Nazi Germany* reveals how humor, indirect coding, absences, and substitutes in Third Reich film comedy helped spectators imagine an abstract Jewishness and a German identity and community free from it. Film comedy's process of identifying and excising the Jewish was parallel and complementary to the mass murder of Jewish people in the Holocaust. In the twenty-first century, resurgent populist nationalism and overt racism on both sides of the Atlantic compel scholars to rethink racism and prejudice in popular culture. Understanding how antisemitism functions in Third Reich film comedy helps us reconceptualize the relationships between film humor, national identity, and race.

The fraught racial politics in the United States in the early twenty-first century, decades after the Civil Rights movement; the backlash in Europe against non-European migrants; and the escalation of overtly racist, antisemitic, and anti-immigrant political rhetoric indicate that challenging racism's most overt manifestations has not been enough to eliminate racism's institutional effects. Critical race studies show that racism comes in many forms, with invisible ideological and structural components that complement more virulent expressions.[6] Like racism, antisemitism is present not only where it is most visible. Although most people today no longer consider Jews to be a discrete race or antisemitism to be racism, Nazi antisemitism was a racial ideology. The Nazis labeled Jews a race and racialized them using scientific, legal, and political discourses, among others. I use the word "race" in this book as appropriate to the historical context and to put Nazi racial antisemitism in dialogue with other racisms. In order to theorize how racisms can infiltrate culture in invisible ways and the complicity of film comedy in that process, I turn to a historical moment in which racial antisemitism and its horrific effects are widely acknowledged and scrutinize cultural productions from which fans and scholars have assumed antisemitism to be absent.

My work complements the rich scholarly literature about the complexity and ambivalence of Third Reich popular cinema. Beginning in the 1990s, Eric Rentschler, Linda Schulte-Sasse, Sabine Hake, and others challenged previous distinctions between propaganda and entertainment films, which divided Nazi-era films into good and bad objects, with the former lauded as classics and the latter criticized for their politics.[7] By complicating this binary, these scholars paved the way for narrower, in-depth studies of specific aspects of Nazi entertainment film, such as female stardom and melodrama.[8] Karsten Witte's *Lachende Erben, Toller Tag: Filmkomödie im Dritten Reich* (Laughing Heirs, Crazy Day: Film Comedy in the Third Reich) was at the vanguard of such scholarship and remains the only monograph to date about Third Reich film comedy. *Lachende Erben* provides an indispensable historical overview and general conceptual framework for understanding these movies. Witte outlines a trajectory in which comedy gradually, unevenly, and covertly—but never thoroughly—conformed to Nazi ideals, masked harsh realities, and built "emotional consensus with party-line propaganda."[9] He examines how fascism appropriated Hollywood and Weimar films' structures and aesthetics, adapting them to its ideological imperatives, social norms, and audiences' desires. According to Witte, most comedies made in the Third Reich not only were escapist in a broad sense but also obfuscated real relations of production and power by hiding them under a comic veneer and distancing plots and settings from spectators' everyday lives. He also shows that despite censorship and increasing nationalization of the film industry, subtle nonconformity was possible due to ambivalences in meaning, a perceived need to respond to audience desires, and some official tolerance of cinema's function as a release valve. Coming from a tradition of leftist ideology critique, Witte's analyses emphasize the political economy of German fascism and, secondarily, gender and sexual politics. His engagement with Nazi antisemitism is minimal. *Lachende Erben* is not unique but rather exemplary in this regard. Overt antisemitism in Third Reich film comedy is scarce, and its absence creates the illusion that comedy had nothing to do with the era's racial politics. My book dispels this illusion, explaining how antisemitism influenced the themes and techniques of Third Reich film comedy, which, in turn, helped spectators envision a Germany free of Jewishness.

Nazi Germany made few overtly antisemitic movies before 1939, and limited filmic representations of Jews to the "role of the nouveau-riche Jew and similar cliché figures" in films set in and critical of the Weimar Republic (1918–33).[10] Between 1939 and 1942, the German film industry produced a wave of explicitly antisemitic propaganda films. The release of these films correlated with the beginning of World War II and the first massacres of Jewish people in Eastern Europe by German soldiers. Nazi officials screened *Jud Süss* (Jew Süss, Veit Harlan, 1940), a commercially successful historical melodrama, and the appalling pseudodocumentary *Der ewige Jude* (The Eternal Jew, Fritz Hippler, 1940) to precipitate and encourage genocidal actions.[11] Accordingly, scholarship on Nazi cinema and the Holocaust emphasizes those two notorious films. Of the other overtly antisemitic films made in the Third Reich, only three are comedies: *Nur nicht weich werden, Susanne!* (Don't Lose Heart, Susanne!, Arsen von Cserépy, 1934/35), *Robert und Bertram* (Robert and Bertram, Hans Zerlett, 1939), and, arguably, *Leinen aus Irland* (Linen from Ireland, Heinz Helbig, 1939). Although the latter is based loosely on a stage comedy, it mostly follows the conventions of a serious drama with a few humorous scenes and minor characters. Neither as vicious as *Der ewige Jude* nor funny, the antisemitic comedies were all critical and commercial failures. No evidence exists of them having been used to prepare soldiers to kill Jews. Therefore, neither scholars of the Holocaust nor researchers of Third Reich popular cinema have prioritized these films. What scholarship there is focuses primarily on *Robert und Bertram*; *Leinen aus Irland* occasionally enters the conversation, and *Nur nicht weich werden, Susanne!* is mentioned rarely.[12]

Restricting analysis of Nazi racial antisemitism to its most overt manifestations limits our understandings of both antisemitism and Third Reich film comedy, a situation that this book remedies. Ella Shohat has argued, regarding American cinema, that "ethnicity and race inhere in virtually all films, not only in those where ethnic issues appear on the 'epidermic' surface of the text . . . ethnicity is culturally ubiquitous and textually submerged."[13] The same can be said about feature films made in Nazi Germany. Antisemitism subtly shaped Third Reich film comedy, which, in turn, propagated fantasies of a Germany freed from the Jewish, fantasies that the Holocaust sought to bring to fruition. Under direct and indirect pressure from the Propaganda Ministry, film studios expelled Jewish filmmakers and excised characters and comic techniques understood as "Jewish." Substitute strategies, characters, and comedians took their places. These substitutes both were marked as "German" and discouraged further "Jewish" incursions. The excisions and substitutions made to film comedy in the Third Reich contributed to visions of a German *Volksgemeinschaft* (racial-national community) without Jews in it.

The Film Industry in the Third Reich and Its Domestic Audiences

When the Nazis took power in 1933, the German film industry was reeling from the Great Depression, which reduced both financing and ticket sales, and from the costs of converting studios, equipment, and theaters from silent film to sound film. The regime wanted to stabilize the industry economically and improve production quality and audience appeal vis-à-vis the foreign competition, and Hollywood in particular. They also wanted to use film to promote the culture and values of the German *Volk* (people), as they conceived of it, and to identify and excise the Jewish. With these aims in mind, the Nazis began a process of restructuring and regulation called *Gleichschaltung* (coordination).[14]

Film financing, production, and distribution were placed under the purview of the Propaganda Ministry, which, as per the Nazi leadership principle, was an authoritarian, hierarchical organization in which Propaganda Minister Joseph Goebbels had the ultimate say. A combination of legislation, restructuring, compulsory professional memberships, and personal pressure expelled most employees with Jewish ancestry rapidly from the film industry.[15] Membership in the *Reichsfilmkammer* (Reich Film Chamber), a state-controlled professional organization, was mandated for all film industry personnel. Rejecting film professionals from the *Reichsfilmkammer* became a way of excluding those whom the regime considered politically or racially undesirable. Film financing also depended on ideological and racial conformity. A state-run loan agency called the *Filmkreditbank* (Film Credit Bank) paired private investors with film projects whose screenplays, personnel, and budgets had been approved by its advisory board and by the *Reichsfilmdramaturg* (Reich Film Dramaturge), who reviewed and censored scripts before and during film production. Postproduction, films had to pass the *Filmprüfstelle* (Film Censorship Board). A ratings system incentivized the production and exhibition of films deemed politically and/or artistically valuable.[16] Propaganda Ministry pressures, incentives, and legislation also regulated cinema ownership and cinema programming.[17] Political groups, such as the Hitler Youth, organized special screenings. *Gleichschaltung* led gradually to the virtual nationalization of the German film industry between late 1936 and early 1938, when the Nazi government indirectly purchased the major film studios through shell companies, trusteeships, and other intermediaries and installed artists loyal to the regime on corporate boards.[18] The film industry was nationalized formally in 1942.[19]

Despite the Nazi regime's political and economic control over the German film industry, there remained some aesthetic and ideological wiggle room. The Propaganda Ministry was a sprawling, overly complicated hotbed of internal power struggles, and, as a result, inconsistent.[20] How much a film could stray from the party line depended on multiple, ever-shifting variables, which included political, economic, and military conditions and individuals' stature, proclaimed political beliefs, and personal relationships with the Propaganda Minister. These variables operated within Goebbels's views on effective propaganda and his business goals, both of which left some space to maneuver: Goebbels believed that subtle rather than explicit propaganda was most effective. Moreover, he wanted both to develop a national cinema and to compete in an international marketplace.[21] To sell pictures, compromises were necessary, despite public rhetoric claiming that "the deeper art is rooted in the national soil, the larger its international significance."[22] Export audiences were uninterested in Nazi propaganda or nationalist bombast, and to develop a popular cinema domestically, studios needed to produce films that both reflected and cultivated audience desires.[23] Genre cinema, such as comedy and melodrama, offered a carefully circumscribed space for transgressive fantasies.[24] It also helped create the illusion of a free public sphere.[25]

Because Third Reich audiences, their movie-going habits, and their preferences were diverse, the Propaganda Ministry took steps to homogenize their cinema experiences and unify the *Volksgemeinschaft*. Throughout the Nazi period, German cinema audiences grew substantially and people went to the movies more frequently than we do today.[26] Between 1933 and 1943, cinema attendance rose from 245 million to 1.12 billion annually, decreasing surprisingly slightly in 1944, given the destruction and air raid conditions in German cities, to 1.102 billion.[27] As admissions increased, however, the diversity of offerings decreased. As described and developed throughout this book, various pressures narrowed the artistic choices possible for German productions. At the same time, tariffs, censorship, and regulations carved out a larger market share for them, building on practices already in place in the Weimar Republic.[28] Between 1933 and 1940, German feature films rose from 56 percent to 83 percent of domestic offerings.[29] During the war, political censorship and a hard-currency shortage limited imports further, and in 1941, Goebbels banned American films.[30] The Propaganda Ministry regulated the cinema program to standardize the viewing experience, beginning by abolishing the double feature in 1933.[31] In fall 1934, the regime mandated the screening of an approved newsreel and *Kulturfilm* (documentary short) before each feature film.[32] Later, to support the war effort, didactic comic shorts featuring characters named Tran and Helle were added.[33] A locked-door policy forbade late admittance, forcing people to view the entire program.[34]

The community addressed in—and in part constituted by—the cinema was meant to be the German *Volk,* racially defined.[35] Both legal restrictions and economic pressures kept Jews from going to the movies.[36] Beginning in 1935, some individual cinema owners and local jurisdictions banned Jewish people from cinemas.[37] After November 12, 1938, the *Verordnung zur Ausschaltung der Juden aus dem deutschen Wirtschaftsleben* (Decree on the Elimination of the Jews from Economic Life) prohibited Jews from attending public cultural events, including film screenings.[38] Erica Carter explains how the architecture of Third Reich movie theaters both brought different classes of the *Volk* together and positioned them hierarchically through a structured system of differently priced seats.[39] In the cinema, racialized spectators became part of what film theorists of the era construed as a collective, intensely emotional *Erlebnis* (experience). This *Erlebnis* encouraged emotional immersion rather than critical thinking, "plac[ed] the spectator firmly within the libidinal structures that constitute imaginary communities inside and outside the theater," and "dissolv[ed]" the individual spectator into the *Volk* body.[40]

Despite the Propaganda Ministry's orchestration of the cinema *Erlebnis* and its community-building functions, the movie house was not a site of total social control. People could choose which movies they wanted to attend, if any, and attendance was not passive. Reports by spies from the security service (*Sicherheitsdienst,* or SD) and articles in the press describe audience members talking, laughing, clapping, whistling, jeering, and otherwise reacting out loud.[41] Some Nazi critics understood such boisterous emotionalism as "a mark of true German character" and in compliance with the Propaganda Ministry's intentions regarding the affective impact of the cinematic *Erlebnis*.[42] Yet people's specific emotions and outbursts did not always comply with the Ministry's intent. Film critics expressed concern about "false laughter" at melodramas, which could ruin both the communal experience and a film's reputation.[43] The SD reported incidences of audience members "hissing at Nazi dignitaries in the newsreels."[44] The infamous baskets of love letters sent to the actor who played the Jewish villain in *Jud Süss* and contemporary accounts of strong negative reactions to *Nur nicht weich werden, Susanne!*, discussed in chapter 2, illustrate that, despite the efforts by the Nazi dictatorship to homogenize film audiences and the *Volksgemeinschaft*, individuals' responses to films and to representations of the Jewish remained heterogeneous.[45]

Imagining the *Volksgemeinschaft* through Comedy

The Propaganda Ministry wanted both the cinema-going experience and the films produced in Nazi Germany to encourage *Volksgemeinschaft*. *Volksgemeinschaft* was "the Nazis' central social concept," a national community unified by race, rather than divided by class or creed.[46] Martina Steber and Bernhard Gotto isolate "five very clear features" of *Volksgemeinschaft*, which "defined the framework for social change in Nazi Germany": *Volksgemeinschaft* was an "imagined order" that was both "ideal" and "template"; it "held out the hope of a brilliant future," materially and symbolically; it "set the dividing lines for a system of dual ascription distinguishing between *Volksgenossen* [racial-national comrades] and *Gemeinschaftsfremde* ('community aliens')"; it "justif[ied] a whole range of actions and positions taken in many social and political spheres"; and, lastly, it "contained within it a call to action."[47] Nazis courted consensus and employed violence to build their imagined *Volksgemeinschaft*.[48] Even as its flexibility, contradictions, and ambivalences left room for negotiation, *Volksgemeinschaft* was central to the Third Reich imagined community, which began with fantasies of a more homogeneous society and ended in genocide.[49] In the Third Reich, film comedy helped people envision *Volksgemeinschaft*. It projected upbeat visions of the German community, encouraged values and behaviors supported by the regime, distinguished between insiders and outsiders, and unified audiences through the shared experiences of visual pleasure and humor. Such functions mirror what scholars have identified as functions of film comedy more broadly.

Although frequently included in genre studies, film comedy is not, strictly speaking, a genre, but rather a mode found across different genres and subgenres, traditionally identified by either the laughter it provokes or narrative features like happy endings.[50] Prevailing theories characterize comedy as "involv[ing] departures of a particular kind—or particular kinds—from what are considered to be the 'normal' routines of life of the social group in question" and the treatment of the gap between real-world expectations and the incongruities or transgressions represented in the filmic world.[51] In its treatment of incongruities, comedy frequently offers the pleasures of both departing from the norm and restoring harmony with a happy ending.[52] Like Nicole Matthews, I consider not only "comic form, but also textual techniques and audience expectations" to identify my objects of study.[53] The films I analyze as comedies were designed to make audiences laugh, an intent indicated by their marketing and reception and their use of comic conventions such as jokes, gags, stock characters, and narrative structures. My analyses emphasize potential social functions, intended and unintended, over aesthetic classifications.

Humor teaches, unifies, and excludes. Its pedagogical and disciplinary aspects made it well suited for building *Volksgemeinschaft*. Michael Billig argues that "ridicule is both a means of disciplinary teaching and the lesson of that teaching."[54] People learn humor through social interactions, through "meta-discourses" about humor, and through verbal and physical cues about what is funny, including their laughter or their choice to withhold it.[55] Disciplinary humor teaches proper social behavior by pitting laughter against the outsider and casting the "normal" as unfunny.[56] People learn what is normal and what to laugh at and fear of laughter and embarrassment encourages people to monitor themselves.[57]

Nazi film theorists were aware of humor's disciplinary functions. Reichsfilmintendant (General Director of Reich Film) Fritz Hippler wrote about comedy's pedagogical potential in 1942: "As is well known, there is nothing more educational than making fun of bad habits. Ridiculousness leads to laughter, and, beyond that, famously, it kills. And what all there would be to kill: intellectualism, snobbism, egoism, individualism and very much else with the same ending; additionally miserliness, conceitedness, envy, narrow-mindedness, to name only a few of the larger concepts."[58] Hippler describes humor as an effective weapon against character traits he casts in a negative light. Within the framework of Third Reich antisemitism, he is targeting the Jewish—not actual Jews, but characteristics Hippler and his contemporaries strongly associated with them. The most recognizable antisemitic tropes in this passage are "intellectualism" and "miserliness."

Overtly antisemitic texts from the period commonly associate all the traits Hippler targets here with Jewishness, and they surface in other texts and films analyzed in this book. Consistent with current understandings of how humor works, Hippler suggests filmmakers can use humor to "kill" these "Jewish" traits.

Humor's disciplinary functions build group cohesion. Because humor is taught, knowing what is humorous is culturally specific and separates outsider from insider.[59] Shared senses of humor promote communal identifications and erect symbolic boundaries between social groups.[60] In contrast to the fear of embarrassment and being laughed at, belonging has strong affective appeal.[61] Through the boundaries and fears created by "laughing at" and the pleasures of "laughing with," comedy disciplines the individual and sculpts the community.[62] Scholarship on the comedy and humor of historically marginalized groups shows how comedy can produce identities and communities and reshape social norms.[63] My book considers the norm-shaping and community-building functions of films produced under a genocidal dictatorship mostly by people who did not identify as Jewish.[64] In focusing on the humor of the hegemonic group, my analysis emphasizes some of the more disturbing ramifications of film comedy's identity- and community-building functions. In Nazi Germany, film comedy helped separate the Jewish from the non-Jewish and build a non-Jewish *Volksgemeinschaft*. According to Martina Kessel, humor in Nazi Germany established a "communicative contract among non-Jews, who used it to act out exclusion and inclusion."[65] "Scorn and derision" demonized and excluded Jewish Germans and humor's entertainment value encouraged the compliance of non-Jewish Germans with the "inclusionary/exclusionary society."[66] My research shows how inclusion, exclusion and the construction of *Volksgemeinschaft* took place in both the style and content of Third Reich film comedy, on both implicit and explicit levels.

Comedies emphasize "familiarity," "cultural specificity," and difference, and adopt, adapt, and discard aspects of comedies from other times and places in order to construct national identity and national cinema.[67] This process of inclusion, exclusion, and recognition of generic features creates not only a domestic market but also a national audience, distinct from others.[68] Referencing Benedict Anderson, who conceives of nations as "imagined communities" created initially by the print media,[69] Juan Egea theorizes the development of a national film comedy in fascist Spain as producing "an *imagining* community," a temporally and medially distinct "refashioning (or reimagining)" of a national community that already has been "imagined" through the process theorized by Anderson.[70] The development of a national German film comedy in Nazi Germany functioned similarly. As it struggled to find its own unique style and to draw boundaries around its own viewership, Third Reich film comedy borrowed and distinguished itself from its own filmic forebear, the cinema of the Weimar Republic, and from contemporary rivals, particularly Hollywood, a dynamic central to films and film criticism of the era. In doing so, it encouraged the imagining of a *Volksgemeinschaft* that was different in composition, taste, and race from Hollywood's and Weimar's cinema publics.

In addition to its engagements with Weimar and Hollywood comedy, Third Reich film comedy imagined and pitted phantasmatic constructs of Germanness and Jewishness against one another, seeking to excise the Jewish from German film. Third Reich film comedy thus participated in a "racial Germanization" analogous to the "racial Spanishization" analyzed by Eva Woods Peiró in Spanish folkloric musicals from the 1920s through the 1950s.[71] Peiró explains how stereotypes of "Gypsies" in folkloric musicals helped spectators imagine a racialized Spanishness, a strategy shared with other racist discourses, and how "Gypsy hypervisibility maintained the imaginary boundary between white European Spain and its internal and external others."[72] Third Reich film comedies exemplify a different method of racialization. Imagining a racialized *Volksgemeinschaft* through film humor did not depend on hypervisibility and stereotypical representations of Jews. Instead, indirect coding of Jewish difference, absence, and substitution were key to imagining *Volksgemeinschaft*.

Third Reich film comedy erected social boundaries and disciplined spectators while imagining a racialized German community. Film comedies and the meta-discourses around them, such as audience reactions and film reviews, taught spectators what was funny, molding a *Volksgemeinschaft* with a shared sense of humor. Nazi film writings emphasize the racial dimension of cultivating shared humor and taste, distinguishing, for example, between German "humor" and Jewish "wit" and "comicalness," which purportedly reflected essential racial traits.[73] The Propaganda Ministry pushed Third Reich film comedy and its audiences toward the former and away from the latter. The resulting comedies helped envision a *Volksgemeinschaft* that excluded the Jewish. Laughter at and ridicule of onscreen characters and events disciplined spectators, schooling them to monitor their own thoughts and behaviors. The comedies spectators laughed at taught them how to behave and whom to exclude in order to imagine *Volksgemeinschaft*. By cultivating a community that laughed together at a distinctively German film humor bereft of Jewish elements, by exploiting comedy's dominant structure of transgression and resolution, and by disciplining behavior through laughter and ridicule, Third Reich film comedies modeled racialized, gendered behaviors and encouraged spectators to conform. Comedy helped shape German national identity and build the Nazi *Volksgemeinschaft*, even as comedy's minor transgressions, pleasures, and ambivalences may have at times thwarted, complicated, or reinforced their own lessons.

Antisemitism and Jewish Difference in Third Reich Film

Defining what was and was not Jewish and segregating the two from one another were fundamental to both Nazi antisemitism and the production of *Volksgemeinschaft*. In Nazi imaginations, Jewishness corrupted German culture from within and without. On the one hand, it adhered to the racialized bodies of people defined by the Nuremberg Laws as Jewish and could be transmitted through blood and sexual contact, which those laws were designed to prevent. On the other hand, Jewishness also circulated as an abstract, free-floating spirit detached from so-called Jews and infecting so-called Aryans and their culture. Put differently, "Jewishness" was a characteristic not limited to those defined by Nazi law and practice as racial Jews.

Nazi political antisemitism had roots in what Shulamith Volkov calls the "new anti-Semitism" of the Wilhelmine era (1871–1918). This new antisemitism was a "cultural code" used to express identification with a suite of conservative, antiliberal, antimodern values and political beliefs that included hostility toward Jews, but was by no means strictly coextensive with it.[74] Wilhelm Marr's popularization of the term "antisemitism" in the 1870s created "a larger semantic space [than older terms for Jew hatred] as a vessel for a variety of desired contents."[75] The new term provided a scientific, modern facelift to Jew hatred and went hand in hand with vague racial notions of the "Semitic," which were aligned neither with religious practice nor, necessarily, with actual Jews.[76] Freeing Jewishness from its associations with religion and with "living Jews," the term antisemitism enabled "the symbolic process through which anti-Jewish attitudes were made analogous for a whole series of other views."[77] Political antisemitism used "wrong metaphor" and "associative merger" to displace the social problems and economic dislocations caused by capitalism and modernity on to the so-called "Jewish question."[78] Antisemitic criticisms of non-Jews' *Judenhaftigkeit* (Jew-like-ness) and *Verjudung* (Judaization) illustrate the concept's extra-racial reach.[79] For antisemites of the Wilhelmine era, Jewishness comprised dishonesty, greed, laziness, cosmopolitanism, commercialism, egotism, capitalism, liberalism, democracy, modernity, and other undesirable characteristics.[80] Nazi antisemitism adopted these associations from its predecessors.[81]

The notion of a free-floating "Jewishness" and the coding of people, ideas, and objects as "Jewish" or "non-Jewish" was not something only Nazis or die-hard antisemites believed in. It was an ordering system in the pre–World War II era in which everyone participated.[82] To better understand Nazi antisemitism and Third Reich film comedy's engagement with the Jewish, it is helpful to analyze it both as a specific historic manifestation and as a part of larger discourses of what Lisa Silverman calls "Jewish difference."[83] Jewish difference is "one of a number of analytic categories or frameworks, like gender and class, that not only intersect . . . and overlap . . . , but also use . . . each others' [sic] terms in order to articulate their power."[84] Similarly to gender, the terms of Jewish difference are frequently conceived of as a hierarchical binary of the "Jewish" and the "non-Jewish," with the latter envisioned in its ideal form as a hegemonic male and the former most frequently imagined as a feminized male Jew. This gendering of the terms of Jewish difference leads to the double marginalization or erasure of Jewish women.[85] Ideals and stereotypes associating Jewishness with wealth similarly erase and marginalize working-class Jews. Silverman's analyses of multiple texts and discourses show how both Jews and non-Jews shape ideals of the "Jewish" and "non-Jewish," that these constructs change over time, and that the binary, hierarchical relationship between the two affects social structures and performances of identities.

Analysis of Jewish difference considers the social construction, coding, and ideological functions of the Jewish and the non-Jewish as powerful paradigms that are not necessarily coextensive with Jews. Antisemitism derives from these larger structures of Jewish difference, for it is an "iteration of the relationship(s) between the mutually constitutive and hierarchical ideals of 'Jewish' and 'non-Jewish.'"[86] Understanding antisemitism as a derivative variant within a larger discursive network of Jewish difference opens up productive lines of inquiry.[87] It offers a way to interpret Third Reich film comedy's specific articulations of the Jewish and the non-Jewish that acknowledges connections with other representations of Jewish difference, particularly those in German-speaking Central Europe, without implying that all such representations are malicious or antisemitic. It understands discourses of Jewish difference as complex, ambivalent, and often subtle or indirect. It enables interpretations of "not only those active, performative gestures that may celebrate or deny traditions, beliefs and practices of Jews, but also those harder-to-quantify gaps, absences and silences that inform so much of German Jewish history."[88] Approaching antisemitism within the framework of Jewish difference emphasizes the coding and decoding of the Jewish and the non-Jewish, their interdependence with class, gender, and other analytical categories, and their performative and textual functions.

Underlying my study of Third Reich film comedy is the premise that Nazi antisemitism was a toxic manifestation within the broader discursive framework of Jewish difference. State-sponsored efforts to eradicate Jewishness and eliminate Jewish people fed on wide-ranging discourses of Jewish difference, many of them preexisting, and not all of them produced with antisemitic intent. The category of the non-Jewish and its assertive, iterative enactment was also fundamental to Nazi constructions of Germanness and a racialized *Volksgemeinschaft*. Defining and regulating the boundary between the Jewish and the non-Jewish was a pervasive political and cultural concern.

Through innuendo, gaps, and displacements, Third Reich film comedy represented Jewish difference in ways that normalized Nazi racial antisemitism and facilitated state-sponsored genocide. Although less explicit and less overtly articulated than more familiar versions of Nazi antisemitism, the form of antisemitism most common in film comedy and emphasized in this book subtly coded Jewish and non-Jewish people, places, and things, naturalized Jewish difference, and used a variety of strategies to exclude or eliminate the Jewish. In so doing, it helped uphold antisemitic structures in society. I call this insidious mode of representing Jewish difference "inferential antisemitism."

For the past several decades, analyses of race and blackness in popular culture have depended on Stuart Hall's distinction between overt and inferential racism. Hall defines ideologies as the naturalized frameworks and accepted "truths" within which identities, speech, representation, and social conditions are produced, frameworks that the media help produce, modify, and perpetuate through repetition and change. Within those parameters, Hall identifies two different ways in which media propagate racist ideologies: "overt racism" and "inferential racism." Overt racism, as the term suggests, expresses hateful or prejudicial views openly. Inferential racism is more complicated. Hall defines inferential racism as "those apparently naturalized representations of events and situations relating to race, whether 'factual' or 'fictional,' which have racist premises and propositions inscribed in them as a set of *unquestioned assumptions*. These enable racist statements to be formulated without ever bringing into awareness the racist predicates on which the statements are grounded."[89] By reproducing racist notions that already have become part of a culture's ideological underpinnings and have been integrated and naturalized as part of its shared values and truths, "inferential racism" perpetuates racist ideologies and buttresses racist social structures without audiences noticing. Inferential racism "is more widespread—and in many ways, more insidious [than overt racism], because it is largely *invisible* even to those who formulate the world in its terms."[90] Using Hall's distinction between overt and inferential racism as a critical lens through which to scrutinize racial antisemitism in Nazi film comedy, I describe explicit Jew-hatred, negative stereotypes, and persecution as "overt antisemitism" and characterize subtle, coded, or covert representations of Jewish difference that naturalize antisemitic premises and encourage viewers to eliminate Jewishness as "inferential antisemitism."

Decoding inferential antisemitism relies on overt antisemitism.[91] Theories of inferentialism in language help explain how this works.[92] Despite everyday connotations that equate "inference" with arbitrary conjecture, the inferential role theory of meaning explains how inference is both socially contingent and normative. The meaning of a word, phrase, or sentence "is a matter of its place in a pattern of inferences," guided by rules that are embedded in social, historical, and institutional contexts.[93] Language use reinforces "commitments" not only to what one intends to say but also to certain ways of thinking and speaking and to particular social practices and hierarchies that depend on the normative meanings of the language used. Speakers also "license" their listeners to infer the socially accepted connotations of their words and phrases, even when they don't mean to. Film and its constitutive elements likewise derive meaning from and contribute to inferential networks and communal norms. Their inferential meaning and significance are therefore heavily context dependent. "Inferences are not subjective mental moves, but rather moves in a certain public intersubjective game, and the rules of the game are constituted together with the constitution of the game itself."⁹⁴ The overtly antisemitic Nazi context licensed and even encouraged audiences to make antisemitic inferences. Whether or not so intended, many representations of Jewish difference reinforced commitments to meanings, practices, and hierarchies the Nazi state advocated.

Nazi institutions built inferential patterns that fortified antisemitic interpretations of Jewish difference. Overt antisemitism was common in the Third Reich, advanced by the Propaganda Ministry through the myriad institutions housed under its administrative umbrella, among them the radio, the press, advertising, literature, theater, film, music, and the visual arts. "If a person could understand German, read a major newspaper, listen to the radio news with some regularity, and view the ubiquitous Nazi political wall newspapers," they would have been well versed in Nazi beliefs and intentions regarding the Jewish people.⁹⁵ The ubiquity of antisemitic tropes put certain "facts" and fictions in the realm of common knowledge, among them notions about Jewish appearance, morals, behavior, and dominance in particular professions and economic sectors, such as banking, the media, and the garment industry.⁹⁶ Hall's account of how overt racism operates in the popular press is relevant here: "It is not only that they circulate and popularize openly racist policies and ideas, and translate them into the vivid populist vernacular . . . it is the very fact that such things can now be openly said and advocated which *legitimates* their public expression and increases the threshold of the public acceptability of racism. Racism becomes 'acceptable'—and thus, not too long after, 'true'—just common sense: what everyone knows and is openly saying."⁹⁷ Institutions not under the direct purview of the Propaganda Ministry, such as schools and universities, also educated the *Volk* about Jewish difference, stressing the need to excise the Jewish and positing the superiority of the non-Jewish.⁹⁸ Where antisemitic values and assumptions were not already the norm, the Nazis strove aggressively and publicly to naturalize them, to root "truths" about Jewish people and their alleged moral failings in racist biology, and to propagate beliefs in a natural Jewish inferiority.

Take, for example, the 1939 exhibition in the Natural History Museum in Vienna (henceforth NHM) entitled The Psychological and Physical Phenotype of the Jews. This exhibition was part of a large scholarly apparatus dedicated to legitimizing Nazi antisemitic policy. Like the better-known Eternal Jew and Degenerate Art exhibitions, which opened in Munich in 1937 and then traveled to major cities throughout the Reich, the NHM exhibition instructed visitors about Jewish difference from an overtly antisemitic perspective and used the museum's authority to validate it.[99]

The NHM exhibition illustrates one of many ways that Nazi institutions created and naturalized a framework of negative inferences around Jewish difference. It also illuminates the reciprocal relationship between Third Reich scientific institutions and the Nazi persecution of the Jews, a relationship in which institutions both profited from and underwrote such persecution. The NHM exhibition included images, casts, anthropometric measurements, and biological samples taken from 440 Jewish men held in the Vienna Stadium on their way to the Buchenwald concentration camp.[100] As illustrated in Figure I.1, an archival photograph of the exhibition, the "data" taken from Jewish prisoners were then displayed to the Viennese public as evidence of their fundamental difference from non-Jews and of the need to separate the Jewish from the non-Jewish. This strategy is similar to that used in Hippler's *Der ewige Jude*, which exploits footage of Jews imprisoned in Nazi ghettos. A sign above the skulls and photos on display posits that there is a Jewish question, in the sense of a problem to be solved, and that there is a difference between non-Jews and Jews. It argues that the two must be separated in order to solve the alleged problem and implies that the exhibition offers supporting evidence. The exhibition's location in the NHM frames its overtly antisemitic presumptions as scientific fact. Thus, the NHM exhibition naturalized Jewish difference, licensed museumgoers to make antisemitic inferences, and legitimized Nazi antisemitic policies.

When positioned within the inferential networks created by Nazi Germany's overt institutional antisemitism, representations of Jewish difference that might otherwise seem banal can be read as inferential antisemitism. Inferential antisemitism, whether or not so intended, naturalized racist assumptions about Jews and grounded Nazi antisemitic actions. The murderous consequences of the norms it reinforced make Nazi-era inferential antisemitism particularly significant. By studying both overt and inferential antisemitism, I broaden the study of antisemitism in Third Reich film to include not only the most egregious examples, which prior scholarship has emphasized, but also more subtle cinematic manifestations of Jewish difference and their imbrication with Nazi antisemitism.

The virulence of overt antisemitism and the institutional structure of the film industry under the Nazi dictatorship framed filmmakers' articulations and audience attitudes in ways that resulted in inferential

Figure I.1. "The Jewish Question is only solvable through a clear separation of the 'non-Jews from the Jews.'" "The Psychological and Physical Phenotype of the Jews," exhibition, Museum of Natural History, Vienna, 1939. Naturhistorisches Museum, Anthropologische Abteilung, Fotoarchiv Inv. Nr. 45. 479.

antisemitism. Subject to pre- and post-production censorship and heavy state control, comedies reinforced a conceptual and moral framework consistent with the regime's imagined *Volksgemeinschaft* and its exclusion of the Jewish. As a result, some of the common conventions of Third Reich film comedy had "unquestioned assumptions" about Jewish difference inscribed in them—independently of individual filmmakers' intentions—that had potential to be mobilized on behalf of Nazi racial antisemitism.

Jewishness as Structuring Absence and a Comedy of *Ersatz*

The project of distinguishing between the Jewish and the non-Jewish, excising Jewishness, and filling the gaps created once Jewishness was expelled shaped the German film industry and film comedy in the Third Reich. Forced "Aryanization," the purging of people with Jewish ancestry, had a pivotal effect on comedy, arguably even greater than on other sectors of the film industry. With the exclusion, exile, and persecution of Jews, German film comedy lost significant talent and professional know-how. Jewish artists had excelled in comedy in the Weimar Republic, including top names in the field such as Ernst Lubitsch, Siegfried Arno, and Curt Bois.[101] Comedy lost more personnel to emigration than did other types of film.[102]

As Klaus Kreimeier has noted, German genre film (including comedy) developed its particularly "German" character during the Third Reich.[103] *Antisemitism in Film Comedy in Nazi Germany* documents how the Propaganda Ministry and film critics promoted a racialized German humor that excluded individuals, ideas, behaviors, and aesthetics coded as Jewish. In the case of film comedy, the Nazi approach defined Germanness less as some positive content of its own than as the absence of Jewishness, contending that Germanness could flourish only once Jewishness was stripped away. Nazi discourses racialized the dichotomy between the non-Jewish and the Jewish and urged the latter's elimination. They encouraged filmmakers to reject abstract values coded as Jewish, such as commercialism and intellectualism, and "Jewish" comic techniques like rapid editing, irony, and witty dialogue. As a result, Jewishness functions as a structuring absence in Third Reich film comedy, a conspicuous elision that mars and distorts the whole. Structuring absence, as defined by Richard Dyer, "does not mean things which are simply not in the text, or which the critic thinks ought to be in the text. . . . A structuring absence . . . refers to an issue, or even a set of facts or an argument, that a text cannot ignore, but which it deliberately skirts round, or otherwise avoids, thus creating the biggest 'holes' in the text, fatally, revealingly misshaping the organic whole assembled with such craft."[104] In addition to the scars left by expunged personnel, attitudes, and techniques, the paucity of Jewish characters in Third Reich film comedy constitutes a structuring absence, a distortion created as comedy participated in the dangerous fantasy of a Germany free of Jews. This paucity of Jewish characters has led to the mistaken impression that "classic" German film comedy is relatively untainted by antisemitism.

To compensate for the absences created by squeezing out the Jewish, the Third Reich film industry turned to substitute personnel, techniques, and content. Although it is difficult to reconstruct how many Jewish people worked in Weimar film, Ofer Ashkenazi estimates that before 1933, around 20 percent of German film industry members were Jewish, including many prominent individuals.[105] Overtly antisemitic Nazi sources identified the proportion of "Jews" in Weimar film as 90 percent.[106] The talent drain caused by Nazis forcing out the film workers they classified as Jewish created many vacancies. Expelling Jewish film talent created career opportunities for "Aryans" as the Propaganda Ministry cultivated a generation of racially and politically approved directors, actors, technicians, producers, and critics, whom the Nazis expected to blossom once freed from Jewish economic and cultural domination. When Jewish comedians were pushed out, artists whom Ronny Loewy characterizes as "the third tier" of comedians in the late Weimar Republic, a cohort including Heinz Rühmann, Hans Moser, and Theo Lingen, stepped up to fill the vacuum and dominated both Third Reich film comedy and postwar German understandings of classic national film humor.[107] This rising talent with more limited, domestic appeal supplanted established comedians and worked with a more limited comic tool kit, which was not supposed to contain strategies associated with Jewish comicalness or wit.

A preoccupation with Jewish difference, a conscious effort to eliminate Jewishness, and the resulting excisions and substitutions created a nationally distinctive style of German film humor in the Third Reich. Discussions of the Jewish and non-Jewish in humor were much older, but the systematic elimination of Jewish humor from German film comedy was an antisemitic development that did not improve German film. In a 1916 interview for the *Kinematograph* with German-Jewish film critic Julius Urgiß, Ernst Lubitsch responded to a question about the overtly Jewish characters and settings of his early comedies: "Jewish humor is, wheresoever it appears, congenial and artistic, and it plays such a large role everywhere, that it would be laughable if one wanted to do without it in film."[108] But that is exactly what Nazi critics wanted and what Third Reich film studios did. Third Reich film comedy replaced techniques coded as Jewish, such as irony and wit, with regime-approved surrogates like wringing comedy from mundane situations in a "natural" or "true-to-life" manner and humorous gestures and facial expressions more subtle than slapstick, which critics of the period deemed crass. I illustrate these stylistic developments in my analysis of *Wenn wir alle Engel wären* (If we all were Angels, Carl Froelich, 1936) in chapter 4. Outsiders have perceived such ersatz German humor expunged of Jewishness as lacking, as demonstrated by the widespread stereotype outside Germany that German cinema is humorless, a stereotype already bemoaned by Third Reich film critics.[109]

In terms of roles and scripts, Third Reich film comedy relied on placeholders and substitutes to execute some of its disciplinary and pedagogical functions. Imagining a Jew-free *Volksgemeinschaft* meant purging Jews from the projected community on screen and Jewishness from films and audiences. To discourage Jewishness through mockery without picturing Jews to mock, Third Reich film comedy relied on comic types that stood in for the Jewish rather than identifiably Jewish characters, among them so-called "white Jews"—in Nazi parlance, "Aryans" who acted too Jewish. These ersatz or white Jews represented the Jewish in the absence of Jews. Films ridiculed these characters in order to "kill" their Jewish traits (as Hippler would have it) or, in Billig's terms, to discipline spectators through humor.[110] Additionally, many Third Reich film comedies grappled with problems of seeing and knowing, appearance and essence, and policing the boundaries between identities. Such films also treated antisemitic preoccupations without bringing Jews into the picture. Common comic devices, such as mistaken-identity scenarios and other comic mix-ups and confusions, substituted for the antisemitic bile that failed to amuse audiences of *Nur nicht weich werden, Susanne, Robert und Bertram,* and *Leinen aus Irland*.

The absence of Jews and Jewishness from Third Reich film humor and the substitutions and displacements it caused have complex relationships to representations and codings of Jewish difference from other historical contexts that, similarly, "operat[e] 'below the level of articulation.'"[111] Ben Urwand argues that Hollywood's economically motivated appeasement of Nazi censors in the 1930s and a desire to avoid reinforcing antisemitic stereotypes "led to the erasure of Jews from the American screen."[112] This "erasure" also had domestic causes. Thomas Doherty attributes "the disappearance of Jews *qua* Jews" from Hollywood film of the 1930s not only to a reluctance to surrender the German market but also to the Production Code mandate that "the history, institutions, prominent people, and citizenry of all nations shall be represented fairly," and to studios' cognizance of the fact that Jewish Americans constituted only 3 percent of Hollywood consumers.[113] Michael Lipiner reads Hollywood's retreat from overtly Jewish plots and characters in the 1930s as a response to antisemitic attacks on Jewish film producers during the Great Depression.[114] Regardless of the causes, the disappearance of overtly Jewish references from Hollywood film looked different and functioned differently from Nazi Germany's. In the United States, Jews remained active as producers and consumers of culture. Films like *The Life of Emile Zola* (William Dieterle, USA, 1937) and *They Won't Forget* (Mervyn LeRoy, USA, 1937), tackled antisemitic injustices—the Dreyfus affair and the lynching of Leo Frank, respectively—even when they avoided the word "Jew."[115] So did Lubitsch's *To Be or Not To Be* (USA, 1942). Charlie Chaplin's *The Great Dictator* (USA, 1940) faced antisemitism head on. In American cinema, Jewish difference not only appears on the surface, but also frequently manifests as what Shohat calls "*inferential ethnic presences*, that is, the various ways in which ethnic cultures penetrate the screen without always literally being represented by ethnic and racial themes or even characters."[116] Ethnically marked performers, like the Marx Brothers, continued to have successful careers. On a larger scale, Jewish characters and themes persisted *sub rosa*.

Henry Bial's theory of "double coding" explains how covert constructs of Jewishness function in Hollywood film. Bial builds on Judith Butler's theory of performativity and Anderson's *Imagined Communities* to argue that a dialectic between coded Jewish performances and an in-group ability to decode such performances has shaped American Jewish identity. Double coding describes "the way [a] work speaks to at least two audiences: a Jewish audience and a general or gentile audience."[117] In the Hollywood films that Bial analyzes, the narrative intended for the general audience is dominant, and "the Jewish reading is . . . *supplemental*" but nevertheless central to the fashioning of Jewish identity and community in the United States.[118] Although the Jewish reading may not be the most obvious reading or even necessarily intended by the filmmakers, it is tenable and compatible with other readings of the text. Ashkenazi analyzes the double coding of genre films in the Weimar Republic, which often both appealed to a non-Jewish audience and could be read by Jews as addressing issues around German-Jewish assimilation. Ashkenazi's work demonstrates the relevance of Bial's theory for the (de)coding and functioning of Jewish difference in Weimar cinema.[119]

Subtextual articulations of Jewish difference, similar to those in Hollywood film, reflect the situational marginality experienced by German Jews in the Weimar era, a context in which Jews had full civil rights but still encountered hostility and discrimination.[120] Kerry Wallach argues that conflicting "impulses to hide and to display Jewishness" drove the vexed dynamics of Jewish visibility in Weimar Germany.[121] The motivations for and consequences of revealing or covering Jewishness or passing as non-Jewish varied according to context, gender, and individual circumstances and attitudes. Jews and non-Jews were thought to read the "signals and codes" of concealed Jewishness differently, and Jewishness was often performed or coded in oblique ways, meant to be legible only to other Jews.[122] Such conflicting impulses around Jewish visibility and the differences and interplay between Jewish and non-Jewish producers and consumers shape Weimar cinema's Jewish codings. They thus differ in important ways from Third Reich cinema's codings of Jewish difference, which were produced by and for non-Jews.

Yet Weimar did offer representational patterns and templates for Third Reich codings of Jewish difference. The signs, symbols, and stereotypes that signified Jewishness in the Third Reich were modeled on those of Weimar Germany. Weimar also offered paradigms for speaking Jewishness through silence. Darcy Buerkle describes Jewishness as "a category that is both powerful and largely unspoken, a category that often functions as an elaborate and circumscribed absence but is not less present for it."[123] Buerkle's work on German-Jewish visual culture and intellectual history in the first third of the twentieth century shows how absences, ruptures, and rhetorical displacements indirectly express affects associated with a Jewish subject position, such as anxiety and shame.[124] These absences and affects are the result of social and symbolic domination, such as the "symbolic public effacement of Jewishness" from advertising images targeted at women in the early 1930s.[125] Consequently, in Weimar cinema, as Wallach argues, "the most desirable displays of Jewishness were . . . highly subtle or visually absent, particularly with respect to women."[126]

German-Jewish filmmakers in Weimar often avoided explicit markers of Jewishness in their work, even as they engaged with Jewish difference.[127] In doing so, they can be described as performing what Elizabeth Loentz calls "authorial passing": "omitting Jewish markers . . . in order to enjoy advantages accorded to the privileged group."[128] "Authorial passing" and the resulting silences and gaps around Jewishness are inherently ambivalent, either validating social hierarchies or showing them to be socially constructed, depending on whether and how such passing is (un)recognized by "dupes" or witnessed by "in-group" members. Within this triangular dynamic, the presence of Jewish witnesses to recognize a successful act of passing as non-Jewish is key to unlocking any of the performance's transgressive potential.[129]

Essential to the functioning of Jewishness as absence in Weimar texts is the dynamic between texts produced by both Jews and non-Jews and a Jewish subject position.[130] On the one hand, "authorial passing," "double coding," symptomatic gaps, and other representational displacements of Jewish difference indicate that before 1933, some German Jews were subject to symbolic and sometimes literal violence that encouraged them to cover the traces of their own existence. On the other hand, such implicit articulations of Jewish difference suggest that Jewish artists, authors, and filmmakers believed that if their films and other works of art engaged Jewish difference quietly and indirectly, there would remain a place for them in the German community.[131] The absences and substitutions that coded Jewish difference in Weimar film provided models for the representation of Jewish difference in Third Reich film, but they expressed more ambivalence and functioned more ambiguously than their Third Reich counterparts.

Earlier representations of Jewish difference by both Jews and non-Jews created templates for coding Jewish difference, inferential antisemitism, and the structuring absences of Third Reich film comedy. Yet their causes and manifestations differed. In Nazi Germany, the Propaganda Ministry controlled who could speak and what could be said. Jews and Jewishness were excised from film production, and the resulting productions addressed differently constituted and differently racialized audiences from those of the Weimar Republic. In the Third Reich, both producers and consumers belonged to an in-group in a situation of extreme ascriptive inequality (unequal social status based on traits construed as inborn). In such a context, absences and substitutions, while they may draw on earlier representations, have very different meanings. By removing Jews from the discussion about

Jewish difference and from the creation, concealment, and interpretation of its markers, the Nazis significantly reduced the ambiguity inherent in the earlier discourses that Third Reich film comedy nevertheless built upon.

The structuring absences and substitutions of Third Reich film comedy, its codings of Jewish difference, its overt and inferential antisemitism, and its community-building functions are a unique variation within larger discursive networks of Jewish difference. My close readings in the following chapters pursue both the salient links and the important differences between the apparent absence of Jewishness and coding of Jewish difference in Third Reich film comedy and representations from other eras.

Methodology

Of "historical narration," Anton Kaes writes, "the way in which the narrative threads are intertwined attaches a certain meaning to the historical event, which by itself has an infinite multiplicity of potential meanings."[132] In my own writing of German film history, I weave the threads to emphasize a particular—and not the most obvious—meaning of Third Reich film comedy over others. It is a critical commonplace that films are polysemic and that different dynamics between text, context, and spectators generate different meanings. In Kaes's terms, films have "an infinite multiplicity of potential meanings" that spectators activate differently, based on their own experiences and subject positions. Theorizing the potential meanings and functions of Jewish difference in Third-Reich film comedies vis-à-vis Nazi antisemitism, I situate close readings of films and other primary texts within salient historical and conceptual frameworks. My analyses uncover the discursive, ideological, and inferential networks within which Third Reich comedies were produced and in which spectators viewed them. Placing seemingly innocuous comedies in dialogue with examples of overt antisemitism reveals the normative inferential patterns available to Third Reich spectators and illuminates "potential meanings" that are lost when these films are viewed in other contexts. Attending to the original production and reception context and reconstructing the inferential patterns available to historical spectators, I am able to interpret these films' potential antisemitic functions and theorize their broader implications.

Because of my emphasis on covert articulations of Jewish difference and inferential antisemitism, readers of earlier drafts of my manuscript have asked why Third Reich filmmakers would have coded Jewish difference implicitly or expressed antisemitism inferentially when there was no social taboo on overt antisemitism in Nazi Germany. Lacking evidence for a more devious motive, I surmise that in a cultural context where antisemitism was so widespread, texts and films likely contain inferential antisemitism, not because authors or filmmakers had something to hide or repress, but simply because the assumed and the obvious do not always need to be proclaimed loudly, and because the commonplace often goes unnoticed. Promoting antisemitism was not the primary goal of most of these comedies; it simply tags along with them, an effect of institutional structures and social norms, contemporary ways of viewing and understanding the world, and longer and broader representational traditions.

For methodological reasons, I prefer not to speculate on individual filmmakers' motives, political beliefs, and psychology. The multiple institutional, political, and economic pressures on filmmakers and the large number of people involved in making a film make it impossible to pinpoint the origin of particular artistic decisions where no concrete evidence exists. Moreover, focusing on "how" comedy works to support racial antisemitism rather than "why" people did what they did in Nazi Germany helps me theorize racism in comedy in a more forward- and outward-looking way. I take my lead here from Barbara Reskin, who has argued that to make more progress in understanding ascriptive inequality, research needs to shift "from motives to mechanisms": instead of asking "why?" scholars should ask "how?"[133] According to Reskin, preoccupation with motives limits scholarship for five reasons: (1) people's true psychological motives cannot be observed; (2) analysis of motives tends to generalize rather than differentiate between members of a group; (3) focus on motives emphasizes intentional acts rather than unintentional ones; (4) motives may not be the sole cause of inequality; and (5) motives do not explain the mechanisms that make inequality work.[134] Reskin's comments offer significant insight into potential pitfalls of working on film and Nazi antisemitism. As witnessed by the popularity of the History Channel, which my graduate school cohort irreverently called the "Hitler Channel," and as testified to by many of my students since, the question of why Germans committed genocide fascinates many Americans. "Ordinary" Germans' psychology, how deeply antisemitic they really were, and their complicity in the Holocaust have also been the subjects of animated scholarly debate.[135] This path is well trodden and leads, at least in the case of Nazi film comedy, to a dead end. Attempting to reconstruct filmmakers' motivations would be a futile distraction, for the reasons Reskin provides. My book thus follows the path she suggests: I analyze film comedies made in Nazi Germany to show how comedy can participate in imagining racialized communities without appearing or even intending to do so. Helping me tease out these films' potential meanings, the resonances between overt antisemitism and inferential antisemitism within the larger analytical category of Jewish difference have much explanatory power.

Structure of the Book

The following chapters explain the effects and promulgation of both overt and inferential antisemitism in Third Reich film comedy; how comedy defined, excised, and substituted for the Jewish; and how it contributed to the process of imagining *Volksgemeinschaft*. I begin with a chapter on Nazi writings about Jews, film, and comedy. Nazi antisemites sought to purge both Jewish individuals and a fluid, abstract Jewishness from the German film industry. Building on widespread notions of Jewish difference in comedy and popular understandings of Jewish wit, they advocated the removal of Jewish comicalness and wit from German humor. Analyzing these Nazi writings about film, I further theorize inferential antisemitism and articulate its relationships both to broader discourses of Jewish difference and to overt antisemitism. I also describe the ideological and institutional contexts that frame my film analyses in later chapters.

Film analyses in chapter 2 complement the textual analyses in chapter 1, expanding on the Nazi antisemitic agenda to Aryanize the film industry, the Jewishness antisemitic film theorists sought to eliminate, and the difficulties they would face in eliminating it. In chapter 2, I put two films into dialogue with one another: *Nur nicht weich werden, Susanne*, an overtly antisemitic satire of the film industry in the Weimar republic, and the popular film operetta *Blume von Hawaii* (Flower of Hawaii, Richard Oswald, 1932/1933), which it parodies. My analysis of these films exposes the tensions between Nazis' overtly antisemitic ideals, genre conventions, and audience preferences in the early to mid-1930s. While *Blume* was a commercial success, *Susanne* flopped and theater owners refused to show the film. The differing reception of Oswald's and Cserépy's films explains why Third Reich film comedy developed as it did. Audience enthusiasm for films that Nazis deemed too Jewish accounts for the persistent diversity of comic styles and their gradual alteration through subtle excisions and substitutions.

Chapter 3 explains how German film comedies in the early to mid-1930s negotiated stylistic questions and audience demand in the new political environment, both integrating and replacing styles the Nazis considered un-German. It analyzes how two paradigmatic, popular, and well-known films, *Viktor und Viktoria* (Victor and Victoria, Reinhold Schünzel, 1933) and *Glückskinder* (Lucky Kids, Paul Martin, 1936), participated in the discussion about developing a new German film comedy within an international cinematic context and a domestic market in which "Jewish" styles still found favor with audiences. On the one hand, *Viktor und Viktoria* and *Glückskinder* strongly feature characteristics of Nazi cinema's adversaries, allegedly Jewish-influenced Weimar and Hollywood cinema. On the other hand, both films propose substitutions for these cultural and stylistic competitors. Analysis of *Viktor und Viktoria* and *Glückskinder* and their reception illustrates how production and criticism of film comedy functioned as sites of contention over humor, style, and racial and national identities on multiple and often inconspicuous levels.

Chapter 4 augments chapter 3's account of the racially motivated stylistic shift in German film comedy in the 1930s and explains the development and promotion of a racialized German film humor. I illustrate this development through a discussion of *Wenn wir alle Engel wären*, the only comedy to have received the highest rating possible in the Nazi film rating system, "politically and artistically especially valuable." *Engel* and its reception helped cultivate "German humor," a humor that sacrificed certain formal elements not only to purge the film industry of Jews, but also to purge German film of purported Jewish features. Close reading of *Engel* in chapter 4 demonstrates how that film exemplified such German humor, distorted by the absence of Jewishness. I argue that *Engel* and the accolades it received offered filmmakers an aspirational model and audiences an example of comedy endorsed by the Nazis. While Third Reich film comedy never achieved stylistic homogeneity, the favored style of humor did shift more generally in the direction urged by the regime, a direction that comedy continued to take in the postwar era. Yet, as apolitical as *Engel* and films like it seem, the decoration and promotion of this style of humor sought to expel and replace persistent elements of "Jewish comicalness" and "wit" as a part of excising the Jewish from the *Volksgemeinschaft*.

Chapter 5 explains how, because of normative inferential networks, stock comic characters and tropes encouraged the segregation of the Jewish from the non-Jewish through disciplinary humor. Scrutinizing

Jewish difference in comedies about capitalism and colonialism, I examine a common character type, the "white Jew," an Aryan who had been corrupted by and behaved as antisemites imagine that Jews do. Interpretations of *April! April!* (April Fools, Detlef Sierck, 1935) and *Donogoo Tonka* (Donogoo Tonka, Reinhold Schünzel, 1935/1936) show how caricatures of white Jews, their economic behavior, and their relationship to colonial situations discourage Jewishness while imagining *Volksgemeinschaft*. Without needing Jewish characters to do so, these films about white Jews and dark continents promote a "non-Jewish" form of capitalism in the service of German colonialism, which would replace the "Jewish" world domination that antisemites feared.

In chapter 6, I trace multiple, indirect connections between representations of masked or assimilated Jews and the ubiquitous mistaken identity comedies of the era, organizing my argument around *Robert und Bertram*. *Robert und Bertram* attacks Jews and "Jewish" capitalism overtly, presents the masked, assimilated Jew as more dangerous than unassimilated Jews, and uses humor to minimize both threats. *Robert und Bertram*'s preoccupation with Jews' ability to pose as non-Jews is an obsession endemic to Nazi propaganda. Nazi anxieties about the lack of visible distinctions between German and Jew are part of larger concerns about the instability of identities and the boundaries between them, anxieties expressed and allayed through the roughly two hundred Third Reich film comedies in which a central figure is mistaken for someone else. These comedies' shared structural and thematic features displace overt preoccupations with masked Jews, moving them to the inferential realm, as they capitalize on comedy's boundary drawing and community building potential.

My explorations of the manifold, indirect relationships between Third Reich film comedy and Nazi antisemitism culminate in chapter 7, which focuses on comedy's escapist functions during the Holocaust and how it encouraged ignorance about uncomfortable realities. Wartime Nazi film comedies engaged the disappearance of Jews and the Jewish while confounding knowing and not knowing, fantasy and reality in pleasurable but problematic ways. Fantasy and uncertainty substituted for knowledge of and responsibility for the persecution and murder of Jewish people. My analyses of *Münchhausen* (Josef von Baky, 1942/43) and *Die Feuerzangenbowle*, the most famous Third Reich film comedies, explain how they accomplished this. *Die Feuerzangenbowle* and *Münchhausen* do not broadcast overtly antisemitic messages or explicitly depict Jews. Yet they both allude to the disappearance of the Jewish and thematize the human body's dissolution into smoke and flame. Surrounding such references, *Die Feuerzangenbowle* and *Münchhausen* create "epistemic murk," a blurring of the fictional and the real that Marcia Klotz locates in overtly racist Third Reich dramas.[136] By mystifying Jewish disappearance and troubling the difference between knowing and not knowing, comedy served as an auxiliary to such dramas, helping spectators maintain a pleasurable distance from wartime atrocities.

The Nazis wove racial antisemitism into the fabric of German society and institutions, resulting in many indirect expressions and effects in addition to the well-known catastrophic consequences. Imagining a racialized *Volksgemeinschaft,* the Nazis sought to remove Jews and Jewishness, as they conceived of them, from German film and the German community. The pressures of institutional antisemitism deformed German film comedy through absences and substitutions, creating a racialized German film humor free of Jewishness and scripts mostly free of Jews. Structured around the absence of Jews and Jewishness, comedies expressed antisemitism inferentially rather than overtly, disciplining spectators through humor and manipulating the boundaries around identities and communities. This book documents and explains these processes. In doing so, it not only sheds more light on a dark period in German film history but also aims to change how we look at comedies in other contexts, with a sharper eye to their potentially racializing, disciplinary, unifying, and exclusionary functions.

Notes

1. Mersch, "Uni-Kultfilm 'Feuerzangenbowle.'"
2. Boerger, "Kultveranstaltung 'Die Feuerzangenbowle.'"
3. Thüna, "Die deutsche Filmkomödie," 317. Distelmeyer, "Übergänge, Kontinuitäten, Brüche," in *Spaß beiseite,* 7.
4. Albrecht, *Nationalsozialistische Filmpolitik,* 110.
5. Welch, *Propaganda and the German Cinema,* 43. For copious statistical information on Third Reich film, see Albrecht, *Nationalsozialistische Filmpolitik.*
6. See, for example, the very influential: Bonilla-Silva, *Racism without Racists.*
7. Hake, *Popular Cinema.* Lowry, *Pathos und Politik.* Rentschler, *Ministry.* Schulte-Sasse, *Entertaining the Third Reich.* Witte, *Lachende Erben.*
8. Ascheid, *Hitler's Heroines.* Bruns, *Nazi Cinema's New Women.* Fox, *Filming Women in the Third Reich.* Heins, *Nazi Film Melodrama.*
9. Witte, *Lachende Erben,* 46–48, passim.

10. Kreimeier, "Antisemitismus im nationalsozialistischen Film," 142.
11. Kreimeier, "Antisemitismus im nationalsozialistischen Film," 142–44.
12. Friedman, *L'image et son Juif,* 35–53. O'Brien, *Nazi Cinema,* 32–45. Schulte-Sasse, *Entertaining the Third Reich,* 233–45. Stern, "Kluger Kommis oder naiver Michel, 50. Tegel, *Nazis and the Cinema,* 113–128. Witte, *Lachende Erben,* 164–67.
13. Shohat, "Ethnicities in Relation," 215.
14. For a more detailed account of *Gleichschaltung* and other transitions in the German film industry between 1928 and 1936, see Hales, Petrescu, and Weinstein, introduction to *Crisis and Continuity,* 7–16.
15. Hull, *Film in the Third Reich,* 19–28. Welch, *Propaganda and the German Cinema,* 15–16. Tegel, *Nazis and the Cinema,* 38–40. Steinweis, "Cultural Eugenics," 23–38. Stahr, *Volksgemeinschaft,* 140–67. Doherty, *Hollywood and Hitler,* 27–29. Analogous processes took place across the arts. For a brief summary, see Friedländer, *Nazi Germany and the Jews,* vol. 1, 9–14.
16. For more on the ratings system, see chapter 4.
17. Kleinhans, *Ein Volk, ein Reich, ein Kino,* 40.
18. Hull, *Film in the Third Reich,* 109.
19. For details, see: Phillips, "Nazi Control," 64.
20. Rentschler, *Ministry,* 9.
21. In the initial period of *Gleichschaltung,* attempts to develop the national character of German cinema were more successful than attempts to expand its international market. Income from German film exports dropped between 1932 and 1936 from RM 12 million to RM 4 Million. Hull, *Film in the Third Reich,* 115. As a percent of industry income, it declined from 12.15 percent in 1934–35 to 7 percent in 1936–37. Phillips, "Nazi Control," 53. The US market for German films shrank substantially. Even US audiences that didn't object to Nazi politics were not impressed by the films' quality. Doherty, *Hollywood and Hitler,* 158–65.
22. "Je tiefer die Kunst ihre Wurzeln in das nationale Erdreich geschlagen hat, um so größer ist auch ihre internationale Bedeutung." Fritzsche, "Dr. Goebbels und sein Ministerium," 342.
23. See Hake, *Popular Cinema.*
24. See Witte, *Lachende Erben.* Heins, *Nazi Film Melodrama.*
25. See Rentschler, *Ministry.* Also, Hake, *Popular Cinema.*
26. Kleinhans, *Ein Volk, ein Reich, ein Kino,* 85.
27. Phillips, "Nazi Control," 53, 62, 63. Kleinhans, *Ein Volk, ein Reich, ein Kino,* 188. Rentschler, *Ministry,* 13.
28. Urwand, *Collaboration,* 47–48.
29. Kleinhans, *Ein Volk, ein Reich, ein Kino,* 105.
30. Phillips, "Nazi Control," 63.
31. Carter, *Dietrich's Ghosts,* 99.
32. Kleinhans, *Ein Volk, ein Reich, ein Kino,* 95–96.
33. Kleinhans, *Ein Volk, ein Reich, ein Kino,* 97. Stahr, *Volksgemeinschaft,* 178–80.
34. Hake, *Popular Cinema,* 74.
35. Carter, *Dietrich's Ghosts,* 87–88.
36. Stahr, *Volksgemeinschaft,* 140–67.
37. Friedländer, *Nazi Germany and the Jews,* vol. 1, 139. Stahr, *Volksgemeinschaft,* 162–163.

38. Carter, *Dietrich's Ghosts*, 93. Hake, *Popular Cinema*, 72–73. Stahr, *Volksgeimeinschaft*, 163. Autobiographies, including Viktor Klemperer's and Ruth Klüger's, indicate that some Jews were able to circumvent the regulations or pass as non-Jewish in order to attend movie screenings. Klemperer, *I Will Bear Witness*. Klüger, *Still Alive*. See also Stahr, *Volksgemeinschaft*, 166–67.
39. Carter, *Dietrich's Ghosts*, 88–95.
40. Hake, *Popular Cinema*, 82. Carter, *Dietrich's Ghosts*, 95.
41. Kleinhans, *Ein Volk, ein Reich, ein Kino*, 88–89.
42. Hake, *Popular Cinema*, 81.
43. Rentschler, *Ministry*, 112–13.
44. Carter, *Dietrich's Ghosts*, 93.
45. Director Veit Harlan is the source of this tale. Friedman, "Male Gaze and Female Reaction," 119, 120–21.
46. Steber and Gotto, "*Volksgemeinschaft*," 2.
47. Steber and Gotto, "*Volksgemeinschaft*," 20–22.
48. Steber and Gotto, "*Volksgemeinschaft*," 16.
49. Steber and Gotto, "*Volksgemeinschaft*," 25.
50. King, *Film Comedy*, 2–5.
51. King, *Film Comedy*, 5.
52. King, *Film Comedy*, 7–8.
53. Matthews, *Comic Politics*, 5.
54. Billig, *Laughter and Ridicule*, 177.
55. Billig, *Laughter and Ridicule*, 183.
56. Billig, *Laughter and Ridicule*, 202–7.
57. Billig, *Laughter and Ridicule*, 200–35.
58. Hippler, *Betrachtungen*, 99.
59. Billig, *Laughter and Ridicule*, 184–89. See also Critchley, *On Humor*, 66–68, 73–75. Medhurst, *A National Joke*, 12–14. The cultural and linguistic specificity of film humor that helps audiences imagine the "national" also helps non-Anglophone film comedies compete with Hollywood in their own domestic markets. Poblete, "Cinema and Humor," 7.
60. Friedman and Kuipers, "The Divisive Power of Humour," 179–95.
61. Medhurst, *A National Joke*, 19.
62. See also Gillota, *Ethnic Humor*, 6. Lionis, *Laughter in Occupied Palestine*, 4.
63. See the following representative examples: Atluri, "Lighten Up?!" 197–214. Bailey, "Fight the Power," 253–63. Bergman, ed., *Camp Grounds*. Cleto, ed., *Camp: Queer Aesthetics*. Distelmeyer, ed. *Spaß beiseite, Film ab*. Georgakas, "Ethnic Humor in American Film," 387–406. John, "Black Film Comedy." Lionis, *Laughter in Occupied Palestine*. Meyer-Sickendiek and Och, eds., *Der jüdische Witz*. Rosenberg, "Jewish 'Diasporic Humor,'" 110–38. Moltke, "Camping in the Art Closet," 76–106. Newton, *Mother Camp*. Reid, *Redefining Black Film*. Robertson, *Guilty Pleasures*. Stratenwerth, "Vorspiel auf dem Theater," 147–65. Weinstein, "Anti-Semitism or Jewish 'Camp'?" 101–21. Winokur, *American Laughter*.
64. Exceptions include Richard Oswald, director of *Die Blume von Hawaii* (The Flower of Hawaii, 1932/1933, to be discussed in chapter 2), who left Germany months after the Nazi takeover, and Reinhold Schünzel, director of *Viktor und Viktoria* (Victor and Victoria, 1933, chapter 3) and *Donogoo Tonka* (Donogoo Tonka, 1935, chapter 5), whose mother's background earned him the legal identity of "half Jew," and who left Germany in 1937.
65. Kessel, "Race and Humor," 380.

66. Kessel, "Race and Humor," 385.
67. Egea, *Dark Laughter*, 10–11. See also Bini, *Male Anxiety and Psychopathology*, 3–5. Gillota, *Ethnic Humor*. Harrod, *From France with Love*, 1–9. Lionis, *Laughter in Occupied Palestine*. Medhurst, *A National Joke*, 6, 10, passim. Poblete, "Cinema and Humor,"12–13. Salys, *The Musical Comedy*, 4–9. Winokur, *American Laughter*.
68. Egea, *Dark Laughter*, 10–11.
69. Anderson, *Imagined Communities*.
70. Egea, *Dark Laughter*, 11–12.
71. Peiró, *White Gypsies*, xi.
72. Peiró, *White Gypsies*, 20.
73. See chapter 1.
74. Volkov, "Antisemitism as a Cultural Code," 25–46, esp. 31–35. Also: Volkov, *Germans, Jews, and Antisemites*, 67–158.
75. Volkov, *Germans, Jews, and Antisemites*, 82.
76. Volkov, "Antisemitism," 38–39. Volkov, *Germans, Jews, and Antisemites*, 82.
77. Volkov, "Antisemitism," 39.
78. Volkov, "Antisemitism," 40–41, 43. Volkov, *Germans, Jews, and Antisemites*, 88–89.
79. Volkov, *Germans, Jews, and Antisemites*, 77.
80. Volkov, *Germans, Jews, and Antisemites*, 99, 117, passim.
81. Volkov, "Antisemitism," 46.
82. See Silverman, *Becoming Austrians*.
83. Silverman, *Becoming Austrians*. Silverman, "Antisemitism," 27–45. Silverman, "Reconsidering the Margins," 103–20.
84. Silverman, *Becoming Austrians*, 6–7.
85. Silverman, *Becoming Austrians*, 80, passim.
86. Silverman, "Antisemitism," 28.
87. See Silverman, "Antisemitism," 28.
88. Silverman, "Reconsidering the Margins," 108.
89. Hall, "Whites of their Eyes," 36.
90. Hall, "Whites of their Eyes," 36–37. See also: Joseph, "Imagining Obama," 393.
91. Joseph shows how "inferentially racist images are reliant upon the overtly racist ones." Joseph, "Imagining Obama," 392–93.
92. For a summary of inferentialism, see Peregrin, *Inferentialism*. On film as a signifying system, see Silverman, *The Subject of Semiotics*.
93. Tirrell, "Derogatory Terms," 46. Peregrin, *Inferentialism*, 10.
94. Peregrin, *Inferentialism*, 12.
95. Herf, *Jewish Enemy*, 15.
96. For more on Nazi attitudes about banking and capitalism, see chapter 5. On the prominence of Jews in the Berlin garment industry, the perception of the industry as a "Jewish" industry, antisemitic attacks against it, and its "Aryanization" in the Third Reich, see Westphal, *Berliner Konfektion und Mode*. Makela, "The Rise and Fall," 185–86, 199–201. Waidenschlager, 'Berliner Mode," 31. Dopp, *125 Jahre Berliner Konfektion*, 50.
97. Hall, "Whites of their Eyes," 37.
98. Hirte, "Vom Antlitz zur Maske," 282.
99. Hirte, "Vom Antlitz zur Maske," 283. See also Taschwer, "'Lösung der Judenfrage,'" 155. For a brief description of *Der ewige Jude* exhibit, see Friedländer, *Nazi Germany and the Jews*, vol. 1, 253. This exhibit showed "an unbearably kitschy commercial production" to exemplify Jewish film.

100. Hirte, "Vom Antlitz zur Maske," 276–77.
101. Distelmeyer, "Übergänge," in *Spaß beiseite*, 7. Loewy, "Ist ein jüdischer Komiker jüdisch-Komisch?" in *Spaß beiseite*, ed. Distelmeyer, 13.
102. Dick, "Flapper, Xanthippen und kleine Männer," in *Spaß beiseite*, ed. Distelmeyer, 85.
103. Kreimeier, "Von Henny Porten," 41–54. Kreimeier, "Antisemitismus im nationalsozialistischen Film," 135, 155–56.
104. Dyer, *The Matter of Images*, 83.
105. Ashkenazi, *Weimar Film*, 159.
106. "Verjudung und Geschäftemacherei," insert. Neumann, et al., Film "Kunst," 26, 39.
107. The quote is from Loewy, "Ist ein jüdischer Komiker," in *Spaß beiseite*, ed. Distelmeyer, 13. See also Distelmeyer, "Übergänge," in *Spaß beiseite*, 7–8. Dick, "Flapper, Xanthippen und kleine Männer," in *Spaß beiseite*, 85–105.
108. Urgiß, "Künstlerprofil," 90.
109. On the stereotype of Germans as humorless, see Critchley, *On Humor*, 70. An example of a Third Reich critic admitting that outsiders don't consider German film funny: "Das Recht auf Humor," 1–2.
110. Hippler, *Betrachtungen*, 99. Billig, *Laughter and Ridicule*, 200–35.
111. Buerkle, "Caught in the Act," 86. Buerkle is building on Steinberg, *Judaism Musical*, 18.
112. Urwand, *Collaboration*, 94.
113. Doherty, *Hollywood and Hitler*, 46–48.
114. Lipiner, "American Jews." Doherty, *Hollywood and Hitler*, 19.
115. Lipiner, "American Jews."
In 1894 a court martial convicted French Captain Alfred Dreyfus, a Jew from Alsace, of espionage, unleashing more than a decade of debate until his exoneration in 1906. Leo Frank was lynched in Marietta, Georgia in 1915, having been convicted under dubious evidence for the rape and murder of Mary Phagan.
116. Shohat, "Ethnicities in Relation," 223.
117. Bial, *Acting Jewish*, 16.
118. Bial, *Acting Jewish*, 17.
119. Ashkenazi, *Weimar Film*.
120. I lean here on Leo Spitzer's account of "situational marginality" as a part of the experience of assimilation. Spitzer, *Lives in Between*.
121. Wallach, *Passing Illusions*, 3.
122. Wallach, *Passing Illusions*, 162; see also Wallach, 62–63, 80.
123. Buerkle, *Nothing Happened*, 3–4.
124. Buerkle, "Caught in the Act." Buerkle, *Nothing Happened*, 3, 4, 18, 19, passim.
125. Buerkle, "Gendered Spectatorship," 626.
126. Wallach, *Passing Illusions*, 89.
127. Ashkenazi, *Weimar Film*.
128. Loentz, "Literary Double Life," 110.
129. Loentz, "Literary Double Life," 130. Loentz extends Amy Robinson's analysis of racial passing to the German-Jewish context. See Robinson, "It Takes One to Know One," 715–36. See also Wallach, *Passing Illusions*, 162–63.
130. See Buerkle's analysis of *Das alte Gesetz*, "Caught in the Act," 91–96.
131. Silverman shows this to have been the case in interwar Austria. Silverman, *Becoming Austrians*, 68.

132. Kaes, *From Hitler to Heimat,* 84.
133. Reskin, "2002 Presidential Address," 1–21.
134. Reskin, "2002 Presidential Address," 4–5.
135. Two well-known, contrasting reference points in the debate about motive are: Browning, *Ordinary Men.* Goldhagen, *Hitler's Willing Executioners.*
136. Taussig, *Shamanism,* xiii, 120–21, 130–33, passim. Klotz, "Epistemological Ambiguity," 91–124.

1

OVERT AND INFERENTIAL ANTISEMITISM IN NAZI WRITINGS AND THE FILM TRADE PRESS

In this chapter, I highlight relationships between overt antisemitism and implicit discourses of Jewish difference in Third Reich writing about film, relationships that explain how antisemitism came to shape German film comedy and that illustrate how inferential antisemitism works. Inferences based on what a word or concept usually means enable speakers and listeners (or writers and readers, filmmakers and spectators, and so on) to communicate with one another and to negotiate the meaning of their communications. Associations with known discourses, patterns, and communal norms, which change based on time, place, and perspective, make such inferences possible. The interplay of inferences made by different individuals results in meaning being contextually dependent and neither fixed nor static. Rooted in communal norms and larger inferential patterns, such inferences are not arbitrary. Speakers license listeners to infer that which is commonly meant or understood by a particular word or phrase. The same is true of visual representations. Therefore, inferences, which are necessary for communication, also tend to have a normative function, perpetuating the concepts, premises, and communicative rules that a statement or representation was based on in the first place.[1] The implicit coding of Jewish difference in some Third Reich film writing and in many Third Reich film comedies licenses inferences linked to the overtly antisemitic discourses around them, generating inferential meanings that naturalize and normalize antisemitic premises. I call this antisemitic residue, licensed by codings of Jewish difference particular to a specific historical-discursive context, inferential antisemitism.

Inferential antisemitism reinforces assumptions, values, tropes, and language fundamental to overt antisemitism without targeting Jews explicitly and without necessarily intending to target them at all. Some instances of inferential antisemitism discussed here unselfconsciously reproduce Nazi-era cultural norms with antisemitic inflections. Other instances mobilize existing tropes of Jewish difference, separate the "Jewish" from the "non-Jewish," and attack identifiable components of the former. The construct of the "Jewish," as inherited and adapted by the Nazis, encompassed a suite of abstract negative concepts, such as intellectualism, cunning, and greed. Within the inferential networks created by overtly antisemitic polemic in Nazi Germany, statements condemning international capitalism—for example, the constraints it imposed on German film art and the sexual immorality it promoted—function as inferential antisemitism. Without naming Jews, such statements echo overtly antisemitic accusations and reject components of the "Jewish," which the Nazis sought to purge and about which they spoke openly and frequently. By expounding on the significance and coding of Jewishness in the Third Reich and emphasizing the conceptual links between overt and inferential antisemitism, this chapter reframes inferential antisemitism in Third Reich film comedy in a way that renders it legible to outsiders.

Some inferential antisemitism is accompanied by innuendo, as described by Theodor Adorno in his essay titled "Anti-Semitism and Fascist Propaganda." According to Adorno, "one of the intrinsic characteristics of the fascist ritual is *innuendo*, sometimes followed by the actual revelation of the facts hinted at, sometimes not."[2] Of innuendo at fascist political rallies, Adorno writes, "For example, the agitator says 'those dark forces, you know whom I mean,' and the audience at once understands that his remarks are directed against the Jews. The listeners are thus treated as an in-group who already know everything the orator wishes to tell them and who agree with him before any explanation is given."[3] Like humor, which separates those who do and do not get the joke, innuendo creates in-groups and out-groups, forging communities who get the allusion and others who don't.[4] Building on the work of Sigmund Freud, Adorno argues that innuendo creates cohesion and identity; it binds "feeling and opinion," "leader and follower," and "conscious and unconscious."[5] Innuendo facilitates imagining a *Volksgemeinschaft* free of Jews. It creates a non-Jewish "us" with a secret code (and, in comedies, a shared sense of humor), opposed to a Jewish "them" that the allusion or joke excludes. Both innuendo and inferential patterns created by overt antisemitism activated implicit codings of Jewish difference in Third Reich writings about film and comedy, resulting in inferential antisemitism.

While theorizing and explaining the relationship between overt and inferential antisemitism, this chapter reconstructs some of the ideological and aesthetic conversations that informed filmmaking under the Nazi dictatorship. It explains the dominant understandings and coding of Jewish difference in relation to German film and film humor in the period. It refines the concept of inferential antisemitism and reconstructs inferential patterns that make it easier to interpret not only the overt but also the inferential manifestations of antisemitism in Third Reich film comedy.

Inferential Networks: Overt Antisemitism, German Film, and German Humor

In Nazi Germany, widespread overt antisemitism created inferential patterns around the coding of Jewish difference, licensing audiences to make antisemitic inferences based on such coding. Building on preexisting understandings of Jewish difference, Nazis insisted that Jews and their power were pervasive and dangerous and that they needed to be eliminated. They misinterpreted Jewish scripture to show how it reflected negative, alien values resulting from the Jewish people's origins in "ancient, unharmonious racial mixings."[6] Josef Keller and Hanns Andersen, for example, in *Der Jude als Verbrecher* (The Jew as Criminal), allege that the Talmud demands Jews follow Jewish law primarily as a tit-for-tat that will make them rich and powerful and that by prohibiting various sexual behaviors and temptations, Jewish religious texts prove Jews to be inherently prone to transgressive sexuality.[7] Keller and Andersen assert that "three features are characteristic of the Jew: unscrupulous lust for power, lust for money, and a high degree of sexual lust, paired with 'morality' that is alien and hostile to us."[8] Nazis conceived of Jewishness as both congenital and infectious. Julius Streicher, publisher of the rabidly antisemitic weekly newspaper *Der Stürmer* (The Stormer), proclaimed that Jews, like bacteria, had infected Germans, their institutions, and their culture with "Jewishness," which needed to be purged.[9] Consequently, the Nazis' obsessive elimination of Jewish influence targeted not only Jewish people but also a disembodied, identifiable Jewishness that existed independently of them. The elimination of real Jews and their influence and the phantasm of lingering, pervasive, and infectious

Jewishness directly motivated the restructuring of the film industry and stylistic and thematic shifts in German film under Nazi leadership.

Imagining a racially authentic German culture depended on separating the "Jewish" from the "non-Jewish." Abstract, racist understandings of Jewishness, the premise that Jewish influence was a *Kulturschande* (a shaming, dishonoring, or deflowering of culture), and the proposition that Jews dominated the film industry grounded Nazi cultural policy. According to *Der Stürmer*, Jews were "the people of decomposition, the people of degradation and destruction" that seduced and preyed upon *Kulturvölker* (peoples of culture) like the Germans.[10] The Nazi position was an extreme version of widespread perceptions of and dissatisfaction with the extensive involvement of Jewish people in German media, literature, and the arts prior to 1933. According to Saul Friedländer, "the 'pernicious' influence of Jews on German culture was the most common theme of Weimar antisemitism. On this terrain, the conservative German bourgeoisie, the traditional academic world, the majority of opinion in the provinces—in short, all those who 'felt German' came together with the more radical anti-Semites."[11]

Within such a conceptual framework, the actual involvement of Jewish people in German cinema during the Weimar Republic metamorphosed, in antisemitic imaginations and rhetoric, into Jewish control and aesthetic and ethical corruption of German film. In 1933, *Der Angriff* (The Attack), the Berlin Nazi newspaper, claimed that 90 percent of the members of the pre-Nazi German film industry were Jewish.[12] For committed antisemites, such inflated statistics substantiated what they perceived as a major problem. Nazis claimed that Jewish domination had made Weimar cinema a decadent commercial product targeted at international markets and lacking in authentic expression of German racial values and artistry. Removing Jews and their influence would enable German film art to flourish.

The distinction between the "Jewish" and the "non-Jewish" was fundamental to Goebbels's vision for the film industry, which emphasized the liberation of German film from presumed Jewish economic and artistic influence. In a major address to 1,500 film industry members at the Krolloper in Berlin on December 14, 1935, Goebbels boasted that "the accomplishment of making the film industry, which at the time of the political transition was almost exclusively in non-Aryan hands, pure German, is so great that it alone could mean a justification of the film politics of the Third Reich."[13] Goebbels, however, did not see his successful removal of people with Jewish ancestry from German filmmaking as having accomplished his ultimate goal; he also wanted to erase what he construed as lingering Jewish effects on the industry. Goebbels and other party ideologues believed that "Jewish" obsessions with profit had damaged film stylistically, turning it into an assembly-line industrial product rather than a work of art. Thus, in his address at the Krolloper, Goebbels called for filmmakers to turn away from "shallow amusement wares" and the "serial production of copycats," both coded as Jewish.[14] Instead, he wanted the German film industry to produce non-Jewish films, or "good and decent" films that reflect everyday life, that are perceived as German by both domestic and export audiences, and that make "contact with the *Volk*," whose taste the artist should guide.[15] To that end, Goebbels announced changes in film production and distribution intended to increase German film's artistic value. Goebbels's scorn for film as an industrial product (Jewish film), Germany's need to produce artistic films that were true to life and to the *Volk* (non-Jewish film), and his desire to cultivate audience tastes appeared often, both in Goebbels's other writings and speeches and throughout much film policy and criticism of the time. While not always stated as overtly as in the speech at the Krolloper, removing both Jews and Jewishness from German film was central to this agenda.

The most detailed formulation of how Nazis conceived of and sought to defeat Jewish influence in film is Carl Neumann, Curt Belling, and Hans Walther Betz's book *Film-"Kunst," Film Kohn, Film Korruption* (Film "Art," Film Cohen, Film Corruption). Neumann, Belling, and Betz all had stature and influence in Third Reich film politics: Neumann was a Nazi functionary and cinema owner, Belling a theorist of film and propaganda, and Betz a film critic. They described their tedious volume as "a brief representation of the National Socialist struggle [*Kampf*] for German film."[16] It is an offensive, factually inaccurate screed, reinventing the history of cinema in Germany, attacking Jewish influence, and proclaiming Nazi victory over it. Presenting lies and falsified statistics as facts, Neumann, Belling, and Betz alleged that Jews dominated the film industry from the beginning—financially, ideologically, artistically, and critically—stunting the growth of an authentically German film art. Imagining a German film art meant, for Neumann, Belling, and Betz, isolating and excising the Jewish. Before 1933, the authors contend, Jews constituted 80 to 90 percent of film personnel and controlled 90 percent of film studios.[17] Despite having hidden behind false German names and masks of respectability, those Jews revealed themselves through their dastardly actions, driven by avaricious, lascivious, and exploitative thoughts. They simultaneously manipulated the capitalist system and disseminated capitalist ideals—dishonestly—and they were also backed by leftists. Jews continued to control film industries globally and to use their influence to make propaganda against Germany. A Jewish-dominated film press promoted their artless productions and anti-German political views.

Neumann, Belling, and Betz claimed that alleged Jewish dominance and Jews' obsession with profits had moral and aesthetic implications. They characterized the history of film in Germany as a "struggle [*Kampf*] between artist and businessman," in which the former was cast as German and the latter as a Jew.[18] Behind this specious dichotomy lurked the core assumption that Jews are, by definition, not German. Making so-called entertainment films, Jews sought to cultivate an international taste, which was that of the lowest common denominator.[19] Films became profit-oriented industrial products, targeting the masses rather than the *Volk* and filling dishonest Jews' pockets. Jewish films capitalized on sensationalism and eroticism and often focused on unsavory social problems.[20] This state of affairs resulted in 99 percent of film production prior to 1933 having been superficial kitsch, and no Jew had made a single decent production.[21] Film in Germany followed the models of American film, likewise controlled by Jews.[22]

Profit-motivated "Jewish" filmmaking, the authors of *Film "Kunst"* argued, suppressed political consciousness and promoted bad morals. The films produced in the Weimar Republic's Jewish studios failed to show that era's true tragedies and how some people were searching for a new direction.[23] Instead, films encouraged "the sober pursuit of ends in their actions and lack of action, the sinister denial of each deeper feeling and each nobler enthusiasm, the undisguised addiction to external pleasure, to empty luxury, and to the most primitive gratification of minor demands, the lack of a higher orientation and more beautiful fulfillment in life."[24] Star culture, like such vacuous films, endorsed foreigners, foreign ideals, and an empty culture of excess and glamour. Casting directors took advantage of the futile hopes of young German women, even as Jews, including the "representatives of 'German humor,'" rose to prominence on screen.[25]

Imagining a truly "German" film required the construct of the Jewish and its elimination. The authors of *Film "Kunst"* would have it that because of Jewish domination, the resulting commodification of Weimar film, and its aesthetic and moral failings, one could not speak of German film in the time before 1933, but only of film in Germany and a "struggle" (*Kampf*) for German film, pioneered by a handful of talented German artists.[26] This struggle was necessary, "if Germany did not want to abstain from someday attaining a film art worthy of its cultural tradition and possessing a film industry in which the principles of the German businessman had currency."[27] For Neumann, Belling, and Betz—as it was for Goebbels—excluding Jewish people from filmmaking was only a preliminary step in the struggle to create worthy German films. An intangible Jewish spirit had infected the whole system. By reorganizing and purging the German film industry, the authors claimed, the Nazis had laid the political, structural, and economic foundations for the development of a truly "German" film.

Central to Neumann, Belling, and Betz's vision for German film was the identification and removal of the Jewish, which is to say, the two categories depended on one another. After Germany eliminated Jews and their business practices from the film industry, the authors of *Film "Kunst"* imagined the development of a uniquely German cinema in an abstract, spiritual sense, a cinema that was free of Jewishness. What these Nazi authors wanted from German film art and entertainment film, regardless of topic, setting, or style was for it to be "conscious of its enormous responsibility toward the soul of the German *Volk* and for that reason to be free of every destructive or international tendency."[28] Applying blood-and-soil rhetoric to filmmaking, the authors proclaimed that "true and pure art can always only come into existence and be effective on the spiritual soil of a racially and folkishly (national) conditioned sensibility. It is the most perfect expression of a community bound by blood through all phases of its historical development."[29] Although film style was crucial in the shift from Jewish to German film and film humor, *Film "Kunst"* is vague on what German film should look like. The book cites positive examples from the past, films with mostly national and political themes and made by prominent Aryan personnel. Yet the examples reveal no consistent aesthetic vision. Instead the authors craved the artistic expression of the *Volk*'s soul.[30]

Jewish difference was key to imagining not only a racial-national German film but also racial-national film humor. According to Nazi theorists, not only serious films but also humorous ones expressed a people's racial character.[31] Siegfried Kadner's *Rasse und Humor* (Race and Humor) was the most extensive and influential work on that topic. Kadner, who had a PhD in literature, began teaching *Rassenkunde* (Racial Studies) at Berlin University in 1929. He joined the Nazi Party in 1933 and became a member of the SS (*Schutzstaffel* = protection squad), an elite Nazi organization whose members were chosen for—and brutally helped enforce—both racial purity and party loyalty. Kadner wrote SS educational materials and spoke as an expert on race and heredity at the district educational office.[32] His *Rasse und Humor* was first published in 1930. This reinforces my point that racialized thinking about film humor in the Nazi era fed on older discourses and did not generate spontaneously in 1933. In German-speaking Central Europe, both antisemitic and philosemitic discussions of comedy and Jewish difference extend at least as far back as the eighteenth century.[33] In the popular imagination and scholarly analyses of ethnicity, comedy, and film, persistent understandings of Jewish humor include a range of purportedly ethnic markers, including irony, wit, cheek, and resistance.[34] Kadner's discussion of Jewish wit is a variation within these larger discourses of Jewish difference in comedy and is only one component of his book, which racializes different types of humor in a sustained way. *Rasse und Humor* appeared in an expanded second edition in 1936 and was reprinted several times. So-called racial scientists, literary scholars, and psychologists cited Kadner's work frequently, and his ideas pervade Third Reich film criticism.

In *Rasse und Humor*, Kadner argues that humor is culturally distinct and racially and biologically determined. On this point, his claims differ from sociological approaches, which similarly describe Jewish humor as culturally distinct, but interpret it as a response to social marginalization.[35] Kadner asserted that "the manifold varieties of humor and comicalness are only to be understood from the bottom up if they are considered not only in a national but also in a racial context" and drew on literature, philosophy, and racist stereotypes to argue that each "race" possessed a unique, characteristic sense of humor.[36] He contrasted honest, introspective, and youthful Germanic forms of "humor" (*Humor*) with the comedy of other races, including not only cynical, word-parsing Jewish "wit" (*Witz*), but also Mediterranean "comicalness" (*Komik*), which Kadner defined as a mechanical comic style that he claimed reflected the superficiality, sensuality, and sociability of Romance-language speakers. Jews also used comicalness. Kadner's distinctions between humor, wit, and comicalness and the racial implications of these terms permeated German film criticism in the 1930s.

German humor, as Kadner conceived of it, was culturally affirmative and free of the racially determined failings of comicalness and wit, as wielded by Jews and other inferior races. He understood the humor of Northern Europeans to be a biologically determined and racially embedded outlook or attitude. He characterized it as a humorous and defiant affirmation of life despite its difficulties, conflicts, and eventual end. According to Kadner, humor, as innate to the Germans, allowed humans to release tension naturally. The further humans developed, the more they became aware of a gap between the superficial world perceived by the senses and the true essence of things, between perceived reality and the ideal, also of the gap between reality and wishes, an awareness that created inner conflict and tension. Kadner claimed that the German race, having developed further than others, was acutely aware of such gaps between perceived reality and ideals and had inherited the resilience to resolve the tensions caused by them. Humor was the primary tool in that struggle.[37]

According to Kadner, German humor expressed the creativity of two related races, the "Nordic" and the "Phalian." "Nordic" people's humor showcased the virtues of this stoic warrior race inclined to moving and expanding. It dealt with serious topics, particularly the gap between appearance and essence; it laughed in the face of hardship, and foregrounded the youthful roguishness of Nordic men. A perfect example of Kadner's "Nordic" humor is Josef von Baky's 1943 *Münchhausen*, starring Hans Albers as the eternally young adventurer (see chapter 7).[38] Kadner argued that Nordic humor often blended with the simple, hearty, and honest humor of the agricultural "Phalian" people, which, like that of the Nordic people, showed the ability to laugh at oneself. Such "Phalian" humor guides films with rustic settings like Carl Froelich's popular and acclaimed *Krach um Jolanthe* (Ruckus about Yolanda, 1934), which revolves around a prize-winning sow, or Karl Ritter's *Weiberregiment* (Women's Regiment, 1936), a humorous battle between the sexes over control of a brewery.

Kadner described Jewish comicalness and wit as alien invaders in German culture. He claimed that Jewish influence in the press, theater, and film had affected German "expressions of comicalness and wit—true humor lies outside the Jewish essence."[39] Whereas German humor was a deeply ingrained, natural attitude, comicalness generated a spontaneous reaction. It was a superficial, mechanical, and vulgar way of inciting laughter. Jewish wit, according to Kadner, was even worse. Wit expressed the sick psychic processes described by Freud, whose sexually obsessed theories applied solely to his "racial comrades."[40] Wit was unacceptably intellectual, schooled by the Talmud in logical and legalistic hairsplitting and clever (mis)use of language, and revealed Jews' inborn dishonesty in an ironic way that sought to render it harmless.[41] Kadner also claimed that

Jews' racial heritage affected the Jewish body and methods of communication, resulting in deformed and exaggerated movements, gesticulation, rhythm, and speech, which non-Jews find both comic and distasteful.[42] Kadner presented an array of purportedly Jewish jokes, some collected by Jewish authors and others that had appeared in antisemitic publications like *Der Angriff*. These jokes highlighted Jews' malice, greed, and essential distance from non-Jews.

According to Kadner, Jewish wit's tone and intent were culturally corrosive. Here and elsewhere, he draws on older discourses of Jewish difference in German language humor and reframes them in the terms of Nazi "racial sciences." In the nineteenth century, what the Brothers Grimm called "thorny, biting wit" was coded as Jewish.[43] Nineteenth-century critics of Heinrich Heine, Ludwig Börne, Moritz Gottlieb Saphir, Karl Kraus, and other political and socially critical authors publicly identified as Jewish drew sharp distinctions between Jewish and non-Jewish humor. Nineteenth-century critics described a Jewish wit that was sarcastic and subversive, characterized by a negative tone, a quick intellect, and a sharp tongue. By contrast, "pure German" humor was understood as affirmative and conciliatory.[44] Kadner evokes these older discourses of Jewish difference in humor when he writes, "In conscious enmity against state and society, church and economy, against the traditional bonds of human communal being, Jewish wit confronts us in its cynical form with acidic acuity and irony in such figures as Ludwig Börne (Baruch) and Heinrich Heine (Chaim Bückeburg)."[45] Heine's and Börne's intellectualism, facility with language, and political opposition through satire made them problematic in Kadner's, his forbears', and his contemporaries' eyes and exemplary of their understanding of Jewish wit.[46]

From Jewish Difference to Inferential Antisemitism: German Humor in the Film Trade Press

German film journalism in the Nazi era, which engages Jewish difference both implicitly and explicitly, was enmeshed in the inferential networks created by overt antisemitism. Reporters regularly maligned common comic strategies coded as Jewish, including wit, irony, intellectualism, exaggerated physicality, rapid rhythm, and superficial, rote comicalness. Analyzed within the inferential networks of Nazi Germany, which built on older discourses of Jewish difference in comedy, the coding and the ease of decoding specific comic techniques as Jewish and the bias against these Jewish techniques becomes evident. Most Third Reich writings on film do not express overt antisemitism. Nevertheless, they activate codes of Jewish difference and naturalize underlying assumptions about the Jewish and the non-Jewish, and many of them promote the latter over the former. Of course, thinking and writing about comedy in terms of Jewish difference, implicitly or explicitly, is not necessarily antisemitic. Both Jews and non-Jews have been known to celebrate Jewish humor. The same was true in German-speaking Central Europe before 1933.[47] By naturalizing antisemitic assumptions about the cultural corrosiveness of Jewish comedy, however, and discouraging Jewishness, Nazi-era film journalists reinforced antisemitic communal norms and promoted key elements of antisemitic film policy and aesthetics. The subtle coding of Jewish difference in Third Reich film journalism and its criticism and rejection of Jewishness helped push comedy in directions urged by Goebbels and other overt antisemites and propagated their values and views. It thus functioned as inferential antisemitism.

Nazi Germany did not have a free press. The Nazis quickly purged the press of racial and ideological outsiders and reorganized it under Propaganda Ministry control, similarly to the film industry. Daily press conferences and printed directives "told the press which stories it should cover, how it should present them, what language to use, and what sources of information to draw on."[48] As described in Kurt Wortig's 1940 doctoral dissertation, the foundations of the Third Reich film journalist's work were the "*Weltanschauung* of the National Socialist state and the regulations for art editors," and the film journalist was expected "to subordinate his private opinion fundamentally to state principles."[49] The regime treated the film press as a vital partner in shaping film style and audience tastes.

In this book, I focus primarily on coverage of comedy in the trade press, periodicals targeted at members of the film industry, because the trade press played a particularly important role in educating film industry members to create *Volksgemeinschaft*. Trade papers reported on film industry goings-on, domestic and international film markets, and artistic and commercial successes and failures. They publicized political developments and mandates and new technologies and techniques. They published editorials on stylistic questions and interviews with artists, producers, and politicians. The trade papers, each with a slightly different professional, regional, or political slant, were the essential go-to guide for how to make movies in Nazi Germany. If, in 1933, you wanted a briefing on the Nazis' reorganization of the German film industry, new policies, and laws, or if, in 1944, you wanted to know which films were big box-office draws for the war-weary public or what rights ticket holders had when film screenings were interrupted by air raids, you consulted the trade press.[50] If you were confused about the kinds of comedy that were considered suitable in the current political situation, the trade press led you through that minefield as well.[51] Writers for the trade press translated Nazi racial and cultural theory into the language of the film business and functioned as communicators of Nazi principles, policy, and aesthetics to film industry members. Inferential antisemitism in the trade press and its complicity in the coding and exclusion of Jewishness encouraged the particular development of Third Reich film comedy.

Inferential antisemitism was a part of both the discussion about film criticism in the trade press and the directions encouraged by that criticism. In 1935, "K." wrote in *Lichtbild-Bühne*, Germany's second-largest film daily, with a circulation of around 3,700, that film criticism should be an "educator," replicating elsewhere in the same article the conceptual framework, language, and imagery found in overtly antisemitic texts.[52] K. understood the film industry similarly to Goebbels, Neumann, Belling, and Betz and wanted critics to push German film away from profit-motivated, repetitive drivel and toward culturally affirmative films that served the *Volksgemeinschaft*. The distinction between commercially motivated cinema and artistically serious cinema was coded as a contrast between the Jewish and non-Jewish. K. accused film critics of having supported the former rather than the latter. In nationalistically loaded language, K. distinguished good criticism from bad and argued that critics needed to move forward with the times and help German film advance. K. criticized the commercialism behind inferior films and the financial relationships that allegedly encouraged some critics to praise those films. In doing so, K. attacked Jewishness without mentioning Jews. K. proclaimed that instead of writing "Schmonzetten" (a Yiddish-derived, French-suffixed word for little bits of kitsch), critics should have a "strong sense of responsibility toward the *Volksgemeinschaft*" and encourage films that would improve it and discourage those that would harm it.[53] By using the word "Schmonzetten," a mix of Yiddish and French, to describe criticism that does not support the *Volksgemeinschaft*, K. invoked both Jewish and French people, whom antisemites associated with what they disliked about modernity.[54] "Schmonzetten" labels criticism that is out of step with the regime as Jewish and foreign. While disparaging the films promoted by such criticism, K. used several metaphors comparing the film industry to the garment industry, again deploying codes of Jewish difference. Historically, Jews were disproportionately represented in the garment industry, particularly in Berlin *Konfektion* (ready-to-wear), which became a major target of antisemitic ire in Wilhelmine, Weimar, and Nazi Germany.[55] Weimar films including Lubitsch's early comedies and other silent "fashion farces" code the garment industry as Jewish.[56] A humorous scene in *Die Stadt ohne Juden* (The City without Jews, Austria, H. K. Breslauer, 1924) posits that if the Jews left Austria, it would ruin the fashion industry. Antisemites wrote about *Konfektion* as a stereotypically corrupt, "Jewish" profession, as, for example, Keller and Andersen did in *Der Jude als Verbrecher*.[57] K.'s metaphors implied that the film industry was rotten in ways similar to *Konfektion*. K. referred to a film requiring deeper scrutiny as being "filmed and woven from eternally old-new fashion fabric."[58] Instead of supporting such unoriginal production, the critic should direct German financial investments into films that benefited the *Volk* and away from "ready-to-wear tricks" (*Konfektionskunststücke*).[59] In a closing anecdote about how studios pressured critics to give them the reviews they want, K. imagined "that the film fashion houses wave triumphantly with newspapers under their arm, 'ha, you unbelievers, here you've got it!' read how wonderfully the others write."[60] Newspapers too represented an industry in which Jews were prominent and which nineteenth- and early twentieth-century Central Europeans understood as "Jewish."[61] Especially in conjunction with the reference to fashion houses, the newspaper in this passage enhances its Jewish coding. While not necessarily referring to Jews, the word "unbelievers" (*Ketzer*) and the use of "ihr" for "you," the informal, second-person plural in German and the formal second person in Yiddish, are suggestive in this context as well. This piece by K. suggested that like Jewish fashion houses, some film studios sought profit rather than the good of the *Volk*. Unscrupulous film critics abetted this behavior. The coded references to stereotypes of Jewishness and antisemitic biases against *Konfektion* in order to distinguish between good and bad filmmaking and film criticism are an example of antisemitic innuendo, revealing the inferential antisemitism in K.'s argument.

By educating filmmakers, the trade press helped shape the new German film humor, another conversation characterized by inferential antisemitism. Goebbels's plans for renewing the German film industry were key here. So too were Kadner's ideas, including his relative valuations of humor, comicalness, and wit. Humor was a racially and politically loaded term in Third Reich film criticism. It was treated as a culturally superior, deeper, and more meaningful form of comedy, suitable to the German *Volk*, and contrasted to inferior forms of comicalness and wit.[62] This distinction, which motivated changes in film style, was racialized and coded as the difference between non-Jewish and Jewish. Several months after the Nazi takeover, Alfred Beierle described a "path to German film comedy" in the *Film Kurier*, the most widely read film trade paper in the Third Reich, with circulation around 8,500.[63] According to Beierle, because political conviction and wit seemed incompatible, other nations thought there was no such thing as German film humor. To combat that notion, Beierle advocated for a national German film humor very much along the lines of the German humor described by Kadner. Beierle claimed that a "sense of homeland and understanding of human nature were the foundations of the humor suited to the *Volk*."[64] Such humor chose material from the "purely human," "lovable weaknesses," and "unconscious strengths" and depicted that material in a subtle way—in pastels rather than in black and white.[65] Beierle's concept of German humor aligned with not only Kadner's but also the culturally affirmative German humor nineteenth-century critics juxtaposed to destructive Jewish satire and wit.[66] Beierle named several non-Jewish film comedians who epitomized a German approach: Heinz Rühmann, Paul Hörbiger, Jakob Tiedke, and Gustav Waldau. He compared German humor to other national humors, contending that French film comedy was materialist and formalistic, recalling Kadner's definition of mechanical, Mediterranean comicalness, and that American comedy was more crude.[67] By contrast, Beierle claimed, German humor was an unacknowledged treasure that could have international appeal because of its "tendency to internalize, love of nature, and emotional turn to contemplative gaiety."[68]

The *Film Kurier* continued to promote a new art of German film humor to replace the corrupt, capitalist (=Jewish) products of the past, as in a telling editorial from late 1933. The author, identified only by the initial "R," used the first-person plural throughout. By using "we," R. spoke on the one hand on behalf of the authors and editors of the *Film Kurier*, and on the other hand, on behalf of those whose thoughts and sentiments aligned with the new regime and with the *Volk*, whose presumed needs and preferences this article invoked frequently. Speaker and audience merged into one, and the author swore clear political allegiances when referring to "the *Volk* movement that has grasped each and every one of us" and "a time 'that places its people before great tasks.'"[69]

R. construed filmmakers as greedy capitalists who had exploited the people and forced inane films upon them. As with K.'s, R.'s text is rich with the coding of Jewish difference, antisemitic innuendo, and inference. Speaking on behalf of the collective, R. wanted to eliminate mechanical, formulaic, and artificial elements from lighthearted entertainment films: "Our thoughts and feelings say adieu and never see you again to the whole comic fuss of yesterday's German film. Without losing ourselves in examples, we gradually want to see liquidated this factory-type attainment of laugh effects through comedian types, dialect jokes, saccharine musical hits, incursions of mistaken identity, pipe dream dolls and whatever else populated the laughter cabinet of yesterday."[70] R. denigrated and wanted to dispose of "yesterday's" comedies as commercial, "factory type" assemblages of stock structures, situations and characters.[71] While not overtly antisemitic, the charges against film industry commercialism in the above quotation and elsewhere in the article—which repeatedly uses nouns such as "wares" or compounds with the word "factory" in them and verbs like "erzielen" (to attain a goal, often in the sense of profits or production)—alluded to the common antisemitic conflation of capitalist and Jew, discouraged aesthetics that antisemites deemed Jewish, and promoted Nazi values.[72] The words "type" and "dialect," used pejoratively, can be read at face value or as discrete references to Jewish "types" and the Yiddish "dialect," as it was sometimes called in German-speaking Europe. Understood in this inferential context and alongside the author's other innuendos, R.'s reference to "types" and "dialect jokes" refers to the influence of the Yiddish theater and ethnically marked Jewish comedians like Lubitsch and Arno.

Drawing on multiple, well-established inferential links, R. advocated that comedy coded as non-Jewish should replace Jewish comedy. Employing a rhetoric of renewal and speaking of "the German cultural revolution," whereby new German films would replace the corrupt, capitalist products of the past, R. called for "revolution all down the line" for film comedy.[73] The revolution R. prescribed for comedy echoed Goebbels's stated wishes: art and artistic motivations should replace commercial concerns. In reality, political, artistic, and commercial motivations all guided the state-influenced financing of Third Reich film through the *Filmkreditbank*. R. wanted to see improvements in comedy's artistic quality and also a turn to the *Volk* and to "earth and a rootedness in the earth, reality and probability," language that, like so much other Nazi discussion of film, praises authenticity and recalls *Blut und Boden* (blood-and-soil) concepts of culture.[74] The piece called for characters integrated "into the territory cultivated by German comedy."[75] R.'s desire for local rootedness and the juxtaposition of nationalistic farming metaphors against the factory metaphors characterizing Weimar film refer to several well-known tropes of Jewish difference. In Nazi parlance, the honest creation and provision of necessary items, in this case nourishment, was productive or "Aryan" economic activity, whereas factory ownership is a form of exploitative or "Jewish" capital.[76] The urban/rural distinction implicit in the factory and farming metaphors was also tied up in longstanding discourses of Jewish difference that construed Jews as cosmopolitan big-city dwellers and Germans as belonging to the land.[77] Tapping in to these inferential networks, R. called for a revolution against Jewish comedy (capitalist, mechanical, artificial) and its replacement with a non-Jewish German comedy (artistic, organic, authentic).

Many Third Reich writings on film comedy promoted a connection to the homeland and a good-natured approach to human foibles and life's minor hardships. The inferential links licensed by the cultural context connect such seemingly innocuous claims to racialized discourses. Expressing an interest in the realistic, everyday experiences of real people, R. asked for a "*reflection* of human weaknesses . . . a life story, a character conflict, a reflection of life in satire or friendly mockery, an example of the *laughing* overcoming of *conflicts* that must be experienced—in the realm of the truthful and probable."[78] As with many other thematic and stylistic features of comedy supported or discouraged by the film trade press, the good-natured approach to mundane conflicts and foibles can be traced back to Kadner, an overtly antisemitic source. In contrast to the mechanical, inauthentic comicalness and cynical wit of Jewish comedy, Kadner praised humor as an essentially German attitude, one that laughed in the face of life's challenges.[79] Characteristic of such humor was "the distance from one's own ego, the gift of being able to smile at, yes even to laugh at, one's self."[80] This self-mocking German humor, according to Kadner, was more modest and affirmative and less ironic, smug, and self-serving than when Jews made Jewish jokes attempting to belittle their own racial flaws.[81] Inferentially rather than overtly antisemitic, R.'s nationalistic program for German film comedy criticized the same features that overt antisemites attributed to Jews, used coding and metaphors associated with Jewishness, and promoted an authentic German humor, grown by German people from the German soil. R.'s program was similar to Kadner's overtly racialized description of German humor.

Throughout the Third Reich, writers for the trade press returned repeatedly to what they diagnosed as the problems of German film comedy and encouraged a humor suited to the German people and the Nazi worldview. These discussions shared terminology, values, and frameworks with overtly antisemitic writings.[82] In 1937, Günther Schwark reiterated that the *Gleichschaltung* of humor need not focus on the political, but rather should spring from "more natural sources" and have an "internal human orientation."[83] Schwark's focus on the natural and the human emphasized values expressed by Goebbels, Beierle, and others and fed into notions of authenticity and *Volk* expression central to Nazi conceptions of German film. According to Schwark, authentic German humor excluded people and comic styles he defined explicitly as non-German and that can be identified inferentially as "Jewish." According to Schwark, German humor demanded a "naturalness and unselfconsciousness" free from "ready-to-wear jokes, childish fatuities, and literary 'Schmonzes.'"[84] The use of the word "Schmonzes," a Yiddish-derived term for blather, the juxtaposition of literary jargon and tomfoolery, and the reference to garment industry humor all alluded to antisemitic stereotypes. Thus, Schwark's innuendo implied, for humor to be in sync with the new order, it had to differ stylistically from Jewish wit, even though it did not need to be explicitly political.

Complementing the critical discussion of German film humor in the trade press, film reviews flagged how well individual comedies met official standards, encouraged and discouraged specific comic techniques, and educated spectators about acceptable taste. Goebbels required film critics to be informed by official principles and regulations and, additionally, knowledge about the art and craft of film; he believed that they should promote high professional and artistic standards, instead of bowing to commercial or personal concerns.[85] He reinforced this agenda with a November 1936 edict banning subjective film criticism (*Filmkritik*) and replacing it with descriptive, politically motivated film observations (*Filmbetrachtung*).[86] The goal of film observations, according to Karl Melzer, business director of the *Reichsfilmkammer*, was: "on the one hand, good film, on the other hand a good public that understands good film and ultimately wants to see only it."[87] Melzer's articulation of this goal acknowledged the discrepancy between public tastes and Nazi cinematic visions, a discrepancy central to the development of Third Reich film comedy. Film journalists were tasked with both correcting this discrepancy and encouraging films that met the regime's standards. Film observations served as important purveyors of Nazi values and aesthetics to film consumers and practitioners. They reveal permitted and encouraged responses to various productions rather than critics' or audiences' honest opinions.

An exemplary film observation that educated readers about German and non-German humor is Hilde Herrmann's "Humor der Völker im Film" (Peoples' Humor in Film).[88] Published in a monthly literary magazine, Herrmann's film observation targeted an educated audience interested in literature and the theater and offers a more sustained example of cultural theory and analysis than a typical film observation in the trade press or a daily newspaper. Herrmann assessed film comedies along the racialized lines drawn by Kadner. She separated authentically Germanic humor from alien wit, promoted the former, and disparaged the latter. Herrmann argued that *Lauter Lügen* (Utter Lies, Heinz Rühmann, 1938), an adaptation of Hans Schweikart's popular stage comedy, exemplified "a particularly German film humor."[89] She praised Rühmann's characteristic "smiling susceptibility to surprise, which stands at the beginning of all wisdom, and which always also spills over a bit into vulnerability; his south German relatives in this are Hans Moser and Paul Hörbiger."[90] Rühmann, Moser, and Hörbiger, as lauded by Herrman, fit Kadner's description of self-critical humor that laughed at serious issues and centered on the boyish German man.[91]

Distinguishing between humor and wit and elevating the former over the latter, Herrmann compared Rühmann's German, "essential humor" to Curt Goetz's "spirited wit" in *Napoleon ist an allem Schuld* (Napoleon Is Guilty for Everything, Curt Goetz, 1938).[92] Although Herrmann's piece is not overtly antisemitic, her language activates codes of Jewish difference in humor. Goetz was an extremely popular comic actor and playwright, known for his sophistication and clever dialogue. His writing was compared frequently to Noel Coward's, George Bernard Shaw's, and Oscar Wilde's. Goetz, who had Swiss citizenship, lived in Switzerland during the early part of the Third Reich, traveling to and working in Germany. In 1939, he emigrated to Hollywood. Nevertheless, his plays were among the most popular and most performed in Nazi Germany.[93] Both the theater and the film industry in the Third Reich benefited financially from having famous film actors appear on stage and popular plays adapted to the screen. Intermedial relationships with theater, such as Goetz's acting, directing, and writing for the screen and Rühmann's adaptation of Schweikart's play, legitimized film as an art form (=noncommercial and therefore non-Jewish). Additionally, by drawing on domestic literary and performance traditions and popular tastes in stage comedy, film adaptations of German authors' plays made film comedy more German. Such adaptations included not only contemporary works but also classics like *Der zerbrochene Krug* (The broken jug, Gustav Ucicky, 1937), based on Heinrich von Kleist's 1811 comedy. The effects of the connections and collaborations between film and theater were frequently consistent with Goebbels's explicit goals and helped make German film comedy less "Jewish." Goetz's involvement in filmmaking, however, did not have an unequivocally Germanizing effect. Film writers' conflicting responses to Goetz's film work highlight how the construct of Jewishness in Third Reich discussions of comedy was not coterminous with Jewish people and how the boundary between the Jewish and the non-Jewish was flexible and mobile.

Goetz was not Jewish by confession, ancestry, or Nazi law. Yet, positioned within the framework of Jewish difference, his comic style was too Jewish. In fact, in November 1923, Goebbels had criticized Goetz's plays for being exactly that.[94] Before Goebbels abolished subjective criticism, some film critics had praised Goetz's witty dialogue in *Glückskinder* as an indigenous alternative to American comedy (and thus, implicitly, as a non-Jewish *ersatz* for it).[95] By contrast, Herrmann's attack on Goetz relies on tropes of Jewish difference. According to Herrmann, Goetz displayed self-confidence instead of introspection; "the polished word, sparkling dialogue that goes hand in hand with his controlled deportment" revealed his weaknesses only in brief moments.[96] Goetz's acknowledgment of personal failings was "more sculpted" in the sense of "western 'humanitas,'" in contrast with Rühmann's more open, "more human," "more German" way.[97] Herrmann repeatedly criticized Goetz's "spirited wit," using the French loan word "esprit" and the potentially racialized and derogatory term "Witz" to connote the foreignness of Goetz's comedy. Goetz's wit, Herrmann argued, missed the mark in *Napoleon*. Of course, the main character's obsession with Napoleon in that film is anti-German as well. Herrmann cast Goetz's verbal wit as alien to the German language. A German with a quick tongue, Herrmann argued, relied more on fact and gesture than the word, because at its root the German language was closer to music than to logic.[98] Moreover, Herrmann claimed that Goetz's rapid-fire dialogue and pointed wit were not suited to the magnification, extension, and proximity of material to the spectator inherent in the medium of film.[99] In short, Herrmann asserted that witty dialogue was both unfilmic and un-German and strongly suggested that it should be avoided. *Napoleon* was Goetz's final film before emigrating to Hollywood. He returned to Europe after the war.

Herrmann's arguments echoed Kadner's, as did those of many other Third Reich film journalists, who promoted less intellectual comedy. Like Herrmann, elevating gesture over language, Hippler proclaimed situation comedy more pedagogically effective than dialogue.[100] Claims that verbal wit and rapid tempo were too demanding for the spectator, likely to be drowned out by audience laughter, and unsuited to the visual nature of film were common in Third Reich film reporting.[101] In Weimar Berlin, the frenetic pace of living and working in the big city was referred to as "Jewish haste," embodied by Arno's performance as Sigi Meyer in *Keine Feier ohne Meyer* (No Celebration Without Meyer, Carl Boese, 1931).[102] A slower pace was coded as nonurban and non-Jewish. Oddly, critics who called for slow-paced, nonintellectual comedy did not acknowledge what their agenda implied regarding the brainpower of German audiences. Intellectualism, cleverness, rapidity, and wordplay were "Jewish," and film writers discouraged them. The linkages between the rejection of "Jewish" comic techniques and Nazi racial antisemitism remain inferential in most cases. Unlike many of her peers, however, Herrmann did articulate a racial aspect of this counterintuitive yet widespread argument against clever comedy: to preserve wit as artificial as Goetz's, despite its unsuitability to the filmic medium, Herrmann speculated, "one must probably be French, or at least Latin."[103] Herrmann's comparison of Rühmann and Goetz defined "German" humor as self-deprecating, "human," blunt, physical, and slow. She dismissed sophistication, self-confidence, and verbal dexterity as alien and the latter as unsuited to the silver screen. Much Third Reich writing on film comedy used similar language and tropes to code Jewish difference and reject Jewishness.

From Inferential Antisemitism in Film Criticism to Inferential Antisemitism in Film

Although articles in the trade press for the most part avoided overt antisemitism, they regularly invoke Jewish difference, coding particular comic techniques as Jewish or non-Jewish, criticizing the former and promoting the latter. The coding of Jewish difference in comedy was well established before the Nazis came to power, and there were both philo- and antisemitic traditions of talking about Jewish wit, Jewish humor, and Jewish jokes. Third Reich film reporters borrowed language and tropes from older discourses, for example, from nineteenth-century criticisms of Jewish wit and capitalism that persisted through the Weimar era and into the Third Reich. Interpreting journalists' codings of Jewish difference within inferential patterns created by the era's overtly antisemitic texts underscores how film reporting normalized negative constructs of Jewish difference, encouraged the expulsion of Jewishness from film comedy, and thus supported the Nazis' antisemitic project. It is in this sense that these examples of film journalism functioned as inferential antisemitism. Inferential antisemitism reinforces the work of overt antisemitism either by unselfconsciously echoing significant values and assumptions or through innuendo that unites speaker and listener with a shared secret code. Overt antisemites argued that Jewish commercialism, greed, and loose morality (both sexual and ethical) had corrupted German film. They sought to purge Jewish people and purported Jewish influence from German film in order to create a new, racially authentic German film art. Without mentioning Jews directly, film reporters discouraged the selfsame traits and techniques identified by overt antisemitic sources as Jewish and promoted the themes and styles those sources praised as German. Such writing pushed filmmaking in the racialized directions conceived of by overt antisemites.

The antisemitic agenda for film comedy and the continuum between its overt and inferential manifestations, as unearthed in this chapter, lay the groundwork for the film analyses in the following chapters. The stylistic dictates stemming from the Nazi obsession with expelling the Jewish from German film more generally and from film comedy in particular were in tension with generic trends and audience preferences. This tension affected the development of film comedy in the Third Reich. Despite directives from the Propaganda Ministry, restructuring of the film industry, and pedagogical pressure from film reporters, comedy fell in line only gradually and inconsistently, for reasons I will soon explain. Overt and inferential antisemitism not only guided the stylistic and thematic development of Third Reich film comedy but also are expressed in different ways as various comedies go about imagining *Volksgemeinschaft*. The coming chapters will untangle the complicated relationships between various texts, films, and the Nazis' antisemitic agenda, isolate the mechanisms for identifying and expelling Jewishness from Third Reich film comedy, and explain how comedies of that era express overt and inferential antisemitism.

Notes

1. There is much rich and dense discussion of inferential role theory in semantics and the philosophy of language. A germinal work in this field is: Brandom, *Making it Explicit*.
2. Adorno, "Anti-Semitism and Fascist Propaganda," in *Stars*, ed. Crook, 228.
3. Adorno, "Anti-Semitism and Fascist Propaganda," in *Stars*, ed. Crook, 228.
4. See introduction.
5. Adorno, "Anti-Semitism and Fascist Propaganda," in *Stars*, ed. Crook, 228.
6. Kadner, *Rasse*, 2nd ed., 222.
7. The Talmud is an important collection of thousands of postbiblical rabbinic writings. Nazi antisemites and their intellectual forbears cited it frequently and inaccurately as evidence of poor Jewish character. Keller and Andersen, *Der Jude*, 138–40. See also: Kadner, *Rasse*, 2nd ed., 216–17, 222.
8. Keller and Andersen, *Der Jude*, 138.
9. Streicher, "Geleitwort vom Gauleiter Julius Streicher," in *Der Jude als Verbrecher*, 9.
10. "Das Volk der Dekomposition, das Volk der Zersetzung und Zerstörung." "Was ist Kulturschande?" 6.
11. Friedländer, *Nazi Germany and the Jews*, vol. 1, 107.
12. "Verjudung," 1. Beilage.
13. S[chneider], "Dr. Goebbels," 1.
14. S[chneider], "Dr. Goebbels," 1.
15. S[chneider], "Dr. Goebbels," 2.
16. Neumann et al., *Film "Kunst,"* 5.
17. Neumann et al., *Film "Kunst,"* 26, 39. The statistics cited above do not square with the different but equally dubious and inflated statistics on page 106. These and other sets of figures in the book illustrate how the authors of *Film "Kunst," Film Kohn, Film Korruption* use spurious, inflated statistics in support of their antisemitic polemic.
18. Neumann et al., *Film "Kunst,"* 26.
19. Neumann et al., *Film "Kunst,"* 29–30.
20. Neumann et al., *Film "Kunst,"* 76.
21. Neumann et al., *Film "Kunst,"* 27.
22. Neumann et al., *Film "Kunst,"* 56.
23. Neumann et al., *Film "Kunst,"* 44–45.
24. "Die nüchterne Zweckverfolgung in ihrem Tun und Lassen, die hämische Verneinung jedes tieferen Gefühls und jeder edleren Begeisterung, die unverhüllte Sucht nach äußerem Genuß, nach einem hohlen Wohlleben und primitiver Befriedigung geringer Ansprüche, der Mangel an einem höheren Ausrichtung und schöneren Erfüllung des Lebens." Neumann et al., *Film "Kunst,"* 44.
25. Neumann et al., *Film "Kunst,"* 67–68.
26. Neumann et al., *Film "Kunst,"* 15.

27. "Wollte Deutschland nicht darauf verzichten, jemals eine seiner kulturellen Tradition würdige Filmkunst zu erreichen und eine Filmindustrie zu besitzen, in der die Grundsätze des deutschen Kaufmanns Geltung hatten." Neumann et al., *Film "Kunst,"* 139.

28. "Seiner ungeheuren Verantwortung der deutschen Volksseele gegenüber bewusst und darum frei sein von jeder destruktiven oder internationalen Tendenz." Neumann et al., *Film "Kunst,"* 153.

29. "Die wahre und reine Kunst kann immer nur auf dem seelischen Boden eines rassemäßig und volksmäßig (national) bedingten Empfindens zustandekommen und wirken. Sie ist der vollkommendste Ausdruck einer blutsmäßig verbundenen Gemeinschaft durch alle Phasen ihrer geschichtlichen Entwicklung hindurch." Neumann et al., *Film "Kunst,"* 166.

30. Neumann et al., *Film "Kunst,"* 137.

31. Herrmann, "Humor," 363–65.

32. Harten et al., *Rassenhygiene,* 263.

33. Och and Meyer-Sickendiek, "Einleitung," in *Der jüdische Witz,* ed. Meyer-Sickendiek and Och, 9.

34. Distelmeyer, "Übergänge," in *Spaß beiseite,* ed. Distelmeyer, 7–9; Loewy, "Ist ein jüdischer Komiker jüdisch-komisch," in *Spaß beiseite,* ed. Distelmeyer, 13–20.

35. See, for example: Och and Meyer-Sickendiek, "Einleitung," in *Der jüdische Witz,* ed. Meyer-Sickendiek and Och, 13. Ben-Amos, "Der 'Mythos,'" in *Der jüdische Witz,* ed. Meyer-Sickendiek and Och, 105. Original text: Ben-Amos, "The 'Myth' of Jewish Humor," 112–31. See also the essays by Micha Brumlik, Limor Shifman, and Sander L. Gilman in *Der jüdische Witz*.

36. "Die mannigfaltigen Spielarten des Humors und der Komik von Grund auf nur zu verstehen, wenn sie nicht nur im nationalen sondern im rassischen Zusammenhang betrachtet werden." Kadner, *Rasse,* 219.

37. Kadner, *Rasse,* 19, 37–41. Kadner adapts Eisler's definition of "Komisch" from his widely used *Handwörterbuch der Philosophie,* 336–37.

38. For Kadner's discussion of Münchhausen in literature, see Kadner, *Rasse,* 86–90.

39. "Äußerungsformen der Komik und des Witzes—der eigentliche Humor liegt außerhalb des jüdischen Wesens." Kadner, *Rasse,* 202.

40. "Rassengenossen." Kadner, *Rasse,* 202–3.

41. Kadner, *Rasse,* 203–8.

42. Kadner, *Rasse,* 2nd ed., 222.

43. Och and Meyer-Sickendiek, "Einleitung," in *Der jüdische Witz,* ed. Meyer-Sickendiek and Och, 11.

44. Och and Meyer-Sickendiek, "Einleitung," in *Der jüdische Witz,* ed. Meyer-Sickendiek and Och, 11–15. See also the essays in that volume by Och, Markus Winkler, and Manfred Schneider, and also Kessel, "Race and Humor," 381–84.

45. "In bewusster Feindseligkeit gegen Staat und Gesellschaft, Kirche und Wirtschaft, gegen die überkommenen Bindungen menschlichen Gemeinschaftswesens, tritt uns jüdischer Witz in seiner zynischen Form in ätzender Schärfe und Ironie entgegen in Gestalten wie Ludwig Börne (Baruch) und Heinrich Heine (Chaim Bückeburg)." Kadner, *Rasse,* 214. Börne and Heine were prominent nineteenth-century political authors who had converted to Christianity from Judaism (Heine later converted back) and who attracted antisemitic ire in their lifetimes and in the Nazi period.

46. On the Nazis and Heine, see Dennis, *Inhumanities,* 109–23.

47. See, for example: Stalzer, "Jüdische Bühnenkünstler," in *Der jüdische Witz,* 226–29. Otte, *Jewish Identities,* 125–280.

48. Herf, *Jewish Enemy*, 25.
49. Wortig, *Der Film in der deutschen Tageszeitung*, 52, 54.
50. "Neuaufbau des deutschen Films," 1–2. Dr. W. M. [pseud.], "Steigendes Interesse für ernste Filme," 2.
51. See, for example: S[chwar]k, "Angst," 1. Many trade press articles focused on comedy and humor and on their relationship to political developments.
52. Sattig, *Die deutsche Filmpresse*, 89; K., "Ist die Kritik als Erzieherin nötig?" 1.
53. K., "Ist die Kritik als Erzieherin nötig?" 1.
54. Spector, "Modernism without Jews," 615.
55. Makela, "Rise and Fall of the Flapper Dress," 185–86, 199–201. Westphal, *Berliner Konfektion und Mode*, 89–91, passim. See also Silverman on the coding of department stores and mass consumerism as Jewish, feminine, and modern. Silverman, *Becoming Austrian*, 82–83.
56. On the fashion farce, see Ganeva, *Women in Weimar Fashion*, 122–30.
57. Keller and Andersen, *Der Jude*, 13, 87.
58. "Aus ewig alt-neuem Modestoff gedreht und gewebt." K., "Ist die Kritik als Erzieherin nötig?" 1.
59. K., "Ist die Kritik als Erzieherin nötig?" 1.
60. "Daß die Filmkonfektionshäuser mit den Zeitungen unter dem Arm triumphierend winken, 'Ha, ihr Ketzer, hier habt ihr's! lest mal wie wunderbar die anderen schreiben.'" K., "Ist die Kritik als Erzieherin nötig?" 1.
61. Friedländer, *Nazi Germany and the Jews*, vol. 1, 79. Spector, "Modernism without Jews," 616. Wallach, *Passing Illusions*, 67.
62. For example: "Mehr Humor in Film," 2; "Maßhalten auch im Heiteren," 2.
63. Beierle, "Der Weg," 3; "Die deutsche Filmpresse," 7; Sattig, *Die deutsche Filmpresse*, 61, 84.
64. "Heimatsgefühl und Menschenkenntnis die Grundpfeiler für den volksgemäßen Humor sind." Beierle, "Der Weg," 3.
65. Beierle, "Der Weg," 3.
66. Och and Meyer-Sickendiek, "Einleitung," in *Der jüdische Witz*, 11.
67. Beierle, "Der Weg," 3.
68. Beierle, "Der Weg," 3.
69. R., "Forderungen," 1
70. "Unser Denken und Fühlen sagt dem ganzen Lustspielgetue des deutschen Films von Gestern lachend Adieu und Aufnimmerwiedersehen. Ohne uns in Beispiele verlieren zu wollen möchten wir diese fabrikmäßige Erzielung von Lacheffekten durch Komikertypen, Dialektscherze, Schlagersüßlichkeiten, Verwechslungseinfälle, Wunschtraumpuppen und was noch alles das Lachkabinett von gestern bevölkerte, allmählich liquidiert sehen." R., "Forderungen," 1.
71. R., "Forderungen," 1.
72. For more on the Nazi-era conflation of capitalist and Jew, see chapter 5.
73. R., "Forderungen," 1, 2.
74. "Erde und Erdhaftigkeit, Wirklichkeit und Wahrscheinlichkeit." R., "Forderungen," 1.
75. "In den Erdraum, den das deutsche Lustspiel bebaut." R., "Forderungen," 2.
76. Brown, *Weimar Radicals*, 52–53.
77. See Schlör, *Das Ich der Stadt*. Lisa Silverman analyzes the function of Jewish difference in the relationship between Vienna and the provinces as well as between different parts of Vienna in: *Becoming Austrians*.
78. R., "Forderungen," 2. Emphasis in the original.
79. Kadner, *Rasse*, 2nd ed., 17–19, also 37–42.

80. Kadner, *Rasse,* 2nd ed., 116.
81. Kadner, *Rasse,* 2nd ed., 221–22.
82. For additional examples, see "Worüber lachen wir eigentlich?" 3; Volz, "Eine zeitgemäße Frage," 2–4; Henseleit, "Heitere Filme," 1.
83. S[chwar]k, "Angst," 1.
84. "'Konfektionswitze, kindliche Einfältigkeiten und literarische 'Schmonzes.'" S[chwar]k, "Angst," 1.
85. "Dr. Goebbels sprach vor den deutschen Kritikern," 2.
86. "Beseitigung der Kunstkritik," 1.
87. "Filmbetrachtung als Erziehungsaufgabe," 1.
88. Herrmann, "Humor," 363–65.
89. Herrmann, "Humor," 363.
90. Herrmann, "Humor," 364.
91. For more on Rühmann, see chapter 4.
92. Herrmann, "Humor," 364.
93. Grange, *Hitler Laughing,* 40–46.
94. Longerich, *Goebbels: A Biography,* 32.
95. See page 123.
96. "Das geschliffene Wort, der sprühende Dialog, dem die sparsame, beherrschte Gebärde bestätigend zur Hand geht." Herrmann, "Humor," 364.
97. Herrmann, "Humor," 364.
98. Herrmann, "Humor," 364.
99. Herrmann, "Humor," 364–65.
100. Hippler, *Betrachtungen,* 100.
101. See, for example: G[eorg]. H[erzberg], "Wortwitz im Film," 1. Also: Eckert, "Filmkomik," 234.
102. Prawer, *Between Two Worlds,* 123.
103. Herrmann, "Humor," 365.
After criticizing Goetz for pursuing a type of comedy alien to his *Volk* and the medium, Herrmann studies and praises Ginnaro Rhigelli's *They've Kidnapped a Man* (1938) as an example of "die italienische Abart romanischen Witzes" and Norman Z. McLeod's "Merrily We Live" (1938) as American "humor" (365).

2

OVERT ANTISEMITISM, JEWISH DIFFERENCE, AND COLONIAL WHITENESS IN EARLY THIRD REICH FILM COMEDY

Nur nicht weich werden, Susanne! *and* Die Blume von Hawaii

IN *FILM-"KUNST," FILM KOHN, FILM KORRUPTION,* NEUMANN, BELLING, and Betz characterize the history of film in Germany as a "fight for German film."[1] Theorized overtly by party ideologues, launched by the Propaganda Ministry, and spread inferentially in film criticism, this antisemitic battle aimed to separate the Jewish from the non-Jewish and to excise Jewishness from film industry practices and products. But antisemitic film crusaders had audiences to contend with. As Katie Trumpener aptly points out, "the cinema of the Third Reich inherited its entire domestic audience from the cinema of the Weimar Republic."[2] Nazis were swimming against a strong current of public tastes. In an article dripping with antisemitic innuendo in the *Deutsche Filmzeitung*, a right-leaning Munich film weekly, Hans Spielhofer bemoaned how the "less talented foreign dominators of German film" and their "speculation on low instincts" had ruined German moviegoers' palates. Comedy and operetta were particularly popular because of "foreign taste," characterized by irony, escapism, and a "'relativity' typical of the foreign spirit"—a swipe at Albert Einstein—which ultimately was to blame for destroying moderation and morality and spreading godlessness. Spielhofer acknowledged that audience preferences were deep-seated and "will" would not be enough to change them quickly, suggesting that "impulse, experience, [and] imagination" could be the harbingers of a "national storm."[3]

Nonpoliticized audience tastes were part of a larger reality faced by antisemitic extremists when the Nazis first came to power: despite widespread prejudices against Jewish people, ordinary Germans were not all that committed to antisemitic fanaticism. Between 1933 and 1935, Hitler showed restraint in his public rhetoric and compromised with more traditional conservative elites on antisemitic policies.[4] Most Germans knew about the regime's antisemitic policies but did not consider them a priority.[5] The public's attention was on political and economic stabilization. Established tastes, habits, and economic anxiety made people unenthusiastic about antisemitic actions. For example, the announcement of a boycott of Jewish businesses on April 1, 1933, provoked questions about the boycott's impact on non-Jewish Germans and "brisk business in Jewish-owned stores . . . ([because] the public did not yet know how long the boycott would last)."[6] Contemporary witnesses described "passive and certainly not hostile" bystanders on the day of the boycott and "many expressions of discontent."[7] Continuing economic difficulties led to "an upswing in anti-Semitism in 1935."[8] Nevertheless, not all Germans were passionately antisemitic at that time either. Small gestures of support by individual "Aryans," their continued friendly relationships with Jews, and openness to self-advocacy by Jewish artists and intellectuals betrayed an "undercurrent of sympathy for the persecuted Jews."[9]

Produced in 1934 and released in early 1935, *Nur nicht weich werden, Susanne!* and its reception provide unique insight into the gap between Nazi antisemitism and audience tastes. The only Third Reich film comedy to voice overtly antisemitic criticisms of the Weimar film industry similar to Neumann, Belling, and Betz's, *Susanne* had all the will in the world to convince audiences to reject "Jewish" film, but at the same time seems to have lacked the impulse and imagination to provide them with a satisfying experience.[10] By parodying the production of Richard Oswald's *Die Blume von Hawaii*, which it codes as Jewish, *Susanne* draws clear boundaries between the Jewish and the non-Jewish to isolate and eliminate Jewishness. *Blume*, by contrast, blurs the boundaries between the Jewish and the non-Jewish through racial performances that assimilate Jewishness into colonial whiteness. Audiences were much less receptive to *Susanne*'s overt antisemitism than they were to Oswald's "Jewish" film operetta. Contrasts between the styles, messages, and reception of *Susanne* and *Blume* highlight the mismatch between the Nazis' antisemitic agenda for German film and the preferences of audiences they sought to reach. Such tensions between ideological dictates and audience tastes were a significant factor in the development of film comedy throughout the Third Reich.

Overt Antisemitism in *Nur nicht weich werden, Susanne!*

A clear example of overt antisemitism with explicitly pedagogical aims, *Susanne* attacks Jews in the film industry, parodies profit-motivated operettas, and proposes more artistic styles of German filmmaking and more wholesome German lifestyles. Directed by Arsen von Cserépy, who became a member of the Nazi party in 1930, and who was known for his Weimar-era *Fridericus Rex* (Frederick the Great) films, *Susanne* is based on a 1933 novel by Willi Krause, published under the pseudonym Peter Hagen.[11] A committed Nazi, Krause served from 1934 to 1936 as *Reichsfilmdramaturg*, a position from which he censored and approved (or shelved) all scripts considered for production in Germany. Krause's position both reflects the confidence Goebbels had in his political and artistic judgment and illustrates that in the crucial transitional period, scripts were controlled by an ideologue who wanted to purge Jewish moral, financial, and aesthetic corruption from German film. *Susanne* was serialized between April 19 and May 31, 1933, in *Der Angriff*, Goebbels's Berlin newspaper, for which Krause was also editor and film critic. Friedrich Bubendey, playwright and author of Nazi political prose, adapted and published *Susanne* as a play in 1934, the same year in which Cserépy made his film.[12] Krause's novel, Bubendey's play, and Cserépy's film all condemn "Jewish" criminal, commercial, and aesthetic practices in the Weimar film industry and offer an allegedly superior alternative. They do this in forms that they subtitle, respectively, "a funny novel," "a comedy in five acts," and "a grotesque from a past time." Cserépy's *Susanne* uses disciplinary humor to teach viewers how to recognize and expunge Jewish influence from German cinema. It satirizes "Jewish" film and proposes a "German" alternative. Cannibalizing its predecessors, *Susanne* also incorporates aspects of Weimar cinema that it criticizes, making the reviled object part of the self.

Multiple strategies in *Susanne* teach spectators to identify Jewish influences in the film industry and advocate for their replacement. *Susanne* classifies various comedic, aesthetic, and commercial practices as positive/German or negative/Jewish. It also instructs viewers regarding sexual, regional, and Jewish difference and inclusion in and exclusion from both the film industry and the *Volksgemeinschaft*. Distinguishing between Jewish and non-Jewish Germans, *Susanne* insists that spectators learn to recognize Jewish difference and to reject Jewishness. It envisions corrupt and criminal Jews producing immoral and laughably bad movies for their own profit and encourages Germans to make serious and realistic film art reflecting on real-life situations instead. Complementing this message, *Susanne* educates Germans to behave as befits their gender and putative race. The narrative, characters, and their dialects encourage cooperation across regional origin and class—the building of a *Volksgemeinschaft*—to entrap and punish criminal Jews. The treatment of the eponymous Susanne (Jessie Vihrog), a pretty blonde extra who wants to be a film star, defines a desired German femininity. Susanne's refusals first to act in a nude bathtub scene and then to act at all, and her ultimately becoming a housewife with a husband, cottage, and vegetable garden, encourage German women to neither serve as display objects nor submit to Jewish machinations, but rather to seek marriage and cultivate fertility. Notions of proper economic production and consumption—in the form of the contrast between culturally corrosive movies and nourishing food—play an important role in this film as well.

The overtly antisemitic representation of Jewish characters in *Susanne* is both malicious and banal. Corrupt, shady figures with stereotypically Jewish names, such as Gold, Silver, Schwarz, and Arschinowitz, populate the film.[13] In addition to their Jewish coding, these aptronyms mark their bearers as money oriented, dark, and—in the case of Arschinowitz—an ass. These stereotypical Jewish figures work in professions frequently targeted by antisemitic criticism in the early 1930s: organized crime, the film industry, the press, and the higher echelons of the police bureaucracy.[14] Even though the actors playing these roles do not necessarily "look Jewish" in a physiognomically stereotypical way, their movements, costuming, and speech conform to antisemitic caricatures of Jews in other Weimar and Third Reich sources, such as *Der Stürmer* (see Figures 2.1 and 2.2). The Jews in *Susanne* strut like puffed-up, arrogant capitalists with prosperously full bellies or fidget fastidiously like neurotic intellectuals. Their costumes include clichéd accoutrements associated with antisemitic stereotypes, such as cigars and round, horn-rimmed glasses. Whereas most non-Jewish characters in this film are marked by strong regional accents, the Jewish characters speak German with varying degrees of Yiddish intonations. This is consistent with longstanding German literary conventions of marking Jewishness and non-Jewishness through language and dialect.[15] The Jews in *Susanne* use Yiddish vocabulary such as *meschugge* (crazy) and

Figure 2.1. Political cartoon with Jewish businessmen, *Der Stürmer*, June 1934 (Issue #26). United States Holocaust Memorial Museum, courtesy of Hans Pauli. The views or opinions expressed in this book, and the context in which this image is used, do not necessarily reflect the views or policy of, nor imply approval or endorsement by, the United States Holocaust Memorial Museum.

Figure 2.2. General Director Gold (Willi Schur) in *Nur nicht weich werden, Susanne!* (1935). The studio director looks like a caricature from *Der Stürmer*. Screenshot.

nebbich (poor clod), gesticulate wildly, and converse primarily about making money through semi-illegitimate businesses or illegal schemes. They brazenly commit fraud, blackmail, and adultery and are smug rather than remorseful about it. The use of such familiar codes tells viewers that Jews are easy to recognize, due to their appearance, speech, and behavior.

Susanne depicts Jews as reprehensible criminal types, who pull the strings behind the film industry. It expects spectators to recognize them based on a suite of characteristics and behaviors and instructs audiences on how to identify and counter the effects of those behaviors. *Susanne* criticizes commercialism in Weimar film as a consequence of Jewish greed and criminality. Through the parodic production of a kitschy musical called *Lieb mich mal in Honolulu* (Love me in Honolulu) and the illegal actions and tasteless debates of its personnel, *Susanne* illustrates "Jewish" moral deficiencies and their commercial and aesthetic effects on cinema. *Susanne* teaches spectators how to recognize such effects and promotes a "German" alternative, by illustrating proper artistic and economic production and consumption.

Films, like the vegetables Susanne grows, should germinate in German soil and be a product of hard work, integrity, and attention to the mundane. They should nourish the nation and generate a subsistence income rather than stimulate frivolous desires in the interest of excessive profit.

Susanne defines and contrasts a "Jewish," commercial view of cinema with an artistic, "German" one, expressing views like those of the party ideologues and film critics discussed in the previous chapter. This contrast is articulated first in a planning meeting for Super-Gigantic-Film's next production, eventually settled upon as *Lieb mich mal in Honolulu*. The producers begin the meeting brainstorming for settings, elements, and a title that will make the film popular. The Jews at the table are most interested in eroticism and "sex appeal," luxury, exotic settings, romance, and music. Mention of other recent productions indicates that the new film will be the next in a series of cookie-cutter projects with only superficial differences between them, all designed to make money. As indicated by both his name and his behavior, Bitter (Eugen Rex), the non-Jewish film director hired for this job, disapproves of his employers' plans. During the meeting, he makes tongue-in-cheek suggestions that the Jewish production team takes seriously. When Bitter proposes, ironically, a "big love scene while surfing the waves," the Jews' enthusiasm for it is ludicrous. This moment is one of *Susanne*'s many uses of mockery as disciplinary humor. To show how bad such ideas really are, Bitter runs his hands through his hair in a frustrated manner and mugs displeasure for the camera. The scene culminates in an argument between him and General Director Gold (Willi Schur) about the nature of cinema and whether it is fundamentally art or commerce, an argument that the aptly named Gold wins because he has the capital. In this debate and throughout the film, Bitter's views echo those of Krause and Goebbels and resonate with commentary in film trade publications, which promoted German/artistic film over Jewish/commercial film.[16] Bitter doesn't want to make films for Gold anymore, because the process is "manufacture" rather than "artistic work." Gold counters this with the claim that film is not art; rather, film is a marketable "ware," analogous to any other type of merchandise. Bitter doesn't care about money and wants to make "a respectable artistic film," a concept that Gold waves aside as an impractical, money-losing proposition. Without money, Gold points out, there is no art, or anything else. And ultimately, he tells Bitter, the film they are planning *is* art and a "magnificent idea." Late-Weimar comedies like *Die Koffer des Herrn O.F.* (The Suitcases of Mr. O. F., Alexis Granowsky, 1931) and *Ein blonder Traum* (A Blond Dream, Paul Martin, 1932) had mocked the seriality and commercialism of Weimar and Hollywood film. By emphasizing the Jewishness and exaggerating the dishonest, manipulative character of the men behind the scenes, *Susanne* pairs similar aesthetic criticism with overt antisemitism.

While the planning scene represents both sides of a debate about the nature of cinema, this representation is racialized and not even-handed; the scene promotes like-mindedness with the German Bitter in several ways. The viewer already knows that the Jewish Gold and Arschinowitz are running their production company as a front for an illegal gambling operation, and their behavior is unsavory. Bitter, so far, is an unknown quantity, but his body language in the meeting—his pulling back and even turning away from the table—illustrates his distance from the crooks. The dialogue reveals Gold's motivation to be profit and Bitter's to be art. Thus, Bitter emerges as the figure with stronger moral character. The camera also encourages sympathy with Bitter. It places him in the front of the frame, larger and closer to the audience. At times, it adopts his point of view, locating the audience literally and figuratively in his corner. The close-ups on his face give his argument greater clarity and import. Yet Bitter is not depicted as a unique, solitary artist. Instead, Gold's use of the plural, informal form of "you" (ihr) in this discussion to refer to Bitter and his ilk positions Bitter as part of a collective opposed to Gold's point of view. Particularly in the context of other cinematic strategies in this scene, this "you" indirectly includes the audience as if it were part of Bitter's group as well, interpellating the spectator as one who shares Bitter's views. This scene and others criticize "Jewish" commercialism in film. The story links such commercialism to "Jewish" criminality and corruption.

Jewish Difference and Colonial Whiteness in *Die Blume von Hawaii*

Die Blume von Hawaii, which *Susanne*'s film-within-the-film parodies, was an adaptation of a popular 1931 Viennese operetta by Paul Abraham.[17] The plot involves an exiled Hawaiian princess returning incognito to the islands from Paris, several tangled love stories, and a thwarted indigenous uprising in Honolulu against the US occupation, all strung together with catchy show tunes. *Blume,* even though it passed censorship and premiered in March 1933, embodied many Jewish-coded features of Weimar cinema, which Nazis criticized. It also addressed Jewish difference indirectly with a mix of comedy, colonial fantasies, and overt racism different from the Nazis': while reifying the superiority of the white colonizer over people of color, *Blume* construed whiteness to include people who could assimilate or pass as white Europeans. Permeable colonial whiteness, defined by appearance and behavior, offered Jews more potential social acceptance than did Nazi racial categories, which excluded them permanently from the hegemonic group because of blood. The composition of the cast and crew, the style, and its deviance from Nazi antisemitic norms made *Blume* the ideal target for Cserépy's parody in *Susanne.*

It was easy for the Nazis to cast *Blume* as a Jewish film, given the prominence of self-identified and perceived Jews involved in this production. Oswald, originally from Austria, was a very prolific film director in the Weimar Republic. He is best remembered by twenty-first century scholars for his film in support of the homosexual emancipation movement, *Anders als die Andern* (Different from the Others, 1919), a film that elicited antisemitic reactions, among others.[18] Oswald made more than a hundred films in a range of genres, from dramas and Expressionist horror films to comedies and operettas. His 1930 film *Dreyfus,* based on France's turn-of-the-century Dreyfus affair, argued against antisemitism and for a just legal system. Paul Abraham, born in Hungary, composed many operettas popular in German-speaking Central Europe and abroad. Both Oswald and Abraham were Jewish, as was scriptwriter Heinz Goldberg. The female lead Marta Eggerth and other members of *Blume*'s cast and crew also had Jewish ancestry. Oswald left Germany in June 1933, after increasing professional difficulties, antisemitic attacks by the press, and a hearing before the Gestapo.[19] Abraham, Goldberg, and Eggerth emigrated as well. The heavy involvement of Jewish people in *Blume* was typical of the genre. According to Steven Beller: "So large was the reliance of operetta on Jewish talent that the Nazi ban in Germany on performing works by Jews to non-Jewish audiences had, by the mid-1930s, effectively destroyed the business model of Viennese operetta."[20]

Blume was a type of film that Nazi restructuring of the film industry intended to make obsolete. *Tonfilmoperetten* (sound film operettas, the forerunner of musical comedy) were already coded as Jewish in the Weimar era and Nazis targeted the genre for reform immediately after taking power.[21] The trade press not only criticized the commercialism of *Tonfilmoperetten,* but also wrote about the genre as being suspiciously foreign. In an inferentially antisemitic attack, the *Film Kurier* described the *Tonfilmoperette* as a profit-motivated product of the ready-to-wear garment industry, a Jewish-coded industry maligned by antisemites.[22] The *Film Kurier* characterized it as a genre "that adorns itself with foreign takes and foreign milieus from the Bosporos to the Eskimos (Nanuk as an operetta tenor admittedly is still absent)."[23] The disparaging tone suggests that spectacles of foreign vistas and visits, often exoticizing and racist in their own right, have an international outlook that was unwelcome. Elsewhere the article argues for more domestic settings in future German films.

Stylistically, *Blume* exemplified aspects of Weimar film that Nazis criticized in both *Susanne* and polemical written texts. Nazis disparaged what they saw as frivolous entertainment, cheap commercialism, and films pandering to base tastes and an international market. While many films made by non-Jews share such flaws, Nazis nevertheless attributed them to Jewish influence. *Blume* happened to fit the Nazis' stereotypes. The commercialism of Oswald's early sound films, which film critics both praised and condemned, was driven by economic circumstances, instinct, and calculation and based on a "recipe for success" that he repeated several times and refined in his extremely popular *Viktoria und ihr Husar* (Victoria and Her Hussar, 1931).[24] Unfortunately, *Blume* conformed to antisemitic stereotypes about Jewish filmmaking. Not only was it formulaic, but also its rapid pace, irony, verbal wit, and physical comedy were much closer to what overt antisemites like Kadner described as Jewish wit and comicalness than to German humor. As did most other films made before Hitler came to power and a significant number of those made after, *Blume* strove to please audiences and make money, not to express the *Volk's* soul artistically, and thus by Nazi standards counted as a "Jewish" film.

As was the case with other *Tonfilmoperetten*, the plot of *Blume* is unrealistic; the characters are undeveloped, and the whole film is an excuse to present musical hits within an appealing spectacle. Yet it was well crafted and very popular. Both positive and negative reviews struggle with this tension. Reviewers concur that the film would be or already was commercially successful, having been based on a very popular stage operetta and executed in the style and tradition of prior successful *Tonfilmoperetten*. *Der Film*, an illustrated weekly edited by Betz with a circulation of about 4,200, was very critical of *Blume*.[25] It nevertheless acknowledged *Blume's* commercial success, which the reviewer attributes—in a barely veiled antisemitic slur—to Oswald's "good nose for business."[26] Despite the existence of a market for this film, however, "in production, there are no delusions about the fact that even the pure entertainment films of the future must bear a different stamp."[27] Even the most glowing reviews noted that *Blume* was out of step with the times. The *Kinematograph* speculates, "In *The Flower of Hawaii* maybe we are seeing the last sound film operetta in the old style. As nice as the script is, as amusingly as the individual events are staged—they have absolutely nothing to do with the needs and wishes of our time."[28] The contradictions between critics' praise of *Blume*'s discrete features and their criticisms of the film and genre as a whole reflect both political and antisemitic bias.[29] They also reflect the tension between audience tastes and the Nazi agenda and critics' function as mediators between them.

Another reason that *Susanne* disparaged *Blume* was that it indulged in internationalism and titillated its audiences with the kind of exoticism criticized by the *Film Kurier*.[30] Various types of exoticism, including Orientalism, Americanism, and other cultural appropriations and misrepresentations, had been quite popular in the Weimar Republic. They were associated with internationalism and cosmopolitanism, which were coded as Jewish and embraced by many. Racial antisemites, however, considered Jews to be a mongrel race and saw the integration of foreign influences as a Jewish-driven racial mixing that poisoned German culture.[31] *Blume*'s hybrid musical style made its internationalism audible. For example, the song "My Golden Baby" blends musical styles marked as European, American, and Hawaiian. The lyrics combine German and English willy-nilly, as in "Du bist mein *Sunshine*/Du bist meine *Lady*/*My beautiful Baby*/Mein Herz *is for you!*" (You are my *sunshine*. You are my *lady*. *My beautiful baby*. My heart *is for you!*) The melody, harmony, and intervals recall Hawaiian music known in Europe at the time, most recognizably "Aloha 'Oe" by Queen Lili'uokalani. The rhythm is a slow foxtrot, and as such closely related to American jazz of that era. The instrumentation and style of "My Golden Baby" are characteristic of *Blume* overall. As described by musicologist Joachim Reisaus, "Above all, in *The Flower of Hawaii* Abraham proves himself master of exotic local color, in that he used both harmonic and instrumental methods that far exceeded the habits of musical entertainment in the interwar period. Next to the classical instruments, the orchestra also includes authentic instruments, such as the steel guitar for the production of characteristic vibrato and glissando sounds, the bird pipe, and the two small single-headed drums of different diameters, called bongos. Even the sousaphone belongs there, a circular tuba that comes from American Jazz and street music."[32]

Blume's exotic setting and costuming also combine multiple cultural influences. They are a bricolage of hackneyed colonial images and reinforce many Weimar and Third Reich preconceptions about non-European peoples and places. The different sets and locations meant to be Hawaiʻi combine tropical foliage, rocky coastlines, and crashing waves, a cavernous ritual space with tiki-lounge decor, and Spanish colonial architecture. The representations of indigenous people are a racial and cultural hodgepodge. They include alternately diffident and defiant native men, African American servants, cartoonish hula girls, and snake-charming fakirs played by Hungarian Roma.[33] The Hawaiians are noble, if somewhat hapless colonial subjects, desiring self-determination but unable to outsmart the Americans.

Blume's cultural hybridity and its Jewishness were at odds not only with Nazi visions for a new German film industry but also with the Nazi placement of Jews in a structured racial hierarchy. Musicals create a fantasy of social harmony, an imagined community in which ethnic relations are negotiated through both presences and absences.[34] In *Blume*, a Jewishness that otherwise seems to be absent is performed indirectly through colonial subjects. In this performance, *Blume* leans on historical antecedents in which colonial whiteness troubled the Jewish/non-Jewish binary.

The position of German Jews vis-à-vis German colonialism and the "relationship between imperial Germany's colonial and antisemitic movements . . . was contradictory and complex."[35] On the one hand, German colonialism promoted racialized thinking and violence that simultaneously fed colonial aggression and extremist antisemitism. In concert with late-nineteenth-century nationalism and racial science, it contributed "to widespread constructions of Jewishness along racialized 'color' lines," treating Jewishness as akin to blackness.[36] On the other hand, colonialism fostered a "new identity, the white colonizer," through which Jews could find acceptance and inclusion alongside German gentiles.[37] Historical circumstances were, of course, very different in the 1930s from those in Wilhelmine Germany. As a result of World War I, Germany had lost its colonial empire, and after 1933, the German state pursued antisemitic policies aggressively. In the Third Reich, some politicians wanted to reclaim Germany's pre-Versailles colonial possessions, desires also expressed in popular culture.[38] Third Reich developments at the intersection between colonial desires, antisemitism, and racial stereotypes were accordingly complex. Nazi racial theorists believed that Jews had strong African traits and blood ties, stemming from earlier racial mixing, and stereotypes of blackness and Jewishness overlapped significantly.[39]

Colonial fantasies in *Blume* blur the Nazi racial boundaries between Aryan and Jew and displace questions of Jewish difference onto differently racialized colonial politics. Through a partial and temporary coding of colonial subjects as Jewish, *Blume* remobilizes the image of the white colonizer as a path to inclusion. In doing so, *Blume* challenges Nazi racial antisemitism while also perpetuating racist stereotypes and colonial fantasies. Nazis understood race as an essential, biological foundation of Jewishness that could not be cast aside with assimilation, naturalization, or religious conversion. *Blume* destabilizes such placement of Jewishness within racial hierarchies by imagining a partially fluid, colonial whiteness that individuals who look and act European can approximate. The film accomplishes this through casting, costuming, and script and its use of blackface and brownface.

European actors play all the Hawaiian roles in *Blume*, all except one in brownface, and perform several variations of "Hawaiianness" with different relationships to racial ideology, whiteness, and Jewish difference. Katrin Sieg coined the term "ethnic drag" to describe performances by actors who identify as members of a different ethnicity from the one they perform, arguing that the functions of such performances are complex, contradictory, and—in the late twentieth and early twenty-first century—controversial. Sieg identifies two different basic styles of ethnic drag: mimesis and masquerade. Mimesis is a naturalistic performance style, in which the performer attempts a convincing portrayal of the character.[40] Masquerade is a nonnaturalistic style that performs a caricatured ethnic type and emphasizes the distance between actor and role.[41] Post-Brechtian intellectual traditions in Germany have criticized mimesis as problematic for naturalizing dominant racial constructions and lauded masquerade as a socially critical practice that stages race and ethnicity as performative constructs.[42] Sieg challenges this reductive approach, demonstrating that the conceptual binary mimesis/masquerade is useful, insofar as performance style is key to interpreting ethnic drag, but that other factors also affect the significance of ethnic performances. To untangle the significance of any specific instance of ethnic drag, Sieg argues that it is essential to consider the performance style, its relationship to the historical, political, and discursive contexts in which it is embedded, and "the question of substitution," in which one ethnicity stands in symbolically for another.[43] All three factors are useful in making sense of *Blume*'s ethnic drag, particularly "the question of substitution." By articulating Jewish difference through performances of Hawaiianness, *Blume* challenges Nazi racial antisemitism but silences and colonizes a nonwhite colonial Other.

Hans Fidesser gives a mimetic performance as Prince Lilo Taro. Both convincing and compelling, Fidesser's performance naturalizes stereotypes of Hawaiianness and their inferiority to their American colonizers with the illusion of verisimilitude. Upon seeing Fidesser during his visit to the film studio, critic Fritz Olimsky described him as "almost unrecognizable under the Hawaiian makeup."[44] Likewise, Fidesser's whiteness and that he wears makeup are imperceptible on screen. Lilo Taro personifies the "noble savage" who is pure and sincere because he is less corrupted by society. His identity is rooted in a strong sense of culture and place, and he sings of his love for his homeland. Yet he bows to the superiority of white men, magnanimously relinquishing his legal right to rule Hawai'i when he urges his betrothed to marry the American captain she loves. Fidesser's mimesis makes the stereotypical construct of Hawaiianness embodied in Lilo Taro seem authentic and his performance supports white colonial hegemony (see figure 2.3).

By contrast, the other performances of Hawaiian men are caricatured and clearly legible as masquerade. These unrealistic portrayals reveal race—at least in this film—to be a performative construct. Ferdinand Hart plays Kanako Hilo and Eugen Rex plays Kililo, shifty figures whose roles slip haphazardly between spies, concert promoters, revolutionaries, and a comedy duo like Stan Laurel and Oliver Hardy, who were well known in Germany at that time.[45] Except for the brownface, Hilo and Kililo differ little from comical petty crooks played by other character actors of the day, such as Oskar Sima and Paul Kemp. In that sense, Hart and Rex make no pretense of authentic Hawaiianness. Instead Hilo and Kililo are rogues, and their brownface, a costume for character actors.

Blackface minstrelsy in *Blume* highlights the artificiality of the film's Hawaiian brownface performances. For the ship voyage to Hawai'i, Hilo and Kililo engage Jim Boy (Fritz Fischer), a white American entertainer who performs in blackface. Jim Boy's musical numbers provide an ironic, self-reflexive perspective on brownface in *Blume*. Figure 2.4 shows a shot of Kanako Hilo backstage with Jim Boy that emphasizes the analogy between

Figure 2.3. Hans Fidesser as Prince Lilo Taro (left); the US governor and military officers (center); and Eugen Rex, Ferdinand Hart, Fidesser, and Marta Eggerth as Kililo, Kanako Hilo, Lilo Taro, and Princess Laya (right). *Die Blume von Hawaii, Illustrierter Film-Kurier* Nr. 680. 1933. Author's private collection.

Figure 2.4. Kanako Hilo and Jim Boy (Ferdinand Hart and Fritz Fischer). Jim Boy's blackface calls attention to other racial performances in the film and the actors' whiteness. *Die Blume von Hawaii* (1933). Screenshot.

Jim Boy's blackface and Hart's brownface. In a dressing gown and without his wig, Jim Boy's costuming highlights what we already know: his blackface performance is an act. Jim Boy's makeup looks like an exaggerated version of Hart's brownface, with dark skin and pale lips. Just as Jim Boy performs blackness on stage for his diegetic audience, Hart, as Hilo, performs Hawaiianness on screen for cinema audiences. Hart's and Rex's caricatured performances, like blackface minstrelsy, exaggerate the distance between actor and role, for Hilo and Kililo are not developed, realistic characters. This distance emphasizes the difference between the whiteness of the actors and the brown people they play and between metropolitan Europe and colonial Hawai'i.

Jim Boy's minstrelsy capitalizes on Al Jolson's fame and the international success of his star vehicles *The Jazz Singer* (Alan Crosland, 1927), the first feature film with synchronized sound, and *The Singing Fool* (Lloyd Bacon, 1928), its blockbuster sequel, both well-known in Germany by 1933.

Jim Boy panders to German audiences' perception at that time that jazz music and minstrel performances represented American cosmopolitanism, by integrating both blackness and Jewishness. It was a "widely held view, in both Europe and the United States, by opponents and supporters of the new music alike, that a special Jewish/black interaction had given birth to jazz."[46] Although German audiences liked it, Nazis understood jazz to be a noxious hybrid of primitive African instincts and Jewish abstract intellectualism that exemplified the worst the United States had to offer.[47] "Hitler and Goebbels above all despised the Americans for the relatively large degree of tolerance they extended to the racial minorities that were being expunged from the German *Volksgemeinschaft*, the blood-based *völkisch* community—namely blacks and Jews."[48]

By invoking Jolson, Jim Boy's blackface performances refer to the challenges of Jewish assimilation and its articulation through discourses of racial difference. In *The Jazz Singer*, a Jewish cantor's son struggles between the values and traditions of his immigrant family and his desire to lead an assimilated, secular life as a jazz singer. Protagonist Jakie Rabinowitz/Jack Robin makes his transition to white Americanness through blackface minstrelsy, as did Jolson.[49] Blackface minstrelsy in Hollywood film of this period played an important role in defining white Americanness and assimilating Jews to it. On the one hand, blackface minstrelsy reflected Jewish immigrants' identification with and sympathy for oppressed African Americans, and, on the other hand, it spoke for African Americans without their consent, appropriated aspects of their culture, and perpetuated damaging stereotypes to redefine Jews as white and American.[50] Jack Robin only pretends to be black in order to become white. Similarly, the Weimar Jewish press seized on Jolson's blackface in *The Jazz Singer* as a "deflect[ion] from the usual antisemitic stereotypes."[51]

Like the Jewish-American performances they imitate, Jim Boy's performances criticize discrimination superficially, yet rely on overt racism and the hypervisibility of performed blackness to emphasize the performer's whiteness. Jim Boy's lyrics advocate for African Americans while makeup, costuming, choreography, and sets reinforce overtly racist stereotypes. In his first appearance, Jim Boy sings that white people ignore African Americans and don't treat them as fully human, even when they pay them to be entertainers: "In the salon or at lunch/everyone avoids me/don't completely count/am not a person/am only a *nigger* [sic]/am only a Johnny/schlep through the world/sing for *money*/dance for money." This seems like an incongruous point to make in context of a performance that mocks people of color, and is thus both ambivalent and ironic.

Despite the self-reflexive irony in Jim Boy's act, it reinforces racist tropes about African Americans: he sings that the European ladies find him "piquant," but he still misses his "homeland" in Kentucky, represented on set by a grass shack with women and children in blackface peeking out of the windows. Jim Boy's lyrics perpetuate stereotypes about black male virility and the temptation of it for European women. His set pictures African Americans' "true" home as "primitive" space. In another problematic musical number, in which Jim Boy objectifies his female costar by comparing her to a doll, a black waiter joins them, acting out the stereotype of black people who sing while working hard to serve white people. Both performance and lyrics exaggerate the trope of a big mouth with white teeth—replicated in minstrelsy makeup—when, with a giant smile, the waiter dances and sings about the doll's white teeth. Jim Boy's performances emphasize differences between black and white, suggesting the former is at home in primitive spaces, whereas the latter belongs in modern Europe.

Jewish difference in film, Laura Levitt argues, operates similarly to colonial mimicry, as theorized by Homi Bhabha.[52] Mimicry describes colonized subjects' response to colonizers' attempts to recreate them in their own image with a performance that is "almost the same, but not quite."[53] This response is ambivalent in that it both expresses a desire to be like the colonizer and criticizes that colonizer; it simultaneously exposes and disavows the differences, slippages, and excesses that mimicry yields.[54] Like colonial subjects, Jews represent an Other who is "almost the same but not quite white."[55] Positioned as Other and disavowing its otherness, cinematic Jewishness as mimicry—as (not) white—appears at the level of "interdiction . . . at the crossroads of what is known and permissible with that which though known must be kept concealed."[56] The articulation of Jewish difference through discourses of race and blackness is one of these crossroads. Jolson's blackface performances in *The Jazz Singer*, which conceal the protagonist's Jewishness on behalf of his professional success, expose Jewishness as a mimicry of whiteness.[57] Similarly in *Blume*, ethnic drag reveals ambivalences around Jewishness as (not) white, which manifest at the level of interdiction.

By the early 1930s, overt markers of Jewishness were already being effaced from German popular culture.[58] Certainly in March 1933, when censors reviewed *Blume,* an explicitly positive treatment of Jewishness and its incorporation into colonial whiteness would not have passed muster. The traditions of Viennese operetta made it easy to avoid this pitfall, however, for in that genre there was already an "absence of explicitly Jewish characters," despite the number of Jewish artists involved.[59] Instead of addressing Jewish difference head on, *Blume* negotiates the relationship between Jewishness and whiteness through performances of colonial difference and Hawaiianness. Jim Boy's reference to Jolson cues spectators to make this connection. By alluding indirectly to Jewish difference through non-Jewish characters, *Blume* functions similarly to the Weimar genre films analyzed by Ashkenazi, which speak covertly of Jewish assimilation, and the 1933 comedies that Hake interprets as indirectly addressing Nazi exclusion of Jews through representations of gender.[60] Beller reads the intersecting racial and colonial narratives in the stage version of *Blume* as expressing the "universalist pluralism of the ideology of Jewish emancipation in central Europe."[61] In expressing a pluralist view of Jewish emancipation, *Blume* submerges the question of difference between the Jewish and the not-Jewish beneath racial and colonial distinctions between white and not-white and codes these distinctions as American.

Princess Laya (Marta Eggerth), the only Hawaiian character not played in brownface, embodies both colonial mimicry and Jewish difference. She is the passing racial Other who assimilates to colonial whiteness in the course of the film. Unlike the other Hawaiians in *Blume*, Princess Laya is light skinned, blonde, European educated, and European mannered. She is also a woman and therefore more easily domesticated and contained within patriarchal structures after being allowed to escape the confines of racial and colonial difference. In exile under the alias Susanne Lamond, Laya is integrated fully as a white Parisian and desired as such by male admirers. When the white American Captain Stone (Iván Petrovich), her love interest, is ordered to find the Hawaiian princess, it never occurs to him that Susanne is the woman he is looking for. At the end of the film, Laya and her betrothed, Lilo Taro, realize she cannot belong to him or to her people. She has become (almost) white and marries Captain Stone. By giving herself to a white man as a wife rather than as a colonial subject, she joins him near the top of the colonial hierarchy that her abdication reaffirms. Mimicry gives Princess Laya the opportunity to marry Captain Stone without the appearance of or prejudice against interracial marriage. It also exposes whiteness as a fluid, constructed category.

While a Hawaiian princess is not to be taken literally as a Jew, the Susanne/Laya character is coded as Jewish. Laya evokes the Hebrew name

"Leah," and, in this case, Leah is mistaken easily for Susanne. Marta Eggerth's mother was Jewish. Laya's ability first to pass as French and then to assimilate to colonial whiteness emphasizes Eggerth's own whiteness and ability to pass as not-Jewish. Frenchness, like Jewishness, was associated with cosmopolitanism and modernity, and considered by the Nazis to be racially and culturally inferior to Germanness.[62] Moreover, Laya's passing and eventual assimilation are consistent with the contemporary notion that Jewish women were more able than men to pass as non-Jews.[63] Laya's ability to pass as white and her successful assimilation to colonial whiteness via Frenchness references Jewish difference and the potential for colonial whiteness to include Jews.

By displacing Jewish difference onto colonial Others, *Blume* deploys mimicry as an ambivalent critical tool, both destabilizing whiteness and embracing its potential for European-looking Others. By combating racial antisemitism with colonial racism, however, this displacement functions as a problematic form of ethnic drag that Sieg calls "surrogation," a performance as a member of another racial or ethnic group that exploits perceived commonalities with that group and disavows significant differences, including any complicity in that group's oppression.[64] By reaffirming American colonialism and using Hawaiianness as a cipher for Jewish difference, *Blume* ignores German colonialism, the involvement of Jewish Germans in it, and its negative impacts on colonized people, including Pacific Islanders. It also reifies stereotypes of Hawaiians and supports the US colonial occupation.

Blume depicts white American colonizers as good natured and benign, and the plot reaffirms their hegemony. The amiable governor (Hans Junkermann), his secretary, Buffy (Ernö Verebes), and his niece Bessy (Baby Gray) provide comic relief. Captain Stone cuts a handsome figure of masculine chivalry. Overall, the colonial regime consists of sympathetic characters and despite the Hawaiians' desire for self-determination, the colonial order is not destabilized. Hawaiian leaders bring back their exiled princess in order to restore her as queen, but her love for Captain Stone quashes the native uprising before the American armada needs to. As the protagonist of the film, the most developed character, and the one with the most screen time, Susanne/Laya invites spectator sympathy and identification. Musical numbers promoting love over duty frame her decision to abdicate as correct. The individualism of this ending is out of line with Nazi *völkisch* ideology, even as it promotes a romanticized, gendered fantasy of benign white colonialism.

Instead of emphasizing differences between Jewish and not-Jewish, as does *Susanne*, *Blume* draws a line between white and not-white, reimagining the colonial whiteness that previously had offered a path to assimilation for some German Jews. In this sense, *Blume* functions similarly to Jewish blackface minstrelsy in the United States, which conflated sympathy with oppressed people of color, cultural appropriation, and overt racism, using performed blackness to construe Jews as white. The overtly racist blackface and brownface performances in *Blume* also underscore differences between people of color and members of other "races" (as understood at the time) who can pass for white, a category that included Jews. Fidesser's mimetic performance depicts Hawaiians as noble savages, rooted to their homeland. Hart's and Rex's masquerades suggest that race is a construct. These alternate representations serve as foils to Eggerth's performance of Hawaiianness in *Blume*, which asserts that assimilation and passing are possible and a member of a marginal group can become white.

Laya can become a white colonizer because she can pass as white and European. Thus, *Blume* proposes assimilation as a viable strategy for those who can pass, framing racial and colonial hierarchy in terms of skin color and cultural identity—areas in which German Jews had hoped to find welcome as Germans. By identifying with the (almost) white Laya and fantasizing kinship with white colonists, Jewish members of the film crew and Jewish audience members might have been able to imagine a privileged position and social mobility denied them by the racial ideologies and policies of the Third Reich. Non-Jewish Germans, composing the majority of this film's audience, could continue to enjoy an exotic fantasy world with permeable racial boundaries. *Susanne* ridiculed the fantasies offered by such a film and sought to replace its audiences' pleasures with comedy of a different sort.

Parody and Other Pleasures: *Lieb mich mal in Honolulu*

Blume's Jewish production team, style, and content all made it a perfect target for *Susanne*, a polemical and overtly antisemitic film comedy about the power and danger of Jews in the film industry. Much of *Susanne* uses dialogue to teach spectators the difference between "Jewish" film commercialism and "German" film art. A scene about the filming of *Lieb mich* attempts to reeducate audiences in film viewing and comic pleasure, teaching viewers whom to laugh with and whom to laugh at, using disciplinary humor, and imagining *Volksgemeinschaft*. *Susanne*'s film within a film mocks and maligns *Blume*. Both the stage original and screen adaptations of *Blume* had been very popular and widely publicized. Even those audience members who had not seen either one would have recognized the reference made by Super-Gigantic-Film's fictional, sappy romantic musical about a member of the Hawaiian royal family returning home. *Susanne*'s staging of *Lieb mich* proclaims that films like the popular *Blume* are poorly made and rotten to the core due to Jewish influence. Audiences are invited to enjoy mocking what Nazi rhetoric rejects.

Cserépy's parody satirizes *Blume* by exaggerating some of its stylistic features to the point of absurdity. These features include those criticized elsewhere in *Susanne* and other Nazi literature. *Lieb mich* is frivolous, inane, artificial, and foreign. The exotic setting and costumes are ostentatious. The "Hawaiian" costuming reveals too much of women's bodies, even as dark wigs and makeup mask their fair appearances, a circumstance highlighted by scenes in the dressing room and canteen. The music combines European operetta with plucking and strumming reminiscent of the ukulele, sliding sounds like those of a steel guitar, and an annoyingly shrill melody line, caricaturing the hybrid style Abraham used for *Blume*. The actors playing the stars of *Lieb mich* grossly overact, in contrast to their less exaggerated acting style in the rest of *Susanne*. This staged overacting is another marker of inauthenticity that makes *Lieb mich* both bad and funny. Close-ups of the actor playing the crown prince of Hawai'i, Tommy Silver (Harry Frank), a conceited and Jewish-coded womanizer, show excessive, unmanly, and unnatural emotion and makeup, as when, moved by his subjects' warm reception of him, he sentimentally wipes a tear from his eye. The close-up shots of his female costar, Hilde Keller (Maly Delschaft), particularly the ones in which she watches him from between bunches of bananas, trivialize the exaggerated sentiments of the indigenous woman she plays. She swoons and throws herself at the prince's feet in a ridiculous gesture of love and subjugation. They kiss in an awkward position that they seem to understand as romantic.

As in the planning scene, here too, the reaction of a sympathetic figure teaches the audience how to respond. Reaction shots show Susanne, an extra in dark makeup, wig, grass skirt, and accoutrements, breaking character and staring puzzledly as the female lead grovels on the steps below the prince. As the stars kiss, we hear a cackling sound from off camera, which another reaction shot reveals to be Susanne laughing hysterically.

She staggers up to the steps where the lovers were embracing; she sits down and continues to laugh, rocking back and forth. The director stops filming and asks what is wrong. Hilde also questions Susanne angrily. Susanne, still laughing, responds that it is all "so funny." After her answer provokes the star further, Susanne finally stops laughing and asks seriously, "Wasn't it supposed to be funny?" Susanne's understanding of the scene is clearly at odds with the production team's and lead actors', who, instead of seeing her perspective as honest and fresh, go on to excoriate her for being a neophyte and not understanding film. Audience members, however, who thought the *Lieb mich* sequence was bad might be more likely to identify with Susanne, Bitter, and all those caught up in the "you" opposed to Gold. That Susanne is a likable and attractive protagonist encourages affinities with her as well.

Lieb mich is staged in an exaggerated way that mocks its fictional makers, even as it both appeals to and pokes fun at real audience desires for romance, music, and the exotic. To reform the German film industry, however, *Susanne* cannot simply rebuff audience desires and belittle their pleasures. Instead, the film within the film offers an alternative to the entertainment it mocks. The parody of *Blume* uses humor to create identifications with an in-group while excluding those it defines as not belonging. Susanne's laughter cues audience members about how to react and signals to them which community they should join. The presentation and framing of *Lieb mich* replace the pleasures of escapism with the pleasure of communal laughing at others, of being part of an "us" with superior standards laughing at an inferior "them."

Susanne casts popular Depression-era *Tonfilmoperetten* as absurd, commercial products of a criminally motivated, Jewish-controlled industry. It uses narrative and character to condemn Jewish people and parody to ridicule their productions. It also offers an alternative through Bitter's repeated claims that film should be artistic—decent, serious, and true to life—and validates these claims through Susanne's desire to make a serious film with Bitter and her scorn for *Lieb mich*.

Despite its impulse to train audiences to like and want films like those Bitter advocates, *Susanne* does not exemplify his aesthetic agendas. As was common among films made in 1933 and 1934, *Susanne* borrows from Weimar-era genre cinema even as it criticizes it, building on its familiarity and popularity, while shifting the construction of its cinematic adversary from Hollywood to the purportedly Jewish-dominated film industry of the Weimar Republic. Weimar genre cinema depicted film production satirically, as in *Ein blonder Traum*, to mock commercial Hollywood practices. In *Susanne*, Jewish greed makes not Hollywood but Weimar films rotten. Yet, even as *Susanne* criticizes Jewish pandering to audience tastes, the film's money laundering, kidnapping, and detective narratives capitalize on its own public's fondness for *Kriminalkomödien* (humorous crime films) set in the film industry, like *Der Schuß im Tonfilmatelier* (The Shot in the Sound Film Studio, Alfred Zeisler, 1930) or *Die Gräfin von Monte Cristo* (The Countess of Monte Cristo, Karl Hartl, 1931/1932). The former involves a murder on set, and the latter, an extra inadvertently becoming a con artist. In the case of *Susanne* as well, an extra goes astray. *Lieb mich* is a front for an illicit gambling operation. The movie's publicity campaign is dominated by the staged kidnapping of Susanne and another extra and the fraud and blackmail surrounding it. As in *Gräfin,* the police ultimately arrest the professional criminals, and the pretty blonde heroine is rehabilitated.

In perhaps its most blatantly hypocritical move, *Susanne* attacks kitschy, exotic productions like *Blume* while using their attractive features to appeal to audiences. Much of *Susanne's* publicity, such as the production still of Maly Delschaft in figure 2.5, featured "Hawaiian" costumes and imagery. Such marketing reveals the studio's commercial cynicism, despite the film's seeming political and artistic commitments. Additionally, it objectifies German women, as do many scenes in *Susanne*, contradicting the film's explicit message regarding the impropriety of such objectification. *Susanne's* dialogue, Bitter's and Susanne's attitudes, and specific scenes in which Susanne refuses to be filmed in a bathtub and ultimately to act in films at all criticize how the film industry puts women on display for cheap titillation, even as Csérepy takes advantage of the Hawaiian setting of the film-within-the-film to insert scantily clad dancers between his characters' moral and aesthetic tirades. In *Susanne*, Csérepy exploits popular comic genres, such as the *Kriminalkomödie* and the *Tonfilmoperette*, to express overt antisemitic criticisms of the Weimar film industry common in Nazi writings. Yet he does not heed his own proscriptions in a consistent or sustained way.

Rejecting Politicized Humor

Susanne is an overtly antisemitic sendup of the German film industry in the early 1930s. Yet, despite its efforts to capitalize on the same popular film genres that it condemns, this comedy resonated with neither critics

Figure 2.5. Publicity still of Maly Delschaft for *Nur nicht weich werden, Susanne!* (1934/35). *Susanne*'s producers exploited the publicity potential of its brief "Hawaiian" sequence, despite the film's overt disdain for exoticism. The Gillespie Collection, Sydney, Australia.

nor audiences and was a box-office failure. Reviews disparaged the film's quality, ineffective satire, and outdatedness, in that it condemned the Jewishness of a bygone film era after the regime had already Aryanized the film industry.[65] They described audience reception that was tepid or worse.[66] The *B.Z. am Mittag* reported audience members hissing at the premiere.[67] David Stewart Hull claims, "Goebbels was astounded when the first night audience on January 24 [1935] booed the film when it was over, an unheard-of experience."[68]

A partial collection of legal and financial paperwork from Cserépy's production company, Normaton, housed at the Filmmuseum in Potsdam, indicates more sustained (and similarly "unheard-of") objections to *Susanne* than audience members hissing and booing in the dark.[69] When *Susanne* was released, cinema owners signed contracts with film distributors in advance, settling on conditions and rates for screening particular films or lineups of films. These practices of "blind booking" and "block booking" protected smaller studios at the expense of theater owners by committing them far in advance to screening films they knew little about. In early 1935, these practices were controversial but had not yet been eliminated.[70] Archival records show that some cinema owners, mostly in larger urban areas, broke their contracts and refused to show *Susanne*. The clearly incomplete surviving paperwork documents eighteen such cases, and references in that paperwork to cases for which there is no other documentation indicate there were likely more. The high number of documented cases of cinema owners refusing to show a particular film is atypical, even considering *Susanne*'s poor quality and the dire financial straits at Normaton, which made Cserépy eager to pursue all funds owed him.[71] Some theater owners defaulted on payment. Others paid but didn't show the film. A few kept requesting deferrals, and several negotiated screenings of another film as a substitute. Only a few documents state potential reasons for the cinema owners' behavior: Christine v. d. Heuvel of the Palast Theater in Dessau refused to show *Susanne* or pay for it, eventually settling out of court to pay Normaton RM 300 instead of the RM 600 she would have paid, had she shown the film.[72] Heuvel argued contractual points, complained that the publicity materials arrived too late, described the film as "unusable" and "deficient," and indicated that even the distributor Neues Deutsches Lichtspielsyndikat had rejected the film.[73] Albert Koch, owner of the Kammerspiel in Weissensee, also refused to show or pay for *Susanne*. In his own defense, Koch cited Normaton's legal representative's admission in a prior court case that the film was bad.⁷⁴ While these explanations may be true, other undocumented reasons were likely also at work. Had theater owners regularly broken contracts with distributors over every bad movie in their lineups, they would have had few German films left to show and even fewer German comedies. Moreover, frequent and widespread breaches of contract would have threatened the entire distribution system.

The most suggestive documents among the files in Potsdam are the cases of Johann Strobel, owner of Metropol Lichtspiele, Nuremberg, and of Gustav Hammer, owner of Union-Lichtspiele in Frankfurt am Main–Niederrad. Strobel offered a settlement of RM 50 and Hammer a settlement of RM 40, for not showing *Susanne*.⁷⁵ Frau M. Pfeiffer, writing on behalf of the distributor Viktoria-Film-Verleih, does not make explicit why Strobel "would and could never show the film" or why Hammer likewise refused to show it.⁷⁶ In both letters, however, written roughly two months apart, Pfeiffer describes the theater owners' refusals to show *Susanne* as being "for the known reasons."⁷⁷ Pfeiffer signs both letters "with German greeting!"⁷⁸ Strobel concludes the only remaining piece of his correspondence about this matter with "Heil Hitler!"⁷⁹ These Third Reich complimentary closings were required by law, although not always used. Their use here indicates that the writers were fully aware of the political context in which their negotiations were taking place and the importance of appearing politically orthodox on paper.⁸⁰ It would have been foolhardy in 1935 to express conscientious objections to *Susanne* in writing. Pfeiffer relies on her reader to infer what the "known reasons" for rejecting *Susanne* are rather than stating them outright. Pfeiffer's prevarication, written in context of the Nazi dictatorship, could easily cloak something more politically sensitive than the film's having been substandard in quality, and I suspect that it did.

Rather than show *Susanne*, cinema owners assumed the financial loss and political risk of breaking their contracts, a risk they may have perceived as substantial, given Krause's power as Reichsfilmdramaturg. There was financial incentive *not* to break these contracts, particularly in the cases in which theater owners agreed to pay or were forced to pay significant sums of money and still refused to schedule a screening, which might have recouped some of their losses through ticket sales. Even though it was a flop, screening *Susanne* to near-empty movie houses would have been cheaper and politically safer than going to court and paying a fine for not showing it. Refusing to screen *Susanne* simply to avoid showing a lousy or unpopular movie makes no political or economic sense. I surmise that at least some of the unexpectedly high number of cinema owners who canceled screenings of and broke contracts to show *Susanne* did so because of the film's overt antisemitism. It is even possible that some of the theater owners who refused to show *Susanne* were Jewish themselves, since cinema ownership was not Aryanized until later in 1935.[81] Yet cinema owners need not have been Jewish or even had strong oppositional convictions not to want to show *Susanne*. They could have found its overt antisemitism overstated, and therefore tasteless, or not minded it themselves but worried that it could alienate their audiences and hurt their business over the long term. They might have wanted to avoid hassle, fearing demonstrations or violence outside their cinemas, as had occurred outside cinemas showing films featuring Jewish actors, or actors perceived as Jewish.[82]

The Swedish import *Petterson and Bendel* (Per-Axel Branner, 1933), an overtly antisemitic film comedy that was released in Germany a few months after *Susanne*, did lead to violence and destruction of property. In *Petterson and Bendel*, a Jewish immigrant's shady business practices threaten honest Swedes' economic and romantic circumstances. Released with subtitles in 1935, in 1938, *Petterson* was dubbed into German, re-released, and advertised as still being timely (*aktuell*).[83] This film served as a supplement to German domestic antisemitism, showing both Jewish thievery and antisemitism to be international phenomena.

Figure 2.6 shows an advertisement for *Petterson* from Hammer Tonfilm Verleih's 1935/1936 catalogue. Hammer, *Petterson*'s distributor, highlighted the film's popularity and international origin and advertised it as a major Swedish comedy. At the same time, Hammer emphasized its alignment with Nazi antisemitic politics. The advertisement notes that censors deemed *Petterson and Bendel* "politically valuable" and "open to all ages" and describes the film as a "full blooded satire."[84] An image of the dark, curly-haired Bendel (Semmy Friedmann) smirking and delicately holding a balloon with the face of a blond, skeptical-looking Petterson (Adolf Jahr) in it, frames this film as a satire of how Jews toy with Aryans.[85]

Petterson was well received in Nazi organs like the *Angriff*, which characterized Bendel as an "authentic representation of the Jewish type," played by a Jewish actor. The *Angriff* also highlighted the international origins and importance of the film, emphasizing that it was: "not ordered by the NSDAP, not written in Nazi Germany, not produced by fascists, but taken first hand from Sweden, written and produced after a prizewinning Swedish novel, with the Jewish role played very originally by a Jew, taken by

Figure 2.6. Advertisement for *Petterson and Bendel* (1933) from the Hammer Tonfilm distribution catalogue 1935/1936. The Gillespie Collection, Sydney, Australia.

the Swedish public as a delectable, authentic comedy, the biggest box office success in a long time, sent as a top film to the international film festival in Venice, screened in America and Denmark."[86] Such prose implied that the Jewishness portrayed in *Petterson* and the antisemitic response to it were global truths espoused not only by the Nazis but also by Swedes, Italians, Americans, and Danes.

Yet the representation of Jewishness that the *Angriff* construed as internationally lauded sparked controversy and violence in Berlin. A Berlin demonstration against *Petterson and Bendel* on July 13, 1935, was met with antisemitic counterdemonstrations, vandalism of nearby cafes that the rioters believed were owned or frequented by Jews, and assaults on Jewish people.[87] Hammer's catalogue references these riots as "quite a stir" (*helle Aufregung*), touting them as a reason to show the film. One might imagine, however, that not all cinema owners wanted controversy and violence outside their doors.

There were other reasons for cinema owners and spectators to reject *Susanne*, even if they didn't object to its overt antisemitism, fear violence, or shun controversy. *Susanne*'s departures from generic norms and audience expectations were likely part of the problem. A self-identified "grotesque," *Susanne* fits uneasily into the genre conventions of early Third Reich cinema. A hybrid form, the grotesque brings together the monstrous and the comic, the repulsive and the humorous. In the case of *Susanne*, parody of corrupt Jewish business practices and degenerate artistic tastes is intended to provoke disgust and laughter. *Susanne* inspired far more of the former than the latter. In the 1920s, the grotesque was a genre of zany comedies characterized by physical or creative excess, such as *Die Mysterien eines Frisiersalons* (The Mysteries of a Hair Salon, Erich Engel and Bertolt Brecht, 1922/23). Departing from what its billing implied, *Susanne*'s humor is not particularly zany, physical, or creative. Its only excess is political. The most overtly propagandistic feature-length comedy from the prewar period, *Susanne* includes more ideological bombast than audiences were accustomed to or would have expected from a grotesque.

It might have made sense for *Susanne* to have been marketed as a humorous *Bewegungsfilm* (movement film), although it would have been an awkward fit in that category as well. The *Bewegungsfilme* were films from 1933 that explicitly promoted the newly triumphant Nazi movement, including *SA-Mann Brand* (SA Man Brand, Franz Seitz Sr.), *Hitlerjunge Quex* (Hitler Youth Quex, Hans Steinhoff), and *Hans Westmar* (Hans Westmar,

Franz Wenzler). These films celebrated Nazi defeats of Weimar-era communists, centered on martyrdom and conversion narratives, and were stylistically similar to late Weimar agitprop.[88] *Susanne* lacks the uniforms, party politics, and street violence of the 1933 *Bewegungsfilme*. Yet it shares some of their narrative and stylistic features. Like *Hitlerjunge Quex* and *Hans Westmar, Susanne* is an adaptation of a Nazi literary work and parrots party rhetoric. Instead of paramilitary street fights against communists, it stages the "fight for German film" and the defeat of Jewish film producers. The protagonist, being a pretty young woman in show business rather than a radicalized young man in the streets, behaves in accordance with Nazi gender ideals. She sacrifices her career, not her life, and is converted to housewifery and gardening rather than party activism. Like the *Bewegungsfilme, Susanne* looks back to Weimar-era battles that were already won and reproduces Weimar filmic styles. Released a little more than a year after the *Bewegungsfilme*, however, *Susanne*'s battles were already old news. Its infusion of humor into an outmoded political genre was indeed grotesque, although presumably not in the way the filmmakers intended.

From Overt to Inferential Antisemitism in Film Comedy

By scrutinizing the reception of *Blume* and *Susanne*, this chapter begins to tell the next part of the story of antisemitism and film humor in Nazi Germany, which complicates the offensive waged against Jewish comedy. Goebbels was opposed for strategic reasons to the ham-handedness of the *Bewegungsfilme* and favored a more subtle approach to disseminating ideology.[89] *Susanne* was a particularly ineffective combination of propaganda and comedy that vindicates Goebbels's strategy.

The Propaganda Ministry hoped to eradicate myriad vestiges of real and imagined Jewish influence and elevate the quality and political effects of German film. Because of greed, criminal inclinations, and a lack of moral character and aesthetic judgment—as antisemites would have it—Jews had corrupted German film. The resulting productions, in the eyes of Nazi film theorists, were inferior, inauthentic products that failed to reflect the everyday life and concerns of the German *Volk*. Jewish films like *Blume* glorified foreign settings, spread alien values, stimulated artificial sentiments, and sexually exploited naive German women. *Susanne* transmitted such negative understandings of Jewishness in film through disciplinary humor.

It mocked *Blume* and caricatured its Jewish producers, directing audience laughter against them while imagining a *Volksgemeinschaft* free of Jews and their influence. *Susanne* was thus aligned with the regime's overt antisemitic agenda for German film comedy, more than any other film of the period, even as it capitalized on aspects of its forbears for which it showed disdain (such as scantily clad women in ethnic drag).

Audiences liked *Blume* and other films like it more than they liked *Susanne*. I cannot verify the extent to which rejection of antisemitism was responsible for the reaction against *Susanne*. I do know that this particular representation of the regime's racial and aesthetic agenda for the film industry, and for comic film in particular, failed at the box office. Audiences preferred Jewish comedy to Csérepy's antisemitic grotesque. In addition to purging Jews and Jewishness, the Propaganda Ministry also struggled to make and keep the German film industry solvent. Filmmakers thus needed to balance the Nazis' political agenda with economic concerns. This dialectic between the regime's agendas and audience desires is at the heart of Third Reich popular cinema.[90] Correspondingly, the need to cater to and slowly redefine audiences' preferences and politics was a significant factor in the development of German film comedy in the Nazi era. The failure of *Susanne*'s overt attempt to educate audiences in antisemitic film aesthetics reveals the distance between audience tastes in entertainment and overt antisemitism. *Susanne*'s failure, despite having made aesthetic compromises (borrowing from the popular Weimar films that it criticized), highlights the limitations of overt antisemitic comedy in trying to bridge that gap. Comedies in which antisemitism remained inferential and the pedagogical impulse more discreet would prove more commercially successful. Various strategies for negotiating the tension between antisemitic ideals and audience preferences would shape the development of Third Reich film comedy in the 1930s.

Notes

1. "Kampf um den deutschen Film." Neumann et al., *Film "Kunst,"* 15.
2. Trumpener, "René Clair Moment," 41.
3. H. Sp. [Hans Spielhofer], "Der neue Geschmack," 1–2.
4. Friedländer, *Nazi Germany and the Jews*, vol. 1, 68–72.
5. Friedländer, *Nazi Germany and the Jews*, vol. 1, 68.
6. Friedländer, *Nazi Germany and the Jews*, vol. 1, 22; on the boycott more generally, see 17–26.

7. Friedländer, *Nazi Germany and the Jews*, vol. 1, 22.
8. Baranowski, *Nazi Empire*, 204.
9. Friedländer, *Nazi Germany and the Jews*, vol. 1, 129.
10. On the parallels between Neumann et al., Film "Kunst," and *Nur nicht weich werden, Susanne!* see: Friedman, *L'image et son Juif*, 35–37.
11. Warnecke, "Bio-Filmographie Arzen von Cserépy."
12. Bubendey, *Nur nicht weich werden, Susanne!*
13. For a Nazi account of how Jewish people acquired "German" names and a description of those names and their significance, see Feder, *Die Juden*, 51–52.
14. The reference here, with the character Schwarz, is to Bernhard Weiß, vice police president of Berlin from 1927 to 1933, who was a frequent target of Nazi vitriol. Apparent contradictions, such as Jews controlling both the underworld and the police or being agents of both Bolshevism and capitalism, were staples of Nazi antisemitism.
15. Loentz, "Literary Double Life," 117–18.
16. See chapter 1.
17. The Bubendey stage adaptation mentions the title of a planned film, *Lieb mich am Ganges* (18), but does not script any part of it. There is no film within a film scene in Hagen's serialized novel in the *Angriff* either.
18. Wallach, *Passing Illusions*, 171.
19. Loacker, "Richard Oswalds Filmschaffen in Österreich," in *Richard Oswald*, ed. Kasten and Loacker, 376–79.
20. Beller, "Right Mélange," 6.
21. Wedel, "Die entfesselte Stimme," 197–237.
22. "Konfektionstyp." R., "Forderungen," 1. For the "Jewish" coding and antisemitic connotations of "Konfektion," see page 48. Also: Westphal, *Berliner Konfektion und Mode*.
23. R., "Forderungen," 1.
24. Wedel, "Richard Oswald und der Tonfilm," in *Richard Oswald*, ed. Kasten and Loacker, 318, 332–33.
25. Sattig, *Die deutsche Filmpresse*, 80.
26. "Spürnase für Konjunkturen." N., review of *Blume*, 2. The review in the *Deutsche Filmzeitung* on March 31, 1933, uses the verb "spekulieren" to describe what the producers did here.
27. N., review of *Blume*, 2.
28. Review of *Blume*, *Kinematograph*, 1–2.
29. Wedel, "Richard Oswald und der Tonfilm," in *Richard Oswald*, ed. Kasten and Loacker, 335.
30. R., "Forderungen," 1.
31. Feder, *Die Juden*, 35. Kadner, *Rasse*, 2nd ed., 222.
32. Reisaus, "Die Wiederkehr der 'Blume von Hawai'" [sic].
33. Olimsky, "Ungarische Version," n.p.
34. Shohat, "Ethnicities-in-Relation," 222.
35. Davis, *Colonialism, Antisemitism*, 23.
36. Wallach, *Passing Illusions*, 31–32.
37. Davis, *Colonialism, Antisemitism*, 23–24.
38. Conrad, *German Colonialism*, 192–93. Schmokel, *Dream of Empire*. Baranowski, *Nazi Empire*.

39. Feder, *Die Juden*, 35. Sander Gilman argues that stereotypes of blackness and Jewishness overlapped significantly in the nineteenth and early twentieth centuries. Gilman, *Difference and Pathology*, 35, passim. Birgit Haehnel investigates such overlaps in the visual culture of the Third Reich: Haehnel, "'The Black Jew,'" 238–59. See also Shohat, "Ethnicities in Relation," 231.

40. On the problems of mimetic ethnic performance, see Sieg, *Ethnic Drag*, 5–6, passim.

41. On the strengths and limitations of masquerade, see Sieg, *Ethnic Drag*, 11–12, passim.

42. Sieg, *Ethnic Drag*, 5.

43. Sieg, *Ethnic Drag*, 5.

44. Olimsky, "Palmen und Frauenträume," n.p.

45. On "Dick und Dof" in late Weimar Germany, see Noack, "Retrospektive Laurel und Hardy im Berliner Babylon." For an example of a Nazi interpretation of Laurel and Hardy as representing American intellectual simplicity, see Macht, "Amerikanischer und deutscher Humor," 11.

46. Rogin, *Blackface, White Noise*, 58.

47. Kater, *Different Drummers*, 29–33.

48. Kater, *Different Drummers*, 30.

49. See Rogin's compelling analysis of *The Jazz Singer*: Rogin, *Blackface, White Noise*, 73–120.

50. Rogin, *Blackface, White Noise*. See also Shohat, "Ethnicities in Relation," 229–33.

51. Wallach, *Passing Illusions*, 84.

52. Levitt, "Redressing Jewish Difference," article 5 (n.p.).

53. Bhabha, "Of Mimicry and Man," 122.

54. Bhabha, "Of Mimicry and Man," 85–92.

55. Levitt, "Redressing Jewish Difference," 1.

56. Levitt, "Redressing Jewish Difference," 1.

57. Levitt, "Redressing Jewish Difference," 8–13.

58. Buerkle, "Gendered Spectatorship," 626.

59. Beller, "Right Mélange," 6.

60. Ashkenazi, *Weimar Film*. Films analyzed by Ashkenazi as reflecting indirectly on Jewish assimilation in the Weimar Republic include (among others): *Ich möchte kein Mann sein* (I Don't Want to Be a Man, Ernst Lubitsch, 1918), *Herrin der Welt* (Mistress of the World, Joe May, 1919/20), *Die Straße* (The Street, Karl Grune, 1923), *Nju* (Nju, Paul Czinner, 1923), *Dr. Bessels Verwandlung* (The Transformation of Dr. Bessel, Richard Oswald, 1927), *Der Himmel auf Erden* (Heaven on Earth, Reinhold Schünzel, 1926/27), *Familientag im Hause Prellstein* (A Family Day at the Prellsteins, Hans Steinhoff, 1927), and two adaptations of *Alraune* (Mandrake, Henrik Galeen, 1927; Richard Oswald, 1930). Hake, *Popular Cinema*, 23–45. Hake frames *Das hässliche Mädchen* (The Ugly Girl, Henry Koster, 1933) and *Viktor und Viktoria* (Victor and Victoria, Reinhold Schünzel, 1933) as commentary on the Nazi exclusion of Jews in 1933.

61. Beller, "Right Mélange," 13.

62. Spector, "Modernism without Jews," 615.

63. See Wallach, *Passing Illusions*, 158, passim.

64. Sieg, *Ethnic Drag*, 13–14, passim. See particularly the chapters on postwar West Germans' performances of Native Americanness.

65. Review of *Susanne! Die Lupe*; R. [pseud.], review of *Nur nicht weich werden, Susanne!*; Ho. [pseud.], Review of *Nur nicht weich werden, Susanne!*; All in *Bundesarchiv-Filmarchiv*, File Folder Nr. 12313 I.

66. Review of *Susanne! Die Lupe*; S. [pseud.], review of *Nur nicht weich werden, Susanne!*; R. [pseud.], review of *Nur nicht weich werden, Susanne! Völkischer Beobachter*, Berlin, January 26, 1935. All in *Bundesarchiv-Filmarchiv*, File Folder Nr. 12313 I.

67. S. [pseud.], review of *Nur nicht weich werden, Susanne!*

68. Hull, *Film in the Third Reich*, 69.

69. Arsen von Cserépy, collected papers, boxes 16.2-11 and 16.2-12, Filmmuseum Potsdam, Collections Department (hereafter cited as Cserépy Papers).

70. S., "Blindbuchen," 1.

71. On June 26, 2014, I consulted with Dr. Peter Warnecke, an archivist at the Filmmuseum Potsdam with extensive knowledge of the materials and the period, who had curated an exhibition on Cserépy. Warnecke said the situation documented in the legal and financial materials about *Susanne* was unusual. He thought that the need to pursue such claims could be explained by Normaton's poor financial circumstances, but that did not explain the volume of cases. He believed the number of cases documented in the files was most likely explained by political objections to *Susanne*.

72. Cserépy Papers. N 003/1081 3731(Nov. 26, 1935).

73. "Unbrauchbar"; "mangelhaft." Cserépy Papers. N 003/1081 3721 (Oct. 21, 1935), 3726 (Nov. 7, 1935).

74. Cserépy Papers. N 003/1090 3858 (Nov. 15, 1935). Koch referred to the case of Schulze from Reinickendorf. No other documentation of the Schulze case appeared in the Cserépy Papers.

75. Cserépy Papers. N 003/1138 4029 (Nov. 30, 1936), 4033 (Oct. 3, 1936).

76. "Den Film niemals spielen wolle und könne." Cserépy Papers. N 003/1138 4029 (Nov. 30, 1936).

77. "Aus den bekannten Gründen." Cserépy Papers. N 003/1138 4029 (Nov. 30, 1936), 4033 (Oct. 3, 1936).

78. "Mit deutschem Gruss!" Cserépy Papers. N 003/1138 4029 (Nov. 30, 1936), 4033 (Oct. 3, 1936).

79. Cserépy Papers. N 003/1138 4026 (Dec. 2, 1936).

80. For more on the use of the "German greeting," see Ehlers, "Der deutsche Gruß in Briefen."

81. Stahr, *Volksgemeinschaft*, 157.

82. For further information about antisemitic cinema demonstrations, see Stahr, *Volksgemeinschaft*, 140–47.

83. Advertisement for *Petterson*. A writer for the *Angriff* also called *Petterson* "aktuell" on July 18, 1935. Cited in: "Für klare Scheidung," 1.

84. *Petterson and Bendel* was the first film import that Nazi censors designated "politically valuable." Wright, *Visible Wall*, 58. "Für klare Scheidung," 2.

85. Most Swedish film critics did not take offense at the antisemitic stereotypes in *Petterson and Bendel*, except "in the Swedish Jewish publication *Judisk Krönika* (The Jewish Chronicle), Holger Ritter accuse[d] Semmy Friedmann of having betrayed his fellow Jews by accepting the role of Bendel." Wright, *Visible Wall*, 56.

86. "Nicht von der N.S.D.A.P. bestellt, nicht in Nazideutschland geschrieben, nicht von Faschisten gedreht, sondern aus erster Hand von Schweden bezogen, nach einem preisgekrönten schwedischen Roman geschrieben und gedreht, in der jüdischen Rolle von einem Juden ganz originell gespielt, von der schwedischen Bevölkerung als ein köstlich-echtes Lustspiel aufgenommen, der größte Kassenerfolg seit langem, als Spitzenfilm zum internationalen Filmkongreß nach Venedig geschickt, in Amerika und Dänemark vorgeführt." *Der Angriff*, July 18, 1935. Cited in: "Für klare Scheidung," 1.

87. "Für klare Scheidung," 1–3. Stahr, *Volksgemeinschaft*, 149–51.

88. Rentschler, *Ministry*, 53–70. Faletti, "Reflections of Weimar Cinema," in *Cultural History through a National Socialist Lens*, ed. Reimer, 11–36. Heinsohn, "Film as Pedagogy," in *Continuity and Crisis*, ed. Hales, Petrescu, and Weinstein, 51–70.

89. Rentschler, *Ministry*, 81 and 333, n. 34.

90. Hake, *Popular Cinema*, 68–86, passim.

3

COMIC *ERSATZ*
Viktor und Viktoria *and* Glückskinder

DESPITE THE NAZIS' DESIRE TO RID GERMAN CINEMA of "Jewish" stylistic influence and their characterizations of Weimar and Hollywood cinema as having been polluted by such influences, throughout the 1930s Third Reich film comedy moved haltingly, unevenly, and never fully away from Weimar-era and Hollywood influenced cinematic traditions coded as Jewish. After all, even after Jews were purged from the film industry and movie audiences, filmmakers' skills and consumers' preferences still had developed in the Weimar Republic. Despite more stringent regulations, cinemas showed Hollywood and other international productions regularly. Imports comprised 44 percent of the German domestic film market in 1933 and remained as high as 27 percent as late as 1940.[1] In fact, the purge of Jewish personnel in 1933 made it difficult for German studios to keep up with cinema owners' needs and audience demand. The relative shortage of German feature films in 1933 made it possible for Hollywood studios to negotiate three years of favorable import quotas for their films.[2] Between 1934 and 1939, Hollywood films constituted "roughly 20 percent" of German feature film distribution.[3] This meant that from 1933 to 1936 and beyond, filmmakers and audiences were cued in to international trends and German productions needed to compete with Hollywood imports. As the Nazis defined German cinema against Hollywood and other international competitors, national cinematic styles coalesced under both international and domestic influences.[4]

This chapter and the following one analyze the styles of German comedies produced between 1933 and 1936, the years in which the Propaganda Ministry restructured and consolidated its control over the film industry. This transitional period was marked by myriad government-mandated institutional changes, large and small, intended to coordinate the film industry institutionally and ideologically with the Nazi regime. There were dramatic shifts in personnel as Jews and political dissenters were forced out and replaced. Keeping one's job and getting one's films produced required a significant degree of compliance, although directors and stars with exceptional box office appeal had more leeway than others. The Propaganda Ministry and the trade press kept filmmakers well informed about new regulations and the changing conditions of film production. Yet what exactly the new political situation meant for the styles and themes of film comedy remained unclear. Both the range of comedies made and explicit discussions in the trade press of what comedy should look like under the new political order reflect such confusion.[5]

Styles of film humor with different national and racial connotations coexisted in Nazi Germany and competed for the favor of audiences, critics, and the government. Audiences voted with their feet and their Reichsmarks, guided in part by personal preferences and word of mouth and in part by film reviews, which, although politicized, continued to exist until late November 1936, when Goebbels mandated their replacement by politically motivated film observations.[6] Dependent on profits from both domestic and international markets, film studios sought compromise between political imperatives and audience demands.

In the years 1933–36, German film studios produced a variety of comedies. The exile and exclusion of many former film industry members, the Propaganda Ministry's increasing control over the film industry, and the adoption of themes and styles more consistent with Nazi attitudes significantly affected film production. At the same time, German film comedies adapted familiar and commercially successful styles and tropes to the new circumstances. Many offerings followed their late-Weimar and Depression-era forebears, setting rags-to-riches stories and mistaken-identity farces in urban milieux. Some directors borrowed techniques from successful Hollywood competitors, imitating the glamour of sophisticated comedies, the fast pace and zany antics of screwball comedies, and the snappy banter of both. Other filmmakers turned to domestic traditions of humor, adapting from the theater, reenvisioning the rural *Volksstück* (people's play) in film form, or otherwise deploying strategies understood as characteristically German. Most commonly, comedies drew on multiple influences, foreign and domestic. The diversity of German film offerings in the early to mid-1930s reflected the skills, experiences, and Weimar pasts of film industry members as well as influences of the international film market. This stylistic diversity increased the domestic popularity and exportability of German film, both of which the government and the film industry's leadership strongly desired.

Despite ideologues' condemnation of purportedly Jewish-influenced Weimar and Hollywood comedy and ongoing discussions of favored strategies for German humor, audiences' and critics' preferences did not follow strong trends in favor of any one particular comic style. Hits from the transitional period include both the bucolic *Krach um Jolanthe* and *Allotria* (Hokum, Willi Forst, 1936), a sophisticated comedy about romantic entanglements among high-society members.[7] While critics often voiced Nazi perspectives, they did not consistently praise films with a recognizably German style or pan those with strong Weimar, Hollywood, or "Jewish" traces.

Between 1933 and 1936, select films and the discussions around them struggled to achieve a nationally and racially grounded comic film style consistent with Goebbels's proclamations, a process marked by substitutions, structuring absences, and inferential antisemitism. The variations in style and reception of film comedies in this period acted out debates about German humor and a nationally and racially determined comic style in public forums. This chapter shows how two well-known films, *Viktor und Viktoria* and *Glückskinder,* participated in this discussion. Both films offered commercially successful approaches that blend a forward-looking, politically conforming agenda for comedy with influences from outside the Third Reich: Weimar film and Hollywood. The hybrid comic styles represented by these two films were neither embraced by the regime nor eliminated fully from the stylistic repertoire of Third Reich directors.

On the one hand, *Viktor und Viktoria* and *Glückskinder* strongly feature characteristics of Nazi cinema's alleged others—namely, Weimar and Hollywood cinema, which were both coded as Jewish. On the other hand, both films depict processes by which to modify or supplant these Jewish styles, creating new alternatives. *Viktor und Viktoria, Glückskinder,* and their reception functioned as sites of contention over what kinds of humor were appropriate for the development of German racial and national identity, as conceived in Nazi Germany. Such concerns pervade these and other Third Reich film comedies on multiple and often inconspicuous levels.

Interpreted against the contested racial and national terrain of film comedy in the mid-1930s, *Viktor und Viktoria* and *Glückskinder* deploy comic strategies coded as foreign or Jewish and stake out a position for them—or their proxies—within the Nazi film industry. *Viktor und Viktoria,* "the biggest box-office hit" of 1933, exemplifies the transition between Weimar cinema and the film of the Third Reich.[8] Its comic and representational strategies are typical of the late Weimar era. Yet it engages simultaneously with Third Reich discussions of race, nation, and comedy, concluding with a vision of both continuity and change. Continuities from Weimar film persist in German comedies well into the 1930s. Hollywood also influenced German comedies in this period, as epitomized by *Glückskinder,* a loose adaptation of Frank Capra's *It Happened One Night* (1934). *Glückskinder* not only illustrates how the German film industry retooled Hollywood elements for its own needs, but also reflects on the process of substitution on multiple levels: on its own role as a substitute for Hollywood comedy, on the comic possibilities of substitution, on substitution as an agent of substantial change, and on the superiority of the substitute over the original.[9] Styles associated with Weimar and Hollywood, which the Nazis believed to be dominated by Jews, remained in Third Reich film comedy and continued to appeal to audiences. *Viktor und Viktoria* and *Glückskinder* represent commercially successful attempts to modify and integrate such styles.

Born Comedians and Weimar Legacies: Reinhold Schünzel's *Viktor und Viktoria*

Viktor und Viktoria, a musical comedy about an unemployed actress who becomes famous as a female impersonator, is arguably Third Reich film comedy's most durable export. Sophisticated and witty, it has a lasting appeal that not only hooked audiences in 1933 but also amuses twenty-first-century American undergraduates, unlike most German comedies from the 1930s. Victor Saville adapted *Viktor und Viktoria* almost immediately for Gaumont British as *First a Girl* (1935) and Karl Anton remade *Viktor und Viktoria* in West Germany in 1957. Julie Andrews starred in a Hollywood adaptation, *Victor/Victoria* (Blake Edwards, 1982), which became a Broadway musical that, in turn, found yet another incarnation as a made-for-television movie in 1995.

Viktor und Viktoria epitomizes a successful comic style that competed against the more German styles of humor envisioned by the Nazis and that encouraged inclusive definitions of German humor and Germanness. It illustrates the persistence of, and advocated for the integration of, "Jewish" elements of Weimar cinema into Third Reich film comedy. A deeply essentialist film on multiple levels, most noticeably regarding gender, *Viktor and Viktoria* displaces the Third Reich's racial essentialism with an essentialism of humor: a double narrative of mistaken identity and revelation, *Viktor und Viktoria* concludes by revealing its female lead to be a born woman rather than the boy others take her for, and its male lead to be a "born comedian" rather than the dramatic actor he imagines himself to be. The replacement of the born woman's career as a female impersonator with the born comedian's serves as an allegory for the replacement of subtle, sensual, and sophisticated Weimar comedy with a blatant, broadly accessible, and less sexual form of humor. In addition, it depicts humor as a natural and inherent identity trait, waiting to be discovered. *Viktor und Viktoria* conceives of German comedy in the Third Reich as partially abandoning and partially adopting elements from Weimar cinema. It uses the figure of the born comedian to embody a new form of humor grounded in identity and fantasizes that the Third Reich's modifications of Weimar cinema would still leave room for the born comedian, no matter his outsider status.

The director of *Viktor und Viktoria*, Reinhold Schünzel, embodied personally the lingering presence of Jewishness and Weimar comic traditions in Third Reich film. Schünzel was a prolific actor and director in Weimar Germany, who made close to 150 films between 1916 and 1933. The Nazis labeled Schünzel a "half Jew"; a "non-Aryan," according to the Law for the Restoration of the Professional Civil Service (1933); or a first-degree *Mischling*, according to the Nuremberg Laws (1935). Having played a major role in *Anders als die Andern*, he also had ties to the homosexual emancipation movement. Because of the quality and popularity of Schünzel's comedies, however, Goebbels gave him special dispensations to continue to make movies after most Jews and leftists had been purged from the film industry. In 1934, internal documents at Germany's largest film studio, Ufa, about the loss of talent due to the Nazi takeover, list Schünzel as one of only nine directors still working for them who were capable of making above-average films.[10] Given the largely forced talent drain from the German film industry, and given Schünzel's abilities, experience, popularity, and willingness to stay, the Propaganda Minister grudgingly granted Ufa permission to hire Schünzel, one film at a time, until he departed for Hollywood in 1937. Despite Schünzel's departure, however, his influence and his films remained in circulation throughout the Third Reich. *Amphitryon* (1935), despite seemingly transgressive elements, continued to be shown in theaters through

1945.[11] Released early in the Nazi period, *Viktor und Viktoria* represented the possibility that German film could include comedies like Schünzel's, which brought with them Weimar and even Jewish traces. To a film industry undergoing a massive transition, *Viktor und Viktoria* offered a model of comedy that was more inclusive of styles and influences coded as Weimar, foreign, or Jewish than turned out to be the case in the longer term, even though remnants of these styles never disappeared completely from Third Reich screens.

Like *Blume*, which negotiated Jewish difference through colonial representations, *Viktor und Viktoria* also engages Jewish difference at the level of interdiction, expressing the unutterable through that which may be spoken. As Hake has argued compellingly, *Viktor und Viktoria* mobilizes Jewish difference indirectly through its overt play with gender roles. *Viktor und Viktoria*'s representation of a woman female impersonator initially seems to promote fluid definitions of gender and sexuality, but ultimately it reinforces heteronormativity and essentialist notions of gender.[12] To understand how the film engages Jewish difference, one must shift the analytical focus away from Susanne Lohr (Renate Müller), the female female-impersonator, to the film's male female-impersonator, Viktor Hempel (Hermann Thimig), a failed tragic actor. Hake interprets Viktor, an outsider, as an indirect reference to the Jews banished from Nazi film.[13] The character's effeminacy and hysteria, showcased in multiple scenes, are consistent with both homophobic and antisemitic stereotypes, which construe Jewish and gay men as not masculine enough, according to dominant cultural standards.[14] *Viktor und Viktoria*'s expression of the Jewish through the queer is another example of surrogation, like brownface in *Blume*, a structure that both expresses solidarity with and fails to recognize the unique positionality of the Other.

In line with my focus on Jewishness and antisemitism, I emphasize the Jewish coding and the Jewish narrative in my discussion of *Viktor und Viktoria*, intending to supplement, not displace, queer readings of this film.[15] Hake shows how Viktor's coding and marginalization reflect changes occurring in German film in 1933 and refer indirectly to the exclusion of Jews from the industry.[16] Building on Hake's analysis, I read this figure slightly differently: analyzing *Viktor und Viktoria* vis-à-vis changes in German film, I find it useful to emphasize not only how Viktor refers to processes of *ex*clusion, as Hake has shown, but also how he goes through a process of *in*clusion. Victor's queer, Jewish characteristics are reclaimed as signs of a born comedian, and he is the entertainer finally put on stage and offered a lucrative contract. The film integrates Viktor into the entertainment industry and he represents a successful comic future.

Part of the integration fantasy involves a process of replacement: replacement of the cosmopolitan woman as entertainer with the male, natural-born comic, reinforcing tropes of comedy as a masculine mode—one that would be dominated in the Third Reich by "little men," middle-class, middle-of-the road, everyday fellows whose masculinity was perpetually troubled.[17] Instead of challenging gender binaries, Susanne's androgyny invokes the New Woman of the Weimar era, only to have her leave the stage for marriage and consign herself to domestic life.[18] When Viktor replaces Susanne as Mr. Viktoria and finally wins the affections of Lilian (Friedel Pisetta), whom he has been courting, heterosexuality, immature or inadequate masculinity (by Nazi standards), and the previously unrecognized comic talent of a born comedian replace Susanne's sensual cosmopolitanism and deceptive androgyny. Viktor's career success and heterosexual happy ending encourage audiences to interpret his effeminacy, cowardice, and neuroses as signs of his comic talent and leave space for them also to be understood as codes of Jewishness. (It helps to think of this character as prefiguring Woody Allen's comic persona.) Fully in line with Nazi film writings, *Viktor und Viktoria* associates androgyny with decadence and replaces it with naive humor. The film weaves its narrowing of sexual possibilities into a discourse of authenticity and nationality that couples heterosexual love with a positive outlook for homegrown German entertainment and the ultimately unrealistic goal that a Jewish comedian could play a role in it.

As it replaces Viktoria with Viktor, *Viktor und Viktoria* advances a gendered shift from female-coded, sophisticated, sensual entertainment to male-coded, juvenile comedy. This shift is characteristic of Third Reich comedy, which reflects concepts of Nordic humor as conceived by Kadner and reaches its apotheosis in Rühmann's boyish comic style.[19] *Viktor und Viktoria* opens with Viktor's uniquely disastrous audition for a dramatic role, and it closes with his comic and heterosexual successes. Viktor's coding initially positions him as a homosexual or Jewish outsider. Yet, the laughter inspired by his cross-dressing reascribes that coding to his status as a heterosexual, cisgender-male, born comedian and offers him a path to career success and social integration. The opening audition scenes establish that Viktor is a ham who does not yet recognize his own comic talent.

Figure 3.1. Susanne (Renate Müller) asks Viktor (Hermann Thimig), "You play Hamlet? . . . I would have sworn you were a comedian." *Viktor und Viktoria* (1933). Screenshot.

Peers and potential employers find him laughable, even though he markets himself as a classical tragedian (see figure 3.1). Viktor's talent is inborn, not studied or practiced, in contrast with the dramatic acting he practices yet fails to perfect. The inborn nature of Viktor's talent is consistent with theories like Kadner's, which define German humor as racially grounded and innate, free from superficial strategies learned from the Jews, Hollywood, or the French. Viktor doesn't need to learn *how* to be a comedian. Instead, he must learn *that* he is a comedian. His apparently Jewish flaws—cowardice, neuroses, and poor acting skills among them—launch him to comic stardom with a pretty girl on his arm. Viktor's rise frees German entertainment from the androgynous cosmopolitanism embodied by Susanne and the dramatic pretensions mocked earlier in the film via Viktor's ludicrous audition. In its impulse to replace androgyny, cosmopolitanism, and high-cultural ambitions with homegrown comedy, Schünzel's *Viktor und Viktoria* echoes important components of Nazi film policy, particularly in its first years. In 1933 public rhetoric condemned individualism, superficial distraction, international styles, market forces, mass publics, and mass production of film. Instead, it advocated for a film industry that would focus on quality rather than quantity, harmonize the personalities of artist and folk, create a national community, provide simple, clean, meaningful artistic entertainment bound to nature and reality, and raise the audience's cultural taste.[20] While consistent in many ways with new film policies and practices, *Viktor und Viktoria* also valorizes diversity in German comedy, diversity still evident in productions and film commentary through 1936, but that several measures that year attempted to contain—among them the special rating of *Wenn wir alle Engel wären,* the topic of the following chapter.

Viktor's effete heterosexuality, his comic potential, and his Germanness are all articulated through his courtship of Lilian, that "shy deer" "from the green shore of the Spree" who trots out numbers before each act in a London variety show. Like Susanne, Lilian represents a cosmopolitan entertainer invited to return to the German fold. Because of her looks, name, high-pitched voice, and mixture of British and German connections, Lilian is an obvious parody of Ufa star Lilian Harvey. She invokes Harvey's dual nationality, her decadent Weimar past, and the recent embarrassment of Germany's most popular star having left for Hollywood.[21] Lilian's position as a German working abroad, and her reference to Lilian Harvey, like Viktor's effeminate and Jewish traits, present a broader vision of Germanness than orthodox Nazi paradigms. *Viktor und Viktoria*'s definition of German comedy includes those with a Weimar past and international connections, which is not surprising given Schünzel's background and legal status.

Although Lilian and Viktor do not conform to Nazi ideals, their Germanness is brought to the fore in a scene that emphasizes their heterosexuality and role as comic entertainers. Crosscutting compares an onstage variety performance with a backstage conversation between Viktor and Lilian, coding them, their simplistic humor, and their seemingly heterogeneous backgrounds as German. Onstage, two small dogs perform a variety act dressed in German women's and men's folk costumes. The dog in a dress sits on a bench while the one in *Lederhosen* begs for her attention. Offstage, Lilian spurns Viktor because he failed to show for a date. Viktor pleads that he had a good reason for missing the meeting, but Lilian claims that she has moved on to Viktor's business partner, Mr. Viktoria, who is a "real man" and her "Mr. Right." At this point, Viktor laughs and whispers in her ear that Viktoria is a woman. The camera shots, editing, and staging create parallels between the humans and the dogs in this scene. Viktor and the dog dressed as a man are on the left side of the screen, Lilian and the dog dressed as a woman on the right. The dogs appear in separate shots as the man-dog approaches the woman-dog, accenting the distance between them. Only when the man-dog is begging are the two in the same frame. The footage with Viktor and Lilian is shot and cut the same way. When Lilian steps away from Viktor, the woman-dog steps away from the man-dog. When Viktor whispers in Lilian's ear, the man-dog licks the woman-dog's ear.

The dogs' German folk costumes and the parallel editing in this scene construe Viktor's and Lilian's banter as German comedy, albeit in a superficial manner—another reminder of the differing degrees to which films of the era embraced purportedly national and racial identities and styles. By signifying Germanness through a variety act in which the performers don't even need to be human to be German, *Viktor und Viktoria* finds room for outsiders in German comedy in a way that official policy did not. Viktor exhibits traits that some spectators would have associated with homosexuality or Jewishness. Lilian is from Berlin originally, yet she lives in London and recalls the cosmopolitan expatriate Lilian Harvey. Schünzel edits these two characters parallel to two dogs in German folk costume. The dogs' recognizably German clothing indicates a focus on German comedy, despite the London setting and the performers' deviance from Nazi ideals of German identity. The editing and costuming, moreover, suggest indirectly that cosmopolitan expatriates and dogs can take on a German guise for the purposes of entertainment, again imagining a relatively broad definition of German film comedy and German national identity. In this film both comedy and national identity, like gender, can be adopted and performed easily. Despite obvious differences, such as species and costume, the behavior, staging, editing, and crosscutting show that the two couples have much in common. This similarity includes the fact that Viktor and Lilian—like the dogs—are capable of humor and heterosexual flirtation, both coded here as German. The humor is intellectually simple; the wit is primarily visual rather than verbal (grounded in physical gestures and editing rather than the dialogue); and human foibles are the butt of the joke. As detailed in chapter 1, criticism of the period treated these comic strategies as essentially German. Additionally, this scene links Viktor and Lilian to the animal world. Compassion for animals was an important component of Nazi notions of Germanness.[22] Indeed, describing "The Path to

German Film Comedy" in 1933, Alfred Beierle lists love of nature as one of the unique features of German humor that could make German comedies marketable abroad.[23]

The analogy made to the dogs' courtship codes as German a heterosexuality that is more wholesome and natural than the sophistication, sensuality, and game playing that characterize the other relationships in the film.[24] Viktor is begging as plainly as the man-dog is, and he wins his intended by whispering in her ear, just as the dog does by licking his mate's. Lilian's attempts to manipulate Viktor appear naive. Her exaggerated gestures and facial expressions look like a poorly acted bluff and indicate that she is lying only to play hard to get. Selecting a female impersonator as a fictional Mr. Right because he is a "real man" is not the most convincing lie, even if one did not know the performer's true gender identification. The rhythm and rhyme of Lilian's banter—which is in verse—accentuate her childishness.

Likewise, the German humor in this scene is rustic and straightforward, and the parallels drawn to the dog act make Viktor and Lilian seem provincial (and, therefore, not Jewish, according to contemporary codes). The dialogue accentuates this. Although Lilian claims not to be as dumb as she looks, she has mistaken a "girl" for a "cavalier." Several scenes show Viktor to be cowardly and clumsy. The parallel editing with the dogs construes both Lilian and Viktor as unsophisticated. It frames their courtship as clumsy, rather silly, and akin to animal instincts. This scene also makes an indirect case for this couple's authenticity. Susanne's cross-dressing, associated as it is with Weimar cosmopolitanism, is mostly successful (of which Lilian reminds us here). Any attempt, however, at deception by Viktor or Lilian is as transparent, silly, and comic as the dogs' disguises.

Viktor is a poor actor and unconvincing female impersonator. But he is an authentic German comedian, a thesis gradually built throughout the film and proven at the end. Viktor's drag flamenco act, which follows the scene with the dogs, demonstrates that he can perform other nationalities and gender roles for comic purposes only. This outrageous musical number convinces the audience that Viktor is anything but female or Spanish. Yet Viktor's voice conveys ambivalent messages about his identity. Viktor screeches hoarsely in a song more suited to Susanne's range. On the one hand, this screech connotes the stereotypical voice of the homosexual or the Jew.[25] On the other hand, Viktor's inability to reach a high pitch asserts his natural masculinity and the depth of his Germanness. It also underscores his consistency. Where Susanne sings different phrases in higher or lower ranges intentionally, Viktor's screech remains in a single range. His use of German lyrics for the same song that Susanne sang in (accented) English reinforces Viktor's Germanness. His clumsy movements for similar choreography show a lack of the feminine graces that she possesses. Whereas the shots of audience reactions to Susanne's performance and spectators' comments reveal desire and admiration for her androgyny, reaction shots during Viktor's performance show mirth. Viktor's flamboyant removal of his wig earns not a gasp, as a similar gesture did for Susanne, but rather, hearty laughter, indicating that the audience was not at all fooled. The film shifts from a stage where identities are fluid and drag is erotic to one where identity is difficult to dissimulate and drag becomes slapstick comedy, a shift parallel to aspects of the transition from Weimar to Nazi film.

Viktor's performance makes him a "born comedian," as proclaimed by Viktoria's impresario (Aribert Wäscher). The impresario's discovery of Viktor affirms the seeming misidentification Susanne makes at the start of the film, when, seeing photos of Viktor in dramatic roles, she erupts with the insulting observation that she would have sworn he was a comedian (figure 3.1). Viktor's performance, the audience's interpretation of it, and the impresario's performative utterance establish Viktor's essential identity, its social desirability, and its financial value. Whereas Susanne's initial misidentification of Viktor lacked the ascriptive authority to recast his outsider traits as comic, the impresario's and audience's reactions to his drag number, backed as they are by power and money, interpellate Viktor as a "real man" and a "born comic." The authorities confirm his gender assignment. Because Lilian spread the rumor that Viktoria was female, the police take Viktor off screen to inspect his genitals. Once the police proclaim Viktor's maleness, based on his anatomy, the entire cast chants joyously in march rhythm that Viktor is a man. They replace this chant with another, with the simple lyric "ha ha ha ha." The ending leaves audiences with the vocal and lyric affirmations of Viktor's masculinity and comic predisposition.

In the final shot, Viktor and Lilian and Susanne and her fiancé, Robert (Adolf Wohlbrück), link arms and skip toward the viewer. The approaching constellation shows the cosmopolitan New Woman has left the entertainment industry for marriage. Escorted by her husband-to-be, Susanne takes a role that puts her on the path to motherhood, so extolled by the Nazi state. Our male lead has had his masculinity reaffirmed and his inherent comic potential discovered. He will replace his failed attempts at tragedy with a bright future in comedy and bring a German woman back home and into respectable heterosexual monogamy. Viktor's ultimate triumph appears to reject what the Nazis saw as the maudlin dramatic pretensions, immorality, and sexual ambiguity of entertainment in the Weimar years. At the end of *Viktor und Viktoria*, a future of born comedians, of happy heterosexuals, of German entertainers returning home from decadent forays into the English-speaking world approaches German spectators—a vision consistent with Nazi entertainment policy.

The vision of German entertainment that *Viktor und Viktoria* presents, is partially consistent with the Nazis', although it also differs in significant ways. *Viktor und Viktoria* simultaneously reflects a transition to a new German comedy and a moderate vision of what that comedy could be like and who could participate in it. Even as it points toward a simpler, less intellectual German comedy, *Viktor und Viktoria* still borrows much of its style and setting from Weimar—so much so that Alice Kuzniar identifies it as part of the queer Weimar cinema.[26] *Viktor und Viktoria* shares features with Weimar urban comedies by Schünzel and others, analyzed by Ashkenazi, that reflect discreetly on Jewish assimilation by conceiving of authenticity as achieved through performance, by negotiating identity between public and private spaces, and by adopting outsider perspectives that allude to Jewishness through a technique of "dual encoding"—the subtle coding of non-Jewish characters and narratives as "Jewish."[27] Both Susanne and Viktor find their authentic selves (the loving wife, the born comic) through performance, a process that takes place between public spaces such as the variety stage and multiple barrooms and private spaces such as dressing rooms and hotel rooms. Also consistent with Weimar film comedy, the film's style of humor relies on sophisticated scenarios and dialogue, sexual tension, rapid banter, and both hetero- and homosexual innuendo for laughs. Yet, as much as it illustrates the persistence of Weimar themes and styles, *Viktor und Viktoria* also deploys strategies characteristic of German film humor, as conceived of by Nazi film critics. The ending promotes the naive, natural comic and a humor based on his clumsiness, cowardice, inability to impersonate others, and other human failings. Scenes throughout the film generate laughter from such elements.

Viktor and Viktoria's heterogeneous styles and messages show that in the first years of the Third Reich, there was room for a new comedy that had Weimar roots yet that differed substantially from its Weimar predecessors. Indeed, influences from the Weimar cinema resonated throughout the Nazi period, at the same time that demagogues denounced the hated Weimar film industry.[28] The regime's tacit tolerance of persistent Weimar styles, however, left space for a few years for diverse film comedies. Official resistance to lingering Weimar presences intensified in the mid-1930s and manifested itself in multiple ways during Schünzel's gradual fall from favor.

Just as *Viktor und Viktoria*'s representation of gender and sexuality allows for some transgression while it ultimately affirms sexual and gender normativity, its representation of new German entertainment enacts fantasies of inclusivity while simultaneously promoting an agenda consistent with the Propaganda Ministry's. *Viktor und Viktoria* promotes nationally defined, simpler-minded comedy, even if produced by cosmopolitan outsiders. Perhaps this nexus of popular cinema that would both reject and subtly draw on Weimar, that would convert markers of Jewishness into signs of the comic, is where Schünzel thought he could fit into an industry where his livelihood, as a "half Jew," was increasingly threatened. Such a conception of Schünzel's own role might explain why *Viktor und Viktoria* rejoices in integrating misfits, outsiders, and returning expatriates into German comedy. One might interpret *Viktor und Viktoria* as Schünzel writing himself into the developing Third Reich film industry and defining this industry in inclusive rather than exclusive terms.

The reviews indicate that Schünzel's vision of a film industry that would have room for Weimar traditions and diverse contributors was not yet entirely out of place. Reviews openly link Schünzel to Weimar cosmopolitanism, beyond frequent references to his past successes. Reviewers compared Schünzel's work to Lubitsch's, invoking Lubitsch's Jewishness and traditions of German-Jewish humor.[29] W. P., writing for the *Deutsche Filmzeitung*, criticized *Viktor und Viktoria* for its lack of originality and called Schünzel's choice of England as the setting for the second part of the film "outdated snobbism," clearly referring to Weimar-era tastes.[30] Yet the same reviewer praised Schünzel as a potential asset to German filmmaking, proclaiming that he had the taste and talent "to eventually make a German film-operetta of consequence" and encouraging Ufa to give him the resources to make one, "instead of immediately connecting new approaches to dated blockbuster practices."[31] W. P. saw the future in Schünzel and his work, even as both were marred by their integration of the Weimar past. Praise of Schünzel and his works encouraged lingering stylistic and (limited) racial diversity in German film comedy, at least through 1937 when Schünzel left, and by which time the Propaganda Ministry had brought the film industry and film commentary much more firmly under government control.

In the early years of the Nazi regime, hopes for continuing polyphony could have been sustained not only by praise for individuals like Schünzel and for Weimar-influenced comedies like his but also by differing, and sometimes conflicting, articulations of overt antisemitism addressed to members of the film industry. For example, on April 7, 1933, the *Deutsche Filmzeitung* reproduced Nazi film ideologue Arnold Raether's pronouncement in front of the Dachorganisation der Filmschaffenden Deutschlands (Umbrella Organization of German Filmmakers = *Dacho*): "We will stand by the decent producer, even if he is a Jew, because the new state is interested in cleanliness, honesty, and openness."[32] Raether's antisemitic comments invite assimilation and conformity and promise a future for Jews who behave as mandated by the Nazi state and who make the kinds of non-Jewish films the regime desired. In hindsight, Raether's comments seem disingenuous, particularly considering that the boycott of Jews from German film studios had already begun on April 1, 1933.[33] To believe in late 1933 that Jews would remain welcome in the German film industry as long as they avoided Jewish business and aesthetic practices would have meant ignoring clear warnings like Dr. N.'s prediction in the *Film Kurier* that "the future German film shall be the child of the German-blooded, race-conscious, creative German person who fanatically loves his *Volk*" or Hitler's speech about cultural politics at the 1933 Nazi party convention, reprinted in the *Film Kurier*, which stated explicitly that "one of the most important tasks of the movement is to declare and execute a merciless battle against these destroyers of our *Volk's* resilience [the Jews], until their complete *extermination* or *subjection*."[34] In keeping with these latter comments, *Viktor und Viktoria*'s fantasized space for outsiders would soon evaporate. Yet Schünzel worked in Nazi Germany until 1937. Between 1933 and 1936, his productions, and his vision of a new German humor that partially incorporated Weimar legacies, remained viable.[35]

Substitution as Comic Strategy: *Glückskinder* and American Humor

Films released in 1933 went into production before (*Blume*) or not so long after the Nazis consolidated power (*Viktor und Viktoria*). Although film studios ejected most Jewish artists quickly, the film industry did not manage to eliminate traits coded and understood as Jewish from film comedy in a matter of months, or even years. A look at the most successful comedies of 1936 and their reception shows that German producers still integrated cosmopolitan and "Jewish" influences from Weimar Germany, other European cinemas, and the United States, and that critics and audiences still embraced them. The mildly risqué *Allotria*, with its high-society flirtations and the glamour of racecar drivers, fashion mavens, and the French Riviera, was the smash hit of the 1936 summer season and was one of the three most successful films that year.[36] Critics lauded Schünzel's *Das Mädchen Irene* (The Girl Irene, 1936) for its British style humor.[37] *Glückskinder*, another popular 1936 film, reworked American comedy for German audiences.[38] Schünzel was an exceptional case of a racialized Jew continuing to work in the Nazi film industry, and his works reflect the influence of Weimar and other European cinemas. *Glückskinder* exemplifies the importance of Hollywood to Third Reich film comedy and of attempts to displace Hollywood hits with local productions that had similar appeal yet were substantively different.[39] In 1936, German censors cracked down on proposed American imports, approving only eight American films, whereas in 1935 they had approved fifty.[40] *Glückskinder* epitomizes the drive to replace those imports. Despite the wealth of good scholarship on *Glückskinder*, this well-known film nevertheless warrants exegesis here for its paradigmatic development and promotion of a comedy of *Ersatz*. As my analysis shows, not only does *Glückskinder* play with substitution as a comic strategy that Germany can adapt from the Americans, but also it stages itself as a successful and superior substitute for American comedy with its own unique German essence.

Because of high consumer demand for American mass culture, which remained available in Germany up through the start of World War II, *Glückskinder* and other Third Reich films aimed to copy and supplant their Hollywood competitors.[41] The best known of such productions, *Glückskinder* is a prime example of the "Germanized Americanism" Witte describes in several 1936 German comedies, which adapted the glamour and modern lifestyles that German audiences associated with Hollywood and America to the Nazi context.[42] Set in New York City and informed by director Paul Martin's and star Lilian Harvey's joint sojourn in Hollywood, *Glückskinder* was seen by its makers and contemporary critics as a successful substitute, an "*Ersatz*," for Hollywood romantic and screwball comedies in general, and for *It Happened One Night* in particular.[43] In *It Happened One Night*, a dashing reporter (Clark Gable) and a runaway heiress (Claudette

Colbert) fall in love. In *Glückskinder*, the hapless reporter Gil Taylor (Willi Fritsch) and the homeless Ann Garden (Lilian Harvey), whom he mistakes for a runaway heiress, fall in love. *Glückskinder*'s American setting, rapid tempo, snappy banter, sexual innuendo, and humorous erotic tension between the protagonists all echo the Hollywood screwball comedy.[44] Lilian Harvey's "sumptuous extravagance and ambitious careerism," which were in better alignment with Hollywood than Nazi ideals, her Hollywood past, and her English name also invoked America for German audiences.[45] As Rentschler has established, *Glückskinder* was a copy that "nonetheless passed for a German original, a cutout with its own shape. It relied on foreign patterns of recognition yet still proudly bore the appellation 'made in Germany.'"[46] *Glückskinder* demonstrated that Germany could copy Hollywood and thereby hoped to displace Hollywood from its niche in the domestic market.[47]

Glückskinder repeatedly points to its own social and economic functions as *Ersatz*. Just as this film positions itself strategically to substitute for American comedy, deliberate substitution occurs throughout the film. Figures attempt to have themselves or their words accepted as something they are not. These gestures result in both humor and confusion. In the final moments of the musical number "I Wish I Were a Chicken," Ann/Harvey wishes to be Mickey Mouse and Gil/Fritsch to be Clark Gable. This is a self-conscious reference to the actors' and the film's own status as substitutes.[48] But the film's interest in substitution extends well beyond this particular moment of self-referentiality. *Glückskinder*, the substitute for American comedy, also organizes itself around the logic of the substitute: it uses substitution to drive plot, humor, and meaning and posits its own ersatz Americanism as superior to the real thing. *Glückskinder* performs Americanness and construes American humor as witty dialogue and narrative based on rapid substitution. This Americanism pleased audiences but found mixed responses among critics, some of whom rejected it because of its impure racial and national origins. The existence of a film like *Glückskinder* and the contradictions and tensions in its reception illustrate not only the ongoing influence of Hollywood on Third Reich film but also the ambiguities around defining a national style of film humor in the mid-1930s.

Glückskinder's investment in substitution draws on but differs slightly from other Nazi-era understandings of Americanism. By the 1930s, conceptions of Americanism in Germany had shifted in emphasis from production to consumption. Fascinations with American products, an imagined

American lifestyle, and the glamour of Hollywood had replaced earlier obsessions with the industrial mass production of Henry Ford and Frederick Taylor. This new Americanism is the reference point for several published interpretations of *Glückskinder*.[49] Yet the film's combination of mechanical plot devices, dialogue, and acting and an emphasis on human interchangeability look back to the Ford and Taylor inspired Americanism of the 1920s. The name of the male protagonist—Gil Taylor—gestures in that direction as well. *Glückskinder* is structured by "the *mechanical* dictates of the confusion of identity, the exchange of social status, and the celebration of minor transgressions" that Witte finds characteristic of film comedies in Nazi Germany.[50] Witte also describes its female lead, Harvey, in mechanical terms: Her face has only one expression, "mechanical good cheer"; she moves like a "wind-up doll," and her voice is driven by "a hurdy gurdy stuck in her throat"; she is "the perfect synthetic actress, whose human features mimic . . . the mechanical ones of cartoons."[51] This mechanical quality accompanies a narrative driven by substitution. People function as interchangeable parts. Although glitches turn up in the system, more substitutions (especially Ann's doubling and her impersonation of Jackson the oil magnate's runaway niece) complete the narrative. Such affinities with the production principles of Ford and Taylor, in which workers are interchangeable, is a central component of *Glückskinder*'s "Germanized Americanism." Several stylized shots and extended montages of printing machinery, which duplicates image after image and story after story, and Jackson's presence also refer to industrial capitalism. The industrial Americanism of the 1920s lurks in the background of *Glückskinder*'s 1930s ersatz Americanism, even as the film emphasizes a logic of substitution subtly different from the seamless functional interchangeability of a Taylorist model. The outcomes of the mechanical substitutions in *Glückskinder* reveal differences between originals and substitutes and result in shifts in meaning. Such shifts expose an underlying assumption that individuals have essentially different identities that can affect the outcome of the substitution process. Therefore, a German substitute for American humor has the potential, because of its different essence, to offer a distinct and superior alternative to the original, a proposition not accepted by *Glückskinder*'s Third Reich critics.

Chains of substitution in the first scene of *Glückskinder*, coded as American through a montage of newspaper headlines and the iconography of the New York newsroom, establish the pace and style of the film's humor as well its central themes. The opening scenes follow what initially looks like a straightforward Taylorist model, where one worker stands in for another to ensure continuous production of the *Morning Post*. The film, however, debunks this model. Court reporter Hopkins (Erich Kestin) calls in to work hopelessly drunk and asks Stoddard (Oskar Sima) to step in for him. Stoddard pawns the job off on Frank Black (Paul Kemp), who owes him money. Frank unsuccessfully attempts to pass the buck to a colleague named Bill. When Stoddard points out—tongue in cheek—that none of them has to go and that Hopkins can simply lose his job if an important case turns up and fails to be reported tomorrow, they get the idea to trick Gil into doing the work. Not only does Gil substitute for Hopkins in court, but also he substitutes for Hopkins by failing to report an important story and losing his job, the fate Stoddard imagined for Hopkins. Purely structural substitution without regard for the nature of the substitute changes the intended product. By ignoring the qualities of the worker substituted (Gil's soft-heartedness and ineptitude), Stoddard and Frank throw a wrench into the system. Instead of reporting, Gil steps in to protect Ann, a complete stranger, from a conviction for vagrancy and ends up marrying her under duress. The *Morning Post* is the only paper that fails to profit from a sensational cover story about Gil's and Ann's marriage.

The scene at the *Morning Post* and later scenes in which Ann poses as Jackson's niece mock a notion of human interchangeability blinded by capitalism and insist on the unique qualities of different individuals. A second kind of substitution, wordplay, recurs in the film and both generates humor and examines relationships between substitution and substance. Much of the film's humor comes from word games, and it codes verbal wit, particularly a mechanical type based on minor substitutions, as American. More narrowly, *Glückskinder* locates such wit among members of the press in New York City—in a city and in an industry broadly construed in both Weimar and Nazi Germany as not only American but also Jewish, even though the main characters in *Glückskinder* are not marked as such.[52] Capitalizing on verbal wit, likewise coded in Germany before and after 1933 as Jewish, *Glückskinder* makes this comic strategy its own. *Glückskinder*'s clever comic dialogue, penned by Goetz, frequently involves characters changing their word choice in successive edits of an utterance.[53] As the chain of substitution proceeds, the meaning of the utterance changes and becomes funny. The courtroom scene offers an excellent example of this comic strategy. Ann appears before a judge for vagrancy. She asks, "Is it a crime to have no money?" The judge's response is telling: "No, but forbidden. Or rather, not forbidden but undesirable. Let us say uncomfortable, as much for you as for us." The judge strings together lexical substitutions describing the relationship of Ann's poverty to the law. The adjectives he uses decrease in intensity, from "forbidden" to "undesirable" to "uncomfortable." By the time the judge reaches "uncomfortable," the shift in meaning is clear and creates humor and irony. "Uncomfortable" does not correspond to the gravity of the situation, the likelihood that he will convict and incarcerate Ann for vagrancy. The final, humorous discrepancy in this witty dialogue shows that both the structure of substitution and its content have social and comic implications.

A similar comic series of substitutions with an absurd, ironic punchline unfolds in a discussion of whose fault it is that Gil has been fired:

FRANK: Actually, it's our fault. We sent Gil to summary court.[54]

STODDARD: It's Hopkins's fault. If he hadn't been drunk, a substitute wouldn't have to have been sent.

FRANK: OK, so we should blame alcohol.

STODDARD: Right.

FRANK: Who actually lifted prohibition?

STODDARD: Roosevelt, but you can't hold him accountable.

STODDARD (TO ANN): We have just simply decided that none of us is guilty. We are simply the victims of political intrigues.

The absurdity and irony of the shifts in meaning underscore the lack of equivalence in the steps and outcome. Stoddard and Frank develop the above chain of scapegoats—substitutes onto whom they displace guilt—at Gil's dining table, while Gil and Ann have a serious talk in the kitchen, in which she says she wants to leave, because it is her fault that they are all out of work. (The chief editor fired Stoddard and Frank for expressing solidarity with Gil.) The dialogue shifts blame among people, objects, and forces. Things go wrong because a substitute goes to court. The characters substitute different agents and actions until they displace their guilt far away from themselves: after this string of substitutions that replace causes, effects, and responsible parties, "none of us" is guilty. Instead, "we" are the "victims of political intrigues." They reassign blame from a person, ultimately, to a structure, within which the individual is conveniently insignificant and helpless, just as Gil is insignificant and helpless within the structure of the

Morning Post. The absurdity of this logic indicates the flaws in Stoddard and Frank's underlying premises. The characters' comedic pretense that each incremental substitution is logical and equivalent not only makes the scene funnier, but also emphasizes that, of course, everybody knows that substitution changes what things mean.

Like Frank's and Stoddard's chain of blame, the song-and-dance number "I Wish I Were a Chicken" plays with structures of substitution, using absurdity and humor to show that people and things are structurally but not substantively interchangeable and that humor based in substitution is valuable. This four-and-a-half-minute interruption falls dead in the center of *Glückskinder*. It seems to be complete nonsense, yet its treatment of substitution anchors the entire film. The four main characters are cooking when Gil says, "I wish I had a chicken. I wish I am [*sic*] a chicken. I wish I were a chicken. I wish I were a chicken." Then he bursts into song and his friends and new wife join him. "I Wish I Were a Chicken" integrates structures of substitution throughout. This musical hit (*Schlager*) underscores the differences between entities and the shifts in meaning that occur during the process of substitution. It reduces these shifts to byproducts of play and suggests that generating comedy from substitution is harmless, worthwhile, and fun. This number begins with a word game, with Gil's verb substitution that leads into the song. Then the others take over the melody and lyrics from Gil, replacing him as the lead vocalist. Next, Ann's wanting to be a man replaces the men wanting to be chickens. Beginning with Stoddard, the men then all take turns as her dance partner. Around the table, each character proclaims a wish that simply replaces the last. A rapid montage of their respective headshots precipitates the close of the song. The structure of substitution is seemingly more important to the song, and to this film, than the nonsense of its manifest content. Yet the staging and the content of the substitutions performed in this number configure a particular understanding of substitution. By celebrating substitution in musical comedy, by having the characters approach it with song and dance, fun and play, the film renders it pleasurable rather than threatening.

The chicken scene illustrates the power of humorous substitution to raise and defuse political tension through the differences and shifts in meaning caused by substitution and the laughter they cause. Such shifts are apparent in the word play leading up to the song. Through pure grammatical substitution, Gil moves from expressing a fairly logical desire for an unemployed man in a kitchen ("I wish I had a chicken") to grammatical nonsense ("I wish I am a chicken") to grammatical sense but logical nonsense ("I wish I were a chicken"). The song's various substitutions, although they otherwise avoid the middle step of grammatical nonsense, jump back and forth between seeming logic and illogic. The humor in the courtroom and the blame scene accentuates the gaps between criminality and social discomfort, between fault and victimization at the hands of politicians, and renders such gaps laughable. The play of substitutions in this song accentuates the gaps between chicken and man, and between man and woman, and shows them not to be socially equivalent. Yet, at the same time, this play turns Gil's desire not to go hungry, Ann's desire to be a man (and her sung criticism of women's work and gender roles), and the men's desires to be chickens, into functional equals—the stuff of nonsense entertainment. This song emphasizes essential differences (chicken/man, man/woman), insists the singers can never change who they are, and trivializes unemployment, hunger, and gender relations, which are depicted as a comic battle of the sexes throughout the film. While coded here as American, comic strategies that emphasized essential differences between identities and trivialized social concerns performed useful functions, unwittingly or intentionally, within the Nazi dictatorship.

Despite the potential political value in its escapism and essentialism, and despite its popularity, "I Wish I Were a Chicken" and the version of Americanism it promoted provoked hostile responses from party ideologues, which provide insight into the racialized battles over German style and humor. According to *Das schwarze Korps* (The Black Corps), the official SS newspaper, and "one of the most popular weeklies of the Third Reich," imitating Anglophone popular culture was unworthy of the German people.[55] The newspaper condemned "I Wish I Were a Chicken," claiming the song exemplified recent trends to remove the most obvious and undesirable African American influences from German popular music, leaving behind an inferior, still corrupt product.[56] According to *Das schwarze Korps*, in racist language that reveals both the tone and attitude of the piece, the music offered in place of "Niggerjazz" in the "transitional period" has been "stripped of the characteristics that were most penetratingly niggerish [sic]" and become the "hit," a creation of the "garment industry Jews" "Cohn & Co.," who transferred their Jewish practices and terminology from the ready-to-wear garment industry to musical theater.[57] *Das schwarze Korps* claimed that German composers had replaced an essentially African-American musical style with an essentially Jewish one.[58] *Glückskinder*'s "I Wish I Were a Chicken" exemplified this phenomenon. The stylistic shift from jazz to the hit was not driven, as the author claimed the public imagines, by "bad-tempered SS men with whips of hippopotamus hide [used in the African colonies] in their hands" standing behind composers to force them to follow an official four-year plan.[59] In other words, composers were not Africans subject to brutal German colonial violence, and the changes they had made were not what the SS wanted. Instead, composers were members of the German *Volk* making poor aesthetic decisions, influenced by the English-speaking world, Jewish capitalism, and mass marketing. From a racial and cultural perspective, *Das Schwarze Korps* saw little improvement here. This article accused "I Wish I Were a Chicken" of being no better than the work of the "enterprising jazzer" of yesteryear and insisted that "this type of artistic production has a hopeless similarity with the behavior of certain firms that certainly scream loud into the world that they are now 'Aryan' but maintain their Jewish methods."[60] "I Wish I Were a Chicken" thus wore a German face but had replaced the African American essence of jazz with a Jewish one. Such a song, like English radio, was not "humor" but "convulsions," characterized for the German listener by a numbing "uniformity" that—like Mickey Mouse films—is intolerable for more than fifteen minutes.[61] English and American popular culture had been corrupted by Jews and African Americans, and German copies of it offered only monotony and quick, cheap laughter. German humor does not lie in repetition, according to this article, or in borrowing from the English-speaking world, but rather in something substantive, creative, and original. "If this humor does not fit the character of our *Volk*—neither the listener nor the composer—then every effort nevertheless to convulsively conjure it up is *an attempt at an unfit object*, which could be stopped one day, and violently."[62] *Das schwarze Korps*'s assessment of *Glückskinder*'s hit song and its central scene show Nazi resistance to German popular culture's borrowing from Hollywood, even though it was a widespread practice. The piece also serves as a forceful reminder that even as popular culture maintained stylistic heterogeneity and remained responsive to foreign influences, loyal Nazis wanted to promote a racially pure national culture, defined in their own terms.

Created and released in a context where Americanism had commercial value yet signified racial alterity and, as a consequence, attracted ideological ire, *Glückskinder* not only enacts but also advocates for what it codes as American-style humor based in substitution that will serve as a superior substitute for American originals. When Ann impersonates the millionaire's niece, the film continues to generate humor from substitution and to show how substitutions cannot erase essential difference; they always result in a shift in meaning. Additionally, in its depiction of Ann Garden and Miss Jackson, *Glückskinder* emphasizes the superiority of the (German-coded) copy over the (American-coded) original. Ann's impersonation relies on physical similarities, a change in costuming, and Ann's taking Miss Jackson's position alongside her uncle. Otherwise, the women's encounter shows them to be completely different, an effect that is ironic, since Harvey plays them both. Ann still makes her snappy comments, yet continues to look innocent in a white feathery dress. Her alter ego, clad in a sleek, metallic gown, is a coolly cynical, glamorous, and worldly woman with a professional boxer for a lover, who speaks an English-accented German, peppered with Americanisms. Schneider, writing for *Lichtbild-Bühne,* calls her "meschuggene [sic]," a Yiddish word for crazy, and a "living parody of American extravagance."[63] Miss Jackson emanates the Hollywood-style Americanism that the film and its public so admired, and Schneider codes it as Jewish. Both urban and urbane, she differs substantially from her middle-class, "German" twin, Ann Garden, a country bumpkin who orders herring and boiled potatoes at a drugstore counter for her wedding meal. The difference between the two characters played by Harvey indicates that even though they look alike and both purport to be Jackson's niece, they are not interchangeable. Garden can pass for Jackson only from a distance. Their personalities and social positions are entirely different and figure 3.2 demonstrates how different they appear close up. This noninterchangeable doubling works because of the versatility of Harvey and her well-known screen persona. Harvey regularly played "the narrative source of turbulent mix-ups that set in motion a comedic carousel of confusion and mistaken identity."[64] Moreover, she plausibly plays both the jaded woman and the "sweet girl," because she is known as both—as the sweet darling of the German screen, as well as for the offscreen excesses of her Weimar and Hollywood days.[65] The film deploys Harvey's bilingualism, her German fame, her well-known British origin, and her Hollywood past here to good effect as well, for Harvey can convincingly play both the American and her Germanized alter ego, shifting her own pronunciation of German as appropriate. In this case, the film steers our sympathies toward the copy who speaks German natively, is one of the common people rather than the elite, and is connected to the land via both her name and her rural origins.[66]

Figure 3.2. The wholesome German *Ersatz* is better than the decadent Jewish-American original. Lilian Harvey (in a double role) and Thomas Czeruchin in *Glückskinder* (1936). Screenshot.

Glückskinder shows the *Ersatz* to be more likeable and morally superior to the original.[67] Gil, our loveable hero, is thrilled that Ann actually is poor and that her role as the millionaire's niece, rather than the young woman from the country lost in the big city, was an act. He likewise is completely unimpressed by the heiress, teaching the audience which woman and which lifestyle is more desirable. The background music, a lyrical love song "Miss Nobody Loves Mr. So-and-So," provides an interpretive frame for Gil and Ann's romance, and emphasizes the value of being a little Miss Nobody rather than the snotty niece of an oil magnate. The "sweet girl" with the unblemished German is our heroine. Here the film makes the case, not that it wishes to be Mickey Mouse (as Harvey sings in "I Wish I Were a Chicken"), but that it is better than any American original. This substitution has resulted in difference, one construed in the film as an improvement.

Glückskinder promotes substitution as a preferred comic strategy that German filmmakers can adopt from the Americans and suggests that when performing as substitutes, German filmmakers will produce films that differ substantively from and constitute an improvement on their American forbears. Promoting both substitution and substantial change, comedies about hopeful Miss Nobodies rather than spoiled millionaire runaways, *Glückskinder* advances a hybrid style. This style, defined by Witte as "Germanized Americanism," adopted and domesticated what the German public enjoyed about Hollywood films, aped Hollywood in many ways, and was marked by the political containment and sexual repression characteristic of the Nazi era; it also dominated German film comedy in 1936.[68]

Members of the German press expressed a range of opinions about the "Germanized Americanism" in *Glückskinder*, the model of humor it provided, and its racial and national appropriateness, illustrating that critics had not succumbed to a hegemonic view of German film humor or reached consensus about the role Hollywood should play as a model for it. *Lichtbild-Bühne*'s Schneider loved the film, proclaimed it a hit, but hedged regarding its status as national or international cinema. Schneider located *Glückskinder* somewhere between American and German film, between international and national appeal: It recalled both *It Happened One Night* and *Allotria* and was positioned to be—in paradoxical phrasing—"a worldwide success . . . wherever German is spoken, or at least understood."[69] Most enthusiastically, F. Röhl, writing for *Der Film*, endorsed *Glückskinder*'s Americanism and assured readers that it was in line both with film critics' wishes and with those of the Propaganda Minister: "We admit that, we have gladly, very gladly, raised American film comedy as an example in the columns of our newspaper."[70] Röhl reminds readers that such an editorial policy and the glowing review are consistent with the Propaganda Ministry's agenda, for Goebbels, in a speech at the Kroll Opera House, announced that German film comedy should deal with real-life topics and named *It Happened One Night* as an example.[71] Thus, positive messages about Americanism in film came not only from filmmakers, critics, and audiences, but from Nazi Germany's highest echelons as well, countering voices hostile to foreign influences.

The production, popularity, and critical reception of *Glückskinder* illustrate the influence of Hollywood on Third Reich film and occupy one of the most important positions in the struggle over a national comic film style. A front-page article in the *Film Kurier* strikingly casts *Glückskinder* and its American orientation as the preferred model for an indigenous

German film humor. The *Film Kurier* calls for a homegrown "style of comedy adapted to our time" and treats *Glückskinder* as a promising model for it.[72] Such rhetoric falls well within a Third Reich norm and echoes sentiments from other enthusiastic reviews of the film. Tellingly, however, as relates to my point about competing paradigms, this praise of *Glückskinder* is not located in a review of that film, but rather concludes an article about *Wenn wir alle Engel wären*'s receiving the regime's most prestigious rating. The article in the *Film Kurier*, however, neglects *Engel*'s specific virtues (although briefly defends it against charges of lewdness), iterates general claims about the importance of comedy in the Third Reich, and on the second page transforms into an argument advancing *Glückskinder* as the ideal German comedy.[73] The *Film Kurier* refuted charges made in "a leading daily paper" that *Glückskinder* relied too heavily on American models.[74] It recalled the tradition of German artists finding inspiration abroad, of first copying superficially and then adapting and propagating foreign influences, as with Renaissance or Gothic styles.[75] In this case, echoing the logic promoted in *Glückskinder* itself, the *Film Kurier* argued that German films needed to learn from Hollywood, and such adoptions will soon "be processed organically through their own creative will into something new and independent."[76] The article also elevates Goetz's dialogue as a successful native element upon which German comedies of the future can build. Unlike Herrmann, who condemned Goetz's style as alien, the *Film Kurier* treated the playwright as a legitimate German artistic source.[77] In line with *Glückskinder*'s suggestion that substitution results in substantial difference and preserves essential identities, the *Film Kurier* recognizes the film's ersatz American humor as its own. The article's conclusion and its emphasis on *Glückskinder* push back against the regime's designation of *Wenn wir alle Engel wären* as the ideal German comedy, even as it uses that rating as a starting point. The *Film Kurier* article thus illustrates one of this chapter's main arguments: contrasting styles of film comedy competed in Nazi Germany, even while critics and filmmakers played conscious roles in efforts to develop German film comedies with a unique national character. Among these competing styles were comedies like Schünzel's, which advocated the integration of successful Weimar traditions, and Hollywood-inspired comedies like *Glückskinder*, both bearing, from a Nazi perspective, taints of Jewish influence. These films and many others like them vied for audience and government favor against films like *Engel*, which the regime lauded as an example of racially and nationally distinct German humor.

Notes

1. Kleinhans, *Ein Volk, ein Reich, ein Kino*, 105.
2. Urwand, *Collaboration*, 62.
3. Führer, "Two-Fold Admiration," 98.
4. See Hake, *Popular Cinema*, 128–48.
5. A few examples: Beierle, "Der Weg," 3. r., "Forderungen," 1–2. "Mehr Humor in Film." S[chwar]k, "Angst," 1.
6. "Beseitigung," 1.
7. Rentschler, *Ministry*, 231, 236.
8. Hull, *Film in the Third Reich*, 41. Hake, *Popular Cinema*, 23.
9. Cf. Rentschler, *Ministry*, 98–122; Witte, *Lachende Erben*, 109–12; Ascheid, "Nazi Stardom," 69; Ascheid, *Hitler's Heroines*, 124–25; Kreimeier, "Von Henny Porten," 47; Witte, "Film im Nationalsozialismus," 130; Hickethier, "Der Ernst der Filmkomödie," 239.
10. Kreimeier, *Die Ufa-Story*, 263, 478.
11. Hans, "Musik- und Revuefilm," 204.
12. See Hake, *Popular Cinema*, 38–45, in contrast to Kuzniar, *Queer German Cinema*, 46–50. Heteronormativity is an ideology that presupposes and promotes heterosexuality and a hierarchical gender binary as natural and normal.
13. Hake, *Popular Cinema*, 39, 42–44.
14. Hake, *Popular Cinema*, 43. Wallach, *Passing Illusions*, 37. These stereotypes persist today.
15. See, for example, Kuzniar, *Queer German Cinema*, 46–50.
16. Hake, *Popular Cinema*, 38–45.
17. On the "little men" comedians as substitutes for Jewish comedians, see pages 136–39.
18. Hake, *Popular Cinema*, 41. Kuzniar, *Queer German Cinema*, 52.
19. See chapters 1, 4, and 7.
20. See, for example: "Film im Dritten Reich," 3; Roemisch, "Was ist ein Volksfilm?" 2; G[eßner], "Freiheit für den Schöpfer!" 1– 2; G[eßner], "'Volk' statt 'Publikum,'" 1–2; G[eßner], "Schluß mit der Einförmigkeit!" 1–2; J. v. B., "Die Aufgaben des volkhaften Films,"1–2; "Niveau auch im Unterhaltungsfilm,"1–2; R., "Forderungen," 2; "Das Filmtheater der Zukunft," 1–2.
21. Readers of the magazine *Licht Bild Bühne* (1 Jan. 1933) voted Harvey their favorite film actor of 1932 with 327 votes. Habich, *Lilian Harvey*, 39. For more on Harvey, her star persona, and her sojourn in Hollywood, see Ascheid, "Nazi Stardom"57–89; and *Hitler's Heroines*, 98–154.
22. Bratton, *The Natural Aryan and the Unnatural Jew*.
23. Beierle, "Der Weg," 3. See also J. v. B., "Die Aufgaben des volkhaften Films," 1–2.
24. See Hake's discussion of British cultural decadence. Hake, *Popular Cinema*, 40.
25. Hake, *Popular Cinema*, 43.
26. Kuzniar, *Queer German Cinema*, 46–50.
27. Ashkenazi, *Weimar Film*, 17–42.
28. Rentschler, *Ministry*, 9; Moeller, *Der Filmminister*, 153; Witte, *Lachende Erben*, 46, 70; Elsaesser, "Moderne und Modernisierung," 24; Kreimeier, "Von Henny Porten," 43, 46; Hake, *Popular Cinema*, x, xi, 9, 11, 12 ff.
29. Review of *Viktor und Viktoria* from the *Nachtausgabe* cited in an Ufa advertisement for *Viktor und Viktoria*, 4.

30. "Veralteter Snobismus." W. P., Review of *Viktor und Viktoria*, 6.
31. "Für die endliche Ausbildung einer deutschen Filmoperette von Rang"; "statt Ansätze zu Neuem gleich mit Schlagerpraktiken ältlicher Art zu verbinden." W. P., Review of *Viktor und Viktoria*, 6.
32. "Dem anständigen Produzenten wird man beistehen, selbst wenn er ein Jude ist; denn es kommt dem neuen Staat auf Sauberkeit, Ehrlichkeit, Offenheit an." "Film im Dritten Reich," 3.
33. Tegel, *Nazis and the Cinema*, 40.
34. "Der künftige deutsche Film soll das Kind des deutschblütigen, rassebewußten, sein Volk fanatisch liebenden, schöpferischen deutschen Menschen sein." Dr. N., "Forderungen an den deutschen Film," 3. "Es wird daher eine der wichtigsten Aufgaben der Bewegung sein, diesen Zerstörern der Widerstandskraft unseres Volkes [den Juden] einen unerbittlichen Kampf anzusagen und durchzuführen, bis zu ihrer vollständigen *Vernichtung* oder *Unterwerfung*" (emphasis in the original). "Des Führers Aufruf an die deutschen Künstler," 3.
35. The lack of clarity about the place of Jews in the film industry at the end of 1933 mirrors perceptions at the national level: "By the end of 1933, tens of millions of people inside and outside Germany were aware of the systematic policy of segregation and persecution launched by the new German regime against its Jewish citizens. Yet, as already noted at the outset, it may have been impossible for most people, Jews and non-Jews alike, to have a clear idea of the goals and limits of this policy." Friedländer, *Nazi Germany and the Jews*, vol. 1, 68.
36. Rentschler, *Ministry*, 236.
37. "Schünzel macht fröhlich," 9.
38. See Witte, *Lachende Erben*, 118.
39. Witte, *Lachende Erben*, 109–12; Rentschler, *Ministry*, 98–122.
40. Urwand, *Collaboration*, 142. The numbers rose again in 1937 and 1938 after Hollywood studios figured out more effective ways of negotiating the German system. Urwand, *Collaboration*, 145.
41. Witte, " Indivisible Legacy," 102–21; Rentschler, *Ministry*, 103–17; Quaresima, "Der Film im Dritten Reich,"16; Cary Nathenson, "Fear of Flying: Education to Manhood in Nazi Film Comedies: *Glückskinder* and *Quax, der Bruchpilot*," in *Cultural History through a National Socialist Lens*, ed. Reimer, 89. See also Hake, *German National Cinema*, 64.
42. Witte, *Lachende Erben*, 102–21.
43. Röhl, Review of *Glückskinder*, 3; Schneider, Review of *Glückskinder*, 2–3; Review of *Glückskinder*, 2; Rentschler, *Ministry*, 98–122; Witte, *Lachende Erben*, 109–12; Ascheid, "Nazi Stardom," 69; Ascheid, *Hitler's Heroines*, 124–25; Kreimeier, "Von Henny Porten," 47; Witte, "Film im Nationalsozialismus," 130; Hickethier, "Der Ernst der Filmkomödie," 239.
44. Rentschler, *Ministry*, 112–17.
45. Ascheid, "Nazi Stardom," 75; Harvey worked in Hollywood for Fox Studios from 1933 to 1935.
46. Rentschler, *Ministry*, 114.
47. Rentschler, *Ministry*, 99–122.
48. Rentschler, *Ministry*, 117; Witte, *Lachende Erben*, 109–10; also Hickethier, "Der Ernst der Filmkomödie," 240.
49. See Witte, *Lachende Erben*, 108–12; Rentschler, *Ministry*, 99–122; Ascheid, *Hitler's Heroines*, 124–34.
50. Witte, "Indivisible Legacy," 27; emphasis mine.
51. Witte, "Too Beautiful to be True," 37.

52. On New York as a Jewish-controlled city in Nazi propaganda, see Herf, *Jewish Enemy*, 40.
53. See pages 53–55.
54. Literally *Schnellgericht*, "quick court," a court with only a judge and no jury and that has brief proceedings and quick decisions. In this case, the German word choice is also a joke, insofar as it is a homograph for quick or preprepared meals.
55. Herzog, "How 'Jewish' is German Sexuality?" 193.
56. "Ich wollt', ich wär' ein Huhn," 12.
57. "Der Merkmale entkleidet, die im besonders penetranten Maße niggerhaft waren." "Ich wollt', ich wär' ein Huhn," 12.
58. By contrast, Karl Holz argues that jazz, not found among African natives, is a pernicious Jewish invention. Holz, "Jüdische Jazzmusik verboten," 6.
59. "Bärbeißige SS-Männer mit Nilpferdpeitschen in den Händen." "Ich wollt', ich wär' ein Huhn," 12.
60. "Diese Art von Kunstproduktion hat eine verzweifelte Ähnlichkeit mit dem Gebärden gewisser Firmen, die zwar laut in die Welt schreien, daß sie jetzt 'arisch' wären, ihre jüdische Methoden aber beibehalten." "Ich wollt', ich wär' ein Huhn," 12.
61. "Ich wollt', ich wär' ein Huhn," 12.
62. "Liegt dieser Humor unserem Volkscharakter nicht – weder dem Hörer noch dem Komponisten, so ist jedes Bemühen, ihn dennoch krampfhaft hervorzuzaubern *ein Versuch am untauglichem Objekt*, das eines Tages und gewaltsam gestoppt werden könnte." "Ich wollt', ich wär' ein Huhn," 12. Emphasis in the original.
63. Schneider, Review of *Glückskinder*, 2.
64. Ascheid, "Nazi Stardom," 63; *Hitler's Heroines*, 118.
65. See Ascheid, "Nazi Stardom" and *Hitler's Heroines*.
66. On the urban/rural distinction as a Jewish/German one, see page 51.
67. Cf. Hickethier, "Der Ernst der Filmkomödie," 241.
68. Witte, *Lachende Erben*, 108–12.
69. Schneider, Review of *Glückskinder*, 3.
70. Röhl, Review of *Glückskinder*, 3.
71. Röhl, Review of *Glückskinder*, 3.
72. "Unserer Zeit angepaßten Lustspiel-Stil." S[chwar]k, "Unterhaltungsfilm gleichberechtigt," 2.
73. S[chwar]k, "Unterhaltungsfilm gleichberechtigt," 1–2.
74. S[chwar]k, "Unterhaltungsfilm gleichberechtigt," 2.
75. S[chwar]k, "Unterhaltungsfilm gleichberechtigt," 2.
76. S[chwar]k, "Unterhaltungsfilm gleichberechtigt," 2.
77. Herrmann, "Humor," 364–65. S[chwar]k, "Unterhaltungsfilm gleichberechtigt," 2.

4

WENN WIR ALLE ENGEL WÄREN AS THE MODEL OF A RACIALIZED GERMAN HUMOR

IN 1936, THE TRANSITIONAL PERIOD WAS DRAWING TO a close. The process of *Gleichschaltung* in the film industry was largely complete; the industry had stabilized financially, and the groundwork was in place for nationalization to begin.¹ The year 1936 was also a turning point in international relations and domestic politics. Having established their government and restored the economy, in 1936 the Nazis shifted from "relative moderation in some domains" to a period of "political radicalization and the mobilization of internal resources ... to prepare the country for war."² Hosting the 1936 Summer Olympics in Berlin, Germany showed the world a conciliatory facade, while becoming more assertive on other fronts. In March, the Nazi regime sent military forces into the Rhineland, violating the Treaties of Versailles and Locarno, and in November signed the anti-Comintern pact with Japan. There were correspondingly aggressive shifts in antisemitic policy in 1936 as well. "Most immediately three main lines of action dominated the new phase of the anti-Jewish drive: accelerated Aryanization [the expropriation of Jewish businesses], increasingly coordinated efforts to compel the Jews to leave Germany, and furious propaganda activity to project on a world scale the theme of Jewish conspiracy and threat."³

Film comedy's support of this new phase of radicalization, mobilization, and antisemitism was subtle and indirect. Jewish filmmakers, themes, and characters had already been expelled. Moreover, Goebbels had decided that overt political propaganda in entertainment film, as in *Susanne,* was largely ineffective. Instead of promoting Nazi antisemitism directly, film comedy helped eliminate the "Jewish" from German culture obliquely.

Inferential patterns and disciplinary humor discouraged Jewish behaviors and attitudes. The present chapter explains the importance of *Wenn wir alle Engel wären* in expelling Jewishness from the style of Third Reich film comedy.

Despite the Propaganda Ministry's having purged Jews from the film industry and restructured it, legacies of Weimar cinema, influences from abroad, and themes and techniques construed as Jewish persisted in German film comedy throughout the 1930s, and audiences continued to respond positively to them. Writers and critics reflected on ways that German film humor might adapt to the racial and national imperatives of the Nazi period, yet in 1936 there remained a gap between the humor prescribed and the film comedies produced. The style of film comedy shifted somewhat after 1933, most noticeably in its sexual restraint, avoidance of topics and viewpoints objectionable to the regime, and alignment with party views on class and gender.[4] Jewish and leftist comedians disappeared. While difficult to quantify, comic techniques discouraged by racial thinkers, like those discussed in chapter one, traits such as irony and verbal wit, seem less prevalent as well. Yet, markedly in the transitional period 1933–36, and to some extent throughout the Third Reich, competing styles of film comedies persisted, reflecting influences from Weimar Germany, from Hollywood, and from other indigenous and international traditions. The public had catholic tastes, flocking to rustic comedies like *Krach um Jolanthe* as well as to more cosmopolitan options like *Viktor und Viktoria* and *Glückskinder*.

Faced with this stylistic diversity, on October 7, 1936, the government made a major symbolic intervention on behalf of nationally and racially defined German film humor. Censors awarded *Wenn wir alle Engel wären*, starring Heinz Rühmann, scripted by Heinrich Spoerl, and directed by Carl Froelich, the highest rating possible in the Nazi film rating system, "politically and artistically especially valuable."[5] This rating conferred prestige, marketing benefits, and tax subsidies on awardees and reinforced Nazi cultural and political norms.[6] *Engel* was the only comedy ever to receive this rating. Most films rated "politically and artistically especially valuable" were ambitious dramas with explicitly political content. Well-known examples include *Der alte und der junge König* (The Old and the Young King, Hans Steinhoff, 1935), a film about the maturation of the Prussian king and military leader Friedrich the Great, and *Jud Süss*, in which a vile court Jew reveals his sinister nature and is hanged for raping a German woman.

Engel's particular artistic or political value to the Nazi regime is not obvious. The film's quality is not extraordinary; other comedies were not decorated so highly; and its story about a husband and wife each trying to conceal a perceived marital infidelity that may not even have occurred does not address socioeconomic or geopolitical issues explicitly. Outside the struggle for a uniquely German comic film style, free from Jewish influences, the rating "politically especially valuable" makes no sense for this film. Its only overt political gesture—a scene in which a German court serves as the arbiter of truth and justice (regarding such nationally insignificant events as extramarital affairs and stolen sheets)—does not rise to the standard of "politically especially valuable," as applied by the censors to other Third Reich films. Scholars have noted the film's value to the regime in setting and enforcing gendered sexual norms.[7] In this, however, *Engel* is fairly typical of Third Reich film comedy, rather than exceptional. Additionally, the film promotes mistrust of foreigners and depicts "a cheerful and happy Germany."[8] While consistent with the Nazi agenda, such representations likewise were relatively common and are not commensurate with the overtly political messages of other films that received this exclusive rating. *Verräter* (Traitors, Karl Ritter, 1936), a spy film that won the highest rating in the same year as *Engel*, cautions against traitors and espionage, and shows how teamwork and Nazi party solidarity will catch the perpetrators and set things right. *Jud Süss* warns audiences against deceptive, assimilated Jews and advocates banning Jews from German lands and hanging them if they have sex with Aryan women.

The reasons for *Engel*'s rating of "artistically especially valuable" are not immediately evident either. Compared to other Nazi-era film comedies, *Engel*'s quality is mediocre. Editing and dialogue are slow and lack the sharp wit, clever juxtapositions, and pointed punchlines of comedies like *Viktor und Viktoria* and *Glückskinder*. Strange lighting favors backgrounds over the actors' faces. Shots are comparatively static, and editing feels slow. Yet a closer look at the film's style helps explain both the film's high artistic rating and its high political rating. My analysis explains *Engel*'s stylistic choices— so unappealing from a twenty-first-century perspective—as absences and substitutions that were part of a move toward a nationally and racially defined German film humor. While a viewer today might question *Engel*'s quality, Goebbels considered it to be one of Germany's finest productions.[9] It was also one of few 1930s German comedies that were genuine crowd-pleasers.[10] At a time when, from a Nazi perspective, techniques understood as Jewish and foreign continued to thrive in German film comedies, *Engel* offered a popular alternative: it served as a paradigm of a racially determined German film humor, well received by audiences, that, once illuminated by its special rating, could serve as a beacon for other films.

An Opportunity to Intervene

Wenn wir alle Engel wären played a unique role in the attempt to establish a distinctively German comic film style. Unlike *Engel*, other box office hit comedies in the mid-1930s did not receive such high honors. *Krach um Jolanthe* earned the rating "artistically especially valuable."[11] *Glückskinder*, *Allotria*, and *Amphitryon*, an irreverent depiction of one of Jupiter's peccadillos, were rated only "artistically valuable"; *April! April!* and *Donogoo Tonka* received no special rating at all.[12] At first glance, *Engel* does not seem substantively better or more political than these other comedies, which, unlike Froelich's films, were and continue to be received by critics as quick, witty, and cosmopolitan.[13] By contrast, *Engel* struck reviewers as "volkhaft" (of the people).[14] The *Berlin Lokal Anzeiger* praised *Engel* for displaying "humor . . . without mockery," "a healthy, refreshing coarseness," and "people deeply rooted . . . in the beautiful land of the Mosel and Rhine."[15] In other words, theme, style, and location had germinated in the German soil, a metaphor that in 1936 had distinctly racial implications. Describing *Engel*'s humor as "healthy" and as lacking "mockery," the reviewer codes it as "not Jewish." By lauding this film's political and artistic worth, the regime promoted its display of a unique and racially determined German film humor at a time in which its competitors did not all follow the recipe for German humor admired in official quarters.

Continuing public and critical favor for wittier, edgier comedies like Schünzel's and Goetz's, and for other successful but less German models of comedy, led the regime to intervene on behalf of the style of humor it favored, including the special rating and promotion of *Engel*. A favorable comparison of Schünzel to Froelich in *Deutsches Wollen: die Wochenzeitung für das junge Reich* (German Will, the Weekly Paper for the Young Reich) reveals that not all film critics had adopted the orthodox understandings of race, nation, comedy, and humor favored by Goebbels. Critics' tastes had not yet been guided or restricted enough to lead them all to laud Froelich's folksy humor over Schünzel's cosmopolitan comedy. In response to the simultaneous premieres of Schünzel's *Das Mädchen Irene* and Froelich's *Engel, Deutsches Wollen* proclaimed, "Schünzel makes [us] cheerful and Froelich makes . . . ?"[16] A pun in the headline, which praises Schünzel for making audiences *fröhlich* (cheerful), accuses Froelich of not living up to his own name. The pun is also an homage to Schünzel's verbal wit and thus, indirectly, a nod to his Jewish humor. Comparing these two films, which opened Ufa's and Tobis's new competing premiere venues in Berlin, *Deutsches Wollen* declared Ufa the winner "by many lengths" with *Irene* over Tobis's *Engel*. The newspaper praised "the English atmosphere" of Schünzel's adaptation of a British comedy and its director's ability to build successfully on his accomplishments in silent film. By contrast, the reviewer upbraided Froelich, "our national prize winner," for his "Rhineland comedy," because the film's sexual morals belonged back in 1930, implying that the film's undignified portrayal of sexuality predated the Third Reich's sexual morality. Such loose morality couldn't even be excused on the grounds of export, argued the reviewer, because the film's use of dialect would make the dialogue incomprehensible to foreign audiences.[17] The review's author cited both Froelich's stature and the local character of his comedy, both of which were strong positives in a Third Reich context; yet they failed to convince the reviewer in matters of taste. Whereas the reviewer praised Schünzel's skill in building on his Weimar-era successes (some of them, in fact, quite risqué), Froelich's perceived throwback to 1930 sexual morality was criticized. In other words, the reviewer rejected Weimar sexual permissiveness but not Weimar cinematic prowess and comic strategies, still preferring Schünzel's cosmopolitan, Weimar-derived, British-influenced (Jewish) wit over Froelich's regional (German) humor.

Despite *Deutsches Wollen*'s party loyalties, the review of *Engel* and *Irene* codes Schünzel's humor as Jewish but does not reject it as such. In another article on the same page, *Deutsches Wollen* denounced Jewish producers abroad, echoing official rhetoric.[18] The paper did not, however, apply an overtly antisemitic perspective to Schünzel's person or to his cosmopolitan wit. Thus, in matters of comic taste and an appreciation for a racially and nationally determined German humor, *Deutsches Wollen*'s anonymous reviewer was not yet fully coordinated with Nazi policies and goals. The contradictions expressed on this single page of *Deutsches Wollen* epitomize one of my major claims: it took time for the Nazi regime to propagate and enforce standards for German racial humor, standards that filmmakers, critics, and audiences in 1936 did not yet always prefer. Actions such as the rating of *Engel* sought to make a more racially and nationally defined film humor the norm.

I argue that censors labeled *Engel* "politically and artistically especially valuable" precisely because many Germans still had an appetite for the more sophisticated Hollywood and Weimar influenced styles coded in the Third Reich as Jewish. In the wake of *Allotria*'s and *Glückskinder*'s box office successes and continued praise for comedies like Schünzel's, critics, consumers, and producers of films needed to be told what a good German comedy looked like. *Engel* epitomized a nationally unique style of German comedy promoted by the Propaganda Ministry. Its special rating instructed filmmakers regarding the model of humor they should follow, and told audiences what they should like. The concurrent tax and marketing benefits not only rewarded the film's creators and motivated distributors but also created broader audiences for the film. Thus, *Engel*'s exceptional rating contributed to attempts to define and promote essentially German film humor and distinguish it from Hollywood, Weimar, and other purportedly foreign and Jewish counterparts.

German Artists Making German Art

Engel represents the ideal German comedy, from a Nazi perspective. Produced by a team of artists heavily identified with the popular culture of the Third Reich, it promotes a film humor tailored to the historical context; exhibits an antimodernist, anti-Hollywood, and anti-Weimar visual style (and therefore, implicitly, an anti-Jewish style); and embodies male, bourgeois German identity through its star, Heinz Rühmann. The film unified audiences in laughter with a suite of themes and strategies that echo discussions of racially defined German humor. Focusing on small-town German life, *Engel* charts a couple's and community's return to wholesomeness after facing several challenges: the gap between reality and ideals, temptations by the urban and the outsider, and mundane human weaknesses such as alcohol, foolishness, and mendacity. Its humor relies on situation, character, and gesture rather than irony, slapstick, or verbal wit, strategies condemned at the time as un-German.

The scriptwriter, director, and star of *Engel* all contributed to the development of a characteristic German film humor during the Third Reich. Although each of these artists' work spanned decades and eras of German cinema, in each case, their work found particular official and public favor in the Third Reich and is prototypical of that era's film production.[19] Heinrich

Spoerl, who wrote *Engel*'s script, was "by far the most popular humorist" of the era.[20] He penned bestselling books, plays, and film comedies such as *Der Maulkorb* (The Dog Muzzle, Erich Engel, 1938) and *Die Feuerzangenbowle*.[21] Spoerl avoided taking a clear position toward the Nazi regime and enjoys a reputation for having been apolitical.[22] Yet his volume of humorous short prose, *Man kann ruhig darüber sprechen* (One Can Easily Talk About It, 1937), engaged its contemporary context and both criticized some Nazi attitudes and reflected and supported others.[23] When one excludes essential Nazi texts such as *Mein Kampf*, which flooded the market, whether or not they were actually read, *Man kann ruhig darüber sprechen* was the bestselling book in the Third Reich, indicating that it appealed to contemporary readers and likely had significant influence on them and on the publishing industry.[24]

Man kann ruhig darüber sprechen illustrates how Spoerl curried public and official favor by developing humor that suited the Third Reich context. The collection's opening essay, "Die Angst vor dem Witz" (Fear of the Joke/Wit), speaks directly to the problem of an appropriate humor for the Third Reich. That editors removed this essay from postwar editions of the book shows that they recognized its particular relevance to the era in which it was first published.[25] At the time of its original publication, "Die Angst vor dem Witz" was distributed widely, having appeared not only at the beginning of one of the Third Reich's bestselling books but also in *Der Angriff* and dozens of other newspapers.[26] "Die Angst vor dem Witz" works through questions similar to those in a *Film Kurier* article in that same year entitled "Angst vor Humor?" (Fear of Humor?), which attempted to resolve filmmakers' confusion about what forms of humor were acceptable under Nazism.[27] These topical questions were connected to broader debates about comedy in the Third Reich. A perceived contradiction between Nazism and comedy initially shut down press discussions of humor, which only began tentatively in 1934 to debate forms of comedy suited to the new Nazi-dominated society.[28] The notion persisted that Nazi comedy was an oxymoron, spurring popular, press, and academic discussion of appropriate forms of German humor, discussions in which the *Film Kurier* article and Spoerl's widely read essay participated.[29]

How Spoerl frames his essay reveals a broader mission to develop suitable humor for the Third Reich. He begins, "First let it be determined: wit is not a Jewish invention; nor is it an instrument of Satan."[30] He concludes with a joke that only made sense in prewar Nazi Germany: "Do you know the difference between a veteran and an 'old fighter'? The number of veterans keeps getting smaller."³¹ While veterans were dying off, the number of "old fighters," people who had joined the Nazi party before 1933, kept growing. This joke mocks those who, jumping late on the Nazi bandwagon, pretended to have been supporters all along, presumably for personal gain. It is a joke that could have been appreciated both by true party loyalists (such as readers of *Der Angriff*) and by those loath to join up. More importantly for our understanding of Spoerl, the joke clarifies the trajectory of his essay and a goal of the collection it introduces, to displace the false premise with which it opens—that wit is "Jewish," even "Satanic"—with a humor specific to Nazi Germany. Seemingly promoting openness, Spoerl's essay argues that wit "doesn't allow itself to be commanded [... or] forbidden" and shouldn't be feared.³² This statement perpetuates a fantasy that humor is free from political control, and can and should remain so. Humor is not merely independent of politics, argues Spoerl, but also essential for their success. He claims wit is needed for "heroic times," a common argument in the 1930s among those attempting to justify lighthearted humor in a serious, Nazi context.³³ When it comes to the specific kind of humor needed to amuse Nazi heroes, Spoerl's argument takes on a more nationalist character: rather than importing jokes from abroad, "we" should make our own.³⁴ The times do—Spoerl admits—pose challenges to domestic production of humor, although not the challenges that the essay presumes the reader imagines (state censorship and somber, heroic attitudes). The only trouble with making jokes in Nazi Germany—according to Spoerl—is that 67% of all jokes begin with the question "Do you know the difference between ... ?" but "we don't know differences anymore."³⁵ On the one hand, this claim is an egregious (and perhaps ironic) mischaracterization of a society structured almost entirely around difference. On the other, the joke's punchline recalls the "illusion of wholeness" that Schulte-Sasse identifies as a primary function of Third Reich film, and, more specifically, points to a dominant function of German humor as theorized and practiced in the Third Reich.³⁶ Patrick Merzinger argues that humorous literature in Nazi Germany had a self-disciplinary and integrative function, finding laughter and understanding for minor transgressions, bringing protagonists ultimately back onto the right path and into the community.³⁷

Structured around minor transgressions and the reconciliation and social reintegration of a petty bourgeois couple, *Engel* is paradigmatic of the disciplinary humorous narratives analyzed by Merzinger.³⁸ The film and its rating also served as proof, at least to the editorial staff of *Lichtbild-Bühne*, that despite fears in 1933 "that the time for laughter was over," "*one can laugh again in the new Germany!*"[39] *Engel*'s rating was a sign that a new humor was ascendant that differed fundamentally from the "cramped," "slippery" "ambivalence" of the Weimar days. Triumphantly, *Lichtbild-Bühne* proclaimed, "And the men, the work of these men, who give us liberating laughter and grins, who breathe healthy wit and humor, *are honored publicly!*"[40] In this particular historical and rhetorical context, praising wit as "healthy" and laughter as "liberating," codes *Engel*'s humor as not Jewish.

Spoerl's script laid the groundwork for *Engel* to exemplify German film comedy. A letter Spoerl wrote to Froelich on October 15, 1936, indicates that such a "cultural mission" may have been a conscious one, or at least one he embraced after the film won the regime's highest rating: "Dear Master Froelich! This morning I read the rating in the *Film Kurier*. I rubbed my eyes, but it is really true: also 'politically.' I rejoiced for three reasons. First of all, overall. Second of all, that your work thus received the highest possible award. And third, that happily humor is starting to be taken seriously, that the cultural mission of such a film is recognized."[41]

A key figure in the Nazi film industry, Froelich realized the potential of Spoerl's script in cinematic terms, translated it into an onscreen vision of German humor, and lent it the necessary stature to win such a favorable rating. Froelich was one of a small cadre of politically committed directors trusted by the Nazi regime repeatedly to make films that were "politically especially valuable."[42] An early film pioneer, veteran of World War I, and loyal member of the Nazi party, Froelich was frequently and highly decorated, as were his films. Due to both his Nazi convictions and his extensive filmmaking experience, he held several influential positions in the Third Reich film industry, and from 1939 on served as president of the Reichsfilmkammer. Froelich won more special ratings for his Third Reich films than any director other than Veit Harlan, signaling "that his films enjoyed a position in Third Reich cinema as exemplary models of Nazism's new popular film art."[43] To be sure, *Engel*'s special rating was yet another way of honoring its director.[44] In addition, the film's special rating singled out and subsidized Froelich's comic style, set new norms for Third Reich film comedy, and promised state support for similar future comedies.[45]

Froelich's films look "off," even incompetent, to eyes used to the speed and shine of Hollywood or the high-contrast lighting and experimentation associated with Weimar. Froelich sought a different path, one that began with German film pioneers like Oskar Messter, with whom he had worked, and bypassed the influences of Weimar and Hollywood.[46] Erica Carter explains how Froelich rejected conventions associated with modernism, German film of the 1920s, and Hollywood, all coded as Jewish. Froelich downplayed point-of-view shots and continuity editing in favor of a detached perspective on framed aesthetic compositions.[47] Other important features of "Froelich's stylistic disavowal of modernism" include his use of single-shot tableaux as basic narrative elements, deep staging, and slow cutting.[48] Lighting functions in his work "as ornament and frame" and to "emphasise . . . the aesthetic ensemble, not the star, as the source of visual pleasure within the camera frame."[49] (See Figure 4.1 and discussion below.) In his heavy reliance on these Wilhelmine-derived, antimodernist techniques, Froelich developed a signature style, which Carter dubs "the *völkish* sublime," to unite and express the spirit of the German people.[50] While Carter is interested in the Third Reich's "film art," not in its lowbrow entertainment, and her analysis focuses on Froelich's National Prize winning *Traumulus* (Little Dreamer, 1936), the stylistic features she ascribes to Froelich can be found throughout *Engel*.

Despite the director's prestige, *Engel* was promoted as and remains known primarily as a Rühmann film, for its male lead. Rühmann's films are a distinctly German variation of what have been theorized in a Hollywood context as "comedian films" or "comedian comedies." Comedian comedies reflect the intermedial influence of humorous short-form stage acts like vaudeville, cabaret, and stand-up comedy on the cinema, and the historical transition of early film comics from popular stage entertainment to the screen. Comedian comedies showcase a star comedian with a well-known signature comic persona and style. They integrate comedians' extra-diegetic comic personas and the show-stopping spectacle of comic gags, bits, or shticks (depending on whom you talk to) into a fictional narrative. Hollywood comedian films in the silent and early sound eras combined the "cinema of attractions," as theorized by Tom Gunning, with narrative cinema, creating tension between the comedian and the diegetic world, and between the character and the social norms that surround it.[51] Embodying conflict between the individual and the community, disruptions caused by the comedian and their eventual resolution have been theorized as destabilizing and/or reaffirming social conventions in different films and historical contexts.[52]

Several aspects of Hollywood and Weimar comedian comedies predisposed them to Jewish coding. Among prominent US film comedians in the 1920s and 1930s—most of them men—were a number of Jewish vaudeville performers, including the Marx Brothers, the Three Stooges, Eddie Cantor, Jack Benny, and George Burns. Similarly, there was a noteworthy Jewish presence in German comedian comedy before 1933, for example, the early Lubitsch, Arno, Bois, Kurt Gerron, and Fritz Grünbaum. These male performers embodied Jewishness and Jewish humor in Weimar film comedy. "Female Jewish characters, in contrast, could be found mainly in supporting or small roles, if they were present at all."[53] Jewish comicalness and wit, as performed in Weimar comedian comedy and spurned by the Nazis, were coded male.

It was not only the contributions of Jewish individuals, however, or the presence of ethnically marked Jewish characters that made comedian comedy Jewish, but also the genre's style and sensibility. Comedian comedy is anarchic and excessive. Bold physical movements, outrageous jokes, over-the-top gags, and the comedian's star persona are disruptive to the narrative economy and to social norms.[54] The protagonists are outsiders and the performers' excesses elude narrative control, even when they are ultimately integrated through a happy ending. The genre creates a liminal space that allows for play with but no escape from ethnic identities.[55]

The figure of the transgressive male (but not overly masculine) outsider, and the comic pathos and critical irony generated by his awkward failures to fit in, were read as Jewish in this time period. (Think back to *Viktor und Viktoria*.) The paradigmatic example is Charlie Chaplin, who, despite being neither religiously nor ethnically Jewish, was perceived as Jewish by both Jews and non-Jews in Germany, the United States, and elsewhere. Many of Chaplin's contemporaries read his physical appearance, his leftist politics, and the gestural vocabulary, outsider status, pathos, and humor of his Little Tramp persona as Jewish.[56] The Nazis' insistent labeling and criticism of Chaplin as a Jew—from Weimar-era press reports through *Der ewige Jude* exhibit, Hippler's film of the same name, and beyond—cast Chaplin as a Jewish clown whose culturally destructive tendencies, promoted by the Jewish-controlled press, harmed the democracies who worshiped him.[57] Third Reich comedians offered a non-Jewish alternative to Chaplin and other Hollywood comedians and filled the vacuum created when Weimar's Jewish comedians left.

Like Hollywood's and Weimar's comedian comedies, Nazi Germany's variation on the genre still foregrounded a well-known comic persona, but the comedians' personae, their comic episodes, and their comic style were less overtly disruptive to narrative flow and to communal norms. Relying on stars construed as representative of rather than isolated from the *Volksgemeinschaft*, comedian comedy was consistent with Third Reich star culture more broadly. The Nazi regime balked at the notion of a filmic firmament far above other members of the *Volksgemeinschaft*, and, presumably, stars who would outshine Hitler. Thus, the role of the Third Reich film star was to perform as part of the onscreen ensemble and the offscreen *Volksgemeinschaft*, dissolve individual identities (including his or her own), and embody the *Volk*'s collective *Persönlichkeit* (personality), racially conceived.[58] Like other aspects of the Third Reich film industry, star culture too reflected the tension between commercial and ideological goals. Stars were essential marketing tools and their personae, which included both their onscreen expressions and the "private" lives and personalities created for them by the press, not only incorporated the people's collective *Persönlichkeit* but also promoted their films and propagated gendered social norms.[59] As with Zarah Leander, the eventual *Ersatz* for Marlene Dietrich's sublimity, these Third Reich stars frequently were "ghosts," whose *Volk*-identified *Persönlichkeiten* replaced the transcendence of stars who had left German film.[60]

"Little men" like Rühmann, Theo Lingen, Hans Moser, and Paul Kemp were the Nazi era's characteristic substitutes for the more anarchic and destructive impulses of Weimar-era "Jewish" comedians.[61] The little men of Third Reich comedian comedy, who replaced Weimar's Jewish comedians, tended to play everyday middle-class people, servants, and members of the lower bourgeoisie. Comic situations arise when they rise above their station or step out of line, and disciplinary laughter reestablishes the social order. A typical example is *Einmal der liebe Herrgott sein* (To Be God One Time, Hans Zerlett, 1942), in which a hotel employee, played by Moser, acts on his desire to run the hotel and chaos ensues. The little men of Third Reich comedy represent community insiders, everyday Germans, with ambitions or minor transgressions that need correcting, rather than true outsiders to the *Volksgemeinschaft*.

In addition to their star personae and characters being a part of the *Volksgemeinschaft* instead of being outsiders, the little men's comic styles were less disruptive of films' narratives than American comedians' shticks and gags. These differences made Third Reich comedian comedy less Jewish, by both US and Central European standards. Rühmann, Moser, Lingen, and other little men like Kemp and Hörbiger were formally trained actors who had acted with major theatrical companies before breaking into film. They also performed in cabaret and variety formats, in which they enhanced their popular appeal and developed signature comic strategies and personae that they would rely on in their film careers. Because of their theatrical training and experience, however, these comedians were accustomed to integrating their humor into narrative, character, and ensemble work, in addition to episodic performances of short gags and bits. The frequency of stage and literary adaptations and the scriptwriting contributions of authors and playwrights like Spoerl and Goetz contributed to Third Reich film comedy's emphasis on narrative, situation, and character. Thus, the starring roles in Third Reich comedian comedy highlight the ridiculousness of a character within a comic situation over isolated episodes of show-stopping slapstick or clever banter. Instead of "Jewish" verbal wit, the little men comedians garner humor and sympathy from their eccentric speech mannerisms and regional accents, which root them in a specific *Heimat* (homeland) within greater Germany. The most acute example of this difference is Moser: his strong Viennese accent, mumbling, grumbling, and tendency to speak in incomplete sentences preclude an emphasis on verbal wit, or, if it is there, interfere with non-Austrian audiences' understanding it.

Rühmann's variation of the comedian comedy was and continues to be understood as particularly German. Many writers have lauded and analyzed Rühmann as the paradigmatic German comedian.[62] His "role as a German 'everyman' led him to be seen explicitly as an icon of the national self image," and helped him serve as a figure of "continuity," "conformity," and "integration" throughout the twentieth century.[63] According to Hake, Rühmann and his performances functioned in Nazi Germany as part of "the strategic use of actors and actresses as part of the phantasmagoria of the racialized body."[64] They rely on strong identifications between actor, role, and national character (in Rühmann's case, as the essential "ordinary German"—in male, petit bourgeois form). Rühmann's performance of contradictions, ambivalences, and tension, and audience identifications with them allow Rühmann to displace social conflict via gender onto individual psychology, which made him particularly popular during the Nazi dictatorship.[65]

In Rühmann's German comedian comedy, the individual is in temporary conflict with the community and he must resolve the conflict and reintegrate himself. His performances of the German everyman, which humorously correct his minor transgressions and reintegrate him into the community are a form of disciplinary humor that fit well within rubrics applied to German comedy in the 1930s: "education to authority," "petty bourgeois gone astray," and "preserving identity in the confrontation with the authorities."[66] Rühmann's "petty bourgeois gone astray" narratives, of which *Engel* is an obvious example, encourage conformity similarly to Spoerl's other humorous writings.[67]

Rühmann's signature style embodies characteristics of ideal German film comedy, as advanced by Third Reich authors and critics. His much-remarked boyish or adolescent appearance and manner (two women in *Engel* actually refer to him as "Bubi," or little lad) exemplify the youthful, roguish man characteristic of "Nordic" humor, as theorized by Kadner.[68] Rühmann's failure to embody mature masculine ideals is one of the sources of his humor: His acting style expresses the frustrations of and compensates for a threatened masculinity and a "body 'too little'" (both in stature and its boyish physiognomy) with a range of strategies including "whining, mumbling, and stammering" and "increased physical activity."[69] Rühmann's gestures of self-belittling self-aggrandizement evoke Beierle's call in the *Film Kurier* to make light of characters' "lovable weaknesses."[70] They are an earlier example of what Herrmann would laud in 1937 as Rühmann's contributions to "a particularly German film humor."[71] These contributions included his characteristic "vulnerability" and "more human" exposure of his own weaknesses.[72] Contextualized within Nazi racial theory, such desires and performances embody Kadner's Germanic humor, which included the propensity to laugh at one's self.[73] The expressions of inadequacy in a physical register, Rühmann's exaggerated facial expressions, frenetic gestures, and emphasis on delivery and tone—or humorous "tonelessness"—rather than witty dialogue fit in well with Third Reich criticisms of verbal wit as alien and preferences for more situational and gestural comedy.[74] Other aspects of Rühmann's comic style noted by contemporary critics, such as his "exaggeration of comic situations" without compromising believability and his ironic and theatrical facial expressions that "make clear the difference between essence and appearance" also echo important language and concepts from overtly and inferentially antisemitic Third Reich discussions of film comedy.[75]

Unmasking Authentic German Humor

Spoerl, Froelich, and Rühmann were all giants of Third Reich popular culture who each contributed to the development of a distinctively German film comedy that differed from cookie-cutter confections like *Blume*, sophisticated, European products like Schünzel's, the Germanized Americanism of *Glückskinder*, and Jewish-coded comedian comedy. Seen from a Nazi point of view, their commercially successful collaboration, *Wenn wir alle Engel wären*, merited the unique decoration (among comedies) "politically and artistically especially valuable." Third Reich film critics urged filmmakers to strip away Jewish comic strategies, including irony, verbal wit, rapid-fire dialogue and editing, and slapstick, and in their place promoted a kind of serious, reflective, forward-looking, and "more human" approach to human foibles, social difficulties, and philosophical questions—an approach exemplified in this film.[76] Thematically in line with critics' injunctions that German humor focus in a gentle, self-critical way on human frailty, *Engel* shows how the larger issues it tackles—the gap between reality and ideals, the threats posed to small-town society by the urban and the outsider—are exacerbated throughout by common human weaknesses: alcohol, sexual temptation, dishonesty, gossip, and stupidity.[77]

According to Kadner, the discrepancy between reality as humans perceive it and their internal ideals was the driving force behind the humor of the Germanic peoples.[78] The gap between appearance and essence, and how to respond to it, constituted a virtual obsession both of Third Reich film and of Nazi racial antisemitism. As will be taken up more thoroughly in chapter 6, the consequences of Jewish attempts to assimilate and the difficulty in recognizing Jews by their appearance were focal points of overtly antisemitic policies and representations. Well-known filmic representations of such anxieties include *Jud Süss* and *Der ewige Jude.* Comedies like *Robert und Bertram* also emphasize how Jews disguise their true essence. Beyond the overtly antisemitic films, Third Reich filmmakers returned repeatedly to plots and themes that explored discrepancies between appearance and essence, which, by buttressing overtly antisemitic preoccupations, functioned as inferential antisemitism. Mistaken identity comedies, which exploited the gap between a character's appearance and his or her "true" identity were widespread.[79] Cross-dressing and performance in *Viktor und Viktoria* lead both protagonists to discover their true selves and create happy endings. In *Glückskinder*, doubling and substitution perform similar functions (among others). Other Third Reich comedies, like *Engel*, played with tensions between surface appearance and authenticity in different ways.

In contrast to *Viktor und Victoria* and *Glückskinder*, which advocate for the rehabilitation or replacement of Jewish comic styles, *Engel* does not valorize performance or substitution. Instead, *Engel* treasures truth and authenticity and depicts dishonesty and deception as alien, threatening to the protagonists' essentially respectable natures, and doomed to fail. Here *Engel* resonates inferentially with overt antisemites' scorn for assimilated Jews, whom they construed as impostors. The small-town, bourgeois respectability to which the protagonists cling is coded as German through Rühmann's person, the physiognomy, costuming, and behavior of other actors, the use of regional dialect, and the small-town Mosel location. Within this German framework, *Engel* condemns liars and impostors and cautions both Germans and German film comedy to remain simple, honest, respectable, and true to community ideals and to avoid toying with deception and pretense. Correspondingly, the central problem in *Engel* is the discrepancies between appearance and authenticity and how they play out in a small-town setting, where they threaten to undermine the protagonists' social positions. Inarguably an effective and widespread comic device, in 1936, the gap between reality and ideal as manifest in dramatic irony and comic misunderstandings could also have been construed as an expression of authentic, racially grounded German humor, as defined by Kadner and spread by film critics. Laughter at failed deceptions in *Engel* also serves disciplinary functions, promoting honesty, authenticity, and conformity with the small-town German community.

At heart, *Engel's* protagonists, Christian (Rühmann) and Hedwig (Leni Marenbach) Kempenich, are a mutually devoted and socially proper petit-bourgeois couple, who are embarrassed to risk not being seen as such. Yet a series of mistakes in judgment lead to the appearance of infidelity and theft—a plot that must be untangled, ultimately, by the courts. The Kempenichs' attempts to protect their reputations (being unable to correct either bad choices or misdemeanors that never occurred) create and reveal more and more dishonesty and increasingly imperil their reputations and social positions. For example, Christian convinces Hedwig's music teacher, Enrico Falotti (Harald Paulsen), to provide a false alibi for him, pretending to have spent the night in the hotel room where Christian's name is on the register. Yet, unlike in *Glückskinder*, which is driven by substitutions, in *Engel*, with its attacks on dishonesty and drive toward authenticity, attempts at substitution are doomed to fail. Hedwig, who was in Koblenz innocently with Falotti on that same night—and believes she cannot reveal it—knows that the claim that Falotti signed the register in Christian's name is a lie. While the lie becomes further proof for her of Christian's infidelity and dishonesty, she cannot confront him with it, for her knowledge of Falotti's actual whereabouts would reveal that she too was away on the night in question with a member of the opposite sex and has been lying to cover it up. That honesty would have been the better course of action for both spouses is made evident by the decline of their marriage, reputations, and financial situation (Christian is suspended from his job) as gossip spreads around the town. The characters' ideals regarding respectability and marriage remain intact. Their bad behavior, their appearance of impropriety, and their fixation upon appearances are shown to be wrong. In a humorous way, the film construes lying, deception, substitution, and imposture as both immoral and ineffective. It promotes adherence to one's proper social position and community ideals, norms, and mores. As the narrative and its agenda unfold, the film repudiates performance, as in *Viktor und Viktoria*, and substitution, as in *Glückskinder*, as solid foundations for either identity or comedy.

The threat to social relations posed by dishonesty, a focus on appearances, and the discrepancy between the visible world and internal ideals is compounded by the city's threat to small town values and institutions, a reactionary theme common in Nazi Germany. *Engel*, shot on location in Beilstein, which today has a population of roughly 160, emphasizes the smallness and the Germanness of the Kempenichs' hometown.[80] The town's nickname, "Sleeping Beauty of the Mosel," not only invites tourists to discover this hidden, sleeping princess, but also emphasizes how the town's half-timbered structures and winding cobblestone alleyways look like something out of a Grimms' fairy tale.[81] *Engel*'s footage of Beilstein delivers "idyllic, peaceful images from the provinces" that are "primordially German."[82] Schneider, writing for *Lichtbild-Bühne*, describes *Engel* as "the film of the German small town," with architecture "for falling in love."[83] The exterior shots of the village consist of a few picturesque locations between which characters walk quickly. When Falotti gives in-home singing lessons, the visual editing and sound editing are independent of one another, so that the sound of the singing lessons continues in the background, even when the camera has moved on to another scene. This asynchronous editing suggests that the town is so small that private singing lessons resonate across it. By contrast, establishing shots when Christian travels to Cologne focus first on the size and scale of its gothic cathedral spires and later on the lights, modernity, and activity of its red-light district. While the cathedral reminds viewers of Cologne's uniquely German heritage and location, other scenes look anonymous and cosmopolitan. The hustle and bustle, chaos, and darkness of the street sequences contrast starkly with Beilstein's picturesque tranquility. A series of scenes at the start of the film where townspeople find out about Christian's impending trip to Cologne for a baptism milk humor out of the temptation and scandal of the great city and small townsfolk's fear and desire of them—temptation and scandal proven to be true when Christian, instead of returning home, visits a burlesque, gets drunk in a private room at a restaurant, and takes a hotel room with a strange woman—the series of events that launches his and Hedwig's marital problems.

The outsider too, in the form of singing teacher Enrico Falotti, while amusing, also poses a threat. Falotti, an aspiring ladies' man who otherwise has no social connections in the village, gropes his pupils, claiming to illustrate how good singing comes not from the mouth but from the heart, chest, and belly. Uninvited, he follows Hedwig on her outing on a Mosel cruise, distracts her so that she doesn't get off the ferry on time to return home with the train, and attempts to book the two of them into a single hotel room, which, the hotel porter reports, earned him a hearty slap on the face. Not only is Falotti a lecherous outsider, but also he seems to be a cultural impostor. Despite his Italian name, Falotti lacks the dark hair and caricatured accent more typical of Italian characters in Third Reich comedy. Indeed, in an era where national origin and physiognomy frequently were stereotyped, the actor's lighter hair and complexion, angular features, and northern German accent would likely have struck Third Reich spectators as distinctly *not* Italian, indicating that the singing teacher is a fraud, pretending to be somebody and something he is not. After Enrico and Christian have adopted the familiar form of address, Enrico tells Christian to understand the name "Enrico" as "Heinrich" and to call him Heini. This reversion from an Italian to a German name raises further suspicions of the character's being an impostor. While not unequivocally coded as Jewish, Enrico/Heini's role as an outsider of dubious national origins and fraudulent identity who attempts to seduce local housewives makes him a distinctly unadmirable character, and one whose negative traits resonate with negative traits frequently assigned at the time to Jews. His departure from the town, with an entourage of suitcases indicating extravagance and luxury, is part of the film's happy ending.[84]

Engel's model of German comedy was not only thematically but also stylistically consistent with Nazism. It illustrates a German style, as defined by its contemporaries. Its story, dialogue, and editing follow a leisurely pace. The director prefers slow panning and tracking over quick cuts. When dialogue speeds up, it is not as part of some clever exchange, but rather as a humorous insight into a situation or a character's frame of mind. Devoid of verbal wit, maligned at the time as a Jewish or French trait, *Engel* relies on situation, character, and gesture for laughs. Drunkenness repeatedly is used to comic effect: on Christian's night out in Köln, when he gets so drunk that he seems completely nonplussed to wake up in a hotel room with a strange woman; on Hedwig's lighthearted cruise down the river, where she sings and laughs and toasts her companions; and elsewhere. Third Reich film critics noted the heavy emphasis on drunkenness in this film. For example, Ewald von Demandowsky organized his review for the *Völkischer Beobachter*, the Nazi party's official daily paper, around the role of wine in the film, as a source of amusement, truth, and good spirits.[85] Twenty-first-century critics explain the drunkenness in *Engel* as a form of Third Reich sexual conservatism, as a way of minimizing or excusing the protagonist's sexual transgression, insofar as he was drunk, and therefore not responsible for his actions.[86] An additional stylistic explanation for the emphasis on drunkenness can be found in contemporary conceptions of German film humor. Such scenes are taken by Gerd Eckert of *Deutsche Volkstum* to exemplify the difference between American and German film comedy, for the latter "looks much harder for the comical in things or in human beings themselves, and it is no coincidence, given this approach, that comic drunkenness plays a role in many German films."[87] If comic drunkenness is exemplary of German film comedy and its emphasis on humans and objects, then its frequent use—if not overuse—in *Engel* can be so explained.

A scene that well illustrates favored techniques for German film comedy, as deployed in this film and deemed exemplary by the censors, is when Christian and Hedwig have each, unbeknownst to the other, been asked to appear before the police because they were registered in a hotel room from which the sheets have been stolen. Each is shocked and embarrassed to find the other at the police station. Both repeatedly change their story because they want to look innocent and because they want to hide from the other where they really were on that night and with whom. This scene showcases not only the director's signature visual style, but also the preferred comic strategies of the era: a focus on character and situation—on human and social foibles, a scripting of situational humor rather than individual jokes or gags, and an emphasis on the subtle gestures and physical comportment of the performers rather than their verbal dexterity and wit.

Froelich's distinctive handiwork, the antimodern, anti-Hollywood, contemplative distancing that Carter terms the "völkisch sublime," also shapes *Engel*. Froelich uses his signature style of lighting, camera, and mise-en-scène to frame the Kempenichs' interrogation at the police station (see Figure 4.1). Beams of light from the window hit and call attention to the wall, the framing function of which is accented by bookshelves, the vertical lines made by the books and files, and a conspicuous painted faux chair rail. While the actors' faces are lit adequately, no star is illuminated above others, and the distracting bright patches on the back wall deemphasize the actors. Both the containment and the parallel lines underscore how entrapped the Kempenichs feel by the awkward situation and the embarrassment of a police inquiry. They also, as is typical of the director, frame an aesthetic ensemble. Several main tableaux dominate the scene and the editing: medium shots of the corpulent police detective, centered, imposing, at his desk; two-shots of the Kempenichs across from him; or shots where the three characters form a triangle, their spatial relationship to one another indicating their shifting solidarity or estrangement. The camera placement and editing likewise emphasize aesthetic choices and groupings rather than using point-of-view shots to build identifications. The camera shows the characters in the dominant tableaux usually from behind or next to the character(s) facing them, often in over-the-shoulder shots, sometimes from a closer position as if the camera were on or at the table. Occasional shots from the side of the room establish the location of all the characters, including a clerk at a desk by the window. The detached shots that compose most of this scene are not so far off 1930s conventions so as to alienate viewers, and, by cutting from one side of the table to the other, to some extent mimic conversation. Nevertheless, by using few point-of-view shots, the camera and editing here mostly avoid the multiple identifications of modernist film and shot/reverse-shot suture, as associated with classical Hollywood cinema.[88] Instead, the camera has an expository quality: it strives to center the actors in balanced shots that emphasize their gestures and facial expressions.

Figure 4.1. Balanced, triangular grouping of actors, framed and contextualized by the background and lighting, and shot from a neutral point of view, rather than a character's, characteristic of Froelich's style. Leni Marenbach, Heinz Rühmann, and Will Dohm in *Wenn wir alle Engel wären* (1936). Screenshot.

Froelich's expository style emphasizes other important features of German humor and film comedy as conceived at the time. The humor in this scene stems primarily from character and situation, from human weaknesses and the resulting conflict, rather than from individual jokes or gags. Each Kempenich wants to behave as a proper bourgeois husband or wife. Such self-identifications and ambitions are established in the first half hour of the film and sustained in the dialogue here. Having been called before the police challenges the Kempenichs' prim image. Encountering each other at the police station (after lying to each other about where they were going) and knowing that this first embarrassment, of the police summons, cannot be kept private, begins to flummox each of them. The police hearing increasingly tarnishes the Kempenichs' proper facade and humiliates them, revealing that each has been up to something that their spouse knows nothing about. Both reveal themselves as liars to the audience, which knows the story, and to the police officer, who keeps catching them in their fibs. Because the Kempenichs refuse to tell the truth, they also appear to the detective to be thieves. This scene mocks the Kempenichs' focus on appearances rather than ideals, their fixation on reputation over honesty. It likewise pokes fun at their cover-up attempts, both verbal and physical.

The dialogue in this scene is not particularly clever, avoiding the verbal wit associated with Jewish and French comics. Ineffectual lying and the police detective's sarcastic remark that forgetfulness frequently creates problems for law enforcement are the highlights of comic cleverness in this scene, so far as dialogue is concerned. Instead, the scene emphasizes the performers' gestures and body movements. The Kempenichs' buttoned up appearances and their bodies' betrayal of their tense emotions in this scene make clear their misplaced emphasis on respectability over honesty. Both wear tailored suits and repeatedly attempt to control their faces and bodies, pursing lips and facial features into properly neutral expressions and bringing limbs and gestures in tight, except in moments of embarrassment or mendacity, which thus appear as loss of control. For example, Hedwig's composure begins to crumble when, just as it seems the couple might be able to leave, the detective gets Christian to admit that he was out of town on the night in question. Her face shifts from a mask of polite interest to one of concern, and her left hand starts picking at the fabric of her jacket. Several times when one of the Kempenichs loses control, the camera cuts to a slightly closer framing of the single agitated character. Such shots emphasize loss of composure and physical manifestations of dishonesty and humiliation: for example, Rühmann's exaggeratedly indignant face when Christian's forgetfulness is challenged, or Marenbach's coughing and fumbling in her handbag when Hedwig is asked where she was while her husband was in Cologne. The scene ends with a hackneyed physical gag: Hedwig is so agitated that she has trouble opening the door to leave. This scene generates humor from common human weaknesses and does so using gesture rather than clever banter. Such strategies are consistent with comic strategies preferred by the era's film critics.

The scene at the police station—like the film as a whole—encourages the viewer to laugh at the absurd situation into which the Kempenichs have gotten themselves and how their desires to hide the truth and keep up appearances repeatedly make things worse. Combined with its drive toward honesty and authenticity, and its emphasis on Germanness, this film's gentle-hearted criticism of common weaknesses and social pressures and its mockery of the gap between surfaces und ideals—as it applies to petty social norms—as much as its anti-Hollywood visual and comic style, exemplify racially inflected German humor as conceived in the Third Reich.

German Humor Moving Forward

Although it seems, on a casual, decontextualized viewing, to be a mediocre, apolitical film, *Engel* epitomizes the subtle yet pervasive influence of racial and national thought on Third Reich film comedy. Coded through character, setting, dialogue, themes, and style as "German," the film envisions simplicity, honesty, openness, directness, authenticity, and small-town bourgeois conformity as central to both German identity and German humor. The film also exemplifies inferential antisemitism, insofar as it rejects a suite of characteristics coded as Jewish, including deception, emphasis on appearances, outsider or multiple perspectives, intellectual humor, verbal wit, disruptive comic bits and gags, and Hollywood and Weimar aesthetics. In its coding, stylistic choices, and structuring absences, this film met imperatives to create a nationally and racially distinct cinema at a time when diverse comic styles and preferences for them persisted. Thus, *Engel* was saluted as not only "artistically" but also "politically especially valuable," encouraging viewership and signaling to audiences, critics, and filmmakers how future German comedies should be.

Despite the beacon raised by *Engel*, however, no other comedy in the Third Reich earned the censors' highest rating. Perhaps in the eyes of the censors, no other films ever reached this standard. Perhaps setting stylistic standards dropped in priority as comedies did fall more closely in line with Nazi ideals of German humor. In any case, after the start of the war, comedy's morale-boosting functions became more important than questions of style, although inferentially antisemitic film criticism continued to promote German "humor" with "heart" and reject comedy "from Hollywood ready-to-wear" and "coldly made comedies, that juggled from punchline to punchline, that hunted after each cheap gag."[89] Influences of Weimar and Hollywood cinemas coded as Jewish became subtler as time passed, but never disappeared. At the same time, many of the features of German humor embodied in *Engel* gradually became the norm for film comedies made in Germany, even as their racial underpinnings remained obscure and largely unremarked by postwar scholars. Such inconspicuous and gradual changes in German film humor, which carried on into the postwar period with little notice, constitute a long-lasting, if peculiar, effect of Nazi-era antisemitism.

Notes

1. Hales, Petrescu, and Weinstein, "Introduction," in *Crisis and Continuity*, 7–16.
2. Friedländer, *Nazi Germany and the Jews*, vol. 1, 179.
3. Friedländer, *Nazi Germany and the Jews*, vol. 1, 179.
4. For a chronological account of Third Reich film comedy that describes many films and analyzes overall trends, see Witte, *Lachende Erben*.
5. Kanzog, *"Staatspolitisch besonders wertvoll,"* 141.
6. Kanzog, *"Staatspolitisch besonders wertvoll,"* 14–47.
7. Courtade and Cadars, *Geschichte des Films* 268. Osten, *NS-Filme im Kontext sehen!"* 83–90, 198–99, 236–38, 277. Kanzog,*"Staatspolitisch besonders wertvoll,"* 147–48.
8. Courtade and Cadars, *Geschichte des Films*, 268.
9. Leiser, *"Deutschland, erwache!"* 20–21.
10. Rentschler, *Ministry*, 112.
11. Albrecht, *Nationalsozialistische Filmpolitik*, 551.
12. Rentschler, *Ministry*, 286, 276, 282, 288.
13. While German film critics continuously have received *Glückskinder* as a rare, witty, and (problematically) apolitical German comedy, praise for revivals of *Wenn wir alle Engel wären* continued into the 1950s and then began to taper off in the 1960s. For example, on July 5, 1963, U. S. of the *Telegraph Berlin-Westsektor* wrote that audiences no longer laughed as they did at the film's 1936 premiere, for "wir haben inzwischen wohl alle ein anderes Tempo am Leibe als früher, auch in puncto Humor und statt Slowfox tanzt man Twist" (since then we all have a different bodily tempo than we had before, also relative to humor, and instead of a slow foxtrot we dance the twist). Review files in Potsdam Hochschule für Film und Fernsehen (HFF). Review clippings of *Glückskinder*. HFF Pressematerialien. Binder: Landesbildstelle Berlin Bibliothek. Medienkundliches Presse-Archiv 551. G. Glückse-God. Review clippings of *Wenn wir alle Engel wären*. Binder: Landesbildstelle Berlin Bibliothek. Medienkundliches Presse-Archiv 551. W. Wenn M. - Wer d.
14. Schneider, Review of *Wenn wir alle Engel wären*, 4.
15. "Humor ... ohne Spott;" "gesunde, erquickende Derbheit;" and "Menschen fest verwurzelt ... in dem herrlichen Land von Mosel und Rhein." Fischer, "Wenn wir alle Engel wären," 7.
16. "Schünzel macht fröhlich," 9.
17. "Schünzel macht fröhlich," 9.
18. "'Deutsche' Filme?" 9.
19. Carl Froelich was involved in German film in multiple capacities from 1906 until 1951. Heinrich Spoerl wrote scripts and his published works were used as source material for films from 1933 (*So ein Flegel!* Robert Stemmle) through 1970 (*Die Feuerzangenbowle* [remake], Helmut Käutner). Heinz Rühmann began his screen acting career in 1926 (*Das deutsche*

Mutterherz, Géza von Bolváry) and appeared in his final feature film in 1993 (*In weiter Ferne, so nah!* Wim Wenders).
20. Merzinger, *Nationalsozialistische Satire*, 298.
21. For more on *Die Feuerzangenbowle*, see chapter 7.
22. Hill, "Humour in Nazi Germany," 4.
23. Hill, "Humour in Nazi Germany," 4–10. See also Kruse, "'Man kann ruhig darüber sprechen," 35–44. Also: Merzinger, *Nationalsozialistische Satire*, 319.
24. Merzinger, *Nationalsozialistische Satire*, 302.
25. Hill, "Humour in Nazi Germany," 10.
26. Kruse, "Mann kann rühig darüber sprechen," 37.
27. Schwark, "Angst vor Humor?" 1.
28. Merzinger, *Nationalsozialistische Satire*, 50–56.
29. Merzinger, *Nationalsozialistische Satire*, 191–202.
30. "Zunächst sei festgestellt: Der Witz ist keine jüdische Erfindung, auch kein Instrument des Satans." Spoerl, "Angst," 7.
31. Spoerl, "Angst," 8.
32. Spoerl, "Angst," 7.
33. Spoerl, "Angst," 7.
34. Spoerl, "Angst," 7.
35. Spoerl, "Angst," 8.
36. Schulte-Sasse, *Entertaining the Third Reich*.
37. Merzinger, *Nationalsozialistische Satire*, 314–15, 325, and more broadly at 297–332.
38. Merzinger, *Nationalsozialistische Satire*, 315. Torsten Körner has also discussed how the self-disciplinary conclusion of *Wenn wir alle Engel wären* is consistent with both bourgeois norms and Nazi society. Körner, *Ein guter Freund*, 179.
39. "Deutschland kann lachen," 1. Emphasis in the original.
40. "Und die Männer, die Werke dieser Männer, die uns das befreiende Lachen und Schmunzeln schenken, die gesunden Witz und Humor atmen, *werden öffentlich ausgezeichnet!*" "Deutschland kann lachen," 1. Emphasis in the original.
41. Letter from Heinrich Spoerl to Carl Froelich, 15 Oct. 1936, reprinted in Körner, *Ein guter Freund*, 179.
42. Kanzog, *Staatspolitisch besonders wertvoll*, 33.
43. Carter, *Dietrich's Ghosts*, 110–11.
44. Kanzog, *Staatspolitisch besonders wertvoll*, 20.
45. Kanzog explains how the rating "staatspolitisch besonders wertvoll" reinforced ideological norms (*Staatspolitisch besonders wertvoll*, 27–47). I extend his argument and claim that the rating system and consequent subsidies reinforced artistic norms as well.
46. Carter, *Dietrich's Ghosts*, 112–18.
47. Carter, *Dietrich's Ghosts*, 112–16.
48. Carter, *Dietrich's Ghosts*, 113.
49. Carter, *Dietrich's Ghosts*, 118.
50. Carter, *Dietrich's Ghosts*, 110–20.
51. Gunning, "The Cinema of Attractions," 56–62.
52. See Krutnik, *Hollywood Comedians*, 1–18.
53. Wallach, *Passing Illusions*, 78.
54. Göktürk, "Strangers in Disguise," 109.

55. Göktürk, "Strangers in Disguise," 108.
56. Pearse, "Charlie Chaplin: Jewish or Goyish?"
57. "Streiflichter," *Völkischer Beobachter*, 1. Neumann et al., *Film "Kunst,"* image plate between pp. 16–17, 77. See also Doherty, *Hollywood and Hitler*, 33–34. The *Ewige Jude* exhibit used Charlie Chaplin as an example of a "Jewish" face and gestures. Friedländer, *Nazi Germany and the Jews*, vol. 1, 253.
58. Carter, *Dietrich's Ghosts*, 26–33, passim.
59. See Ascheid, *Hitler's Heroines*. Hake, *Popular Cinema*, 87–106.
60. Carter, *Dietrich's Ghosts*.
61. Rainer Dick, "Flapper, Xanthippen und kleine Männer: Der Wandel im Typenarsenal des komischen Films nach dem Exodus seiner exponiertesten Darsteller," in *Spaß beiseite*, ed. Distelmeyer, 101, 95–102.
62. A few of many examples: Lowry, "Heinz Rühmann," 81–89. Hake, *Popular Cinema*, 87–106. Herrmann, "Humor," 364. Beierle, "Der Weg," 3. On the opening page of their biography, Franz Josef Görtz and Hans Sarkowicz cite many examples from the popular press: Görtz and Sarkowicz, *Heinz Rühmann*, 7.
63. Lowry, "Heinz Rühmann," 81.
64. Hake, *Popular Cinema*, 88.
65. Hake, *Popular Cinema*, 87–106.
66. Lowry and Korte, *Der Filmstar*, 38.
67. Lowry and Korte, *Der Filmstar*, 47. Merzinger, *Nationalsozialistische Satire*, 314–315.
68. Hake, *Popular Cinema*, 90, 102–3, 105; Lowry, "Heinz Rühmann" 81, 85; Lowry and Korte, *Der Filmstar*, 33, 59; Kadner, *Rasse*, 69–95.
69. Hake, *Popular Cinema*, 102. Lowry and Korte make a very similar claim: *Der Filmstar*, 53. Many of the little men, their Weimar predecessors, and Hollywood competitors appear on screen to be physically small. Rühmann was 1.65m tall (5'5"). https://geboren.am/person/heinz-ruehmann, accessed August 10, 2017. Moser was even shorter, at 1.57m (5'2"). http://www.steffi-line.de/archiv_text/nost_film20b40/35_moser.htm, accessed August 10, 2017.
70. Beierle, "Der Weg," 3.
71. Herrmann, "Humor," 363.
72. Herrmann, "Humor," 363–64.
73. Kadner, *Rasse*, 95ff.
74. Brinker, *Heinz Rühmann. Hertha Feiler. Er und Sie* (Berlin: Wilhelm Gründler, [1941]), 13–14, cited in Lowry and Korte, *Der Filmstar*, 54.
75. Citations here from Lowry and Korte, *Der Filmstar*, 58.
76. For more on this critical discussion, see chapter 1.
77. The trope of the threat posed by the urban and the outsider to small-town life continue uncritically in postwar German film and TV, such as in Edgar Reitz's *Heimat* series (Homeland, 1981–84).
78. Kadner, *Rasse*, 14–24.
79. Witte, *Lachende Erben*, 46. Moeller, *Der Filmminister*, 163. Witte, "Die Filmkomödie im Dritten Reich," 352.
80. "Beilstein in vergangener Zeit." "Beilstein."
81. "Beilstein."
82. Körner, *Ein guter Freund*, 180.
83. Schneider, Review of *Wenn wir alle Engel wären*, 4.

84. Courtade and Cadars, *Geschichte des Films*, 268.
85. D[emandowsky], "Ein neuer Froelich-Film."
86. Hake, *Popular Cinema*, 97. Merzinger, *Nationalsozialistische Satire*, 315.
87. Eckert, "Filmkomik," 890.
88. Silverman, *The Subject of Semiotics*, 201–15.
89. "Aus der Hollywooder Konfektion." "Kalt gemachten Lustspielfilmen, die von Pointe zu Pointe jonglierten, die jeden billigen Gag nachjagten." Utermann, "Der deutsche Lustspielfilm im jetzigen Kriege."

5

CAPITALISM, COLONIALISM, AND THE WHITE JEW IN *APRIL! APRIL!* AND *DONOGOO TONKA*

IMAGINING A *VOLKSGEMEINSCHAFT* FREE OF JEWS, ONLY A handful of Third Reich film comedies include Jewish characters—who were not needed to encourage audiences to reject Jewishness. A few Third Reich comedies make obvious antisemitic innuendos, such as Froelich's unsavory depiction of Weimar-era political and financial elite in *Die Umwege des schönen Karl* (The Detours of Handsome Karl, 1937/38). Most antisemitism in Third Reich film comedy, however, is inferential, mobilizing tropes of Jewish difference in ways that seem innocuous when viewed out of context but are troubling when understood within Nazi Germany's inferential networks. By separating the "Jewish" from the "non-Jewish," rejecting the former and embracing the latter, such films augment the Nazis' antisemitic agenda in indirect, subtle ways and support the purging of Jewishness from a non-Jewish *Volksgemeinschaft*.

Through mockery of familiar stock characters, Third Reich comedies took on disciplinary functions, discouraging traits the Nazis deemed Jewish. To show how this works, chapter 5 scrutinizes the stock figure of the greedy capitalist, a figure that Third Reich cinema inherited from Weimar film. As Derek Penslar notes, "Throughout the modern Western world, . . . the Jews' economic influence has been often exaggerated, not only by anti-Semites searching for a culprit for overwhelming social ills, but also by philo-Semites identifying material manifestations of Jewish chosenness."[1] German-speaking Central Europe was no exception, and well before the Nazi Party came into existence, business acumen was already coded both positively and negatively as Jewish. Humorous depictions of capitalist profiteers were common in Weimar and Nazi cinema, and capitalist antagonists and negatively portrayed supporting characters from the 1920s and 1930s frequently have multiple stereotypically Jewish characteristics. Such capitalists, crooks, and speculators, like the unscrupulous Latin American industrialist in Harry Piel's *Die Welt ohne Maske* (The World Without a Mask, 1933/34), who attempts to steal an invention from an eccentric German craftsman/genius, need to be understood in the context of widespread coding of capitalism as Jewish and of pervasive antisemitic anticapitalist discourses. *Nur nicht weich werden, Susanne!, Petterson and Bendel, Robert und Bertram,* and *Leinen aus Irland* mock and attack Jewish capitalists overtly and extensively. Most Third Reich comedies with capitalist antagonists, however, do not identify or attack the Jewishness of such characters explicitly. Even if filmmakers had wanted to, it would not have been necessary. Shady capitalist characters resonated by default with the omnipresent, frequently overlapping antisemitic and anticapitalist discourses of the time. The historical construct of the "white Jew," or the Aryan who has become too Jewish, is a useful analytical tool for understanding Third Reich representations of capitalists, the inferential networks in which 1930s German audiences would have situated them, and the disciplinary functions of their humorous portrayals.

This chapter offers a case study in how stock characters and disciplinary humor can result in inferential antisemitism, explaining how two representative comedies from the 1935–36 film season engage with Jewish difference as they weave together colonial fantasies and critiques of capitalism. The humorous anticapitalism in *April! April!* and *Donogoo Tonka* is typical of comedy made around the time of the Great Depression, not just in Germany, and can be read productively alongside anticapitalist comedies from other countries and periods.[2] What interests me here, however, is the particular significance of these films' engagement with capitalism, colonialism, and Jewish difference in a Third Reich context, and the inferences that these representations and others like them could have licensed for Third Reich audiences.

April and *Donogoo* use humor to criticize greedy capitalists and promote colonialism. Because of their production context, *April* and *Donogoo* needed to reconcile their critiques of capitalism with their colonial fantasies. Capitalism and imperialism are interdependent. Yet in the Third Reich, these already overdetermined concepts collided with antisemitic rhetoric of Jewish global domination. Considering the inferences licensed by the social norms and discursive patterns of Nazi Germany enables a more nuanced reading of *April* and *Donogoo*, illuminating how they caricature the Jewish and promote the non-Jewish, and thereby encourage productive economic activity and imperial expansion free of Jewish influence.

April and *Donogoo* are perfect examples of how culturally embedded and insidious inferential antisemitism is. It is not an intentional strategy of politically committed directors, nor a type of purposefully concealed ideological content, but rather the product of normative patterns and the inferences they license in a specific discursive context. The directors of *April* and *Donogoo* were not Nazis. As discussed in chapter 3, Schünzel, the director of *Donogoo*, was a legal "half-Jew," working under special dispensation, who left Germany in 1937. Detlef Sierck, *April*'s director, was one of many newcomers tapped from the theater to fill the vacuum created when the Nazis expelled Jewish people from the German film industry. After *April*, Sierck became well known for his melodramas starring Zarah Leander. For political reasons and to protect his Jewish wife, actress Hilde Jary, Sierck emigrated to Hollywood in 1937, where he became Douglas Sirk. Since the 1970s and the rise of auteurist film criticism, scholars have lauded the ambiguity and stylistic excess of Sirk's melodramas. Although Sirk's reputation makes *April* more noteworthy from a film-historical perspective than other run-of-the-mill German comedies made in 1935, my analysis resists the temptation to use Sirk's later oeuvre, or his auteurship, as it were, as an analytical lens. *April* was not a project controlled by an established, artistically independent director with a recognizable stylistic signature and social agenda. Sierck's first feature film, *April*, is a typical 1935 comedy by the Ufa studio, the same studio that produced Schünzel's *Donogoo* several months later. Ufa not only emulated Hollywood's studio system, resulting in fairly standardized products, but also operated under significant Propaganda Ministry influence. *April* and *Donogoo*, despite their directors' biographies and skill, share many stylistic features, character types, and narrative tropes with other film comedies of their time—features, types, and tropes that had proven themselves commercially viable as well as acceptable to censors. Whether or not so intended by Schünzel, Sierck, or by any individual director, some of these stock features of Third Reich film comedy functioned within Nazi Germany's discursive networks as inferential antisemitism.

Anticapitalism, Antisemitism, and Non-Jewish Imperialism

April and *Donogoo*'s negative views of capitalism and positive views of colonialism are consistent with the economic climate of the early to mid-1930s. Weimar Germany had struggled economically, burdened in multiple ways by the debt and reparations incurred from World War I, including the catastrophic hyperinflation of 1921–23. In 1929, the Great Depression hit. Between 1928 and 1932, when prices and wages fell to "rock bottom," the Gross National Product dropped from 89.5 billion Reichsmarks to 56.6 billion Reichsmarks, and unemployment rose from 1.4 million to 5.6 million.[3] The economy began to improve in 1933, due to a suite of state interventions begun in the Weimar Republic and continued by the Nazis, similar to strategies pursued in other countries, like Roosevelt's New Deal.[4] The German economy reached full employment in 1936, and 1937–39 saw a "short burst... of high growth."[5] In the early to mid-1930s, however, still grappling with the effects of decades of economic stagnation and crisis, Germans had many reasons to criticize capitalism and distrust capitalists. Germans' personal income, purchasing power, and standard of living were dramatically lower than the Americans' or the British people's and had been since World War I.[6] According to economic historian Adam Tooze, "It cannot be stressed too strongly, that in the early 1930s Germany looked back on almost twenty years in which economic decline and insecurity massively outweighed the experience of prosperity and economic advancement.... In light of this experience, one did not have to be a radical right-wing ideologue or paranoid anti-Semite to doubt the efficacy of the liberal doctrine of progress."[7]

The economic precarity Germans had experienced since World War I led many to be skeptical of capitalism. And in the Weimar and Nazi periods, anticapitalist criticism was inextricable from constructs of Jewish difference. An important strain in Nazi antisemitism blamed the hyperinflation of the early 1920s, the Great Depression, mass unemployment, and other German economic woes on the Jews and those tainted by them—on "the *Volk* comrades alien to their own kind, those acquainted with business, the stock market, and speculation, the nouveaux riches, foreigners in Germany, and their followers."[8] Viewpoints like this one were not exclusive to Nazi antisemites and had been common accusations made against Jews and the "Jewish" behaviors of their alleged collaborators in the Weimar Republic and prior.

Nazi anticapitalism reflected conflicts and tensions in the party around economic policy and other Nazi ideals. The Nazi party (National Socialist German Workers' Party) imagined a *Volksgemeinschaft* that was united by race rather than divided by class. It envisioned prosperity and a standard of living corresponding to the *Volk*'s cultural superiority.[9] Expansionism, antisemitism, and—by the mid-1930s—colonialism figured strongly among the party's social and economic visions. In its early years, the Nazi Party had included strong socialist voices. Party leaders continued to deploy anticapitalist rhetoric long after Ernst Röhm, the loudest advocate for socialism among the Nazi leadership, was executed on July 2, 1934, as part of the Night of the Long Knives. In contrast to persistent anticapitalist utterances, as the economic crisis tapered off, the regime's actions favored private enterprise (when in "Aryan" hands), for example, reprivatizing firms between 1935 and 1937 that had been nationalized in 1931 and 1932.[10] Despite struggles between more traditionally leftist socialists and the economic policies that emerged as dominant in the party, the Nazi party did not abandon anticapitalism, albeit an inconsistent, contradictory, and "essentially irrational and emotional" anticapitalism.[11]

Anticapitalism and socialism, as conceived by the Nazis as supporting members of a racially defined *Volksgemeinschaft*, were predicated on antisemitism. Jews stood in for the evils of capitalism. Joseph Goebbels wrote, "As socialists we are foes of Jews, because in the Hebrew we see the incarnation of capitalism, that is, of the misuse of the people's goods."[12] In this extreme view, Nazism racialized and acted on premises theorized by a diverse array of early twentieth-century economic thinkers, Jewish and non-Jewish, Marxist and non-Marxist, that Jews represented not only a people but also a social class and even an economic system.[13] Images of the Jew as the *Drahtzieher* (wire puller) "transformed class conflict between capital and labor into a national and racial battle between Jews and the German masses."[14] There was substantial redistribution of wealth in the Third Reich, but rather than from the bourgeoisie to workers, as in other versions of state socialism, in Nazi Germany property was transferred from Jews to non-Jews as Jewish businesses were Aryanized and Jewish people were forced to surrender their property, whether they were executed, deported, or able to emigrate. Nazism conflated Jews and capital, proposing that the expropriation and defeat of the former would lead to economic justice. Such conflation of anticapitalism and antisemitism, of the capitalist and the Jew, had been common in Weimar-era journalism and would have been a familiar thought pattern for German film spectators in the 1930s.[15]

Nazi anticapitalism tapped into longstanding antisemitic strains in German anticapitalism more broadly.[16] Nazism shared a symbolic and rhetorical association between capitalist and Jew with Marxism, although it otherwise looked very different.[17] Whereas Marxism espoused internationalism, for example, in the oft-sung "Internationale," Nazism was a profoundly nationalist movement that positioned itself in opposition to both communism and capitalism, each construed as the domain of "international Jewry."[18] Both the theory and practice of Nazi anticapitalism had racial elements. As Brown describes, "Alongside the anticapitalist theory of people such as [Gottfried] Feder [who distinguished between productive and exploitative, or 'Aryan' and 'Jewish,' capital] and [Otto] Strasser [who likewise promoted 'racialized anticapitalism'] was a heartfelt rank-and-file anticapitalism fused in many cases with a thinly veiled class resentment, an emotive soldierly idea of socialism as a community of shared sacrifice, and a vague but powerful myth of the *Volksgemeinschaft*."[19] The German socialism advanced by the Nazis promoted ideals of "German work" dating back to the nineteenth century. German work was productive, in contrast to a perceived Jewish lack of work ethic. Both capitalism and Bolshevism were functions of Jewish parasitism, whereas German socialism was "designed to restore joy in work and to reintegrate the workers into the body of the nation. A class free *Volksgemeinschaft* was to be created, one based on an altruistic work ethic."[20]

As the economy stabilized and Germans had been put back to work through a variety of programs, the Nazis increased their efforts to extract economic resources from racial outsiders. The Aryanization of Jewish property accelerated after the Nuremberg Laws in 1935 and intensified further in 1936, when the new economic Four Year Plan, focused on military mobilization, came into effect.[21] "By late 1937, . . . the enforced Aryanization drive had become the main thrust of the anti-Jewish policies, mainly in order to compel the Jews to emigrate."[22] In this same time period, the colonial issue moved from the back burner, " to ever more definite and menacing demands for colonial restitution, while the whole apparatus of official Nazi propaganda was enlisted to convince the public in Germany and abroad, that in that way alone could Germany's economic difficulties be solved."[23] In 1936, "the colonial problem [stood] in the forefront of public discussions in Germany."[24] Hitler gave major speeches in the Reichstag on March 7, 1936, and at the Nazi Party congress in Nuremberg on September 9, 1936.[25] Extensive arguments were made on both economic grounds and "moral" ones, that Germany wanted not only more territory, resources, and markets, but also "equality of status" with European colonial powers.²⁶ In negotiations with other European nations, Germany increasingly emphasized its demands for the return of its pre–World War I colonial possessions.²⁷

The racialized dichotomy between productive and exploitative capital colored the colonialism debate of the mid-1930s and produced interesting ideological inconsistencies. In the 1920s, Hitler had "dismissed the beginnings of a new colonial agitation [in Germany] as a 'Jewish swindle' aimed at diverting attention from real issues."²⁸ Goebbels railed against Germany having become "an exploitation colony of international Jewry."²⁹ Yet once they came to power, the Nazis wanted more *Lebensraum* (living space) and economic resources for the German *Volk*, and pursued an imperial agenda. To both reclaim former colonies and imagine themselves free of exploitative, "Jewish" practices, the Nazis needed to envision a non-Jewish imperialism. The racialized juxtaposition of productive vs. exploitative capital, as theorized by Feder, played a major role in drawing this distinction. It is also a dominant theme in Third Reich colonial films. For example, *Der Kaiser von Kalifornien* (The Emperor of California, Luis Trenker, 1935/36) contrasts Johann Sutter's will to build a productive agricultural colony with the destructive greed of gold prospectors. *Ohm Krüger* (Uncle Krüger, Hans Steinhoff, 1941) illustrates how British financial interests and materialism led to their domination of the hard-working, agricultural Boers and the conquest of South Africa, an effort spearheaded by Cecil Rhodes (Ferdinand Marian), a white Jew. Both *Der Kaiser von Kalifornien* and *Ohm Krüger* insist that farming is more virtuous than speculation or prospecting for precious metals and that hard-working Germanic people (Swiss and Boer) are the people most worthy of subduing colonial lands and subjects. Wanting to pursue a colonial agenda, promote economic growth, and exclude the "Jewish," as they understood it, the Nazis imagined the possibility of non-Jewish forms of capitalism and colonialism that were productive rather than exploitative. Films that ridiculed greedy capitalists, or white Jews, indirectly supported this fantasy, discouraging "Jewish" economic behaviors.

The White Jew

The concept of white Jews, which dates back to Hartwig Hundt-Radowsky's early-nineteenth-century writings, was an established part of Third Reich vocabulary and thought.³⁰ "'Weisse Juden' in der Wissenschaft" ("White Jews" in Science), by Johannes Stark, 1919 Nobel Laureate in Physics and long-time supporter of Adolf Hitler, exemplifies Nazi writing about white Jews. Stark's article, which was published in 1937 in *Das schwarze Korps*, disparages racial, radically segregationist antisemitism as "primitive" and proposes what the author posits as a more sophisticated model. Stark illustrates how, for some Nazi fanatics, the elimination of so-called "racial Jews" did not constitute the entire Nazi antisemitic project. Instead, some Nazis conceived of antisemitism in broader terms and looked to rid the German people, culture, and economy of perceived Jewish influence. Awareness and elimination of white Jews, Aryans who think and behave as Jews do, were central to such a project. According to Stark: "If we would fight the Jews by the old, not even unmistakable features of hooked noses and frizzy hair, then this fight would be a fight against windmills. The fact, however, that we had to fight Jewish influence on politics and cultural life and that we still have to fight Jewish influence on the German economy already proves that it doesn't have to do with the Jews themselves, but instead with the spirit or specter that they spread, with even that which one calls influence."[31] Stark dismisses equating antisemitism with eliminating Jews as simplistic. His article serves as a reminder that different kinds of antisemitism, antisemitic fantasies, and antisemitic representations existed in the Third Reich and that individuals had different modes of reading and recognizing Jewishness. More precisely, Stark's views exemplify a current in Nazi antisemitism that fixated on covert, widespread Jewish influence, detached from the racialized bodies identified in Nazi Germany as Jews. Films like *April* and *Donogoo* do not provide fodder for the explicitly racial, corporeal antisemitism that Stark dismisses as "primitive" but rather appeal—wittingly or unwittingly—to the antisemitic perspective that Stark characterizes as more sophisticated and enduring: the struggle to recognize and fight diffuse Jewish influence.

Nazi antisemites used the term "white Jew" to condemn specific individuals and rhetorically evoked types who think or behave in ways construed as Jewish. Stark's text clarifies its meaning in the Third Reich context:

> For the *racial Jew* himself was not dangerous for us, but the *spirit* that he spread. And if the carrier of this spirit is not a Jew, but a German, then to us he must be twice as worth fighting as the racial Jew, who can't hide the origin of his spirit.
> *Jews in Mindset*
> The people have coined the term "white Jew" for such bacterial carriers, which is exceedingly fitting, because it broadens the concept of the Jew beyond the racial. One could speak in a like sense also of Jews in spirit, Jews in mindset, or

Jews in character. They have submissively absorbed the Jewish spirit because they lacked their own.³²

According to Stark, due to a lack of personal character, some Germans absorb Jewish ways of thinking, feeling, and behaving and carry these mindsets and behaviors like bacteria. Because such white Jews hide the Jewish origin of their infectious spirit, they are twice as dangerous and a twice as worthy target of the antisemitic struggle. The bacterial metaphors and Stark's venomous tone parallel language about so-called "racial Jews" in unapologetically antisemitic venues like *Der Stürmer* or *Der ewige Jude*.

The term "white Jew" was imprecise; it could refer to a variety of negative stereotypes and behaviors coded as Jewish. Goebbels defined white Jews in 1932 as "swine among us, who, although they are Germans, oppress their own folk- and blood comrades using immoral methods."³³ Goebbels's following words imply that non-Nazis also spoke of "white Jews": "But why do you call them white *Jews*? You, therefore, understand *Jewishness as something inferior and despicable.* Just like we [Nazis] do. Why do you ask us why *we* are *opponents of Jews*, when you, without knowing it, are one yourself?"³⁴ In this passage, Goebbels addresses a "you" skeptical of Nazi antisemitism. The reader he posits, however, despite not self-identifying as an antisemite, used "white Jew" as an epithet. Goebbels's rhetoric suggests that individuals existed in 1932 who didn't think of themselves as antisemites or Nazis but who nevertheless cursed white Jews. In using such rhetoric, Goebbels implies that the concept was current not only among the Nazi faithful.

A decade later, Hippler wrote about white Jews in the film industry as: "pompous eager beavers with much sentimentality, but without heart, much experience without prowess, spinelessness without conformity, defeatism without gravitas, boundless self-conceit without a trace of personal substance."³⁵ Stark defined white Jews as "worshippers of a hairsplitting intellect" who were characterized by an "uncontrollable self-importance" and "propagandistic business operations."³⁶ "White Jew" was shorthand for Germans who lacked strong character and authentic, regime-, *Volk*-, and nation-affirming values (or who were anti-Nazi) and who exhibited inflated self-worth, greedy, business-oriented behavior, intellectualism and cunning, or undeserved influence over others. Antisemites believed that such individuals spread the "Jewish spirit" despite their "Aryan documentation" and needed to be stopped.³⁷

I revisit Third Reich film comedy and its relationship to the era's antisemitism with Stark's claim in mind that "a wide field on which to pursue an active antisemitism still remains, even if there is not a single hooked nose in the whole empire."[38] Outside the cinema, Third Reich audiences were inundated with overtly antisemitic texts and images and encouraged to seek out Jewish traces even in places where not a single "hooked nose" or racially marked Jew was visible. Overtly antisemitic films warned them to stay vigilant. The inferential patterns created by overt antisemitism and everyday insults in Nazi Germany licensed spectators to interpret certain comic types in Third Reich film as white Jews. Even if audience members did not consciously identify white Jews as such, these characters facilitated the mockery and vilification of traits coded as Jewish. White Jews thus had narrative, comedic, and ideological functions with potential to reinforce antisemitic agendas. Without depicting Jewish characters, comedies featuring white Jews both imagined a Jew-free *Volksgemeinschaft* and reinforced "'moral pictures' . . . underlying configurations of moral thought, perception, and feeling"[39] consistent with Nazi antisemitism, encouraging "German" values and belittling values ascribed to Jews, whether or not their makers or viewers were aware of it.

Disciplinary Humor and a Non-Jewish *Volksgemeinschaft*: *April! April!*

Like other Depression-era comedies, *April* continues Weimar-era film conventions and expresses anticapitalist sentiments and fantasies of individual economic gain. In his well-known 1927 essay, "Little Shop Girls Go to the Movies," Siegfried Kracauer argues that film, as a capitalist product, both reflects the daydreams of its audiences and protects the status quo. In doing so, film reflects society not as it appears on the surface, but rather, society's internal mechanisms and the wishes and ideologies that drive it.[40] Kracauer describes fantasies of upward social mobility, nestled in comic escapism, and explains how such fantasies support capitalism.[41] Ulrich von Thüna describes similar escapism and secretaries marrying "the bank director as a modern fairytale prince" in comedies made between 1930 and 1933.[42] *April* ends with the secretary Friedl Bild (Carola Höhn) riding off to Africa with a handsome prince (Albrecht Schönhals), and existing analyses interpret the film in this vein. Witte invokes Kracauer's claim that Rolls Royce owners dream of scullery maids dreaming of rising to their level and frames

April as a capitalist projection of young working women's fantasies.[43] He describes the film as a "daydream of petit-bourgeois class reconciliation," fulfilled through the rational alliance between the scions of noodle and flour manufacturers and the reward of an undemanding secretary with a modern Prince Charming.[44] Trumpener focuses on the representation of servants in *April*. She highlights the contrast between the ineptitude of the Lampes, the owners of a noodle factory, and their staff's competence and how the film reveals both to be motivated by dreams of a prince's impending arrival.[45] As Kracauer asserts in his essay, and as Trumpener interprets *April*, dreams of nobility keep incompetent capitalists in their positions and employees serving them efficiently. Thus, while *April* mocks industrialists' wealth, greed, pomp, and aristocratic pretensions and appears to criticize the social and economic order, its narrative fantasies of upward mobility and the double marriages at the film's conclusion reinforce rational capitalist hegemony and reward humility.

Like many other German film comedies of this period, *April*'s social and economic fantasies are consistent with fascism, as Witte has already shown.[46] Further analysis of this film reveals the relationship between film comedy's support for the fascist economic system, normative gender and sexuality, and Nazi racial ideology. *April* sells hope and dreams of upward mobility through felicitous marriage, rather than criticizing a broken system. Yet, even as *April* propagates fantasies underlying the capitalist status quo, it also adopts an anticapitalist tone, mocking the Lampe family throughout. In addition to criticizing specific capitalists while inspiring fantasies of success within the current economic system, *April*, like Nazism, promotes a postclass *Volksgemeinschaft*. The film concludes with a tableau of renewed, happy society united by affective bonds and appropriate behavior rather than one that is divided by class. This tableau illustrates some of the racial implications of the film's class politics: the secretary and her prince ride off to Africa on a horse-drawn cart full of bags of flour. This shot symbolically unifies German white-collar workers, the nobility, and the agrarian in colonial pursuits. *April*'s economic and social fantasies are interwoven with colonial fantasies. What is less visible in this shot and in prior analyses of this film is that *April*'s anticapitalism connects to strands in Nazi antisemitism.

In the Weimar Republic and the Third Reich, caricatures of *nouveaux-riches* Jews were an antisemitic standard and central to the mythical conflation of capitalist and Jew. Many such caricatures appeared both in the pages of *Der Stürmer* and in more moderate publications.⁴⁷ Some representations of Jewish *nouveaux riches* also perpetuated older stereotypes of parvenu Jews embracing German high culture as a mark of assimilation and purchasing socially advantageous marriages for their daughters.⁴⁸ Lubitsch good-naturedly mocked such notions in *Die Austernprinzessin* (The Oyster Princess, 1919), also a mistaken-identity comedy involving a prince and an industrialist family, in which—unlike in *April*—the industrialist's daughter does win the prince in the end.⁴⁹ In 1939, *Robert und Bertram* ridiculed *nouveaux-riches* Jews' attempts to assimilate and to wed their daughter to a nobleman in a grossly antisemitic way. *April* falls between *Die Austernprinzessin* and *Robert und Bertram* in both production date and tone: the Lampes' efforts to fit in and their daughter's attempts to sing poetry by Goethe, behave like a lady, and marry a prince result in repeated humiliation. In this, *April* resembles nineteenth-century Jew farces, which mocked Jewish parvenus, and on which *Robert und Bertram* was based.⁵⁰

April lampoons the Lampes, wealthy capitalists who live in luxury due to industrial noodle production rather than hard work or noble birth. The first scene establishes that the Lampes occupy an economic station to which they were not born, that they use money to present themselves as upper-class Germans, that they fancy themselves better than others, and that their social connections dislike them for it. In the opening scene, pictured in figure 5.1, the Lampe daughter Mirna (Charlott Daudert), accompanied on the piano by Reinhold Leisegang (Werner Finck), the sensitive flour dealer who wants to marry her, sings loudly before guests in her palatial home.⁵¹ Although the audience applauds, many guests look uncomfortable, as if they were only showing polite interest. Mirna's mother (Lina Carstens) brags about Mirna's expensive voice lessons, cuing eye rolling from her guests. Mirna announces that she will sing a final piece with lyrics by German literary icon Johann Wolfgang von Goethe and accompanying music by Leisegang, at whom she gazes affectionately. This introductory sequence illustrates the Lampes' social ambitions: to purchase the ability to perform German high culture, an audience to witness it, and a husband to accompany the performance. The Jewish characters in *Robert und Bertram* perform a similar scene.

The Lampes' social climbing is shown from the outset as negative. The exaggerated arrogance of Frau Lampe, snide comments by the guests, and gossip about the Lampes' lowly origins (Herr Lampe formerly was a baker and Frau Lampe a cook) encourage viewers to scorn the Lampes' social aspirations. The public's negative view of the Lampes is cemented when, after

Figure 5.1. Reinhold Leisegang (Werner Finck) and Mirna Lampe (Charlott Daudert) at the piano (center). Erhard Siedel as Julius Lampe (bottom left). Lina Carstens as Mathilde Lampe gossiping with her friends (top) and alongside her daughter (bottom right). The Lampes' social pretensions lead to their humiliation. *April! April! Illustrierter Film-Kurier* Nr. 1158. 1935. Author's private collection.

receiving an April Fools' call from a friend named Finke (Paul Westermeier) announcing a visit the next morning by the Prince of Holsten-Böhlau, Frau Lampe abruptly withdraws her hospitality from her guests, insisting they all leave immediately so that she can prepare for his majesty's visit. The film does not rely on audience members' own standards to judge Frau Lampe's sudden ejection of her guests as rude. Guests' physical and verbal reactions show that they judge her poorly as well. Finke regrets his mean-spirited April Fools' joke, but after Frau Lampe's pompous announcement, he proclaims the Lampes can wait for their fictional prince to come "until they turn black," a metaphor for rot that also, in its use of the word "black," conjures racial associations.[52] With their inappropriate behavior, the Lampes have earned the disappointment and humiliation that will follow. Finke's April Fools' prank and its humorous consequences perform didactic functions for both the Lampes and the audience.

Excess and exaggeration in *April* generate humor and cast the Lampes' behavior as inappropriate. The Lampes' palatial home and its rococo decor are out of place in the twentieth century and visually assert a noble heritage that the Lampes lack. By contrast, the elegant economy of the art deco furnishings in the prince's office show that instead of lingering on the past he has kept up with the times. Like her home, Mirna's dress is both over the top and out of style. Instead of accenting her silhouette with the long lean lines of the mid-1930s, this ridiculous white confection overwhelms Mirna in flounces and frills. Her costumes in other scenes are likewise ostentatious and unflattering. Her heavy makeup and her hairstyle, bleached platinum blond and set in curls, appeal to standards of artificial rather than natural beauty. Friedl's girl-next-door look highlights Mirna's artificiality. Mirna's voice is too loud and too shrill. The low camera angle during her vocal performance exaggerates her large, wide-open mouth and intensifies the humorous effect of her failure to present herself as either talented or classy. Mirna's mother brags that she pays thirty marks an hour for singing lessons not for "a little bit of singing," but for "our social standing." While Frau Lampe's appearance is more staid than Mirna's, her dialogue and behavior are more exaggerated. She performs her oversized fantasies of gentility assertively and forces her family members and friends to participate in them, even when she becomes a target of laughter and scorn. The gendering of the Lampe's social climbing is consistent with gendered understandings of Jewishness in the Weimar Republic: Jewish women were seen as both prone to opulent excess and more desirable when assimilating successfully.[53] As a counterpoint to his wife and daughter, Herr Lampe's (Erhard Siedel) behavior emphasizes his ambivalence toward adopting upper-class habits. He sleeps through Mirna's performance and seems generally uninterested in his wife's soiree and demonstrations of social superiority. When dictating a letter, he has no idea how to address a prince. He relies on Friedl to coach him in the proper language and stumbles repeatedly attempting to use it. Although the caricature of the Lampes in *April* recalls representations of *nouveaux-riches* Jewish industrialists, such as those in *Die Austernprinzessin*, it does not explicitly target Jews, as defined racially in the Third Reich. The film gives spectators little reason to assume the Lampes are Jewish, although in Nazi Germany there well could have been spectators who understood them as such. Neither does the dialogue refer to the Lampes as Jews, nor do they exhibit any Jewish religious practices. They do not have stereotypically Jewish names or physiognomies, and they do not speak broken pseudo-Yiddish accented German, as do Jewish characters in *Susanne, Robert und Bertram, Jud Süss*, and other overtly antisemitic Nazi-era films. Nevertheless, the *nouveau-riche* Lampe family embodies numerous characteristics long coded in German-speaking Central Europe as Jewish, notably greed, immodest social-climbing, and extravagant behavior. Viewed in concert with Nazi antisemitic anticapitalism and notions of white Jews, *April* can be seen to supplement the antisemitic project by discouraging behavior and economic practices antisemites construed as Jewish and promoting those the Nazis defined as non-Jewish, by using the Lampes as stand-ins for Jews. In this film, the "non-Jewish" characters are more likable and reap better rewards than the mocked and humiliated characters whose behavior is too culturally and economically "Jewish." Inferentially rather than overtly antisemitic, *April* paints a "moral picture," patterns of thought, emotion, and behavior, conducive to the larger Nazi project. From a Nazi perspective, *April* helps create *Volksgemeinschaft* through ridicule, by teaching Germans to exclude and not to be white Jews.

Reviews of *April* functioned alongside it pedagogically, connecting it to inferentially antisemitic discursive networks. They lingered on the Lampes and their inappropriate social ambitions.[54] In doing so, they reinforced the film's moral picture. Some reviewers praised the actors playing the Lampes and their obnoxious yet laughable social posturing, while others, such as E. K. of the *Deutsche Filmzeitung*, found the representations of the Lampes excessive and overdone.[55] Even reviewers who found the Lampes funny characterized their behavior as distasteful. In addition to using an assortment of negatively connoted words and phrases related to snobbism, pretension, and social climbing, reviewers described Herr Lampe as a "wannabe" (Gernegroß) and called the Lampe women names like "Fräulein Neureich" (Miss Newlyrich) and "Mathilde Nudelreich" (Matilda Noodlerich).[56] These names not only make fun of the characters' *nouveau-riche* status but also invoke stereotypically Jewish names that are compound words connoting wealth (i.e., Goldstein, Silberberg). Moreover, the word "neureich" (newly rich) had specifically antisemitic connotations. Klaus Kreimeier notes, "This term was already used in the nineteenth century first and foremost in connection with prosperous Jewish families, mostly from Galicia, who were assumed to have come into their wealth in a shady way, or at least at the expense of honest Germans."[57]

Several reviewers described the Lampes as "Raffke," or money-grubbers, a word used in Weimar and Nazi Germany to describe World War I profiteers and stock market speculators, categories of individuals frequently targeted by antisemitic screeds.[58] The stereotype of the *nouveau-riche Raffke* had existed since the imperial era and surged in popularity during the hyperinflation of the early 1920s.[59] Some films depicted *Raffke* as *nouveaux-riches* Jews, for example, *Alles für Geld* (Everything for Money, Reinhold Schünzel, 1923) and *Familientag im Hause Prellstein* (Family Day in the Prellstein House, Hans Steinhoff, 1927).[60] The Lampes recall such representations through their absurd social pretensions and their ostentatious wealth—cast as undeserved in that wealth is new to this generation and from an industrial source.

The language of E. K.'s review in *Deutsche Filmzeitung* also activates inferential patterns. The review describes "the clash of two milieus... the upstart milieu...and the pureblooded milieu of old tradition."[61] German film reviewers had used the word "milieu" to describe Lubitsch's early comedies, set in the recognizably Jewish milieu of the Berlin garment district, and the word may have connoted a Jewish milieu for readers of this review as well.[62] Film journalists would also use the word "milieu" to describe wealthy Jewish society in *Robert und Bertram*.[63] E. K.'s deployment of the term "pureblooded" (echtbürtig), used in Nazi Germany to refer to someone's genuinely Germanic origins, also hints at potential racial connotations of the class and milieu conflict in *April*.[64]

The ridicule in *April* disciplines both the Lampes and, by extension, the audience, to avoid pretentious "Jewish" behavior. *April* mocks the "upstart milieu" represented by the Lampes and repeatedly shows the negative consequences of such foolishness and misguided social ambition. The Lampes, unable to distinguish between pomp and nobility, honor tie-salesman Müller (Hubert von Meyerinck), whom they hired to impersonate the prince, because of his dapper appearance and haughty behavior. They insult the real prince, who arrives on foot and therefore must be an impostor. A garment industry employee, a master of deception and disguise, and a profiteer who exploits others' weaknesses and benefits from their humiliation, Müller exhibits several Jewish-coded characteristics. Falling for Müller's disguise and rejecting the true prince, who dresses and behaves more modestly than they expect him to, the Lampes fail to realize that honest, down-to-earth "non-Jewish" behavior, such as the prince's, is superior to extravagant superficial displays of wealth, coded as Jewish. For this they are punished: first wining and dining Müller at great expense, and then owing him a fee for his performance, the Lampes fund their own humiliation. Mirna's attempts to curry favor with the prince, in hopes of a royal marriage, also backfire. Sent to the prince's office to apologize because her family failed to recognize him, Mirna collides with the prince on the stairs. Still failing to recognize him, she rebukes him, "Such shamelessness," presuming her own social superiority to any man she would meet in a stairwell. The prince's ironic response, "I think so too," reinforces all the other negative coding around Mirna and this incident and emphasizes that she and her family are the ones who are shameless. Mirna continues up to the prince's office, puts on airs in front of his secretary, claiming to know the prince personally, only to learn that the man on the stairs was the prince. Ashamed and not wanting to return to her chauffeur right away—and thus reveal that she didn't spend any time with the prince—Mirna hides in the elevator. Her pearl necklace breaks in the hallway. When the prince's secretary leaves the office and trips on Mirna's pearls, she picks them up and keeps them for herself. By the time Mirna comes out of hiding, she has lost her pearls and her chauffeur has left. She goes to a café to drown her sorrows in whipped cream, even as her mother spreads rumors that she is dining with the prince. Mirna's arrogance and disdain for others as well as her family's inappropriate, *nouveaux-riches* actions and assumptions have cost her time, wealth (the lost pearls), and esteem. After many similarly humorous scenes of public and private humiliation, the Lampes learn a lesson and, instead of winning the prince, Mirna marries the foppish, clumsy, and inept Leisegang (=soft step). All the other characters push Leisegang around. He gets drunk on cherry brandy, thinking it is juice, is friends with a dapper necktie salesman, and has a hysterical, squeaky voice when irate.⁶⁵ Leisegang's effeminate and ineffectual coding marks him as comic relief, not as romantic lead. Mirna can only have a happy ending by reducing her social and marital ambitions. The audience learns to deride such ambitions.

By contrast, the pairing of Friedl and the prince represents the unification of social classes around non-Jewish behavior and an imperial mission. Friedl, the Lampes' secretary, attracts the handsome, assertive prince, despite all her efforts to push him away. Although he is noble and rich, the prince's unaffected behavior and attempts to convince Friedl that he is an average, working man prove his willingness and ability to join the *Volksgemeinschaft*. A deserving partner, the prince unites with Friedl and rides off into the sunset on a wagon laden with bags of flour. E. K. found it implausible that on her first date with the incognito prince, Friedl orders modestly, relishes her simple meal, and says she prefers men who save their money.⁶⁶ Yet *April* celebrates such idealized behavior and identity: Friedl's and the prince's unpretentiousness and restraint are rewarded with romance and the promise of an African adventure, affirming "non-Jewish" modesty and parsimony, in contrast to the Lampes' extravagance.

There is a *völkisch* cast to *April's* anticapitalism, to its impulse to merge social classes, and to its colonial aspirations. *April* mocks the Lampes to caricature and criticize greed and ambition, traits that the era's antisemites understood as Jewish, while promoting an imperial economy and a *Volksgemeinschaft* that otherwise unified previously separate social castes. Although the nobility lost their privileges in the Weimar Republic, *April* takes place in a world where a prince commands much wealth, attention, and respect and in which his title still matters. Those around him—and the audience—need to learn, as Mirna admits, accepting Leisegang as a husband, that "a prince is nothing better," though of course he is. The prince, a very positive figure, already knows this. Despite his status, the prince enters the film prepared to join the common folk. He walks among them rather than having a chauffeur drive him to the Lampes' factory. Throughout the film, the prince's attitudes, expectations, and behavior are entirely different from what the Lampes and Müller presume they will be. Neither arrogant nor demanding, but rather modestly dashing, the prince passes as a common salesman and prefers a simple woman to an extravagant one, and a simple meal with her to a banquet. Once Friedl discovers his true identity, the prince must convince her that he is as good as the common salesman he pretended to be. His persistence ultimately leads her to accept him as an ordinary man and a partner.

Friedl's and the prince's union brings together different classes of the non-Jewish to pursue a joint imperial venture. When Friedl embraces the prince on behalf of the *Volksgemeinschaft*, she commits to joining him in Africa, validating colonial fantasies. The prince's occupation as an African explorer points to the brief and bygone days of German empire, where the pride and identity of the nation relied on both royalty and colonies. The African art on his walls evokes the colonial legacy and emphasizes the prince's whiteness, which, along with his modest behavior, predetermines his integration into the *Volksgemeinschaft*. Their decorative fusion with his modern furnishings depicts a new imperial future that integrates modernity, colonialism, and hereditary royalty, if they unite with the common people. The first shot in which we see the prince, reading a paper and smoking a pipe, balancing the symmetry between an art deco lamp and an African statue, envisions such a combination as a harmonious one. (See Figure 5.2.)

The colonial impulse in *April* hearkens back to an earlier era and imagines a modern hybrid of *Volksgemeinschaft* and imperialism. After having convinced Friedl he is as authentic and humble as a salesman, the prince is rewarded with a pragmatic, capable, and attractive companion to journey with him to Africa, a woman who can help him transition from exploration to settler colonialism. This representation suggests the *Volk* will embrace such nobles as are willing to join them and that if they work together they can rekindle Germany's colonial aspirations. This vision is in contrast to the greed, self-absorption, and flamboyance of the seemingly non-Jewish Lampes, who, as white Jews, provide a target for spectators' anticapitalist and antisemitic inclinations. Ridicule of white Jews and reward of their opposites had disciplinary functions whether or not these characters were intended to be or were recognized as such: *April* taught behavior suitable for the Nazi *Volksgemeinschaft* and promoted industrious colonial conquest over *Raffke*-style capitalism. Having maligned and disciplined domestic, industrial food producers, *April* ultimately unites a healthy young German couple from formerly disparate classes and sends them off to Africa for new discoveries and conquests. After correcting greedy, social-climbing "Jewish" behavior and its influences on the domestic, industrial economy, the ending of this film romanticizes *Volksgemeinschaft* and imperialism.

Figure 5.2. Our first view of the prince (Albrecht Schönhals). *April! April!* (1935). Screenshot.

The Use Value of the White Jew: *Donogoo Tonka*

Like *April*, *Donogoo* romanticizes imperialism and caricatures capitalists negatively in ways that resonate with Nazi-era antisemitic codings of Jewishness and Jewish behavior. Unlike *April*, however, *Donogoo* construes the behavior of white Jews as a necessary evil and foundation for imperial success. The film uses the concept of a strong work ethic to rehabilitate capitalism and colonialism, a rehabilitation consistent with Nazi ideals of a non-Jewish or Aryan capitalism. Using characters that are white Jews, rather than "black" or "racial Jews," whose racial makeup cannot be altered, enables such rehabilitation and redemption. Honest labor and the application of true German values can overcome the Jewishness of white Jews, capitalism, and imperialism.

Nazi-era critics understood *Donogoo* as a film exposing capitalism's dark underbelly. F. R., who reviewed *Donogoo* for *Der Film*, described it as "a caricature of the banking world that works with shady means with a sturdy comedy format."[67] In Nazi Germany, it was widely reported that the "the banking world that works with shady means" was contaminated by international Jewry. Thus, Nazi-era films usually portray bankers and capitalists negatively and exclude them from the community, as in *Die Welt ohne Maske*, *April*, and *Die Umwege des schönen Karl*. *Donogoo* treats its white Jews differently. Even as *Donogoo* mocks and criticizes its white Jews, it also casts them in roles essential to the development of a lucrative, organized, and modern settler colony in South America.

While no one in *Donogoo* is labeled a Jew, several supporting characters have multiple features coded as Jewish. Miguel Rufisque (Paul Bildt) is a quack scientist named for a Senegalese port town, which connotes foreignness, blackness, and Islam. The Nazis believed North Africans, Arabs, and other non-Aryan Muslims were racially inferior, although they admired Islam's history of conquest. Nazi leaders also understood collaboration with some Muslim peoples to be strategically advantageous, particularly in the war against the British Empire.[68] Islam—an Abrahamic religion originating among what racial scientists then considered the Semitic peoples of the Middle East—is a surrogate for Jewishness in *Donogoo*, and the two characters linked to Islam are marked by a number of Jewish traits. Rufisque practices psychotherapy, a profession that was roundly condemned by antisemites as Jewish, because of the founding role of Sigmund Freud and the prominence of Jewish people among early psychoanalysts. Rufisque presents himself as an experimental scientist, complete with humorous, innovative technologies. Yet his technology and understanding of human beings are both sorely lacking, coding him as a Jewish pseudoscientist, obsessed with theory rather than pragmatic observation. Dramatic irony reveals Rufisque's complete misreading of the protagonists' psyches. Rufisque misinterprets Pierre's (Viktor Staal) pretending to jump into the Seine as a suicide attempt, which leads to his psychotherapeutic treatment of Pierre and his girlfriend Josette (Anny Ondra). Rufisque is overconfident, incompetent, and coded as Jewish. His diagnosis and prescription keep the plot in motion, leading Pierre and Josette to Professor Trouhadec (Heinz Salfner), whose problems inspire their colonial venture.

Like Rufisque, Trouhadec has a number of Jewish-coded features. Trouhadec is a fussy academic, whom Pierre and Josette meet in front of a mosque. This direct reference to Islam is an indirect reference to Jewishness, operating at the level of interdiction. In Third Reich film comedy, the Jewish could not be spoken or represented openly in anything other than an overtly antisemitic way, particularly not by Schünzel, a "half Jew" whose career depended on Goebbels's whims. Trouhadec's proximity to the mosque links him associatively with the Semitic. His main character traits are those antisemites understood as Jewish, among them vanity, intellectualism, neurosis, and dishonesty. Trouhadec is being blackmailed by a con man, Broudier (Oskar Sima), because he has built his scholarly career writing about Donogoo Tonka, a nonextant colony in South America. Broudier, a clever, petty crook with a dark and greasy appearance—a stock character in Austrian actor Sima's repertory—also plays to antisemitic stereotypes.

The most powerful and dishonest character in *Donogoo*, the key to the film's ability to maneuver between Jewish capital and non-Jewish imperialism, is bank director Margajat (Aribert Wäscher). The character's name, Margajat, is the name of a Brazilian tribe, which has been used in French since the nineteenth century to signify both language that makes no sense (as in, "it's Greek to me") and, when applied to a person, a scoundrel. Thus a Margajat is both foreign and dishonest. Like Sima, the dark, corpulent Wäscher specialized in shady characters. In addition to Wäscher's typecasting and the character's descriptive name, his profession as a rich banker occupied a prominent position in the antisemitic imaginary. Film critics emphasized the inferential linkages here. The reviewer for the *Deutsche Filmzeitung* called Margajat "a larger than life shyster" (Schieber), using a word common during the hyperinflation of the Weimar Republic and in Third Reich antisemitic/anticapitalist rhetoric.[69] Günther Schwark, of the *Film Kurier*, made a more pointed reference to both hyperinflation and to antisemitic stereotypes when he wrote "involuntarily one is reminded of the inflation era, when operators had similar *chutzpah*."[70] Schwark's use of the Yiddish word "chutzpah" (nerve) refers to the stereotypical Jewishness of Margajat's behavior, and is a barely concealed antisemitic innuendo. Goebbels, for example, understood the word "*Chutzpah* [as] a typically Jewish expression that really cannot be translated into any other language, since *chutzpah* is a concept found only among the Jews. Other languages have not needed to invent such a word, since they do not know the phenomenon. Basically, it means unlimited, impertinent, and unbelievable impudence and shamelessness."[71]

The Jewish-coded speculator Margajat has power, money, and financial acumen, but no scruples. He controls the fate of others without caring what happens to them. In this, he is a humorous analogue to Fritz Lang's Dr. Mabuse, whom the right-wing press understood as Jewish.[72] Looking forward, Margajat also has features in common with Max Bialystock (Zero Mostel) in Mel Brooks's *The Producers* (1967), a post-Holocaust Hollywood comedy that garners sympathy for Jewish crooks. Margajat appoints Pierre president of the Donogoo Tonka swindle, not because he intends to let him found a real colony, but so that he will be the one held accountable if the fraud is revealed. Margajat also has lecherous tendencies that could have been understood as Jewish. He showers Josette with expensive presents, exploiting her naiveté, and seemingly angling for sexual favors, even though his secretary is already his mistress. Margajat's cunning and lack of compassion not only threaten those closest to him—the naive couple that came to him for help, his employees, his wealthy investors—but also have negative consequences for common people he has never met. The publicity Margajat launches for the fictional Donogoo Tonka and its gold mines convinces not only wealthy investors to give him money but also masses of unemployed men to sail across the Atlantic and search the South American wilderness for the elusive colony.

Surprisingly, however, given their Jewish coding and therefore potentially antisemitic resonances in a Third Reich context, Margajat's shady deeds, and those of the other white Jews in *Donogoo*, do not lead to disaster, humiliation, or punishment but rather to successful colonization and wealth. This is because of the handsome, blond, upstanding, and hardworking protagonist, Pierre, whose response to fraud is to turn it into a legitimate enterprise. Pierre's efforts convert Jewish speculation into non-Jewish productivity. Feder wrote that "the Jews are almost completely alienated from the soil, but even the products of the soil and human industriousness are more foreign to them than pure money."[73] Pierre introduces the non-Jewish elements of work and soil into the colonial project and in doing so reverses both Trouhadec's academic dishonesty and Margajat's Ponzi scheme. Pierre founds a real colony named Donogoo Tonka where the fabricated one should have been and leads the hopeful gold prospectors in the difficult project of building a productive and prosperous colony. The various falsehoods and frauds made for personal gain become *ex post facto* legitimate. Soil-based productivity grounds a colonial economy instigated by speculation. Within the ideological and rhetorical framework of Nazi anticapitalism and German socialism, Pierre's founding of a genuine colony converts the economic system in the film from an exploitative, Jewish one to a productive Aryan one. (See Figure 5.3.)

Donogoo is problematic for many reasons, including its support for colonialism and its fantasy of South America as a virgin landscape awaiting better colonizers—fantasies that echo the nineteenth-century discourses

Figure 5.3. Lobby card advertising *Donogoo Tonka* (1936). The "white Jews" in the background enable the blond, young couple to raise a model colony. Stiftung Deutsche Kinemathek.

analyzed by Suzanne Zantop, which helped justify German colonial ambitions.[74] Schünzel's colonial fantasies not only promote colonialism but also highlight the contradictions in the Nazi antisemitic critique of capitalism, which existed alongside significant colonial ambitions. Finance capital and investment are necessary for the colonial enterprise, which, if it succeeds, ultimately converts speculative or "Jewish" capital into productive or "Aryan" capital and blurs the distinction between the two. *Donogoo* uses character, narrative, and humor to highlight this process, showing that colonial fantasies depend, indirectly, on "Jewish" investment. The realization of such fantasies requires hard work.

Film comedy's ambivalent structure of transgression and resolution and its humorous mode allowed for modest deviations from Nazi racial orthodoxy when it came to colonial representations. For example, *Quax in Afrika* (Quax in Africa, Helmut Weiss), filmed in 1943, depicts Africans in a racist, "primitive" way, yet Quax (Heinz Rühmann) marries a black African woman—only to leave her soon thereafter.[75] *Die Blume von Hawaii* destabilizes Nazi racial categories, replacing the fixed and putatively biological binary of Aryan/not-Aryan with a semipermeable binary of white/not-white, with whiteness open to individuals who look and act European. *April* excluded Jewishness, as expressed in the social and economic behavior of white Jews, from the *Volksgemeinschaft* and its colonial expeditions. By contrast, in *Donogoo,* white Jews contribute to the growth of a working colony. The protagonist forces exploitative, greedy capitalists to make their speculative investment productive, and thus mobilizes an economic position coded as Jewish as a first step on the way to Aryan imperialism. The film implies that a successful colonial enterprise needs "Jewish" financiers as well as non-Jewish labor. As did *Blume*, *Donogoo* incorporates Jewishness into the community of colonizers. By extension, it suggests a potential reading in which Germans need Jews to help fulfill their expansionist dreams and Nazism needs the Jewish to work.

Non-Jewish leadership and labor, *Donogoo* implies, can convert white Jews and turn their crimes to the community's advantage. This was the takeaway message highlighted by the press. According to Albert Schneider of *Lichtbild-Bühne*, Schünzel's comedy illustrated "that any business offense can lead to something good."[76] If young men work honestly and hard, *Donogoo* suggests, "Jewishness," in the form of dishonest, speculative capitalism, can be turned to serve the *Volksgemeinschaft* and the individuals infected by it can be rehabilitated. Thus F. R. describes Margajat in his review as a "cheating banker, who subsequently finds the right path again."[77] While *Donogoo's* explicit cooptation of business practices decried by the Nazis as Jewish and its rehabilitation of characters marked as such are both unusual and provocative, they are also consistent with shifts in Nazi policy in respect to the former German colonies. Although Hitler had once called colonial fantasies a "Jewish swindle," by 1936, when *Donogoo* was released, he wanted Germany's former colonies back and was ratcheting up the campaign to reacquire them. The "Jewish swindle" of German imperialism needed to become Aryan.

Aryanizing Capitalism and Colonialism without Jews

Caricatures of wealthy entrepreneurs and bankers, such as those in *April* and *Donogoo*, were fairly typical of German film comedy in the 1930s. Widespread antisemitic and anticapitalist discourses and Nazi condemnation of white Jews contributed to preexisting inferential networks that would have licensed audiences to interpret these characters and/or their behaviors as Jewish. Understanding the Jewish coding of such characters elucidates their function in relation to Nazi visions of the *Volk*. White Jews stood in for the Jews absent from Third Reich film comedy and satirizing them was a form of inferential antisemitism. Mocking white Jews served disciplinary functions and taught spectators to police and regulate their own behaviors, reinforcing distinctions between insiders and outsiders consistent with Nazi ideology. *April* mocks and punishes the Lampes, teaching viewers not to behave that way. By witnessing the Lampes' ridicule and laughing at them together, audience members learn as a community to reject Jewish behaviors (in antisemitic terms), even as other, positively depicted, characters model values and behaviors more consistent with the Nazis' imagined *Volksgemeinschaft*. Thus *April* illustrates how the standard character tropes and narrative patterns of German film comedy in the early to mid-1930s were consistent with the Nazis' moral pictures and conducive to the building of a Nazi *Volksgemeinschaft*, whether or not filmmakers intended them to be so.

Donogoo too positions white Jews vis-à-vis the *Volksgemeinschaft* and its goals and juxtaposes their behaviors with more desirable models of non-Jewish industriousness. As in *April,* these representations and juxtapositions have disciplinary and community-building functions. Yet, while ridiculing quack scientists, neurotic intellectuals, crooks, and shysters, *Donogoo* nevertheless construes such characters as necessary, if distasteful, facilitators of colonialism. The blond, hard-working protagonists need them in order to secure themselves a stable future. Given that *Donogoo*'s protagonists start out broke, in contrast to *April*'s prince, who can fund his own African expedition, *Donogoo*'s integration of and reliance on white Jews appears pragmatic. Yet it also envisions a more inclusive colonial community. Instead of humiliating and discarding its white Jews, *Donogoo*, like *Die Blume von Hawaii*, imagines a community of white colonizers with room for the Jewish, even though Jews never enter the narrative. In fact, *Donogoo* posits that "Jewish" capitalists are necessary for the Reich to realize its imperial ambitions. The ambivalence of this paradox is symptomatic of the vexed positions of Jews and antisemitism in Third Reich film comedy—on the one hand, both were seemingly absent, and, on the other, contextualized decoding reveals them to have been significant underlying factors, factors that may well have been needed in order to make Third Reich film comedy work.

Notes

1. Derek Penslar, foreword to *The Economy in Jewish History*, ed. Reuveni and Wobick-Segev, vii.
2. On the relationships between *April*, Weimar, and French cinema, see Trumpener, "The René Clair Moment," 33–45.
An earlier version of my analysis of *April!* was published as: Weinstein, "'White Jews' and Dark Continents," 132–48.
3. Overy, *Nazi Economic Recovery*, 14.
4. Overy, *Nazi Economic Recovery*, 3, passim.
5. Tooze, *Wages of Destruction*, 141. Overy, *Nazi Economic Recovery*, 1.
6. Tooze, *Wages of Destruction*, 135–43.
7. Tooze, *Wages of Destruction*, 144–45.
8. "Die artfremden Volksgenossen, die mit Handel und Börse und Spekulation Vertrauten, die Neureichen, das Ausländertum in Deutschland und ihre Gefolgschaft." H. Sp., "Der neue Geschmack," 1.
9. Tooze, *Wages of Destruction*, 135.
10. Bel, "Against the Mainstream," 34–55.
11. Brown, *Weimar Radicals*, 53.
12. Goebbels, *Die verfluchten Hakenkreuzler*, 18.
13. Reuveni, "Prolegomena to an 'Economic Turn' in Jewish History," in *The Economy in Jewish History*, ed. Reuveni and Wobick-Segev, 3–11.
14. Herf, *Jewish Enemy*, 33.
15. Schäfer, *Vermessen, gezeichnet, verlacht*, 43–44, 53, 271–360.
16. Lange, *Antisemitic Elements*.
17. Benz, *Bilder vom Juden*, 24–25.
18. Goebbels, *Die verfluchten Hakenkreuzler*, 6.

19. Brown, *Weimar Radicals*, 52–53.
20. Campbell, *Joy in Work*, 312–336.
21. Baranowski, *Nazi Empire*, 222.
22. Friedländer, *Nazi Germany and the Jews*, vol. 1, 247.
23. Amery, *German Colonial Claim*, 15–16.
24. Johannsen and Kraft, *Germany's Colonial Problem*, 9.
25. Johannsen and Kraft, *German Colonial Claim*, 6, 34–35.
26. Johannsen and Kraft, *German Colonial Claim*, 34.
27. Amery, *German Colonial Claim*, 123–25.
28. Amery, *German Colonial Claim*, 14.
29. Herf, *Jewish Enemy*, 37.
30. Hundt-Radowsky, *Die Judenschule*. Koonz, *The Nazi Conscience*, 207–12.
31. "Würden wir die Juden nach den alten, nicht einmal unverkennbaren Merkmalen der krummen Nasen und krausen Haare bekämpfen, so wäre dieser Kampf ein Kampf gegen Windmühlen. Die Tatsache aber, daß wir den jüdischen Einfluß auf die Politik und das kulturelle Leben bekämpfen mußten und den jüdischen Einfluß auf die deutsche Wirtschaft weiterhin bekämpfen müsssen, beweist bereits, daß es nicht um die Juden 'an sich' geht, sondern um den Geist oder Ungeist, den sie verbreiten, eben um das, was man Einfluß nennt." Stark, "'Weisse Juden,'" 8.
32. "Denn nicht der *Rassejude* an sich ist uns gefährlich gewesen, sondern der *Geist*, den er verbreitete. Und ist der Träger dieses Geistes nicht Jude, sondern Deutscher, so muß er uns doppelt so bekämpfenswert sein als der Rassejude, der den Ursprung seines Geistes nicht verbergen kann. *Gesinnungsjuden*. Der Volksmund hat für solche Bazillenträger die Bezeichnung 'Weißer Jude' geprägt, die überaus treffend ist, weil sie den Begriff des Juden über das Rassische hinaus erweitert. Man könnte im gleichen Sinne auch von Geistesjuden, Gesinnungsjuden oder Charakterjuden sprechen. Sie haben den jüdischen Geist willfährig aufgenommen, weil es ihnen an eigenem mangelt." Stark, "'Weisse Juden,'" 8.
33. "Schweinehunde unter uns, die, obwohl sie Deutsche sind, nach unsittlichen Methoden ihre eigenen Volks- und Blutsgenossen unterdrücken." Goebbels, *Die verfluchten Hakenkreuzler*, 18.
34. "Aber warum nennst Du sie weiße *Juden*? Du verstehst also unter *Judensein* etwas *Minderwertiges und Verachtenswertes*. Genauso wie wir [Nationalsozialisten]. Warum fragst Du uns, wieso *wir Judengegner* sind, der Du, ohne es zu wissen, selbst einer bist?" Goebbels, *Die verfluchten Hakenkreuzler*, 18–19. Emphasis in the original.
35. "Gschaftlhuber mit viel Rührseligkeit, aber ohne Herz, viel Routine ohne Können, Rückgratlosigkeit ohne Anpassung, Miesmacherei ohne Ernsthaftigkeit, maßlose Selbstüberhebung ohne eine Spur persönlicher Substanz." Fritz Hippler, "Ein Hauptproblem: Der Filmstoff," in *Wunderwelt Film: Künstler und Werkleute einer Weltmacht*, ed. Siska, 55.
36. "Anbeter eines spitzfindigen Intellekts." "Unkontrollierbare Selbstherrlichkeit." "Propagandistischen Geschäftsbetrieb." Stark, "'Weisse Juden,'" 8.
37. Stark, "'Weisse Juden,'" 8.
38. "Daß es für aktiven Antisemitismus immer noch ein breites Betätigungsfeld verbleibt, selbst wenn es im ganzen deutschen Reich keine einzige Krummnase gibt." Stark, "'Weisse Juden,'" 8.
39. Rodriguez, "Ideology and Film Culture," 268.
40. Kracauer, "Little Shop Girls," 291–304.
41. Kracauer, "Little Shop Girls," 291–304.

42. Thüna, "Die deutsche Filmkomödie," 317.
43. Witte, *Lachende Erben*, 97.
44. Witte, *Lachende Erben*, 96.
45. Trumpener, "René Clair Moment," 38–41.
46. Witte, *Lachende Erben*, 95–98.
47. Schäfer, *Vermessen, gezeichnet, verlacht*, 43–44, 53, 271–360.
48. Kaplan, *The Making of the Jewish Middle Class*, 99–104.
49. Weinstein, "(Un)Fashioning Identities," 130.
50. See Sieg, *Ethnic Drag*, 38–47.
51. The actor playing Leisegang, Werner Finck, was a cabarettist whose cabaret was closed in May 1935 and who spent a brief time in a concentration camp.
52. The use of "schwarz" (black) to refer to people of African descent was established well before 1935, as in "die schwarze Schmach" (the black disgrace), a Weimar term referring to the occupation of the Rheinland by French colonial troops. Sander Gilman argues that stereotypes of "blackness" and "Jewishness" overlapped significantly in the nineteenth and early twentieth centuries. Gilman, *Difference and Pathology*, 35, passim. Birgit Haehnel investigates such overlaps in the visual culture of the Third Reich: Haehnel, "'The Black Jew,'" 238–59. See also Heinig, *The "Black Jew,"* 43–46. Wallach, *Passing Illusions*, 31–32.
53. Wallach, *Passing Illusions*, 7, 45, 88–95, 97, 102–10.
54. For example, S[chwar]k, Review of *April! April!*, 2.
55. E.K., Review of *April! April!*, 5.
56. S[chwar]k, Review of *April! April!*, 2. L., Review of *April! April!*, 6.
57. Kreimeier, "Antisemitismus im nationalsozialistischen Film," 148.
58. L., Review of *April! April!*, 6. E. K., Review of *April! April!*, 5. S[chneider], Review of *April! April!*, 3. For more on *Raffke*, see Owen Lyons, "'Denn Gold ist Glück und Fluch dieser Welt': Examining the Trope of 'Gold' in *Gold* (1934) and *Der Kaiser von Kalifornien* (1936)," in *Crisis and Continuity*, ed. Hales, Petrescu, and Weinstein, 94–96.
59. *Fräulein Raffke*, directed by Richard Eichberg, 1923. Carl Sieber, *Raffkes: Schwank in 3 Akten* (Stuttgart: O. Wizemann, 1923). Arno Krugel, *Raffkes Werdegang* (Berlin: Hansa-Verl. f. Literatur u. Kunst Leo Kajet, 1923). Artur Landsberger, *Raffke und Cie, die neue Gesellschaft: Roman* (Hannover: Steegeman, 1924). Hermann Meister, *Also sprach Raffke: Die 222 besten Raffkewitze* (Heidelberg: H. Meister, 1924). Friede Bierkner, *Raffkes neuer Chauffeur: humoristischer Roman* (Leipzig: F. Rothbarth, 1924).
60. Frank Stern, "Kluger Kommis oder naiver Michel: Die Varianten von *Robert und Bertram* (1915, 1928, 1939)," in *Spaß beiseite*, ed. Distelmeyer, 51–52.
61. "De[n] Zusammenstoß zweier Millieus, . . . das . . . Emporkömmlingsmilieu und . . . das echtbürtige Milieu alter Tradition." E. K., Review of *April! April!*, 5.
62. Weinstein, "Anti-Semitism or Jewish 'Camp'?" 101–2.
63. Schneider, "Robert und Bertram," 3.
64. Euphemismen.de.
65. Sabine Hake argues that Viktor Hempel's voice in *Viktor und Viktoria* (1933), which, like Leisegang's, is at times high-pitched and hysterical, can be read as "Jewish" or "homosexual." Hake, *Popular Cinema*, 43. Gilman has located multiple intersections between stereotypes of homosexuality, Jewishness, and hysteria in sexology, psychoanalysis, and literature in many places in his work. For example: Gilman, *Difference and Pathology*, 214. Gilman, *Jew's Body*, 125, 133, 196. See also Wallach, *Passing Illusions*, 36–37.

66. E. K., Review of *April! April!*, 5.

67. "Eine Karikatur der mit dunklen Mitteln arbeitenden Bankierwelt mit handfestem Lustspielformat." F. R[öhl], Review of *Donogoo Tonka*, 9–10.

68. See Nicosia, *Nazi Germany and the Arab*; Motadel, *Islam and Nazi Germany's War*.

69. Review of *Donogoo Tonka*, 3–4. Lyons, "'Denn Gold ist Glück und Fluch dieser Welt,'" in *Crisis and Continuity*, ed. Hales, Petrescu, and Weinstein, 94–96.

70. "Unwillkürlich wird man an die Inflationszeit erinnert, wo mit ähnlicher Chuzbe operiert wurde." S[chwar]k, Review of *Donogoo Tonka*, 2.

71. Goebbels, "Mimicry."

72. *Dr. Mabuse, der Spieler* appeared in two full-length parts, *The Great Gambler: an Image of our Time* (*Der große Spieler: Ein Bild unserer Zeit*) and *Inferno: a Game of People of our Time* (*Das Inferno: ein Spiel von Menschen unserer Zeit*). These films were followed by *The Testament of Dr. Mabuse* (*Das Testament des Dr Mabuse*, 1932/33) and *The 1000 Eyes of Dr. Mabuse* (*Die tausend Augen des Dr. Mabuse*, Ger./Fr./It., 1960), as well as a number of postwar Mabuse films by other directors. On the press reading Mabuse as Jewish, see Rentschler, *Ministry*, 156, 359, n. 38.

73. Feder, *Die Juden*, 37.

74. Zantop, *Colonial Fantasies*.

75. *Quax in Afrika* was approved for all ages (Jugendfrei) in February 1945, but did not premiere in the Third Reich due to war conditions.

76. Schneider, Review of *Donogoo Tonka*, 3.

77. F. R[öhl], Review of *Donogoo Tonka*, 9–10.

6

MISTAKEN IDENTITY AND THE MASKED JEW IN *ROBERT UND BERTRAM*

Hitler's oft-cited Reichstag speech on January 30, 1939, in which he "made his first unequivocal public threat to exterminate (that is, murder)—not merely to remove, deport, or defeat—'the Jewish race in Europe' in the event that 'international finance Jewry inside and outside Europe' brought about a new world war," began a new intensified phase of radical antisemitism in German propaganda.[1] In this speech, Hitler announced that Germany would produce antisemitic films to counter Hollywood anti-Nazi productions.[2] Most of Nazi Germany's overtly antisemitic films were released in the next twenty-two months, including *Robert und Bertram, Leinen aus Irland, Jud Süss, Der ewige Jude,* and *Die Rothschilds: Aktien auf Waterloo* (The Rothschilds: Shares in Waterloo, Erich Waschneck, 1940). *Robert und Bertram* premiered on July 7, 1939. The other films were released after Germany invaded Poland on September 1, 1939. As illustrated by the French poster advertising *Leinen aus Irland* (*Les Rapaces*) pictured in figure 6.1, the overtly antisemitic films made in Nazi Germany were shown not only in the Reich proper but also in occupied Europe, presumably to stoke antisemitic sentiments.

The wave of overtly antisemitic films produced in 1939 and 1940 accompanied Germany's increasing control over vulnerable Jewish populations as a result of its military conquests. In 1939 and 1940, German authorities relocated Jewish people and concentrated them into designated areas such as "Jew houses," camps, and ghettos. They began the first deportations of German and Austrian Jews to Eastern Europe. The Germans forced Jewish people they deemed fit into labor and restricted their access to food and other resources. Jewish people under Nazi rule were subject to tyranny, violence, sickness, and starvation.

Figure 6.1. French poster advertising *Leinen aus Irland* (1939; in French, "Birds of Prey"). The Gillespie collection, Sydney, Australia.

Anti-Jewish violence escalated in 1941, after the invasion of the Soviet Union. Hundreds of thousands of Jewish civilians were murdered. German soldiers shot them *en masse*; non-Jewish local populations killed them in pogroms; and, by the end of the year, Germans were gassing Jews and Roma to death in vans at Chełmno. In other words, the emphasis shifted in 1941 from relocation and exploitation to mass murder. According to Shelley Baranowski, "the wholesale slaughter of Jews that unfolded in the Soviet Union, Eastern Galicia, and Romania represented a turning point for Germany and its allies."[3] Nazi Germany's most overtly antisemitic films were released well before this turning point.

Between 1939 and 1945, Nazi propaganda characterized antisemitism, World War II, and the extermination of the Jewish people in Europe as responses to a global Jewish conspiracy.[4] Notions of Jews as chameleons who could disguise signs of their Jewishness had been part of Weimar discourses of Jewish difference, not limited to antisemites.[5] The idea that Jewish "chameleons" were difficult to recognize became a central tenet of the Nazis' genocidal antisemitism (hence the mandate that Jews wear the yellow star).[6] A distinct feature of Nazi propaganda was the claim "that the Jews were experts at camouflage and that as a result a massive effort at 'public enlightenment' was needed to expose them and their aim of world domination. If not identified and destroyed, the Nazi propagandists feared, Jewry would annihilate the German people."[7] The Third Reich's overtly antisemitic films reinforced this belief. In this chapter, I explain how Nazi Germany's best-known antisemitic comedy, *Robert und Bertram*, invokes the figure of the masked or camouflaged Jew both directly and indirectly, stimulating and assuaging anxieties around it. *Robert und Bertram*'s ambivalence is related both to its treatment of the masked Jew and also to its comic strategies, which rely on disguise and misrecognition.

Mistaken Identity and Third Reich Film Humor

Disguise and misrecognition and the accompanying irony, incongruity, and humor were standard comic devices in the Third Reich, particularly in the era's numerous *Verwechslungskomödien* (mistaken-identity comedies). I argue here that there is an indirect link between such comedies and antisemitic preoccupations with the masked Jew. Nazi anxieties about the lack of visible distinctions between German and Jew were a subset of a larger constellation of concerns about the instability of identities and the boundaries between them, anxieties expressed and allayed through the roughly two hundred Third Reich film comedies in which central figures disguise themselves as or are mistaken for someone else. These comedies' shared structural and thematic features displace overt preoccupations with masked Jews, moving them to the inferential realm, as they capitalize on comedy's humorous boundary-drawing and community-building potential.

The problem of not being able to rely on visual cues to decipher someone's identity, the instability of identity itself, and the comic potential of misrecognition dominated Third Reich film comedy. The dissolution of identity and "a persistent anxiety over questions of identity" were recurrent themes in both comedy and other modes.[8] In her analysis of "Jewish" and "non-Jewish" coding of Third Reich sexuality, Dagmar Herzog argues that "assumptions about the fluidity and instability of identity categories (Jewish versus German, homosexual versus heterosexual) were essential to Nazism's ideological effectiveness."[9] Such assumptions are particularly obvious in *Verwechslungskomödien*, which exemplify concerns about identity and recognition expressed in Third Reich cinema more broadly. Mistaken identity is a stock comic strategy common in film, inherited from European theatrical traditions—Shakespeare, Goldoni, and Molière, for example. Yet, despite the prevalence of this strategy, there is no concept of mistaken identity as a discrete genre in Hollywood film. By contrast, the German language reflects an understanding of mistaken-identity comedy as a genre. *Verwechslungskomödie* is not a rare or scholarly coinage. German-language film criticism, film reviews, and popular sources like descriptions on movie schedules commonly use the term. That is, the *Verwechslungskomödie* is part of studios' marketing strategies and the established patterns in which consumers group film. The term creates a horizon of expectation for audiences, an important function of filmic genre.

Verwechslungskomödie was a major comic genre in Nazi Germany.[10] Witte claims that German film in the 1930s relied much more heavily on the narrative device of mistaken identity than did Hollywood in the same period.[11] While difficult to quantify, Witte's comparison is consistent with my observations. *Verwechslungskomödien* constituted a striking share of feature films produced in Nazi Germany. The admittedly imperfect method of cross-referencing Gerd Albrecht's list of Third Reich H-films ("heitere," or cheerful, films) against available plot summaries suggests that 194 feature films made in Nazi Germany (37% of the humorous films made, or 18% of total feature film production) could be described as *Verwechslungskomödien*, and that *Verwechslungskomödien* were made and released throughout the period, albeit at a somewhat uneven frequency.[12] In these films, commoners are mistaken for millionaires (*Glückskinder, Umwege des schönen Karl,* and *Kleider machen Leute* [Clothes Make the Man, Helmut Käutner, 1940]) and celebrities and nobility pass as commoners (*Die Blume von Hawaii, April! April!,* and *Die Frau meiner Träume* [The Woman of my Dreams, Georg Jacoby, 1943/44]; women dress as boys (*Viktor und Viktoria, Capriccio* [Capriccio, Karl Ritter, 1938]) and the reverse (*Charleys Tante* [Charley's Aunt, Robert Stemmle, 1934]), and many other absurd and implausible mistaken-identity scenarios drive plots and humor. Some of the era's many *Verwechslungskomödien,* such as *Viktor und Viktoria* and *Die Feuerzangenbowle,* remain well known today. Many more, however, like *Capriccio,* do not appeal to contemporary tastes and have attracted less scholarly attention.[13]

Verwechslungskomödien generate humor out of two complementary elements, figural and narrative. Neither of them is inherently Jewish or antisemitic, although both can engage Jewish and other kinds of difference on multiple levels, depending on the context, the normative commitments made, and the inferences they license. In a typical *Verwechslungskomödie,* a central figure passes for someone or something else, and other characters in the film fail to recognize this figure's "true" identity. The misunderstandings and dramatic irony created as the plot unfolds are humorous for the cinema audience, which recognizes those other characters as dupes. Spectators occupy an ambivalent and mobile position in this triangular structure—at times identifying with the figure in disguise because they are in on the joke, and at other times identifying with the dupes, as surrogate spectators within the film.[14] The ambivalence and mobility of the spectatorial position in *Verwechslungskomödien* mean that these films can yield contradictory readings and function in either transgressive or normative ways.

The central narrative problem of *Verwechslungskomödien* is an inability to distinguish between appearance and essence, a problem that Third Reich critics theorized as fundamental to the comic mode. In 1938, playwright Sigmund Graff defined the comical entirely in terms of appearance and perspective, claiming that the comical was not an inherent trait, but rather an appearance (*Anschein*) something takes on in a particular light.[15] According to Graff, comedy offers a distanced point of view on incongruencies, fallacies, and illogic: "'Comical' is each recognition of a discrepancy between essence and appearance, between demand and output, concept and reality. In one word: each 'incongruity' is comical. Everything is comical that doesn't completely 'jibe,' that doesn't perfectly 'match up.'"[16] Graff's theory of comedy as something that exposes incongruities and treats life's serious issues was not new or unique. It is derivative of a long philosophical-theoretical tradition including thinkers such as James Beattie, Henri Bergson, Immanuel Kant, Søren Kierkegaard, and Arthur Schopenhauer.[17]

Kadner articulates a similar theory of comic misrecognition, filtering it through the lens of German racial superiority and Jewish difference. Kadner conceptualizes incongruity and the discrepancy between appearance and essence in German humor similarly to Graff.[18] Unlike Graff, however, who identifies philosophical seriousness, a lighthearted perspective on life's failures, and an interest in the gap between appearance and essence as fundamental traits of the comical more generally, Kadner identifies them as characteristics of a racially determined, essentially German humor.[19] Whereas Kadner construes Germans as wanting to plumb the depths between *Schein* and *Sein*, he positions Jewishness as part of the hidden truth that Germans want to uncover. Kadner cites Jewish physiognomy as an example of deceptive appearance: "It occurs often enough that external appearance does not correspond to the soul's character, that, for example, a Phalian person is in an Eastern [Alpine] shell, and the other way around, yes, that even an appearance that at least at first glance looks Nordic can belong to a Jew."[20] Highlighting deceptive Jewish appearance, as Kadner does, within an argument that Germans can use humor to dissipate the tension generated in the gap between appearance and essence, implies that German humor can help reveal the masked Jew. The dramatic irony of the *Verwechslungskomödie*—in which spectators recognize identity differently from characters in the film—creates a discrepancy between surface and interior, appearance and essence, which Graff sees as the heart of the comical, and Kadner as motivating German humor and as managing the anxieties that such discrepancies create. In mistaken-identity narratives, a key figure's imposture ensnares unwitting dupes, whereas dramatic irony provides moviegoers the distanced perspective described by Graff, which makes the gap between appearance and essence humorous, warns spectators about the pitfalls of recognition, and positions them (at least in this instance) as the ones able to see and know the truth.

Most *Verwechslungskomödien* made in Nazi Germany were not overtly about Jews, although lots of Jewish coding typically surrounds outsider figures whose "true" identities are "mistaken" by others. Moreover, contemporary antisemitic discourses understood deception and disguise in and of themselves to be Jewish. Therefore, for spectators sensitized to Jewish difference, the central figures of mistaken identity comedies always already occupy a "Jewish" role in the narrative. *Verwechslungskomödien* analyzed in other chapters of this book, including *Die Blume von Hawaii*, *Viktor und Viktoria*, *Glückskinder*, *April! April!*, and *Die Feuerzangenbowle* all represent variations on (mis)recognition narratives, figures who pass, and their intersections with codes of Jewish difference. Nazi-era discourses of masked Jews are part of the inferential patterns that make the Jewish codings of these intersections legible.

The Masked Jew

The Nazis fixated on the difficulty of identifying Jews visually. They construed Jews as masters of deception and disguise, and emphasized the supposed ability of assimilated Jews to pass as German, despite their alleged differences. Such Nazi paranoia builds on older discursive traditions, both Jewish and non-Jewish, questioning the dissimulation and abandonment of authenticity presumed to be inherent in Jewish assimilation.[21] As far as the Nazis were concerned, the ability to disguise their Jewishness made Jews exceptionally dangerous. A cartoon by Mjölnir from a pamphlet by Goebbels (Figure 6.2) illustrates the widespread notion of the Jewish mask and the imperative to strip it off in order to reveal the danger underneath.[22]

Mjölnir's cartoon depicts the Jew, a scowling, obese man in a business suit, as having appeared previously in multiple disguises—as a Christian, a German citizen, a German nationalist, and a harmless passerby. The "wakening Germany," however, a giant Nazi with a hatchet, advances threateningly on the Jew, telling him that his days of disguise are over and that "we see through all your masks!"[23] The Nazis, this cartoon promises, will recognize and destroy the Jew—imagined here as male—despite his clever disguises.

Less overtly antisemitic sources also emphasized the dangers posed by disguised Jews. For example, on January 4, 1939, the *Film Kurier* reported that two Jews by the names of Aronsohn and Adam had been arrested. Under false Aryan names, the misuse of the German greeting, and the pretense that they were influential in the film industry, the two men were alleged to have been seducing teenage girls with the promise of helping them break in to the film business.[24] At first glance, this story does not seem worth

Figure 6.2. "Wir durchschauen alle Deine Masken!" (We see through all your Masks!). Mjölnir, *Die verfluchten Hakenkreuzler*, 1932. Harvard University. Collection Development Department. Widener Library. HCL.

reporting. Neither the seduction technique nor the arrest of Jews in 1939 is particularly novel or newsworthy, and the writer of the article claimed not to be surprised that Jews would behave in such a way. Whether or not intended to foment antisemitism, however, this *Film Kurier* story provided readers with a concrete example of Jewish cunning, criminality, and sexual appetites and, above all else, of the risks of mistaking Jewish impostors for non-Jewish Germans.

The problem with the masked Jew, according to Nazi sources, was the Jews' ability to influence and exploit the naive and gullible. Third Reich texts imply that differences in intelligence, perception, education, and experience made Germans more or less able to recognize assimilated Jews and their deceptions. These differing abilities could have sexual and racial consequences. The *Film Kurier* article about Aronsohn and Adam not only highlighted the methods and motives of Jewish con men but also presented the story as "an unbelievable chapter of teenage imprudence and gullibility."[25] How could the girls have been so stupid as not to notice the scam and to think that sex rather than talent could get them into film?[26] According to this news report, inexperience and naiveté, particularly on the part of young women, could lead directly to *Rassenschande* (racial defilement). Sexist assumptions about women's lack of intelligence and self-control, antisemitic notions of Jewish masking and lechery, and the sexual and racial/genetic implications of both were not only standard features of Nazi propaganda but also a significant component of the legal discourse around the Nuremberg laws.[27]

The Third Reich's overtly antisemitic films—propagandistic documentaries, dramas, and comedies—warned spectators to watch for hidden, dangerous Jews. The title of the 1938 compilation film *Juden ohne Maske* (Jews without Masks) emphasizes the trope of the masked Jew and the importance of removing and seeing behind the mask. This film, only a fragment of which survives, was produced by the NSDAP Reichspropagandaleitung (Nazi Party's Reich Propaganda Office) to accompany the traveling *Ewige Jude* exhibit. *Juden ohne Maske* spliced together footage of Jewish actors playing unsavory characters and implied a counterintuitive role reversal: the parts they played were the Jews' authentic identities and acting their natural state.

Der ewige Jude, a more extensive and better preserved documentary-style antisemitic compilation film, juxtaposed appalling images, egregiously false and biased voice-overs, and footage of people confined by the Nazis in ghettos, in order to teach viewers to recognize, fear, and hate Jews. Because of Hippler's access to ghettos and Jews, as defined by Nazi law, he was able not only to represent and caricature Jewish behavior, faces, and bodies, but also to make the claim that the Jews in his film were authentic, not played by non-Jewish actors as they were in Nazi-era feature films. *Der ewige Jude* makes such reality claims in a series of dissolves between images of clean-shaven men dressed in modern, Western European clothing to their images in the guise of bearded, Eastern European Jews, accompanied by the following voice-over: "The Jews alter their outward appearance when they leave their Polish haunts for the rich world. The hair, beard, skullcap, and caftan make the Eastern Jew recognizable to everyone. Should he remove them, only sharp-eyed people can spot his racial origins. An essential trait of the Jew is that he always tries to hide his origin when among non-Jews." This voiceover introduces a sequence focusing on the alleged danger posed to Germany by its assimilated Jews, who pass as Germans and feed off their unknowing host. *Der ewige Jude* insists upon an essential and dangerous German-Jewish nature, part of which involves hiding its racial origin and which, therefore, cannot always be detected through visual clues. In this account, the assimilated German Jew blurs the distinctions between Eastern Jew and non-Jewish German, a blurring *Der ewige Jude* struggles to contain by dissolving the difference between Eastern and Western Jew. By using dissolves rather than cuts, this scene visually creates not merely analogies but continuums between Eastern Jews and German Jews. These continuums, moreover, appear not as recognizable or realistic sequences of human actions, but as special effects. The dissolves in this well-known sequence from *Der ewige Jude* provide visual evidence for the claims made in the voice-over—that Jews pass from an authentic appearance to an inauthentic guise—and they render the transition unnatural or magical. They also reveal how Jews, even if they look different from one another, are all fundamentally the same. The film attempts to liquidate distinctions between Jews with different costumes and customs and to reestablish barriers between Jews and non-Jews, despite the apparent lack of visible differences between them.[28] It purports to reveal an essential Jewishness, schools viewers in Jewish physiognomy, and warns them to watch for it—even when it has been stripped of Jewish speech, mannerisms, behavior, and cultural markers such as beard, sidelocks, and costume.

Antisemitic feature films also emphasized the danger of mistaking masked Jews for non-Jews. *Jud Süss*, a fictionalized account of Joseph Süss Oppenheimer (Ferdinand Marian), an eighteenth-century German-Jewish banker, provides an excellent example. In an oft-noted scene from this much-discussed film, hot-headed Faber (Malte Jäger), whose fiancée Dorothea (Kristina Söderbaum) has caught a ride into Stuttgart in Oppenheimer's carriage, outs him as a Jew. Faber tells the elegantly dressed, clean-shaven Oppenheimer that there are no inns for Jews in Stuttgart, and Oppenheimer compliments him on his "knowledge of human nature." A close-up on Oppenheimer's face here seems to have a pedagogical function, teaching viewers not to rely on costume alone, but to look more closely at physiognomy, facial expression, and behavior to recognize assimilated Jews.[29] Marian, however, was not Jewish and his casting and this use of his face to illustrate what a Jew looks like challenge the notion of visible difference between Aryan and Jew.[30] Instead of relying on physiognomic difference, Marian performs Jewishness through uncouth "Jewish" speech and mannerisms and sinister behaviors, such as financial exploitation, behind-the-scenes exercise of power, womanizing, and rape. Süss's voice, actions, and associates reveal him to be a Jew. Other explicitly antisemitic feature films from the Third Reich also teach spectators to watch for disguised Jews and mark characters' Jewishness using similar techniques. For example, in *Leinen aus Irland* the financial machinations and inappropriate marital ambitions of the assimilated antagonist Dr. Kuhn (Siegfried Breuer) are exposed to spectators as Jewish through the caricatured Eastern European Jewish behavior and heavily Yiddish-inflected language of his Uncle Siggi (Fritz Imhoff).

In Nazi Germany's antisemitic feature films, non-Jewish actors perform Jewishness as a suite of ugly behaviors, recognizable as Jewish to the wary eye. The casting of non-Jewish actors to play Jewish roles could be seen as blurring boundaries between the Jewish and the non-Jewish, criticizing Jewish difference as a logical ordering system. Yet, performed as well-established racial stereotypes using conventions dating back to the nineteenth century, ethnic drag in these films undermines confidence in physiognomy or phenotype as reliable indicators of difference more than it undermines the logic and hierarchy of difference itself. Caricatured performances of Jewishness by non-Jews in which actors' original racialized identities remain legible (masquerade) reassure spectators that Jews are inherently different from non-Jews and reaffirm the hierarchy of the non-Jewish over the Jewish.[31]

Overt Antisemitism, Inferential Antisemitism, and Humorous Displacement: *Robert und Bertram*'s Masked Jews

Robert und Bertram, the third of four films based on Gustav Raeder's 1856 farce of the same name, explicitly treats the imagined problem of masked Jews with the tools and strategies of mistaken-identity comedy.[32] In the Zerlett version, the eponymous vagabonds disguise themselves and steal a suitcase of jewels from wealthy Jews in order to free an innkeeper and his daughter from their debt to an overbearing moneylender. *Robert und Bertram* follows traditions of the Jew farce. "The genre, which flourished in the early nineteenth century, lampoons the Jew as usurper, who attempts to buy and cheat his way into communal acceptance and respect, but is unfailingly exposed and cruelly punished."[33] The Jew farce "addresses the spectator as racial detective who will not be duped by the Jew's dissimulations" and, performed for Christian audiences, helps them imagine themselves as Germans.[34] *Robert und Bertram* not only uses an established generic framework to deliver overtly antisemitic content but also, in doing so, exposes the connections between the pleasures of comedy, anxieties over identity, and obsessions with Jewish disguise in Third Reich film. It presents spectators with the problem of the masked Jew in three different registers: overt antisemitism, inferential antisemitism, and humorous displacement. In the overtly antisemitic register, *Robert und Bertram* mocks Jewish attempts to disguise their Jewish nature. At the inferential level, the film implies that masked or assimilated Jews are particularly dangerous. Simultaneously, the pleasure and humor produced by disguise and deception are displaced on to the film's protagonists, turning the problem of the masked Jew into German humor.

Robert und Bertram's overtly antisemitic representation of the Ipelmeyers, a wealthy Jewish family, and the guests they invite to a masquerade ball emphasizes Jewish ambitions to assimilate and to disguise their true nature, and trivializes the threat through stereotypes and mockery. To varying degrees, all the Jews at the Ipelmeyers' are stereotypically Jewish looking; the illustrated fan magazine *Mein Film in Wien* called them "black skinned, black haired, black bearded."[35] To be precise, black beards mark only male Jews in the film. Consistent with social and visual codes predating the Nazi era, dark coloring and extravagance mark the Jewish women. The Ipelmeyers and their acquaintances, men and women, are lecherous, greedy, pretentious liars, who speak a language peppered with Yiddishisms and French malapropisms.[36] They worship a sterile, cosmopolitan high culture, starkly contrasted with the sentimental German folk culture shown earlier in the film at a rural wedding celebration.[37] The Jews at the Ipelmeyers love social posturing and disguising themselves. Despite their attempts to blend in, however, those who know what to look for can recognize them.[38]

In several scenes, *Robert und Bertram* mocks Jewish desires to fit in and their obliviousness to their own legibility as Jews. Having come to Berlin to defraud Herr Ipelmeyer (Herbert Hübner), Bertram (Kurt Seifert) first recognizes him "by his profile," referring to Ipelmeyer's prodigious nose.[39] Bertram follows Ipelmeyer into Café Kranzler, and—after a staged conversation between himself, pretending to be Professor Müller, and Robert (Rudi Godden), pretending to be the Count of Monte Cristo—is able to initiate a conversation with Ipelmeyer. Ipelmeyer asks "Müller" to bring the count to his home, but first he must entrust him with a secret: "I am an

Israelite." Bertram responds in kind with his own secret, introduced with great drama: "I have a belly." The two portly men in their finery, sitting across from one another at a small table smoking cigars, look and move almost like twins—both crooks aspiring to a social class to which (from the perspective of the film) neither is worthy. Yet there is a difference that is so obvious and so grounded in the physical body that it is as obvious as Bertram's substantial girth: Ipelmeyer is a Jew. The joke about the men's secrets uses irony to call attention to how open Ipelmeyer's "secret" really is. With his nose, his pretensions, and his accent, Ipelmeyer could not be mistaken for anything but a Jew. This scene and others featuring Herr and Frau Ipelmeyer and their servant Jack suggest that while Jews attempt to disguise their true nature, they are incapable of doing so.

The masquerade ball at the Ipelmeyer mansion at which (literally and figuratively) masked Jews are exposed, mocked, and humiliated perpetuates myths of masked Jews while trivializing any threat they pose or anxieties they could provoke. This scene features major and minor Jewish characters at differing stages of assimilation and dishonesty and emphasizes how different they are from Germans. Even doubly disguised, with a literal mask over their usual metaphoric mask, Jews cannot hide their true identities or their desire to conquer the world. Mary-Elizabeth O'Brien notes how the Jews' chosen costumes "illustrate their ridiculous desire to be powerful rulers of foreign cultures that they do not understand"[40] and that these costumes suit them ill: "Mr. Ipelmeyer masquerades as 'Louis Quartose the fifteenth' [sic], his wife as Madame Pompadour, . . . and his daughter Isidora as 'Queen Kleptomania,' alias Cleopatra. Samuel the Jewish bookkeeper likewise tries to adopt the identity of a powerful, honorable knight by donning a suit of armor, but he cannot walk in it, let alone fight or make love when the opportunities arise."[41] Jews are recognizable, however, not only because their costumes reflect their megalomaniacal ambitions, but also because their grotesque bodies, voices, and sexual desires give them away. A bearded, masked, obese sultan grabs the breast of an equally voluptuous masked woman in silk. "Take away your hand, Forchheimer," she reprimands. "You recognized me. How?" he asks. "Because of your feet," she answers. Despite their disguises, Jews are recognizable because of their lechery, their feet, their Yiddish pronunciation, and their butchered grammar and syntax.[42]

In the eighteenth and nineteenth centuries, both Jews and non-Jews understood the Jewish voice to be a dominant marker of Jewish difference. The Yiddish language and the Jewish voice were coded as "deceitful and ugly," in contrast to the German, which were "beautiful and true."[43] This marker became a central characteristic of performed Jewishness in nineteenth-century Jew farces.[44] Between script and performance, these farces developed different degrees of "lexical, syntactic, and phonological markers" that betrayed characters' Jewishness.[45] Nazi Germany's overtly antisemitic feature films adopted these markers. A devil greets Louis XIV as "Herr Ipelmeyer," who asks, "How do you know that I am Herr Ipelmeyer?" with pseudo-Yiddish syntax, pronunciation, and polite form of you.[46] The devil answers in similarly Jewish-coded language and inflection, "Nu, if I wouldn't notice it because of your pronunciation, I would notice it because of your infatuated glances at the solo dancer."[47] Voice and lust reveal the Jew. Even though spectators have not previously encountered Ipelmeyer's companion, Dr. Corduan (Walter Lieck), his syntax and pronunciation and the kinky hair and hooked nose protruding from his mask tell spectators that he too is a Jew.[48] Jews can be recognized, according to this sequence, by their bodies, speech, ambitions, lust, and disguises, which are ornate, overly ambitious, and woefully inadequate.

Using non-Jewish actors, *Robert und Bertram* attempts to school audience members in recognizing Jews. This pedagogy is accomplished partially through Frau Ipelmeyer's (Inge van der Straaten) recognition of Forchheimer (Erwin Biegel) and partially by allowing the audience to recognize her when she is in disguise. Van der Straaten's body, voice, and face are all obvious, and not at all disguised by the tiny mask over her eyes. By layering these with phony Jewish speech and extravagant clothing, the film deceives the audience into believing it has successfully recognized a Jew, when it has really only recognized the actor and the role she is playing. As with Marian's performance of Süss Oppenheimer, the casting of Aryans as Jews might seem to trouble *Robert und Bertram*'s pedagogy here. Yet van der Straaten's exaggerated performance style, an ethnic masquerade, consistent with the film's satire, helps distance performer from role in a way Marian's mimetic acting style does not. A cartoon and caption in a publicity pamphlet from the Tobis studio refers to van der Straaten's performance of Frau Ipelmeyer as a "mask." (See figure 6.3.) *Robert und Bertram*'s masquerades counter the irony that all of the film's Jews are played by Aryan actors. By exaggerating their performances of Jewishness, the actors disavow the similarities that their ethnic cross casting seems to imply. Just as the Ipelmeyers and their guests cannot disguise their Jewishness, Aryan actors cannot disguise their own true nature.

P 15   M. Zeichnung: Trautschold — Tobis
Inge von der Straaten
in der Maske der jüdischen Bankiersfrau Ipelmeyer — einer Hauptfigur der Hans H. Zerlett-Produktion der Tobis „Robert und Bertram"

Figure 6.3. Caricature of "Inge von [sic] der Straaten in the mask of the Jewish banker Ipelmeyer's wife." Publicity pamphlet for *Robert und Bertram*, Tobis Filmkunst, 1939. The Gillespie collection, Sydney, Australia.

Stereotyping of the Ipelmeyers and the actors' transparent ethnic masquerades establish "the illusion of an absolute difference between self and Other," which Sander Gilman identifies as the primary psychological function of the stereotype.[49] Contemporary film reporting explained *Robert und Bertram* in this way. The January 1939 announcement of the film's going into production described the antics at the Ipelmeyer ball as "a single great satire of the at that time recently ennobled Jewish community" and at the same time as "monstrously authentic."[50] A review in July echoed that paradox, describing it as "an astonishingly authentic caricature."⁵¹ Proclaiming *Robert and Bertram*'s overtly antisemitic stereotypes to be authentic urges readers and spectators to accept such stereotypes as true and to understand the actors' masquerades as mimesis.⁵² The seeming contradiction inherent in this kind of praise, which sees comic caricatures of Jews as both satirical and true, predates the Nazi era. Similar formulations can be found, for example, in the promotion and reception of Lubitsch's Jewish milieu comedies of the 1910s (among which was an earlier version of *Robert und Bertram*).⁵³ The press's praise for the authenticity of satire and caricature in *Robert und Bertram* builds on their rootedness in a long tradition of similar stereotypes, from Jewish and non-Jewish, philo- and antisemitic perspectives, including performances of Jewishness like Lubitsch's, which made fun of stereotypes from the inside, and have been accused of "self hatred."⁵⁴ Similar stereotypes were deployed to combat antisemitism in the 1924 Austrian film *Die Stadt ohne Juden* (The City without Jews), based on Hugo Bettauer's 1922 novel of the same name, and criticized on similar grounds by Jewish film critics.⁵⁵ The familiarity of the stereotyped Jewishness in *Robert und Bertram* helped the press read the actors' performances as both satiric and authentic, verifying the differences between Jews and non-Jews.

The performances of the Ipelmeyers and their social circle mocked Jewish attempts to mask themselves. These performances and the overt antisemitism in *Robert und Bertram* create a generational and gendered view. The Nazi film press emphasized the lesson taught by the figure of Ipelmeyer's "already dangerously assimilated daughter," Isadora, played by Tatiana Sais, whose difference from non-Jews is more subtle than her parents' and who therefore is more seductive.⁵⁶ This character was consistent with "perceptions that Jewish women were more likely to be able to disguise their Jewishness," perceptions that were already "widespread" in the Weimar Republic.⁵⁷ According to Georg Herzberg of the *Film Kurier*, "Ipelmeyer's daughter is already no longer born in Łodz, and raised instead in Berlin for expensive money. She speaks French, is embarrassed by her parents, and is already no longer comical, but instead a confident and clever person, who loses her composure only seldom and as a type has contributed decisively to the successes of the Jews before 1933. Tatjana Sais provides in so few scenes a whole chapter of the Jewish Problem."⁵⁸ Isadora Ipelmeyer, a character very similar to *April! April*'s Mirna Lampe, personifies "the comic stock type of the salacious and ambitious 'aesthetic

Jewess,'" who has assimilated with the host people through her "cultural accomplishments" and hopes to seduce its ranking members (shown by her desire to wed the Count of Monte Cristo, whom she does not recognize as a fraud).[59] Isadora embodies the stereotype of Jewish women as "the ultimate consumers and seducers," as sophisticated, educated ladies, who fetishize the latest, most expensive fashion and culture from Paris in order to appear not Jewish.[60] Isadora wants to assimilate via wealth and Frenchness, but the stereotyping here construes Jewish women as different from non-Jewish women, precisely because of their extravagance and cosmopolitanism, mapping Jewish difference onto class difference and onto the urban/rural divide. Isadora differs radically from the honest, hard-working, and virtuous German Lenchen (Carla Rust), also an unmarried young woman, and has more in common with her Jewish parents than with her Aryan counterpart. Recognizably more assimilated than her parents, Isadora Ipelmeyer still shares a number of their characteristics, including her social pretensions, frivolous lifestyle, love of wealth, admiration of all things French, and aggressive sexuality. Beyond gender and age, she has little in common with the innkeeper's daughter.

The Ipelmeyers and their friends perpetuate comic traditions of Jewish stereotypes, and highlight both the pleasures and the nasty underbelly of those traditions, reinforcing the illusion of Jews being clearly Other. In the course of this overtly antisemitic representation, Zerlett construes Jews as willfully deceptive, but not dangerously so. The Ipelmeyer family and their associates, although accused by the film of financial chicanery, lusty sexual appetites, and unseemly social pretensions, are anything but sinister. According to Herzberg, Jewry becomes "target of a superior and sure to be effective mockery."[61] The depiction is so comic that Albert Schneider, writing for *Lichtbild-Bühne*, bemoaned the fact that "as well as the Jewish milieu . . . is portrayed in its ridiculousness, one very much misses a single visible proof of the dangerousness of the typical stock market speculator."[62] Wolfgang Martini of the *Deutsche Filmzeitung* made a similar complaint.[63]

The overt antisemitism in *Robert und Bertram* is so exaggerated that it is easy to miss less ham-handed antisemitic innuendos and inferences licensed by more ambiguous aspects of the film. For evidence of Jewish dangerousness in *Robert und Bertram*, a viewer has to look beyond the Ipelmeyer household and the Ipelmeyer guest list and scrutinize another character in the film marked by codes of Jewish difference: the antagonist, Herr Biedermeyer (Arthur Schröder), a middle-aged businessman. Biedermeyer wants to marry Lenchen, whose father owes him money. Supplementing the overtly antisemitic portrayal of the Ipelmeyers, *Robert und Bertram*'s ambiguous portrayal of Biedermeyer as potentially *either* a white Jew *or* a "black-" or racialized Jew, addresses the problem of the masked Jew on an inferential level.

Biedermeyer embodies both the economic threat and the sexual/racial threat posed by masked Jews—in that he either is one of them, or has been corrupted by them. Although he gets little screen time, Biedermeyer motivates the plot of *Robert and Bertram* and is central to its preoccupation with unrecognizable Jews. The opening minutes establish Lenchen's choice of suitors as the driving issue in the film. The first thing shown after the credits is the boyish Michel (Heinz Schorlemmer) carving a heart and Lenchen's name into a tree. A dissolve to the ham she is packing for Michel's uncle brings the camera's gaze to Lenchen. A zoom out and pan up to her face shows her gaze, and the film cuts to follow it, showing Herr Biedermeyer arriving at the inn. The following dialogue makes clear that Biedermeyer is an unwelcome suitor and that Lenchen wants neither him nor Michel, who is not yet mature and assertive enough for her. At the same time, the mise-en-scène, acting, and cinematography show that Michel and Lenchen could be a good match for one another, whereas Biedermeyer is an interloper. Both Michel and Lenchen are young and blond and wear rustic clothing. They both work with their hands in traditionally gendered ways—his carving wood, and hers packing food. The dissolve, linking his heart to her ham, shows the affinity between the two. By contrast, the cut from Lenchen's disapproving look to Biedermeyer immediately signifies a lack of connection between them. The following dialogue emphasizes this gap: Lenchen rebuffs Biedermeyer and explicitly tells him that he does not attract her. Their body language, where he moves toward her and she pulls away, expresses opposite desires. Their differing appearances—hers young, simple, and light; his older, sophisticated, and dark—show them to be ill matched. This mismatch is even more obvious after Biedermeyer takes his leave and Michel and Lenchen have a private conversation, which is characterized by awkward flirtation yet clear affection. These opening moments draw the audience's attention to Lenchen and her suitors, even though the primary narrative will follow, as the credits make clear, the protagonists Robert and Bertram and their ascension to heaven for the virtue of gratitude. Ultimately, the two plotlines are connected: to express their gratitude to Lenchen and her father, Herr Lips (Alfred Maack), Robert and Bertram rob the Ipelmeyers and give Lenchen's father the booty, so that he can pay off his debt and free Lenchen from Biedermeyer's clutches.

Despite the director's intending him to be Jewish, Biedermeyer is a weirdly illegible character, both today and at the time of the film's release. In an interview with the *Film Kurier* on January 17, 1939, Zerlett called Biedermeyer "a disagreeable Jewish admirer."[64] His profession as a moneylender; his dark curly hair, mutton chops, and mustache; his urbane suit, which looks too formal and out-of-place in the village setting; his greed; his persistent wooing of Lenchen; his sing-song voice, and the suspicious dark shadows usually hiding his face, all connote Jewishness according to Third Reich filmic codes. Yet, aside from the *Film Kurier* interview with Zerlett, the press coverage doesn't discuss Biedermeyer as a Jew. Film reporters described Biedermeyer in decidedly negative terms: he was a "cunning bachelor" who had an effect on the viewer that was "very uncomfortable."[65] The business dealings that put Lenchen's father in Biedermeyer's debt and his pressure to have her marry him were described as "the mesh of a swindler's net" and "the machinations of a Jewish clique."[66] Yet reporters for the trade press didn't explicitly identify the character as a Jew. Herzberg omitted Biedermeyer from his lengthy discussion of Zerlett's skilled treatment of the Jewish problem and his sensitivity to the *Volk*'s taste in such matters.[67] Schneider and Martini both complained that all the Jews in *Robert und Bertram* were too comic and harmless.[68] If they recognized Biedermeyer as a dangerously assimilated Jew threatening Lenchen's virtue and the purity of the German race, they did not mention it. Either reporters failed to make the antisemitic inferences licensed by Biedermeyer's coding—serving as a reminder of just how elusive and situational inferential antisemitism can be—or the Propaganda Ministry didn't want Biedermeyer's Jewishness emphasized. Postwar scholars, when they mention this character at all, rarely describe him as Jewish.[69] This is not so much an oversight on their part as an indicator of the figure's illegibility.

Biedermeyer's name, despite its suggestive "Jewish" spelling with a y, refers to his origin in the bourgeoisie and additionally conveys ambivalent messages about his identity and significance.[70] Ernst Jerosch of *Der Film* describes *Robert und Bertram*'s central conflict in the following terms: "The poor child [Lenchen] is pressed to marry a Herr 'Biedermeier' for financial reasons, who is most unpleasant not only for her but for all spectators, when she would really much rather have 'Michel,' a blond, good chap, who is currently serving his years in the military."[71] Jerosch adds, "Zerlett even puns very nicely with the names here."[72] The significance of Michel's name is straightforward. Michel, whose military service changes him from a timid boy into confident man, is the German Michel, an allegorical figure who "has symbolized Germany's good-natured but sleepy People unable to forge a successful revolution."[73] The significance of the name "Biedermeyer" is overdetermined. Biedermeyer is "named after the allegorical figure of the petty bourgeois philistine who had come to embody the entire restoration [Biedermeier] period."[74] His name thus connotes both the materialism and the bourgeois domesticity of that era. In addition, the name is coded as Jewish, in a roundabout way. Biedermeyer is not a stereotypically Jewish-sounding surname. Yet the use of "meyer" in both Ipelmeyer and Biedermeyer's names, albeit common in farce, serves as a constant reminder of the similarities and connections between the two men.[75] The interconnectedness of bourgeois and Jewish identity implied by the matching suffixes in Ipelmeyer's and Bidermeyer's names also was part of the Nazi understanding of the Biedermeier period. Jerosch described *Robert und Bertram* as "a mockery of that time that we and also others before us label satirically with the word 'Biedermeier,' and that was more *Meier* [a name that means steward or dairy farmer] than *bieder* [upright]. It is the time of the large Jewish immigration into Germany, the time of Mendelssohn and Meyerbeer, who began at that time to make central European 'culture.'"[76] Jerosch characterizes the Biedermeier period as an era most notable for the increasing Jewish influence on German culture and for its business orientation rather than its ethics. Thus, his interpretation of Herr Biedermeyer's name as a pun suggests that Jerosch understood Biedermeyer to embody Jewish influence on the German bourgeoisie. Intended by the director to be Jewish, Biedermeyer reads as an unsavory bourgeois businessman of indeterminate origin. Biedermeyer's illegibility draws our attention back to the problematic blurring of the categories of capitalist and Jew in the Nazi imaginary and to the construct of the white Jew, elaborated in the previous chapter. Third Reich spectators could have understood Biedermeyer as either a Jewish person or a white Jew, an Aryan corrupted by Jews and who now thinks and behaves like one. Perceiving Biedermeyer as Jewish would reframe his actions from an attempt by a wealthy businessman to marry a pretty young woman to *Rassenschande,* in Nazi terms. The seriousness of such a crime by Third Reich standards would explain the film's otherwise puzzling ending, in which Robert and Bertram are rewarded for their virtues by flying to heaven in a hot-air balloon.

Robert und Bertram engages Jewish difference and the trope of the masked Jew on multiple levels. The overtly antisemitic stereotypes of the Ipelmeyers reinforce messages spread in other Nazi propaganda about both the masked Jew who wants money and power and Jews' essential inferiority to non-Jews. The coding of Biedermeyer as Jewish inferentially emphasizes the threats of covert or masked Jewish influence, Jewish economic practices, and potential miscegenation. *Robert und Bertram*'s engagement with Jewish difference, however, extends beyond the film's antagonists. Costumes, music, speech, and settings all connoting the German *Volk* clearly code Lenchen and her father, Michel, the constables, and all the other provincial residents as non-Jewish. Yet the protagonists Robert and Bertram have a number of characteristics frequently associated with the Jewish and which mirror Jewish characters in the film.[77] Blending Jewish and non-Jewish coding with humor, the portrayal of Robert and Bertram diffuses anxiety by reversing the film's central concerns and displacing them onto more pleasurable figures in a way similar to the era's *Verwechslungskomödien*.

If viewed through an unsympathetic lens, Robert and Bertram could be interpreted as a variety of white Jew, not in the sense of being capitalists, but as dishonest, rootless wanderers with no work ethic who disguise themselves in order to steal working people's money. O'Brien discusses several ways in which Jewish and non-Jewish characters in *Robert und Bertram* bear an "uncanny resemblance" to one another.[78] Bertram, like the Ipelmeyers and their servant Jack, has language difficulties and confuses words in a humorous way.[79] Witte notes that even though Jack calls Isadora Queen Kleptomania (a malapropism for her Cleopatra costume), Robert and Bertram are the real kleptomaniacs.[80] Kleptomania, "an overdetermined embodiment of the desire to consume," was coded as a "female" or "Jewish" pathology.[81] Jack's malapropism has multiple functions. It shows that Jews are so pretentious and linguistically deficient that even the servant in the Ipelmeyer household tries to use fancy words that he fails to master. It labels the Jewish woman a thief, with a stereotypical pathology. The use of the word "kleptomania" also calls attention to the protagonists' thievery and suggests that it is something they have in common with their Jewish hosts. Additionally, the pathology feminizes them (as does their later cross-dressing), a gendering they share with male Jews in both this film (for example, Samuel the bookkeeper) and Central European discourses more broadly.[82] Jews and Aryans react similarly to Robert and Bertram's disruptions of their festivities—the wedding, the costume ball, and the fair. This is highlighted cinematographically: "All three scenes are characterized by rapid editing (twelve to eighteen shots in quick succession), a mobile camera at the center of the crowd, and a narrow, contained mise en scène filled with many obstacles. Even the shot of a screaming Jewish girl followed by a close-up of a screeching parrot finds its complement in the shot of an irate Aryan crowd followed by a close-up of a frenzied monkey."[83]

Robert and Bertram's "Jewishness," however, is neither mocked like the Ipelmeyers' nor rendered uncomfortable like Biedermeyer's. These characters' portrayal is very sympathetic. As the protagonists, they are spectators' primary point of identification. They are good natured, (sometimes) funny, and the film's main source of entertainment through both their humorous entanglements and their musical numbers. Robert and Bertram's skills as tricksters and con men and their repeated acts of disguise and deception are a part of their humorous appeal. For this, they rely on dramatic irony, incongruity, and the gap between appearance and essence as comic elements, as theorized by Graff, and as are central to *Verwechslungskomödien* and to German humor, according to Kadner. Robert and Bertram sneak out of prison, fool the constables looking for them, pose as nobility, and defraud the Ipelmeyers. Dressed as women, they attract the attentions of the same prison superintendent who mistakenly let them go in the first place. Confusion about identity is displaced in a pleasurable way from the Jewish characters onto the protagonists, who repeatedly disguise themselves from others. Schulte-Sasse points out that Robert and Bertram's Jewish coding contributes to the film's pleasurable effects. She concludes that "the 'fun' of *Robert and Bertram* lies in the fantasy of reversing *Jew Süss*, allowing 'Aryan' figures to invade 'Jewish' space and make the Jew laughingly visible. Robert and Bertram beat the Jew at his own game, not only by moving in on him and causing upheaval, but by satirizing 'Jewish' masquerade themselves."[84] While pleasurable, this displacement of deception, disguise, and unclear identity onto Robert and Bertram is also ambivalent, for, as O'Brien asks, "Are the Aryans outwitting the Jews at their own game, or is this merely another example of how the Aryan and the Jew resemble each other?"[85]

There are several essential differences between Aryan and Jew in *Robert und Bertram*'s depictions of masking and (mis)recognition. Robert and Bertram are good at imposture, unlike the Ipelmeyers and their guests, and they trick the Ipelmeyers successfully. The protracted banter with the constables shows that their wit serves admirably as a good disguise, even from discerning non-Jews, whose job is to catch crooks. Initially charmed by witty repartee and clever excuses, the constables eventually determine that Robert and Bertram must be the fugitives they seek. Prison Superintendent Strambach (Fritz Kampers) is too slow to stop their jailbreak. Later, at a fair, he lustily flirts with what he takes to be hearty womenfolk and only recognizes that they are Robert and Bertram in disguise when another woman snatches Bertram's bonnet. Robert and Bertram's ability to pass can be interpreted as the difference between non-Jewish and Jewish performance, or between mimesis and masquerade. According to Sieg, from the Enlightenment through the Nazi era, mimesis was theorized as a privilege of "Christian, male, heterosexual bodies," in contrast to Jewish masquerade or mimicry, which attempts mimesis, yet fails to reproduce its object convincingly.[86] Another important distinction between Robert and Bertram's deceiving the Ipelmeyers and their other acts of criminal deception is that the duping of Jews is not seen to be a crime by God or the government. The king forgives them, and when they ascend in a hot-air balloon, the pearly gates open to let Robert and Bertram in to heaven. The non-Jewish protagonists, Robert and Bertram, exploit the pleasures of disguise, deception, and misrecognition central to mistaken-identity comedies. The film distinguishes between the Jewish and non-Jewish variations of these Jewish-coded traits in terms of their mimetic success and their larger social and communal functions. Money and self-enrichment are inappropriate goals, whereas gratitude, helping others, and rescuing non-Jews from Jewish intrigue redeem behavior that might otherwise be coded as Jewish.

Robert and Bertram's ambivalent representation of Jews construes them as the same as and different from Aryans, as alternately funny and feared. It also takes an ambivalent attitude toward their performed inclination to deceive—either almost undetectable or laughably obvious, it can be trumped by the actions of the film's Aryan protagonists. Yet, even while stimulating anxieties, *Robert and Bertram,* via its comedy and displacement, tells the viewer that there is little to worry about. Although they may be taken in temporarily, Aryans in the film are not as naive and gullible as the girls in the *Film Kurier* story. Also, some non-Jews have the wherewithal to best the Jews at their own games. Thus, while *Robert and Bertram* raises and allays some anxieties about Jewish assimilation, the dissolution of identities, and the masked Jew, it also reveals the limitations of comedy, with its inherent ambivalence, as a vehicle of unequivocal antisemitic messages. The comic mode lends itself much better to inferential antisemitism and to the indirect treatment of anxieties around identity, a role filled by the Third Reich's many *Verwechslungskomödien*.

Humorous Displacement: *Verwechslungskomödien* and Jewish Difference

The central figures and narratives of *Verwechslungskomödien* offer filmmakers a ready-made suite of common comic elements—irony, incongruity, performance, and misperception, among others. With spectators positioned as witnesses with shifting knowledge and identifications, these elements, particularly in conjunction with one another, are ambiguous and frequently ambivalent. They make *Verwechslungskomödien* well suited to infinite variations and multiple cultural and political contexts. The mistaken identity comedy is by no means in and of itself antisemitic, nor is, necessarily, the related motif of the Jew who passes as a non-Jew.

The renowned Hollywood anti-Nazi films *The Great Dictator* (Chaplin, 1940) and *To Be or Not to Be* (Lubitsch, 1942) are both mistaken identity comedies that engage and problematize Jewish difference in order to criticize Hitler and the Third Reich. *The Great Dictator* and *To Be or Not to Be* stage two major preoccupations of Third Reich film to anti-Nazi ends: like the Nazi propaganda they seek to refute, these films ask whether there are differences between Germans and Jews and how viewers can know what those differences are, when they cannot be seen. In *The Great Dictator*, a Jewish barber with a toothbrush mustache is mistaken for an antisemitic megalomaniac dictator named Adenoid Hynkel (both played by Chaplin). In *To Be or Not to Be*, members of a theater troupe in Nazi-occupied Poland disguise themselves as Nazis to save themselves and help the resistance. These comedies use mistaken identity narratives and central figures who pass to exploit the glaring paradox central to Nazi antisemitic propaganda: Jews were despised, different, subhuman; at the same time, they were difficult to identify. Chaplin's and Lubitsch's comedies stage confusion between the Jewish and the non-Jewish to challenge the Nazis' claim that Germans and Jews are fundamentally different and to insist that the individuals in both groups are, ultimately, human, and equal to one another—a parity marked by visual likeness.

Chaplin's and Lubitsch's films emphasize visual similarities between Nazis and Jews not only to mock Nazis as buffoons, but also to challenge Nazi racial antisemitism. These Hollywood productions imply that the lack of visible differences between "Aryans" and those they oppress means that any differences between Jews and non-Jews are social rather than biological, performed rather than essential. This message is punctuated at the end of *To Be or Not To Be* with a modified version of Shylock's monologue from William Shakespeare's *The Merchant of Venice*, delivered by Greenberg (Felix Bressart), a Jewish member of the theater company resisting the Nazis. Shylock's speech insists that both Jews and Christians are human organisms. *To Be or Not To Be* removes the words "Jew" and "Christian," using "we" instead, in a way that linguistically dissolves such religious distinctions and he puts this speech in the mouth of an angry Jewish Pole confronting a fake Polish Hitler in front of Nazi soldiers who believe this Hitler to be real. Greenberg's recitation of Shylock's monologue in this scene points to the biological, human kinship between Jews and Germans as well as the injustice of Nazi antisemitism: "Aren't we human? Have we not eyes? Have we not hands, organs, senses, dimensions, affections, passions, fed with the same food, hurt with the same weapons, subject to the same diseases, healed by the same means, cooled and warmed by the same winter and summer? If you prick us, do we not bleed? If you tickle us, do we not laugh? If you poison us, do we not die? If you wrong us, shall we not revenge?"[87] The earnest caesura in *To Be or Not to Be* created by Greenberg's monologue emphasizes a message that otherwise Lubitsch's film delivers via comedy and mistaken-identity gags, that there is no essential difference between Jew and non-Jew, and that the distinctions made by the Nazis are arbitrary and cruel. Chaplin makes a similar point with his dual performance in *The Great Dictator*, reinforcing it with his famous antifascist speech at the close of the film.

Third Reich *Verwechslungskomödien* deploy similar motifs in a different cultural context. They react to perceived shifts that took place in Germany in the early twentieth century and in the Weimar Republic: a putative social and cultural homogenization caused by mass production and mass culture, including film, increased class mobility, changing gender roles, Jewish assimilation, and social and cultural shifts associated with political change. Comedy, because it invests such disjunctions with pleasure, became a privileged way to address them. *Verwechslungskomödien* destabilize central figures' identities by having them appear to others in the film as something or someone other than what the audience knows them to be. Ultimately, the "truth" is revealed, social order seems to be restored, and identity seems to be fixed in place with a happy ending. Yet, after the pleasures of sustained transgressions, the pat narrative resolutions typical of *Verwechslungskomödien* do not necessarily uphold traditional configurations of identities.

Verwechslungskomödien stage the dissolution of the boundaries between social identities and in doing so reshape these identities and redraw the boundaries between them.[88] This is similar to what we see in *Robert und Bertram*, which highlights Jewish-coded propensities for deceptions and disguise and uses stereotypes to promote illusions of Jewish difference, even as its comic strategies emphasize similarities between Germans and Jews.

Third Reich *Verwechslungskomödien* express, exploit, and assuage anxieties that traditional identities could no longer be recognized in their established forms and perhaps no longer existed. *Blume* blurs and manipulates the boundary between white and nonwhite in a way that challenges the boundary between the Jewish and the non-Jewish. *Viktor und Viktoria* and *Capriccio* trouble traditional gender roles in order to update them for the contemporary political context.[89] *Glückskinder, April! April!, Umwege des schönen Karl, Kleider machen Leute*, and dozens of other films like them enact the dissolution of class distinctions and seek a harmonious post-class social order—the fantasy of the *Volksgemeinschaft*.

Verwechslungskomödien use identity's fluidity and the difficulty in determining identity through visual cues as basis for comedy. The humorous perspective of the *Verwechslungskomödie* invests the dissolution of identity with pleasure, even as it cues spectators to keep their eyes open for deception. The anxiety around the instability of identity that was characteristic of German modernity and of Third Reich film was cathected onto Jewish people.[90] The concept of the masked Jew is a particularly dense locus of this anxiety. The many *Verwechslungskomödien* made in the Third Reich and the anxieties and pleasures they express are connected, albeit indirectly, to this particular antisemitic preoccupation. The central trope of this obsession, the figure of the masked Jew, exploits a similar gap to the *Verwechslungskomödie* between inside and outside, appearance and essence. In face of the masked or assimilating Jew, as antisemitic voices would have it, Germans must avoid becoming dupes. As Third Reich film comedy imagined it, the *Volksgemeinschaft* should notice Jewish difference and laugh.

Notes

1. Herf, *Jewish Enemy*, 5.
2. Urwand, *Collaboration*, 204.
3. Baranowski, *Nazi Empire*, 325.
4. See Herf, *Jewish Enemy*.

5. Wallach, *Passing Illusions*, 129–30.
6. Cf. Herf, *Jewish Enemy*, 151.
7. Herf, *Jewish Enemy*, 7.
8. Hake, *Popular Cinema*, 13. See also Witte, *Lachende Erben*.
9. Herzog, "How 'Jewish' is German Sexuality?" 186.
10. Witte, *Lachende Erben*, 46. Moeller, *Der Filmminister*, 163.
11. Witte, "Die Filmkomödie im Dritten Reich," 352.
12. Albrecht, *Nationalsozialistische Filmpolitik*, 545–57. There were noticeable peaks in the production and release of *Verwechslungkomödien* in 1933, 1937, and 1944, and a dip in 1941–42.
13. Weinstein, "Third Reich Film Comedy," 85–104.
14. On the triangulation of passing, dupes, and witnesses, see Robinson, "It Takes One to Know One," 715–36; Loentz, "Literary Double Life," 130.
15. Graff, "Was ist komisch?" 1.
16. "'Komisch' ist jede Erkenntnis eines Mißverhältnisses zwischen Sein und Schein, Anspruch und Leistung, Begriff und Realität. Mit einem Wort: Komisch ist jede 'Inkongruenz'. Komisch ist alles, was sich nicht restlos 'deckt', was nicht vollkommen 'übereinstimmt.'" Graff, "Was ist komisch?" 2.
17. Morreall, "Philosophy of Humor."
18. See pages 44, 140–41.
19. Kadner, *Rasse*, 19, 37–41, passim.
20. "Es kommt häufig genug vor, daß dem äußeren Erscheinungsbild die seelische Beschaffenheit nicht entspricht, daß in einer ostischen Hülle z.B. ein fälischer Mensch steckt und umgekehrt, ja selbst daß eine, wenigstens auf den ersten Blick nordische wirkende Erscheinung zu einem Juden gehört." Kadner, *Rasse*, 2nd ed., 32.
21. Sieg, *Ethnic Drag*, 39–40, 47.
22. Goebbels and Mjölnir [Hans Schweitzer], *Die verfluchten Hakenkreuzler*, 17. Mjölinir was "the leading Nazi poster artist in the 1920s" and became the "Reich representative for the creation of artistic form" in 1936. Herf, *The Jewish Enemy*, 29. The motif of masking and unmasking was part of broader discourses of Jewish difference in the Weimar republic, not limited to antisemites. Wallach, *Passing Illusions*, 135–36.
23. Goebbels and Mjölnir, *Die verfluchten Hakenkreuzler*, 17.
24. "Wie ist sowas nur möglich?" 2.
25. "Wie ist sowas nur möglich?" 2.
26. "Wie ist sowas nur möglich?" 2.
27. Szobar, "Telling Sexual Stories in the Nazi Courts," 146–47. The Nüremberg Laws were legislation passed in 1935 that used descent to determine who was Jewish and to deny them citizenship, the right to marry or have sexual relations with non-Jews, and other rights.
28. Cf. Karsten Witte's interpretation of this dissolve as a demasking of the Jew that masks the technologies of cinema: Witte, "Film im Nationalsozialismus," 149.
29. Schulte-Sasse, *Entertaining the Third Reich*, 66.
30. Weinstein, "Dissolving Boundaries," 508.
31. See Sieg, *Ethnic Drag*; also Silverman, *Becoming Austrians*, 71, 88–90.
32. *Robert und Bertram. Die lustigen Vagabonden* (Robert and Bertram, the Funny Vagabonds, Max Mack, 1915); *Robert und Bertram* (Rudolf Walther-Fein, 1928); *Robert und Bertram* (Hans Zerlett, 1939); *Robert und Bertram* (Hans Deppe [BRD], 1961).
33. Sieg, *Ethnic Drag*, 38.

34. Sieg, *Ethnic Drag*, 32, 34.
35. Jockisch, "Vagabunden seit 83 Jahren!" 8.
36. See also: O'Brien, *Nazi Cinema*, 38–39.
37. Schulte-Sasse, *Entertaining the Third Reich*, 239–40. O'Brien, *Nazi Cinema*, 40–41. O'Brien adds, however, that irony and parody of both types of culture may have partially undermined the distinction.
38. O'Brien, *Nazi Cinema*, 38.
39. On Jewish noses, see Gilman, *Jew's Body*, 179–93. Wallach, *Passing Illusions*, 38.
40. O'Brien, *Nazi Cinema*, 41–42.
41. O'Brien, *Nazi Cinema*, 42.
42. On feet, see Gilman, *Jew's Body*, 38–59. Also: Silverman, *Becoming Austrians*, 76.
43. Sieg, *Ethnic Drag*, 35. For a more extensive discussion of stereotypes of the Jewish voice, see Gilman, *Jew's Body*, 10–20.
44. Sieg, *Ethnic Drag*, 39.
45. Sieg, *Ethnic Drag*, 40.
46. "Wieso kennt ihr, dass ich bin der Herr Ipelmeyer?"
47. "Nu, wenn ich es nicht würde merken an der Aussprache, würde ich es merken an die verliebten Blicke, was Sie man werfen auf der Solotänzerin."
48. In the Weimar era, dark, curly, or frizzy hair had also been considered "signifiers of embodied Jewishness." Wallach, *Passing Illusions*, 47.
49. Gilman, *Difference and Pathology*, 18.
50. "Ungeheuer echt." Jerosch, "Aufnahmebeginn bei 'Robert und Bertram,'" 10.
51. "Eine verblüffend echte Karikatur." Martini, "Robert und Bertram," 3.
52. Cf. Kreimeier, "Antisemitismus im Nationalsozialistischen Film," 7. Enno Patalas quoted in Dammeyer, *Der Spielfilm im Dritten Reich*, 72. Kreimeier and Patalas both suggest that the "banal," "everyday" antisemitism in the representation of the Ipelmeyers could indirectly promote Nazi extermination strategies by linking them to a long, seemingly harmless comic tradition. Karsten Witte also sees *Robert und Bertram* as fomenting antisemitism that would lead to the Judeocide. Witte, *Lachende Erben*, 167.
53. For example: Advertisement for *Schuhpalast Pinkus*. Review of *Schuhpalast Pinkus*.
54. Weinstein, "Anti-Semitism or Jewish 'Camp'?" 101–21.
55. Silverman, *Becoming Austrians*, 72–79. Spector, "Modernism without Jews," 618. Wallach, *Passing Illusions*, 78–79.
56. Martini, "Robert und Bertram," 3.
57. Wallach, *Passing Illusions*, 158.
58. Herzberg, "Robert und Bertram/Ufa-Palast," 3.
59. Sieg, *Ethnic Drag*, 38–39.
60. Silverman, *Becoming Austrian*, 85, 79–87.
61. Herzberg, "Robert und Bertram/Ufa-Palast am Zoo," 3.
62. "So gut das jüdische Milieu . . . in seiner Lächerlichkeit gezeichnet ist, so sehr vermißt man einen einzigen sichtbaren Beweis der Gefährlichkeit des typischen Börsenjobbers." Schneider, "Robert und Bertram," 3.
63. Martini, "Robert und Bertram," 3.
64. "Eine[n] lästigen jüdischen Liebhaber." "Landstreicher im Himmel," 3.
65. "Hinterhältige[r] Freier." "Höchst unangenehm." "Robert und Bertram." *Paimann's Filmlisten*, 53; Jerosch, "Der Schritt zur Filmposse," 6.

66. "[Die] Maschen eines Gaunernetzes." "Die Machenschaften einer jüdischen Clique." Herzberg, "Robert und Bertram/Ufa-Palast," 3. "Heiterkeit und Spannung," *Der Film*, 28.

67. Herzberg, "Robert und Bertram/Ufa-Palast," 3.

68. Martini, "Robert und Bertram," 3; Schneider, "Robert und Bertram," 3.

69. Most scholars interpret Biedermeyer as a nefarious Jewish-influenced Aryan businessman, the type of character I analyze in chapter 5 of this book as a "white Jew." Examples of such an interpretation include Schulte-Sasse, *Entertaining the Third Reich*, 237; and Hollstein, *Jud Süss und die Deutschen*, 200.

One example of scholarship treating Biedermeyer as a Jew is: Rentschler, *Ministry*, 153.

70. The press uses the spelling "Biedermeier," but in the film, the spelling "Biedermeyer" appears on the letter from Ipelmeyer that Robert and Bertram find in Biedermeyer's (stolen) wallet. According to Schulte-Sasse, "meyer" is "the more common spelling for Jewish names." Schulte-Sasse, *Entertaining the Third Reich*, 237.

71. Jerosch, "Der Schritt zum Filmposse," 6.

72. Jerosch, "Der Schritt zum Filmposse," 6.

73. Schulte-Sasse, *Entertaining the Third Reich*, 242. See also O'Brien, *Nazi Cinema*, 37.

74. O'Brien, *Nazi Cinema*, 38. See also Schulte-Sasse, *Entertaining the Third Reich*, 235.

75. Schulte-Sasse, *Entertaining the Third Reich*, 237.

76. " . . . eine Verulkung jener Zeit, die wir – und andere vor uns auch – satirisch mit dem Worte 'Biedermeier' bezeichnen, und die mehr Meier als bieder war. Es ist die Zeit der grossen Judeneinwanderung in Deutschland, die Zeit der Mendelssohn und Meyerbeers, die damals anfingen mitteleuropäische 'Kultur' zu machen." Jerosch, "Aufnahmebeginn bei 'Robert und Bertram," 10. Jerosch probably is referring here to the composer Felix Mendelssohn-Bartholdy, who was from a Jewish family but was baptized Lutheran. The Mendelssohn name, however, also invokes the rest of the famous family, including Mendelssohn-Bartholdy's grandfather Moses Mendelssohn, who combined Jewish thought with the Enlightenment and was an advocate for assimilation and emancipation. Giacomo Meyerbeer (born Jakob Liebmann Meyer Beer) was a German opera composer of Jewish extraction who also worked in Italy and France. His success in Paris—coupled with Richard Wagner's lack of it—resulted in the latter's antisemitic tract on Jews and music.

77. For more on doubling and mirroring between Jew and non-Jew, see pages 223–24, 234.

78. O'Brien, *Nazi Cinema*, 39.

79. O'Brien, *Nazi Cinema*, 39. Schulte-Sasse, *Entertaining the Third Reich*, 239.

80. Witte, *Lachende Erben*, 166.

81. Silverman, *Becoming Austrians*, 82.

82. See: Gilman, *Difference and Pathology*; Silverman, *Becoming Austrians*.

83. O'Brien, *Nazi Cinema*, 39.

84. Schulte-Sasse, *Entertaining the Third Reich*, 239. See also: O'Brien, *Nazi Cinema*, 41–42.

85. O'Brien, *Nazi Cinema*, 41.

86. Sieg, *Ethnic Drag*, 12, 42–45.

87. Cf. William Shakespeare, *The Merchant of Venice*, Act 3, Scene 1, lines 49–56.

88. Weinstein, *Mistaken Identity*.

89. Weinstein, "Third Reich Film Comedy," 85–104.

90. Baumann, "Allosemitism," 149–50.

7

JEWISH ABSENCE, EPISTEMIC MURK, AND THE AESTHETICS OF CREMATION IN *MÜNCHHAUSEN* AND *DIE FEUERZANGENBOWLE*

IN A WELL-KNOWN ARTICLE BY THE SAME NAME, Karsten Witte asks, "How fascist is *The Punch Bowl*?"[1] His answer is that fascist ideology in *Die Feuerzangenbowle*, as in other Third Reich comedies, manifests not so much in the dialogue as in other structural and stylistic features.[2] In questioning the politics of *Feuerzangenbowle*, which, as described in the opening of this book, remains one of Germany's best loved classics, Witte's iconoclastic article proposed that "Nazi film comedies provide West German [television] stations a convenient way of sneaking propaganda fare from the Third Reich into their programs and putting it on parade, dressed up, so to speak, in civvies."[3] Witte did not write about potential connections between *Feuerzangenbowle* and Nazi antisemitism. Published in West Germany in 1976, his article was more than provocative enough without linking a national film treasure to the Holocaust. As a US scholar revisiting this film decades later, I occupy a historical and cultural space and have a set of analytical tools that enable me to answer the question that was, for Witte, unspeakable: what do *Feuerzangenbowle* and the other seemingly innocuous film comedies that he characterizes as "propaganda fare" have to do with Nazi antisemitism?

In this chapter, I explain a different type of relationship between Third Reich film comedy and Nazi antisemitism, namely comedy's escapist function during the Holocaust. Before the war, film comedies helped in imagining a non-Jewish Germanness and creating a *Volksgemeinschaft* purged of Jewishness. During the war, comedy also offered distraction and boosted morale. This chapter theorizes the type of escape wartime comedies offered. *Münchhausen* and *Feuerzangenbowle* are two of the most famous and successful comedies from this period. Despite their problematic historical origins, both films have remained popular. Here I argue that *Münchhausen* and *Feuerzangenbowle* were not only passively escapist in regards to the fate of Europe's Jews, but also actively so. By this I mean that these two films are not simply about something more innocent and distracting than the Holocaust. They cultivate ignorance and blindness, which were components of film comedy's larger escapist functions. Scholars have interrogated the implicit politics of both *Münchhausen* and *Feuerzangebowle*, but no one has discussed them as a pair or placed the Nazi Judeocide at the center of their analysis.[4] Revisiting these films with a focus on their relationship to the Holocaust allows me to explain their complicity in politically and culturally sustained blindness. Such blindness empowered many Germans to not know about the Holocaust, despite the evidence in front of their eyes. *Münchhausen* and *Feuerzangenbowle* actively steer the gaze away from what German people were doing to Jewish people by romanticizing not knowing, not looking, and human beings' dissolution into smoke. Neither *Münchhausen* nor *Feuerzangenbowle* is overtly or intentionally antisemitic. Nor is my primary interest in this chapter these films' occasional moments of disciplinary humor and inferential antisemitism. By the time *Münchhausen* and *Feuerzangenbowle* were released, the Nazis were murdering Jews on an unprecedented scale. The enormity of the Holocaust dwarfs these comedies' mild mockery of purportedly Jewish characteristics like intellectualism and greed.

Between Knowing and Not Knowing: Epistemic Murk and the Final Solution

Between early 1941, when planning for *Münchhausen* began, and early 1944, when *Feuerzangenbowle* was released, Germans systematically murdered millions of Jews. Massacres in Eastern Europe and deportations from Western and Central Europe were well underway by mid-1941. On January 20, 1942, top government officials met in Wannsee near Berlin to coordinate the logistics of what they called the "Final Solution," the extermination of the remaining Jewish people in Europe. That year, the mass murder of human beings in gas chambers began at Auschwitz-Birkenau, Belzec, Sobibor, Treblinka, and Maidanek. "By the end of 1942, an estimated four million of the roughly six million Jews who lost their lives during the Holocaust had already been killed."⁵ By mid-February 1943, "some 75 to 80 percent of Holocaust victims were already dead, and a mere 20 to 25 percent still clung to a precarious existence."⁶ The Nazi media did not report the gory details of the genocide to the German population, but they made no secret of the government's removal of Jewish people from German territories. On November 7, 1941, the Jewish Telegraphic Agency summarized news reports from Berlin that "the Nazi government is determined to make the Reich [unified Germany and Austria] 'entirely Judenrein' [Jew free] by April 1, 1942," a deadline they did not meet.⁷ Throughout 1943, Nazi officials openly proclaimed one jurisdiction after the next *Judenrein*.⁸ Already in 1941 and 1942, diary entries by Germans in different cities described rumors of mass shootings, deportations, and gassing of Jewish people.⁹ Even if they did not know the details of the genocide, members of the *Volksgemeinschaft* knew, at a minimum, that their Jewish neighbors had disappeared, deported by the Nazis to who-knows-where.

The Nazi news media released just enough information about the Judeocide to make Germans feel complicit in an unspoken, dirty secret.¹⁰ Jeffrey Herf's research shows that:

> during World War II anyone in Nazi Germany who regularly read a newspaper, listened to the radio, or walked past the Nazi political posters between 1941 and 1943 knew of the threats and boasts of the Nazi regime about intentions to exterminate European Jews, followed by public assertions that it was implementing that policy. Claims of ignorance regarding the murderous intentions and assertions of making good on such threats defy the evidence, logic, and common sense. With confidence we can say that millions and millions of Germans were told on many occasions that the Jews had begun a war to exterminate the Germans, but that the Nazi regime was exterminating the Jews instead.¹¹

The German press did not report the details of the Holocaust (nor did it report accurately on German casualties and defeats). Yet press reports, official rhetoric, omnipresent wall newspapers, and other propaganda asserted that the Jewish people needed to be destroyed, using words like "*Vernichtung* (extermination) and *Ausrottung* (annihilation)" noneuphemistically to refer "to a policy of mass murder."¹² According to Nicholas Stargardt:

> The media avoided inviting wide-ranging or open discussion of what was going on; yet at the same time, it provided a series of rhetorical justifications for extermination, and drip-fed innuendos which allowed people to connect the

abstract threats of Goebbels and Hitler with the specific details of mass executions that circulated privately. What was being created was a sense of "knowing without knowing," which did not invite any kind of public commitment, affirmation or feeling of moral responsibility; and it could work as long as no one broke the artificial limit on what could be said.[13]

A "small minority" of Germans were fanatical, genocidal antisemites, and Nazi propaganda built a "moderate, rather than genocidal" antisemitic consensus among the general population.[14] "The mixture of blunt speech and suppression of the facts was adequate to consolidate a 'covenant of gangsters,' while offering to the silent, indifferent, and uncurious majority a fig leaf of plausible deniability."[15]

Third Reich film comedy did not depict the Holocaust. Instead, it contributed to the silence regarding Germany's atrocities and to the general population's in-between state of "knowing without knowing." Goebbels conceived of propaganda in terms of an "orchestra principle," in which different media, genres, and works had discrete but complementary parts to play in a harmonious symphony.[16] During the war, newsreels, documentary shorts, the Tran and Helle series, radio, and the press tended to play the more propagandistic parts of the score, and feature films played mostly entertaining melodies. The war was good for the film business.[17] The larger audiences initially drawn in by newsreels returned for distraction, yielding returns that Goebbels called "real war profits."[18] Hollywood imports were banned in 1940. This resulted in both a larger market share for domestic productions and more thorough control over audiences' ideological and aesthetic diets. By 1941, the Nazi film industry was "truly dominant" in Europe and on solid financial footing; military conquests and "a vast pan-European infrastructure for the distribution and exhibition of German movies" expanded domestic and export markets.[19] In 1942, Goebbels fully nationalized and consolidated the remaining German production companies under Ufa (renamed Ufi) and ordered them to cut costs and churn out primarily entertainment films.[20] As the war progressed, other public entertainments were limited and Germans became avid moviegoers.[21] Following the Wehrmacht's pivotal defeats at El Alamein and Stalingrad in the winter of 1942–43, Third Reich cinema's popularity peaked. In a decade, cinema admissions had quadrupled, from roughly 250 million annually in 1933 to roughly one billion in 1943.[22] In that year Germans attended the cinema, on average, twenty times each.[23] Thirty-nine of the eighty-three productions that year (47%) were comedies.[24] As members of the *Volksgemeinschaft* sat together in the dark and laughed, there were many things that film comedy helped them not to see.

Film comedy helped create an indeterminate space between knowing and not knowing that enabled Germans to both accept and deny the extermination of the Jewish people. Klotz has argued convincingly that feature films spawned a "gray area that lies between the realms of 'knowing' and 'not knowing'" that upheld Nazi ideology, racial policy, and violence.[25] In this gray area, also shaped by the "the mixture of secrecy and blunt talk" that Herf and Stargardt describe, Germans could both tacitly consent to and deny Nazism's inconsistencies and atrocities.[26] To theorize this media-generated gray area between knowing and not knowing, Klotz draws on Taussig's notion of "epistemic murk," a discursive fluidity between fiction and truth in colonial situations, which enables colonial violence. According to Taussig, those in power control the "truth," which is infused with fiction; at the same time, they emphasize uncertainty and doubt, in conjunction with the truths they have produced, to generate fear and to justify domination of the oppressed.[27] Klotz analyzes how overtly racist colonial and antisemitic biopics rated politically valuable by Nazi censors created epistemic murk. She argues that *Jud Süss*, *Ohm Krüger*, and *Carl Peters* (Herbert Selpin, 1941) blend history and fiction and generate fear and doubt in service of Nazi racism, antisemitism, and colonialism.

Klotz's, Herf's, and Stargardt's work all emphasize the importance of a media-generated space between knowing and not knowing in situating the German public in relation to the Holocaust. Following Klotz's lead, I borrow Taussig's term "epistemic murk" to describe this space and argue that film comedy participated in carving it out. Propaganda Minister Goebbels held the entire media apparatus in his hand and assigned different media different roles. Nazi news sources—paper, radio, newsreels—posed as sources of truth, despite their omissions and fictions. Feature films blurred truth and fiction in auxiliary ways. It is in this sense that escapist film comedies helped generate epistemic murk. When it destabilized the boundary between fact and fiction, film comedy challenged audiences' ability to know and reinforced the state of knowing/not knowing about the Holocaust established by Nazi print media. It facilitated audiences' blindness to and mental escape from German war crimes.

Münchhausen and *Feuerzangenbowle* offer two variations on a multipronged strategy that surrounds Jewish disappearance with epistemic murk and both evokes and dismisses knowledge about the Holocaust. Engaging

Jewish difference and Jewish disappearance differently, both films blur the boundaries between fantasy and reality and aestheticize cremation, alternately romanticizing and obscuring the murder of Europe's Jews. According to *Münchhausen*, truth is hard to recognize and the eye can be deceived: you can never be certain what to believe. Staging the disappearance of a sinister magician coded as Jewish, *Münchhausen* construes Jewish disappearance as an illusion or cinematic trick that benefits the non-Jewish protagonist. Motifs of fire and smoke and repeated use of the cinematic dissolve allude to the Holocaust and imply that death is natural and cremation beautiful.

Like *Münchhausen*, *Feuerzangenbowle* is heavily engaged in the production of epistemic murk, although its connection to Jewishness is more abstract. In *Feuerzangenbowle*, Jewishness is a structuring absence, visible only obliquely through other types of lack. The film fosters uncertainty and apathy regarding that lack. *Feuerzangenbowle* depicts truth as subjective and malleable—it can become whatever you wish it to be—and concludes that neither truth nor individual lives matter. It celebrates the destruction of truth and the dissolution of the individual when, at the close, its protagonist dissolves into flame. *Feuerzangenbowle*'s nihilistic conclusion dismisses the truth or significance of everything outside the viewer's imagination, an everything that in 1944 included war and genocide.

In *Münchhausen* and *Feuerzangenbowle*, numerous strategies engender epistemic murk around the tropes of absence and Jewish disappearance. These films' whimsical approaches to illusion and reality highlight and disavow the disappearance of the Jewish from German culture and perpetuate discrete ways of both knowing and not knowing about this disappearance. Revealed and disavowed, mystified and romanticized, Jewish disappearance recedes into a cloud of smoke and uncertainty that enables blindness and deniability. These films' escapism, silences, the epistemic murk they create, and the ways in which they romanticize humans' combustion illustrate two different ways in which film comedy helped German people look away from the horrors the Nazi regime executed on their behalf.

Münchhausen

An extravagant early Agfacolor film meant to rival *The Wizard of Oz* (USA, 1939) and *The Thief of Bagdad* (UK, 1940), *Münchhausen* was produced to celebrate Ufa's twenty-fifth jubilee on March 3, 1943.[28] Goebbels authorized

Ufa to exceed usual budgets and hire whomever they wanted, including superstar Hans Albers and banned author/scriptwriter Erich Kästner.[29] The resulting film became one of the Third Reich's top ten moneymakers and has had many successful postwar revivals.[30] There was much fanfare at the premiere, which took place two nights after the worst bombing raid on Berlin to date and a month after the radio announcement of the defeat at Stalingrad.[31] Goebbels spoke and handed out awards to film industry luminaries. Ufa General Director Ludwig Klitzsch gave a speech about Ufa's history, which, in his revisionist account, had been "defenselessly exposed to Jewish and economically irresponsible powers" before the Nazis took over the film industry.[32] Klitzsch's speech "showed how exceedingly hard a few patriots had to fight against Jewish-American efforts at control of the German motion picture during *Systemzeit* (the Weimar Republic)."[33] Klitzsch framed *Münchhausen* as celebrating Ufa's triumph over Jewish domination. In his 1992 history of Ufa, Kreimeier highlights a number of noteworthy absences from Klitzsch's speech. He writes about the people who were erased that night from Ufa's past, such as Berlin residents killed or dislocated by the bombings and actors and filmmakers who resisted the regime. Among the missing were Jewish Ufa employees who had been driven into exile, suicide, concentration camps, and death.[34] Kreimeier asks whether any of the "illustrious guests at the Jubilee" noticed that their former colleagues were gone and implies that Jewish and non-Jewish Ufa employees had worked together too closely and that Jewish filmmakers had made too large of a contribution for their absence not to be felt.[35] Having helped build Ufa's pre-1933 successes, Jewish artists and technicians were not simply not there. Rather, the structuring absence created by their forced departure defined the triumphant Ufa celebrated by Klitzsch and Goebbels. *Münchhausen* both acknowledges and disavows this absence.

Münchhausen depicts Jewish disappearance within an epistemological gray zone, in which a protagonist with eternal youth blurs the boundaries between truth and lie, between knowing and not knowing, and between fantasy and reality, and finally dissolves into a puff of smoke. In other words, it creates epistemic murk around Jewish disappearance and romanticizes smoky death. Based on the tales of the so-called "lying baron," Karl Friedrich Hieronymus Baron Münchhausen, collected and expanded by Rudolf Erich Raspe and later Gottfried August Bürger, *Münchhausen* takes its protagonist and its viewers on fantastic adventures: from eighteenth- to twentieth-century Braunschweig, the baron's ancestral home, to Catherine the Great's Russia; from the Ottoman sultan's palace, to Casanova's Venice; and to the moon and back. *Münchhausen* blends fictional and factual places and people, weaving them into narratives presumed to be lies. *Münchhausen* produces pleasure by confounding fiction and reality as people go up in smoke.

To create epistemic murk in support of racial domination and violence, the oppressor must both control the truth and undermine the audience's confidence in its own ability to ascertain the truth. The Nazi film program split this task. After the newsreel and the *Kulturfilm* propagated "truths" trafficked by the Nazi regime, feature films like *Münchhausen* and *Feuerzangenbowle* questioned knowledge and perception. If audiences were suspicious of the "fake news" (to use today's term) presented in the Nazi newsreels—and evidence suggests that they were—the feature film complemented that uncertainty by celebrating how nobody can ever be certain about what is really true anyway.[36] Within the epistemic murk that it creates, *Münchhausen* raises and dismisses the specter of Jewish disappearance and aestheticizes and trivializes the human body's dissolving into smoke.

Epistemological Framemurk

Münchhausen's cultural and narrative frameworks position spectators as always already uncertain about what they know. Prior knowledge of the Münchhausen figure establishes viewer expectations of a series of tall tales. A frame narrative introduces the storyteller/protagonist, disguised as his own descendant, preparing to tell his implausible story to a young couple. This frame reinforces the epistemological uncertainty inherent in legends of the lying baron. It begins with an eighteenth-century portrait of Baron Münchhausen (Albers) winking complicitly at the viewer. One of numerous self-reflexive moments in the film, the shot of the winking portrait foregrounds the magical effects of film technologies and their ability to make images move.[37] In addition to reveling in its own fictitiousness and demanding audience members' passive complicity, this opening shot introduces several important guidelines: not all is what it seems; objects and people will not behave as expected; and the film's playful approach will mix life, representation, and illusion in unexpected ways. The first full scene, a masquerade ball on the baron's estate, sustains these sentiments. Elaborate costumes and baroque decor trick viewers into thinking the film begins in the eighteenth century. When, roughly seven minutes in to the film, the baron reaches for an electric light switch, it jostles the audience into recognizing that the setting is Nazi Germany (viewers soon see a Nazi flag on a car parked outside). Smeared makeup exposes the baron's exotically clad black servant as a white actor in blackface.[38] The baron himself, however, isn't in disguise. The costume ball masks his true guise as the eighteenth-century baron. These revelations remind viewers how difficult it is to distinguish truth from lie, a concept central to the film.

Not only narrative, costume, and character, but also *Münchhausen*'s genre and technology establish favorable conditions for epistemic murk. A fantasy in the comic mode, or a fantastic comedy (and either way, unique in Nazi Germany), *Münchhausen* asks viewers to suspend disbelief, accept magic, and ignore the boundaries between reality and illusion. Cinematic technologies in *Münchhausen* assist in this task, helping create a space between knowing and not knowing. A dissolve from the baron's face to the cover of *The Wonderful Journeys and Adventures of Baron Münchhausen* is one of many effects that connect and confound past and present, truth and lie. It equates Baron Münchhausen, about to tell his own story, with the book, construing him as both storyteller and character in his own fiction. The visual "lie" of special effects created by Konstantin Irmen-Tschet, who had worked on *Metropolis* (Fritz Lang, 1925/26), *Viktor and Viktoria*, and *Glückskinder*, among other films, reinforces the "lie" of narration.[39] *Münchhausen*'s trick shots took ten months to stage and edit and were more elaborate than any German use of special effects since the silent era.[40] They conflate fantasy and reality by making the impossible appear possible and the imagined real. When Münchhausen's servant Kuchenreutter (Hermann Speelmans) and his son smear special hair-growing salve on their faces, giant mustaches sprout. A jacket bitten by a rabid dog infects a wardrobe full of clothing, which begins to bark and fly around the room threateningly until shot. Verbal and technological falsehoods make fantasy appear to be real. Thanks to special effects, the audience witnesses the impossible—notes frozen into some bugles defrost, and the horns dance and play madly until crushed; the legs of the fastest man in the world fly in a blur of speed; and Münchhausen rides a cannonball into a Turkish encampment. Woven in with recognizable historical figures and dates, these events are construed as part of history, although they are as implausible as Kuchenreutter's rifle, which enables users to see for leagues, aided by the not-very-special effect of close-ups and reverse-shot editing. The special effects in *Münchhausen* detach seeing from knowing: the eye is easily deceived, with the result that all narrative and all events witnessed are suspect, including the disappearance of the Jewish, envisioned near the middle of the film.

Disavowing Jewish Disappearance

The prime locus of Jewish difference in *Münchhausen* and the center of the film's fetishistic disavowal of Jewish disappearance is the magician Cagliostro (Ferdinand Marian), a character based loosely on a historical Freemason, alchemist, and accused swindler. To summarize briefly what Rentschler and Schulte-Sasse have each detailed previously: Cagliostro's shady appearance and behavior, his sinister ambitions, his comments about his profile being unsuitable to appear on currency, and Münchhausen's characterization of him as a usurer all code him as Jewish.[41] The casting of Ferdinand Marian, who played Jew Süss, anchors this character's Jewish coding. Marian frequently played "the Third Reich's prototypical racial others and screen villains. His Austrian accent, dark hair and eyes, and heavy features facilitated his casting as all-purpose alien."[42] The caterwauling of a black cat announces Cagliostro's entrance into the film, and Kuchenreutter calls him an "uncanny crook." The black cat, its repulsed reaction, and Kuchenreutter's use of the word "uncanny" cast Cagliostro as demonic and his powers as dark magic, referencing historical discourses and licensing antisemitic inferences that link Jews, the devil, and dark magic. Mysterious symbols on Cagliostro's wall in St. Petersburg resemble Hebrew or Cyrillic letters, evoking types of racial and cultural alterity that the Nazis considered inferior and alluding to the perceived threat of a secret Jewish language.[43] (See Figure 7.1.)

A "Jewish" illusionist, Cagliostro uses magic to manipulate his surroundings. He has an uncanny ability to hear things said when he is absent. With the tap of his glass on the side of a pitcher, he can transfer wine from one vessel to the other. With the snap of his fingers or a simple hand gesture, he can conjure violin music out of thin air or reposition a reclining nude in a painting for a frontal rather than a rear view. Cagliostro's invisible Jewish power is both magical and political. In an obvious allusion to Nazi tropes of the Jewish wire puller, Cagliostro proposes that he and Münchhausen take over Courland and together become king, with Münchhausen's face and lineage in the foreground and Cagliostro behind the throne. Cagliostro is also coded as Jewish through tropes of crime, moneymaking, and usury—which had been considered Jewish and sinful in Christian Europe for centuries. Münchhausen claims the "dumb" of the world need Cagliostro, because "he lends them his imagination, at usurious rates, of course," and Kuchenreutter's description of Cagliostro as a "crook" (*Gauner*) has antisemitic connotations.[44]

In its representation of Cagliostro, *Münchhausen* codes deception and illusion as Jewish. Yet special effects, lies, and illusions are sources of visual and comic pleasure and strongly associated with the protagonist. Both Rentschler and Schulte-Sasse describe Cagliostro as Münchhausen's *Doppelgänger*, the dark side of the baron's mastery of time, space, and illusion.[45] Münchhausen has multiple "Jewish" features.[46] Like the Jew of antisemitic fantasy, he is an omnipresent power who masters space, time, and narrative and seduces beautiful women. Individualistic, mysterious, and powerful, he controls his own image and others' gazes. He tricks and defeats his rivals and superiors.[47] Like his Jewish counterpart, Cagliostro, Münchhausen is "a shape-shifter and nomad."[48] To translate these traits into well-known antisemitic tropes: Münchhausen resembles the masked Jew and the wandering Jew, emphasizing the ubiquity and invisibility of Jewish influence.

However, as strongly as Marian's physical appearance and star persona code Cagliostro as Jewish, Albers's appearance and persona code Münchhausen as non-Jewish. The blond-haired, blue-eyed Albers embodied Nazi Germany's masculine ideals and, as Rentschler aptly describes, "is the closest one comes to a Siegfried among the Third Reich's male leads."[49] Agfacolor emphasized Albers's racialized appearance, because, as Albers quipped in an interview, "now eyes really will appear blue and hair really blond."[50] The two characters operate within different value systems, Jewish and non-Jewish, which becomes evident when Münchhausen refuses to help Cagliostro conquer Courland. Whereas Cagliostro wants money and power, Münchhausen seeks entertainment and adventure.[51] He is the epitome of the roguish hero of Nordic humor, theorized by Kadner.[52] Cagliostro's methods of getting what he wants are more ominous than Münchhausen's. The former uses dark magic, and the latter, imagination and storytelling. This binary too relies on tropes of Jewish difference. As discussed in chapter 1, antisemites construed Jewish forces as destructive and sinister and non-Jewish, Aryan forces as creative. Just as the Aryan hero turns "Jewish" fraud into colonial triumphs in *Donogoo Tonka* (see chapter 5), the non-Jewish Münchhausen converts dark "Jewish" magic into humorous escapades. The mastery over youth and illusion that Cagliostro gives Münchhausen is an allegory for the transfer of Ufa's magic from

Jewish influence to non-Jewish control.[53] Because of his non-Jewish values and coding, Münchhausen's "Jewish" powers lead to conquests presented as whimsical adventure rather than sinister world domination, as he bests Russian, Turkish, and Italian adversaries portrayed as his physical, intellectual, and moral inferiors.

By depicting Cagliostro as his dangerous, magical double, the protagonist/narrator justifies the former's elimination from the narrative and his own subsequent use of Cagliostro's power. A look at mechanisms of epistemic murk in a colonial context—a related form of racialized othering—is illustrative here. Münchhausen's account of Cagliostro deploys the same "magic of mimesis [that] lies in the transformation wrought on reality by rendering its image," which colonists use to create epistemic murk and justify their own violence.[54] Taussig construes storytelling as a form of magic that transforms reality.[55] He describes a mimetic relationship between the "magic" and "savagery" that colonial storytellers attribute to indigenous peoples and the "magic" of colonial storytelling and "savagery" of colonial violence. Indigenous people's purported "magic" and "savagery" are a reflection of the colonists' real storytelling "magic" and violent "savagery." Colonial storytelling transforms the indigenous Other into a violent and magical savage. The results of this magical transformation justify colonists' own savage violence against indigenous peoples. The doubling in *Münchhausen* works similarly. *Münchhausen* celebrates the non-Jewish protagonist's creative powers of storytelling and demonizes Cagliostro's magical powers. In doing so, it self-reflexively celebrates Ufa's newly non-Jewish creative powers and, perhaps, surreptitiously criticizes a regime and worldview built on lies.[56] Immediately after Cagliostro's disappearance, the baron's twentieth-century interlocutors question the protagonist's veracity. The lying baron's version of history features a dark reflection of himself. His tale discredits his Jewish *Doppelgänger* and justifies his own actions. Like colonial narratives that depict the colonized as magical savages, displacing the colonizers' characteristics onto them and using that displacement to justify colonial violence and expropriation, the lying baron's account of Cagliostro demonizes and submits him to the symbolic violence of erasure when, chased by the czarina's secret service, he vanishes permanently from the film. Münchhausen profits from his *Doppelgänger*'s disappearance, inheriting a golden ring and magical powers that lead him triumphantly through colorful adventures.

The scene in which the Jewish Cagliostro disappears both hints at and disavows what Germany was doing to Europe's Jews. This scene stages Jewish disappearance surrounded by smoke and flame. At the same time, however, it construes this disappearance as willful, symptomatic of Cagliostro's continuing dark and manipulative powers, and a boon to the German protagonist. Cagliostro's disappearance is framed as *both* illusory *and* beneficial. Under the pretense of needing a wound treated, Münchhausen visits Cagliostro in St. Petersburg to warn him about his impending arrest. In thanks, Cagliostro gives Münchhausen an invisibility ring and fulfills his wish to remain young as long as he desires. The czarina's soldiers arrive immediately after the puff of smoke that results from Cagliostro's granting Münchhausen's wish. When told he is under arrest, Cagliostro laughs, approaches Münchhausen, takes a ring out of his pocket, admires it, and puts it on. A slow dissolve takes Cagliostro from opaque, to transparent, to nothingness, as he asks Münchhausen to greet Catherine the Great for him (Figure 7.1). Münchausen studies his own ring. In the guards' ensuing confusion, two fly to the side as if pushed by an imaginary force. The door opens and shuts, and we hear Cagliostro's menacing laughter as the screen fades to black. A flame fills the center of the dark screen. We hear the sound of someone blowing it out, and the scene brightens to a close up of the twentieth-century baron lighting a cigar, his face partially masked by its smoke.

The sequence described above stages the disappearance of Jewishness in an oblique way that primarily obscures and justifies the Holocaust. This scene indirectly shifts responsibility for Jewish disappearance from the German hero onto the Jewish antagonist himself and recasts that disappearance as self-serving. Although Münchhausen dislikes Cagliostro, he warns him that the police are after him, giving Cagliostro the opportunity to escape and absolving himself of any complicity in Cagliostro's potential arrest. Cagliostro needs to flee and his disappearance is construed as a deception rather than a real absence: Cagliostro's disappearance fools the police, is explained diegetically as a magic trick, and is created using recognizable trick cinematography. The trick cinematography used to make Cagliostro's body disappear is a dissolve from a shot of him and Münchhausen to an identically composed shot with Münchhausen standing alone (Figure 7.1). While many of *Münchhausen*'s special effects were "state-of-the-art wizardry" in 1943, Cagliostro's disappearance was not.[57] It relied

Figure 7.1. The magical disappearance of the Jew. Ferdinand Marian and Hans Albers in *Münchhausen* (1942/43). Screenshot.

on a long-established cinematic technique, the dissolve. The dissolve was an old technology, used by Georges Méliès as early as 1899 to join multishot films.[58] Its use in trick filmmaking for disappearances and metamorphoses predates the standardization of classical editing conventions around 1917 by more than a decade.[59] The dissolve was also a familiar and characteristic trope of Nazi cinema, used to search for origins and authenticity, as in *Jud Süss* and *Der ewige Jude*, to regress historically and socially, as in *Feuerzangenbowle*, and to enhance cinema's illusions, as in *Münchhausen*.[60] By staging Cagliostro's disappearance narratively and cinematographically as a trick, *Münchhausen* suggests that Jewish disappearance is all smoke and mirrors. Jewish disappearance is a clever, self-interested illusion, and the Jewish remains an invisible lingering threat.

Although Cagliostro vanishes and does not appear again, the disappearance scene indicates that he remains a dangerous force, alluding to the ominous, behind-the-scenes Jewish power that Nazis invoked in other contexts to justify the elimination of Europe's Jews. Cagliostro's conversation with Münchhausen, disdain for the police, and triumphant, sinister laughter emphasize that his illusory disappearance is willful and temporary. He is not really gone. Viewers know that the invisibility ring Cagliostro gave Münchhausen works for only an hour and can infer that the one he uses himself has similarly limited powers. The sound of Cagliostro's voice, even when he is not visible, broadcasts the character's lingering presence. The guards who lunge out of the way as if pushed and the opening and shutting of the door appear to be an effect of Cagliostro's continuing embodiment and strength. The disappearance scene suggests that the Jewish-coded Cagliostro remains a threat and that his disappearance is an illusion he created in order to escape the police.

Cagliostro's disappearance scene depicts this Jewish-coded character as tricky and dangerous and, although invisible, not really gone. It suggests that Jewish disappearance is impermanent and inadequate. In so reframing Jewish disappearance, *Münchhausen* muddles viewers' perspective on what was really going on with Europe's disappearing Jews. At the same time, however, an allusion to the Holocaust is buried in the transition from this scene to the next, even as diegetic logic encourages viewers to understand the two scenes as separate. At the end of the disappearance scene, Cagliostro vanishes before the audience's eyes, his body dissolving into nothingness. Blackness, fire, and smoke replace his image and voice. The smoke and fire are not narratively, spatially, or temporally part of Cagliostro's disappearance from his St. Petersburg apartment. Yet the editing from blackness to the close up of a flame provides no establishing shot or clarifying sound cue to orient viewers. It delays explanation for the fire, smoke, and puffing sound until after Münchhausen's face appears and the audience can see that he is dressed in his twentieth-century clothes and lighting a cigar. In those seconds of disorientation, the audience must struggle to figure out what is going on. In the midst of the uncertainty it creates, the montage connects Jewish disappearance with burning. In so doing, *Münchhausen* references what audiences both did and did not know about their Jewish neighbors. Europe's Jews were disappearing. The editing of this confusing transition enables viewers *either* to conclude that Jewish manipulators have faked their own disappearance and remain an invisible threat *or* to make the cognitive jump needed to infer that Jewish people were being blotted out and consumed in flame. The ambiguity and ambivalence around Cagliostro's disappearance promote epistemic murk around the contemporaneous disappearance of Jewish people from German-occupied Europe.

The Aesthetics of Cremation

In addition to creating epistemic murk around Jewish disappearance and both justifying and disavowing the elimination of the Jewish, *Münchhausen* romanticizes death and combustion. In 1874, with regenerative furnaces developed for glassmaking, Friedrich Siemens resurrected the practice of cremation in Germany, which Charlemagne had banned as unchristian in the late eighth century. Inspired by the new technology, reformers in Wilhelmine and Weimar Germany agitated to replace burial with cremation on "hygienic and economic as well as aesthetic and ideological grounds."[61] Challenging both Christian and Jewish traditions prohibiting cremation, these reformers romanticized the return of human bodies to nature as ash, representing "a peaceful state of unity and holistic integration."[62] Simone Ameskamp describes how "metaphors and images employed in poems, songs, and declarations stemmed from the realm of nature, in particular the four elements and above all fire. The flames freed the spirit—*Geist*—from its mortal remains to return to its source."[63] The Nazis turned the cremation movement to their own ends, infusing it with *völkisch* nationalism, legalizing and regulating cremation on a national level, and deploying the same technologies to dispose of the victims of mass murder at concentration and death camps.[64]

Münchhausen advances an aestheticized, romantic view of cremation consistent with modern German cremationists and with National Socialism. Scenes in which characters die and dissolve into smoke simultaneously entice viewers to acknowledge what was going on in gas chambers and crematoria and cloud their vision by picturing smoke as part of a beautiful death. One example of how *Münchhausen* aestheticizes cremation is the scene on the moon when Münchhausen's valet and friend Kuchenreutter dies. Having escaped from Venice in a hot air balloon, the baron and his valet land on the moon and soon observe in the ripening of cherry trees and the rapid changing of the seasons that on the moon a year passes each day, a fanciful interpretation of theories of time and space, such as the Copernican rotation of the planets or Einstein's theory of relativity, though Nazis rejected Einstein's work.[65] In the course of minutes, Kuchenreutter's hair whitens, his face ages, and he succumbs to old age and death, dissolving into a puff of smoke as the moon people do. Kuchenreutter's death scene posits that despite their relationships with one another, humans are insignificant relative to the rest of the universe. In contrast to Münchhausen, who expresses love, regret, and grief when Kuchenreutter dies, the moon people are nonplussed by Kuchenreutter's passing. When the moon man caring for the gourds out of which moon young are born matter-of-factly tells his wife's portable head that the old earthling is dying, she responds in a cold voice, "Yes, carry me away." These comments, of course, come from people who grow on trees, have detachable bodies, and enjoy a life span of days. In this universal context, Kuchenreutter and his death are ordinary. This scene illustrates the baron's "Copernican" worldview that the individual is insignificant in the universe, a philosophy that he expounds when speaking to his guests. Münchhausen's so-called Copernican worldview and perspective that the individual doesn't matter are consistent with official Nazi views on religion. As summarized in 1941 by Martin Bormann, Hitler's party deputy, in a letter to all party district leaders (*Gauleiter*), the individual is insignificant in the universe and unworthy of the attention of an anthropomorphized deity.[66] Such a view is also consistent with Nazis' disregard for human life, evident in their military and genocidal actions as well as in their ethic of martyrdom on behalf of the *Volk*.

Kuchenreutter's death scene romanticizes death and aestheticizes cremation (Figure 7.2). This scene, like the baron's narrative trajectory, establishes that it is natural, ordinary, and right for people to die, and beautiful when they disappear in a puff of smoke. The final dialogue between Kuchenreutter and Münchhausen depicts Kuchenreutter at peace with his own passing, and Münchhausen as increasingly uneasy about his own unnatural longevity and resulting alienation from other human beings. When Kuchenreutter stops moving, his face, in the center of the frame, begins to dissolve into smoke. The composition of the shot is harmonious and balanced, with Kuchenreutter's face dividing the screen symmetrically. Lines, angles, and shapes become soft, with the smoke. The complementary pinks and greens and the blacks and whites blur together, until shapes, shades, colors, distinctions, and Kuchenreutter vanish. Kuchenreutter's dissolve into smoke shows the ephemeral nature of his life and its equivalence to nothingness, a point made explicit in the following scene. Cigarette smoke veiling his face and matching the preceding shot of Kuchenreutter, the modern baron says to his listeners: "The human being is like smoke, which rises and blows away." Münchhausen's figurative language renders poetic an image that many Germans were witnessing firsthand during bombardments, on battlefields, and in death camps. In March 1943, no one living in Germany or occupied Europe was far removed from death in smoke

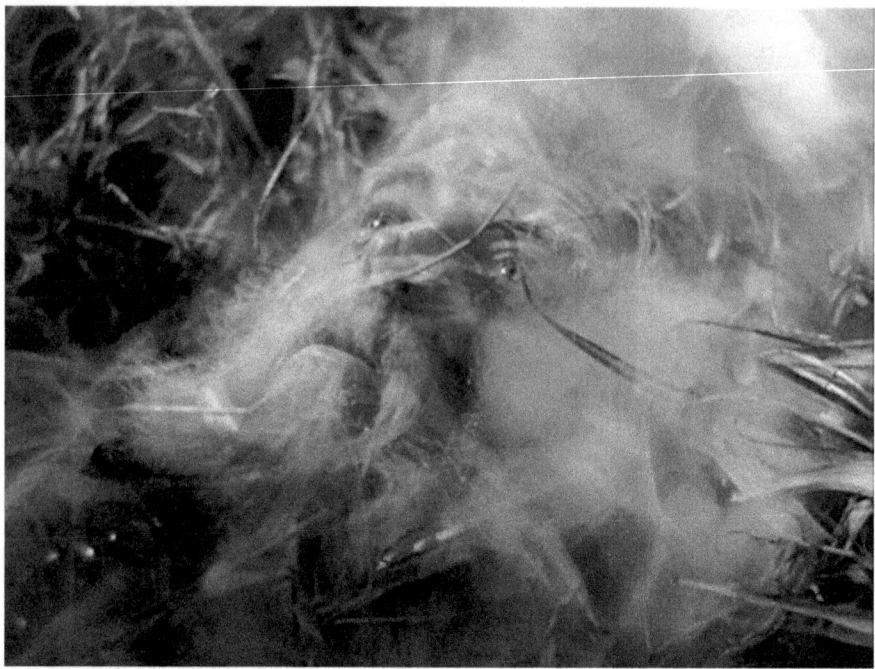

Figure 7.2. Kuchenreutter's death. The human body dissolves into smoke. Hermann Speelmans in *Münchhausen* (1942/43). Screenshot.

and flame. The moral of the baron's story, which he proclaims needs to be learned with the heart, is that human beings are insignificant and transitory and that the fantasy of humans ascending and dissipating as smoke is creative, poetic, and beautiful.

Münchhausen's thematic strands come together in its final scene, which blurs the boundaries between reality and illusion, romanticizes death, and aestheticizes cremation. In this scene the contemporary baron reveals that he is also the historical baron who has never aged, and his horrified young guests depart hastily. Muted colors and dim lighting create a somber mood and make it difficult to distinguish what is happening onscreen, increasing viewers' uncertainty. The colors and lighting also signal nightfall after a day of storytelling, and, symbolically, the dusk of Münchhausen's life. A lengthy shot of an owl with glowing eyes as the Münchhausens and their guests return to the house gives the scene a haunted feel, as does the smoke from Münchhausen's cigar. Recalling Kuchenreutter's death, this smoke visually reinforces Münchhausen's comment about humankind being as ephemeral as smoke, and it foreshadows the choice he makes at the end of this scene to age and die. This dark mood and Münchhausen's statement that others grew to fear him as he failed to age, put a glum finish on a primarily carefree and fantastical film. Living among illusions and a belief in eternal fun and youth is not, *Münchhausen*'s ending suggests, to be taken completely lightheartedly.

When *Münchhausen* turns away from its own escapism and reveals the threatening side of illusion and purportedly fascist fantasies of eternal youth, it seems to reject fascism. Yet fascist sympathies are found in Münchhausen's acceptance of his death, which makes it seem more pleasant and meaningful than it was for those dying in and because of the Third Reich.[67] Münchhausen tells his wife he does not want to live after she has gone, and he relinquishes his eternal youth, aging—almost—before our eyes. (A cut here functions as a sleight-of-hand.) The scene closes with a zoom into a close-up of the baron's portrait, which, in a set of trick shots, blows out candles in a candelabra carried by the butler. In a close-up, the smoke from the last candle spirals up to spell "the end." In these final shots, the baron is replaced first by his magical portrait and then—as was Kuchenreutter—by a wisp of smoke. The final moments in which the magical portrait blows out the candle continue to merge illusion and reality. They remind viewers that the individual is as insignificant as a puff of smoke. Smoke serves again as a metaphor for a beautiful death, one the baron has chosen to share the fate of the woman he loves. This romantic conflation of smoke and death downplays the horrors of war and the chimneys at Auschwitz.

Münchhausen creates a window between knowing and not knowing and offers viewers several escape routes to avoid seeing what Germany was doing to Jewish people. Characterized by unreliable narration, uncertainty, and cinematic tricks, *Münchhausen*, on a fundamental level, undermines the distinction between fact and fiction and the link between seeing and knowing in multiple ways, suggesting that truth is unknowable, even for witnesses. Within this framework, *Münchhausen* uses a crooked magician to embody Jewishness and erases him from the narrative, transferring his magic to the non-Jewish hero. The staging of Cagliostro's departure suggests Jewish disappearance is a trick and that the Jewish magician is still pulling the strings behind the scenes. At the same time, its ambiguous depiction allows spectators to see, or not see, in his combustion the fate of real Jewish bodies. This combustion is linked to motifs of smoke, disappearance, and natural, beautiful death throughout the film. *Münchhausen*'s romanticization of death and aesthetics of cremation could ease the consciences of those who, despite the epistemic murk, manage to see the flames.

Die Feuerzangenbowle

Whereas *Münchhausen* justifies, mystifies, and aestheticizes Jewish disappearance, *Feuerzangenbowle* does not reflect on disappearance per se. Instead, the Jewish is absent and only indirectly visible. *Feuerzangenbowle* does not reflect on this absence; it cultivates blindness, retreating to an interior world and asserting that reality is simply what people pretend is true. *Feuerzangenbowle*'s central assertion is both complicit with fascism and exposes its methods. The Nazis believed that they could influence reality via illusion, hence the attempts of the Propaganda Ministry to influence the *Volk*'s perceptions and experiences.[68] While their efforts were not necessarily consistent, coherent, or effective, the Nazis' attempts were in this sense successful: the realities of Germany and Europe from 1933 to 1945 and beyond were indelibly stained by Nazism's fictions, including antisemitism. *Feuerzangenbowle* demonstrates how staging elaborate illusions can transform reality. By calling attention to and generating pleasure from this process, *Feuerzangenbowle* injects uncertainty into the Propaganda Ministry's audience. As part of Goebbels's multimedial orchestration of truth, fiction, and propaganda, comedies like *Feuerzangenbowle* contributed to the culture of simultaneous knowing and not knowing and a broader pattern of epistemic murk in Third Reich media. Control over narrative and the concurrent stimulation of uncertainty enable racial domination and violence.[69] Asserting that perceived reality is no more real or substantial than fantasy or fraud, *Feuerzangenbowle* encourages viewers to disregard what they might hear about Nazi atrocities. After undermining viewers' confidence in their ability to know, *Feuerzangenbowle* takes a nihilistic turn. Ultimately, the film celebrates the inability to know the truth and the dissolution of the individual, as both are consumed in flame, another example of an aesthetic of cremation.

Jewishness as Absence

Feuerzangenbowle is about absence and the fantasy of recreating the missing. The protagonist, Johann Pfeiffer (Rühmann), is an older man attempting to live out a youth he never had by pretending to be a prankster schoolboy, a fantasy he cannot sustain. Not only the plot and protagonist, but also the film itself, attempt to recreate a lost past. *Feuerzangenbowle* is a remake of *So ein Flegel* (Such a Rascal, Robert A. Stemmle, 1933/34), a typical mistaken-identity comedy of the transitional period, also starring Rühmann.⁷⁰ In *Flegel*, Berlin playwright Hans Pfeiffer (Rühmann) is struggling with a play about high school. When mistaken for his brother Erich, a rebellious small-town schoolboy (also Rühmann), Hans trades places with him, and mayhem ensues. The memory of the earlier film, which still would have been fairly fresh in 1944, haunts the remake, calling attention to what is missing.

Feuerzangenbowle is remarkably different from *Flegel* in tone, style, and narrative detail. These differences reveal structuring absences that provide brief and indirect glimpses of missing Jewishness. Rühmann's 1944 performance lacks the innocent, lighthearted quality of his performances a decade earlier. Of course, there were ample reasons for Rühmann's and his audience's youthful exuberance to have faded, including war, hardship, and the murder of Europe's Jews. The stylistic differences between *Feuerzangenbowle* and *Flegel* also reflect loss. Filmed in late 1933, around the same time as *Viktor und Viktoria*, *Flegel* has many stylistic elements typical of that moment, retaining Jewish traces of Weimar and Hollywood influence. For example, Dr. Joh. of the *Film Kurier* wrote that if *Flegel*'s shots and editing were not so rushed, it would have been a perfect "Schlemihl" film.⁷¹ Haste was coded Jewish, as was the "Schlemihl," Yiddish for an unlucky, foolish character.⁷² "Schlemihl" also invokes Adelbert von Chamisso's *Peter Schlemihl*, a Romantic *Doppelgänger* novella, in which the eponymous protagonist sold and was pursued by his shadow. I will reflect more on the Jewishness of the *Doppelgänger* below. Despite its Jewish traces, Betz praised *Flegel* as "something new," proclaiming that by adapting a Spoerl novel, the director "broke through the pink front of trusted Riviera operettas," emphasizing how literary adaptation could ground a new German film humor, and situating *Flegel* on the front lines of what he would later describe as the "battle" over German film.⁷³ *Flegel* was an early foray into the racialized German humor theorized and cultivated in Nazi Germany, which was exemplified by *Engel* (chapter 4) and culminated in *Feuerzangenbowle*. As I have explained, this German humor purged of Jewishness is dominated by lack: the absence of irony, verbal wit, rapid tempo, and other comic strategies coded as Jewish, and of visual conventions associated with modernism, Weimar Cinema, and Hollywood, which also were understood as Jewish.

The disappearance of Pfeiffer's brother Erich is another structuring absence in *Feuerzangenbowle* indicating the loss of the Jewish. The elimination of this major character cuts a number of scenes, alters the protagonist's motivations, and leads to significant narrative restructuring. Erich's absence from *Feuerzangenbowle* can be construed as a case of missing Jewishness. Joh. writes about Rühmann's having split his "individualism" in *Flegel* between the successful Pfeiffer and his "alter ego," his feckless brother.[74] The modernity of split subjectivity and the psychoanalytic terminology Joh. uses were both coded Jewish, as was the structural position of the alter ego, or *Doppelgänger*. Particularly in Nazi Germany's numerous mistaken-identity comedies, the *Doppelgänger* is related to the trope of the masked Jew, who looks like the self but actually is a manipulative Other (chapter 6). As in the example of Cagliostro, above, Jewish coding around the *Doppelgänger* can be explicit and both highlights the non-Jewishness of the protagonist and enables the protagonist's achievements. The oil magnate's "meschuggene" niece in *Glückskinder* casts Ann Garden's non-Jewishness in a favorable light and is the plot device that makes Gil recognize it and accept her as his wife in more than name (chapter 3).[75] The fake prince in *April! April!* occupies the same Jewish structural role. Actually a clothing salesman and a successful impostor (both coded Jewish), the fake prince highlights the real prince's non-Jewishness and worthiness to join the *Volksgemeinschaft* and facilitates the series of events that lead him to the right female partner for his colonial escapades (chapter 5). Lazy, deceitful, disrespectful, and yet still funny, Erich Pfeiffer uses comic strategies associated with Jewish humor and a stock character type that Lubitsch made famous in his early comedies like *Schuhpalast Pinkus* (Shoe Palace Pinkus, 1916). Erich even helps out in a Berlin underwear shop—a stereotypically Jewish space—rather than fulfilling Hans's obligations at the theater. In *Feuerzangenbowle,* Rühmann no longer splits his subjectivity and deletes the Jewish-coded brother from the story. Unlike colonialism in *April* or Münchhausen's European conquests, Pfeiffer's liberation from objective reality works without a Jewish alter ego. By 1944 the vast majority of European Jews had been exterminated, and the *Volksgemeinschaft* largely had been purged of Jewishness. Moreover, fascist fantasy production no longer needed the Jewish to work.

Fantasy, Reality, and Epistemic Murk

Another structuring absence in *Feuerzangenbowle* is the omission of Hans's play, which motivates his disguise in *Flegel*. This particular absence does not necessarily signify missing Jewishness, but it creates the conditions for epistemic murk and willful blindness. Without the play as motivation for Hans's transgressions, the causal relationship between fantasy and reality changes. In the earlier film, Pfeiffer needs real experience to create successful fiction. In the remake, Pfeiffer's fictions transform the world around him. In other words, representation is no longer grounded in reality. Instead imagination and representation produce new realities. In redefining what is true, the film rejects modern epistemology and inductive reason, the practice of drawing conclusions by proceeding logically from observable fact. The alternative truth that *Feuerzangenbowle* promotes—memories, dreams, and desires—offered 1944 audiences a mental escape from the mass slaughter outside the cinema.

Feuerzangenbowle blurs distinctions among fantasy, representation, and reality and, like *Münchhausen,* uses the dissolve to enhance the epistemic murk created by the script. A series of dissolves takes *Feuerzangenbowle* from a smoky barroom to the schoolyard and Pfeiffer from an adult to a fictional schoolboy. These dissolves and their counterpart at the end of the film, when Pfeiffer dissolves back to an adult, emphasize the permeability of the boundaries between imagination, representation, and reality. During the initial sequence of dissolves of Pfeiffer's changing face, Pfeiffer describes what he must do to become a schoolboy. His mustache vanishes; his hair becomes shorter; wire-rimmed glasses appear on his nose; and finally he is revealed in school cap and suit, books under his arm. Instead of describing the pragmatic method by which Pfeiffer assembles his disguise, as in the novel, where Pfeiffer goes to the barber, shops for new clothes, and so on, the film mystifies the connection between the two Pfeiffers.[76] The final shot of Pfeiffer as a schoolboy, but still in his original location, quickly dissolves into a full shot of Pfeiffer from the back in a busy schoolyard, yet still is accompanied by the adult Pfeiffer's voice-over. The voice-over and dissolve blend the old setting with the new as Pfeiffer's change of size, body position, and setting moves us to the internal narrative. The audience is denied a clear cut that would establish a true jump in space and time, and the resulting visual fluidity, while providing the first clue that the interior narrative may be an extension of the external narrative, also would seem to depict history as a series of magical transitions rather than as a human-structured narrative. In the dissolve back to the frame at the end of the film, in the midst of a monologue in which he confesses that he fabricated the whole story, the school, and the people in it, the face of Pfeiffer the schoolboy, sitting on a teacher's desk, dissolves into the face of Pfeiffer, standing in the barroom where he and his old friends first lit the flaming punch. The perfect match of position and size represent Pfeiffer as a single continuous individual as his background shifts. He continues his dour monologue, claiming, with a strange tic in his right eye, that even he is an invention and all that is true is the flaming punch of the film's title and "the memories that we carry with us, the dreams that we spin, and the desires that drive us."

Feuerzangenbowle dismisses objective, external truth and troubles the relationship between fantasy and reality, showing how the former can alter the latter and rendering the distinction between the two unknowable. Many instances in *Feuerzangenbowle* illustrate how people's lies influence reality. These instances include not only Pfeiffer's impersonation of a schoolboy but also the mischief he instigates in that role. During a chemistry lesson on the creation of alcohol, Professor Grey (Erich Ponto) gives the boys each a tiny taste of blueberry wine.[77] Using the code word "valerian," which signals the entrance into an alternate reality, Pfeiffer cues students to behave as if they were drunk, inciting humorous classroom chaos. While Grey grows more flustered and puzzled—for a small sip of his wine, with a 13% alcohol content, hardly should have intoxicated these boys—he concedes to a disruption as authentic as it would have been had the boys truly gotten drunk, one that has equally real consequences. When Director Knauer (Hans Leibelt) enters the classroom, he sends the boys home to sober up and begins to chide Grey for having poisoned his senior class. Here Pfeiffer realizes the consequences of his pretenses, revealed by cinematography that emphasizes the fluidity between imitation and real life. In a shot framed by the classroom doorway, the camera shows Knauer upbraiding Grey. Pfeiffer walks to the door, and as his face comes closer and more into focus, faculty members begin to blur. Rühmann adopts a series of facial expressions to show comprehension, regret, and shame and shuts the door on the camera. The handle latches and, in a quick transition effect, the shot of the door flips upside down and over, and is replaced by a shot of Pfeiffer sitting in solitary confinement. These final shots show Pfeiffer's recognition that his play-acting has had a serious impact. The transition represents his decision to reverse it and to accept the responsibility and consequences for what really happened.

The most elaborate example of pretense overtaking an initial reality and creating a new one occurs when Pfeiffer and a friend hang a sign on the school gate that school has been canceled because of construction work. Seeing the sign when they get to school, all the students turn around and go home. The teachers' response to this debacle underscores how unstable and malleable reality is. The teachers initially agree to punish the guilty party but quarrel over whether it would be just to punish all the students if they cannot locate the guilty one. Agitated discussion ensues until Professor Bommel (Paul Henckels) suggests they do nothing. His words stressed by a panning, zooming camera that centers him large and prominently in the frame, Bommel declares, "Whether a forgery exists, Mr. Director, is dependent upon us. We play completely dumb and say, 'the sign is real. We hung it out ourselves because of the construction work.'" The only problem is that the school is not under construction. Bommel promises to fix that, and a dissolve shows him from a comically high angle, framed by the school's architectural features, standing on a banister and dumping a bag of cement dust over construction equipment. This dissolve signifies the becoming real of Pfeiffer's fictional proclamation about the school being closed for construction. In dissolving between old and new realities, this dissolve functions like the dissolve in the prologue that makes Pfeiffer a schoolboy. A cut to a classroom of excited boys shows them reacting to the events and Rosen threatening to tell the truth and turn Pfeiffer in. The boys are not yet aware that reality, and thus truth, has changed. Rosen bears the brunt of this lesson. When Rosen denounces Pfeiffer to Grey, he finds himself in a losing verbal battle with his teacher, being insulted, having his grammar corrected, and eventually being told that the sign was put up because of school construction. The sequence is punctuated with reaction shots of Pfeiffer, the wonder growing on his face, and concluded with a close-up of a classical bust of Zeus on the wall, panning down to Grey's face as the bust goes out of focus. New realities proclaimed in the present are clearer and more substantial than the inherited knowledge that seemed so solid and upon which the teachers' authority rests.

Through these and other scenes of Pfeiffer's pranks, *Feuerzangenbowle* establishes a regime in which truth is unstable and uncertain and tricks and lies reshape reality. Additionally, *Feuerzangenbowle* illustrates how the epistemic murk created by such a regime can hide transgression, deny lack, and disavow difference. This point is made most forcefully in a scene in which Grey discovers that a boy has drawn a naked girl on the blackboard. (See Figure 7.3.) Pfeiffer saves his schoolmate from punishment by telling Director Knauer that it is an unfinished drawing of a boy. Grey discovers the drawing when he asks a student to flip over his blackboard and sends for the director rather than handling the situation himself. The camera

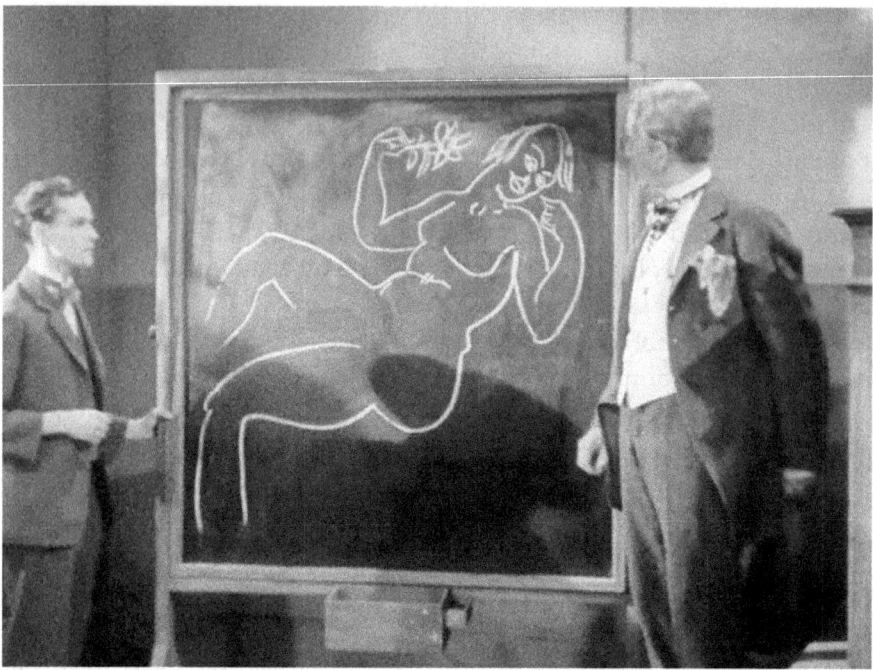

Figure 7.3. Strategic epistemic murk. Pfeiffer will soon convince Director Knauer that the drawing on the chalkboard is an unfinished drawing of a boy. Professor Grey (Erich Ponto) and one of his pupils. *Die Feuerzangenbowle* (1943/44). Screenshot.

pans from Grey's face to Zeus's bust on the wall, which dissolves into a close-up of Knauer, who berates the boys about his disappointment in their moral decay. This odd shot shows the transfer of authority from Grey back to the classical patriarch, who is embodied in the modern day by the director (whom the boys call Zeus). Yet for this new patriarch, reality is flexible, which allows subversive art and its interpretation to be turned to his advantage. Pfeiffer stands and volunteers that he finds the picture pretty. Knauer expresses his shock and dismay and talks about the young woman's shame. At this point, Pfeiffer corrects him, stating that the nude on the blackboard is actually a picture of a boy that they had no time to finish. Although this is patently not the case, mutual consent to accept a new reality and ignore the old resolves the situation. Knauer admits that he had suspected something like that and states: "I appreciate it extraordinarily that this embarrassing situation has found such a harmless explanation." As with the construction incident, manufacturing new truths is preferable to the embarrassing truth. Yet such sleight of hand does more than alleviate shame. It also integrates the artists and formerly unruly schoolboys into the school's authority structure by ignoring their transgression and asking them to interpret it in the director's favor. This act comments not only on authority but also on the flexibility of representation, interpretation, and reality. The resistant artwork may be advantageously interpreted and assimilated into the status quo. Through a performative speech act and a simple act of consent, Pfeiffer and Knauer detach the sign from referent and reassign it elsewhere by agreeing that a curvaceous feminine nude, with shapely breasts and hips, reclining while holding a flower, is truly an unfinished boy. Thus, they demonstrate that representation and reality (because of the consequences for the boys) are malleable and adaptable and that strategic epistemic murk creates space to deny transgression, difference, and lack (the feminine) that are there for all to see.

Feuerzangenbowle is ambivalent toward the epistemic murk it presents. In the interior of the film, illusion is pleasurable and backed by the most likable characters. Pfeiffer's deceptions are a source of joy for his companions and the audience, made clear in the students' laughter at his jokes, their willingness to follow his lead, and girls coming to meet him in the school "jail" when he sits there in punishment. Converting illusions to reality averts scandal and preserves authority within the school. Several scenes make this clear: the teachers' conference where they agree to pretend that the school was under construction; the episode where Director Knauer embraces Pfeiffer's tale that the female nude is an unfinished boy, and a final scene where Knauer begs Pfeiffer to impersonate Professor Grey, after having made him miss an important inspection by resetting his alarm clock.

Cremating the Self

Although the internal narrative construes illusion as pleasure, the frame narrative casts this entertaining interior in cynical terms, envisioning it as the product of dark magic—an allusion to cultural Otherness. The original convocation around the punch bowl that launches the whole fantasy is portrayed in a sinister light. The cramped interior of the tavern is lit in high contrast, with smoke wafting through the scene, looking much like German Expressionism's "haunted screen."[78] Men dressed in dark suits circle the punch bowl like a Shakespearean witches' brew. Flames from candles and the punch add to the ritualistic atmosphere. Pfeiffer's skeptical, gloomy attitude and his dialogue express cynicism. This cynicism is particularly evident at the end of the film, during Pfeiffer's dour monologue, in which he reveals that fiction poses as truth, and that the only real truth is in memories, dreams, and desires. According to *Feuerzangenbowle*, what we recognize as reality is manufactured from dreams, and those are the conditions under which "we" must live. Beyond that, nothing is solid or true. Pfeiffer's closing words, like the dissolves and filters between the frame narrative and the internal narrative, blur what the film posits as fiction and what it posits as true, and depict a careful ambivalence about the possibilities of such confusion. The realistic representational techniques in the inner story and the more heavy-handed filmic effects in the frame further confound this distinction and heighten the ambivalence around it, for the play-acting school scenes appear more real and familiar than does the gentlemanly witches' coven, which the film initially presents as true.

Feuerzangenbowle contends that what looks like experience and the self may be fiction and that there are limits on what is true and how we know it. If spectators submit to epistemic murk, they can deny the evidence before their eyes, be it the body of a female nude or the disappearance of Jewish people. In *Feuerzangenbowle*'s final moments, addressing spectators directly and telling them that all they have seen was a lie, Rühmann states that feeling is more authentic than seeing, expressing the film's epistemological cynicism. *Feuerzangenbowle* limits not only how viewers can know but also what can be known: namely, subjective internal phenomena. Although this focus on interiority would seem to promote individuality and selfhood, the narrow range and the limited ability to know result in the erasure of the speaking self of the story. At the moment Pfeiffer admits that he too is a fiction, he is consumed visually by the flames of the punch bowl, flames that eventually fill the screen. He tells us these flames are the one "true" thing in the story and, as such, an analogy for "our" "true" memories, dreams, and desires (see Figure 7.4). As representation of the interior, the flames consume the physical body and the material world around it, expressing not only epistemological uncertainty but also the immortality of something like a soul in the face of bodily destruction.

Feuerzangenbowle's epistemological skepticism and privileging of interior over material existence can be interpreted as a response to its historical context, a context alluded to indirectly when Pfeiffer disappears behind a wall of flame. When *Feuerzangenbowle* was made and released, flames were consuming too many people—soldiers on battlefields, civilians during air

Figure 7.4. Erasing the self and aestheticizing cremation. Heinz Rühmann in *Die Feuerzangenbowle* (1943/44). Screenshot.

raids, Jews, Roma, LGBTQ people, people with disabilities, dissidents, and other Nazi prisoners. In face of mass immolation, *Feuerzangenbowle* incinerates the face of its protagonist, invoking both genocide and war and letting them drift away. This escapist film, on the one hand, is jaded, bitter, and wistful regarding the regime's illusions and, on the other hand, disavows the material realities concomitant with the war's impending loss. According to Witte: "When [*Feuerzangenbowle*] premiered, the turning point of Stalingrad lay a year behind, the Allies were in Sicily, the Warsaw ghetto had been destroyed, Hamburg and Berlin were bombed out, and the German army had been decimated by one-half. Goebbels's edict that reorganized wartime film production around features with 'predominantly entertaining contents' had been in effect for two years. The flight from reality had thus become state policy."[79] For Witte, escapism in *Feuerzangenbowle* goes hand in hand with its juvenile regression.[80] Its light-hearted interior narrative offers a humorous recess from the war and attempts to recapture a lost childhood. It reflects on how fantasy can reshape reality and how a dynamic exchange between the two can undo transgressions and disavow loss. Yet the film's framing device indicates a cynical embrace of psychic life over either illusion or material reality. This cynical turn inward can be read as a response to the war and potentially also to filmic bombardment by entertaining fictions and ideological bombardment by less entertaining ones. *Feuerzangenbowle*'s escapism also directs the individual to escape within and flee material reality, for rather than revealing authentic "archetype" and "primordial shape,"[81] the dissolves in *Feuerzangenbowle* represent the uncertain relationships between illusion and reality that result from the potential of fictions to be staged as truths and a doubt that anything authentic exists outside the mind. The outside world is deceptive and unknowable, and the boundary between reality and fiction is illusory. By embracing such epistemic murk, looking inward, and letting the self dissolve, audiences could blind themselves to what was going on around them.

Feuerzangenbowle's nihilism can be read as responding to the impending loss of the war and failure of a regime whose dreams and illusions deeply impacted Germany's material reality and also as manufacturing consent to and denial of that regime's actions. Spectators are encouraged to content themselves with introspection and turn away from the material world. This message could serve as a palliative prescription for all experiencing the harsh conditions of the final years of the war: as life gets even tougher, be assured and soothed by fact that life is a dream. For Nazi believers, the epistemic murk and cynicism might have helped prepare them for all that they held to be true to be disproved or destroyed. More subtly, *Feuerzangenbowle* might be interpreted as suggesting that if all is illusion, then the atrocities of World War II do not really matter. If nothing is certain, how can one know or understand what is going on?[82] It is in this sense that *Feuerzangenbowle* contributes to epistemic murk and thus to people's inability to see the genocide: it promotes epistemological uncertainty and apathy, an attitude that "I don't know and I don't care."

How Fascist Is *Die Feuerzangenbowle*?

At the end of *Feuerzangenbowle*, Pfeiffer, like Münchhausen, questions truth, gives up his unnatural regression, embraces his own dissolution, and disappears in flame. Both films create epistemic murk through plots in which pleasurable fictions pass for reality. If, in *Münchhausen*, illusion ends with the protagonist's acceptance that human life is insignificant and transitory, in *Feuerzangenbowle*, the vacillation between reality and fiction leads to the replacement of the self with the "truths" of memories, dreams, and desires—subjective forms of knowledge ambiguously figured in collective language. No doubt different spectators understood the ending of *Feuerzangenbowle* differently: as a call to preserve an authentic internal self from the encroachments of fiction; as a nihilistic response to the impending loss of the war; as disillusionment with the fictions and realities created by the regime; or as a call to collective organization around subjective, affective concerns as all that used to be true goes up in flames. The same can be said of *Münchhausen*, which as an escapist publicity vehicle may have promoted Nazism indirectly, yet which also made riskily "subversive subtextual references," and at the same time either criticized or advertised Nazism's illusionism and regression, promoted self-sacrifice, and aestheticized cremation.[83] The complexity, ambiguity, and polysemy of these two films generate multiple potential meanings and paths to escape knowledge of the disappearance of Europe's Jews. Among these films' escapist strategies are not only their humor, imagination, and entertainment value, but also their extension of epistemic murk, their differing methods of disavowing absence, and their aesthetics of cremation.

How fascist is *Die Feuerzangenbowle*? On the one hand, it encourages its public to accept illusion, escapism, regression, self-erasure, and a comfortable disavowal of and "not knowing" regarding material reality, when in 1944 material reality was quite ugly. On the other hand, this comedy also exposes its own mechanisms, showing itself, perceived reality, and authority to be based on fiction if not outright lies. The technology used to promote fascism also unveils its own workings. *Münchhausen* functions in a similar way.

Feuerzangenbowle and *Münchhausen* offered Third Reich audiences escape from wartime realities by generating epistemic murk—a gray zone of knowing, not knowing, and ambivalence—and render it appealing through humor and visual pleasure. Both films, made in a time of mass murder and cremation, culminate in wistful embrace of an aestheticized, smoky death. Despite their troubling origins and original escapist functions, both these films have fans today, fans who may be troubled by my claim that their beloved "classics" have any relationship to the Holocaust other than a critical one. Is *Münchhausen* or *Feuerzangebowle* inherently antisemitic? Not overtly, no. Does watching these movies turn people into Nazis or make them commit genocide? Hardly. Are you an antisemite if you like one or both of them? Of course not. But if you ask whether threads within the complex weaves of these films can be tied to the Nazis' antisemitic agenda during World War II, the answer has to be an uncomfortable "yes." And what do we do with that?

Notes

1. Witte, "How Fascist," 31.
2. Witte, "How Fascist," 31.

According to Witte, the dissolve from the protagonist as a mature man to his disguise as a schoolboy is part of an "infantilization" masking the loss of childhood for wartime youth. It also functions, as do other fascist dissolves, such as those in *The Eternal Jew*, to search for origins, authenticity, and nature and to regress historically, socially, and evolutionarily. *The Punch Bowl* regresses nostalgically, pedagogically, and sexually and displays fascism's "compulsion to legitimate and pursue feats of conquest with the power and myth of youth." It encourages conformity by marginalizing women and promoting discipline and "reversion into nature." ("How Fascist," 32–36.)

3. Witte, "How Fascist," 36.
4. For example: Witte, "How Fascist," and *Lachende Erben*. Rentschler, *Ministry*. Schulte-Sasse, *Entertaining the Third Reich*.
5. Baranowski, *Nazi Empire*, 332.
6. Browning, "One Day in Jozefow," 196.
7. "Nazis Determined."
8. Results for search term "Judenrein," *JTA Daily News Bulletin*, accessed July 13, 2017, www.jta.org/archive.
9. Stargardt, *German War*, 255.
10. Stargardt, *German War*, 245–46.
11. Herf, *Jewish Enemy*, 267.
12. Herf, *Jewish Enemy*, 267.
13. Stargardt, *German War*, 247–48.
14. Herf, *Jewish Enemy*, 277, 268.
15. Herf, *Jewish Enemy*, 269.
16. Rentschler, *Ministry*, 20.
17. Kreimeier, *Die Ufa Story*, 374–77.
18. Stahr, *Volksgemeinschaft*, 175.
19. Martin, *The Nazi-Fascist New Order*, 191.
20. Rentschler, *Ministry*, 259. Hull, *Film in the Third Reich*, 206.
21. Stahr, *Volksgemeinschaft*, 183.
22. Kreimeier, *Die Ufa Story*, 377.
23. Rentschler, *Ministry*, 262.
24. Hull, *Film in the Third Reich*, 206.
25. Klotz, "Epistemological Ambiguity," 91.
26. Herf, *Jewish Enemy*, viii; Klotz, "Epistemological Ambiguity," 121–24.
27. Taussig, *Shamanism*, xiii, 120–21, 130–33, passim.

28. Hull, *Film in the Third Reich*, 252–60. Kreimeier, *Die Ufa-Story*, 386. Rentschler, *Ministry*, 194. Schulte-Sasse, *Entertaining the Third Reich*, 302.
29. Kreimeier, *Die Ufa-Story*, 386.
30. Rentschler, *Ministry*, 267, 196, 213.
31. Kreimeier, *Die Ufa-Story*, 373, 379–80.
32. Kreimeier, *Die Ufa-Story*, 379.
33. Translation from Goebbels's diary, cited in Hull, *Film in the Third Reich*, 259. Rentschler, *Ministry*, 202, 263. Cf. Neumann et al, *Film "Kunst."*
34. Kreimeier, *Die Ufa-Story*, 382–86.
35. Kreimeier, *Die Ufa-Story*, 382.
36. Stahr, *Volksgemeinschaft*, 181–82.
37. Cf. Rentschler, *Ministry*, 198. Schulte-Sasse, *Entertaining the Third Reich*, 304.
38. For more on blackface, see pages 73, 74, 76–78.
39. Kreimeier, *Die Ufa-Story*, 387.
40. Hull, *Film in the Third Reich*, 253.
41. Rentschler, *Ministry*, 205. Schulte-Sasse, *Entertaining the Third Reich*, 309–11.
42. Carter, *Dietrich's Ghosts*, 186.
43. See Gilman, *Jewish Self-Hatred*.
44. See chapters 5 and 6.
45. Rentschler, *Ministry*, 205, 210–11. Schulte-Sasse, *Entertaining the Third Reich*, 311–12.
46. Schulte-Sasse, *Entertaining the Third Reich*, 308, 311–12.
47. Schulte-Sasse, *Entertaining the Third Reich*, 308, 311–12.
48. Rentschler, *Ministry*, 211.
49. Rentschler, *Ministry*, 198–200.
50. Hans Albers, from the *Berlin Lokal-Anzeiger*, in Rentschler, *Ministry*, 203.
51. Schulte-Sasse, *Entertaining the Third Reich*, 311. Rentschler, *Ministry*, 205.
52. See page 44.
53. Cf. Rentschler, *Ministry*, 211–12.
54. Taussig, *Shamanism*, 134.
55. Taussig, *Shamanism*, 134.
56. Cf. Rentschler, *Ministry*, 198, 211–12. Schulte-Sasse, *Entertaining the Third Reich*, 304, 316–17. Hull, *Film in the Third Reich*, 253.
57. Rentschler, *Ministry*, 196.
58. Salt, "Dissolved Away," 79.
59. See Hennefeld, "Destructive Metamorphosis," 176–206.
60. Rentschler, *Ministry*, 158–64. Schulte-Sasse, *Entertaining the Third Reich*, 75. Weinstein, "Dissolving Boundaries," 508–9. Witte, "Film im Nationalsozialismus," 117–66. Witte, "How Fascist is *The Punch Bowl*?" 33.
61. Ameskamp, "Fanning the Flames," 94.
62. Ameskamp, "Fanning the Flames," 101.
63. Ameskamp, "Fanning the Flames," 105.
64. Ameskamp, "Fanning the Flames," 106–8.
65. See: Stark, "Weisse Juden," 8.
66. Bormann, "The Relation Between," 103.
67. Rentschler, *Ministry*, 212.
68. Rentschler, *Ministry*, 16.
69. Taussig, *Shamanism*, xiii, 120–21, 130–33, passim.

70. Both films are adaptations of Heinrich Spoerl's popular 1933 novel, *Die Feuerzangenbowle*. On Rühmann's and Spoerl's important roles in shaping Nazi Germany's "German humor," see chapter 4.

71. Dr. Joh. [pseud.], review of *So ein Flegel*, 2.

72. See page 55.

73. "Durchbrach die rosa Front trauter Rivieraoperetten." Betz, Review of *So ein Flegel*, 4; Neumann et al., *Film "Kunst,"* 5. See chapters 1 and 2.

74. Dr. Joh., Review of *Flegel*, 2.

75. Schneider, Review of *Glückskinder*, 2.

76. Spoerl, *Die Feuerzangenbowle*," 14–16.

77. This is another example of drunkenness functioning as German humor. Eckert, "Filmkomik," 890.

78. Eisner, *The Haunted Screen*.

79. Witte, "How Fascist," 32.

80. Witte, "How Fascist," 32–34.

81. Witte, "How Fascist," 33.

82. See Klotz, "Epistemological Ambiguity," 91–124.

83. Schulte-Sasse, *Entertaining the Third Reich*, 312. Rentschler, *Ministry*, 193–213.

CONCLUSION

Overt and inferential antisemitism persist. The virulent overt antisemitism of the radical right is the more urgent threat. Yet foregrounding such explicit hate obfuscates the naturalized assumptions off which it feeds. Despite perceptions that Jewish Americans enjoy all the privileges of whiteness, recent political discourse demonstrates that a boundary remains between the Jewish and the non-Jewish, even if that boundary is situational and permeable.[1] Across the spectrum, US political rhetoric deploys codes of Jewish, racial, sexual, gender, and class difference—among others. During the 2016 US presidential campaign, opponents of both major party presidential nominees coded the candidate they despised as Jewish. The most notorious example of this was when Donald Trump tweeted an image of Hillary Clinton in front of a heap of money and emblazoned with a Star of David reading "Most Corrupt Candidate Ever."[2]

Although President Trump justifiably has been accused of pandering to antisemites in his white supremacist base, his critics also use terms of Jewish difference to describe his failings. Ted Cruz faced blowback for referring to Trump's "chutzpah."[3] Yet Cruz is one of many to blow that dog whistle. A Google search of "Trump + chutzpah" yields more than 232,000 hits, including major news sources, which use this Yiddish word to code Trump's attitude and business practices as Jewish.[4] As noted in chapter 5, Goebbels argued that only Yiddish had a word to capture the uniquely Jewish failing of *chutzpah*.[5] Using *chutzpah* as an insult *schleps* Jewishness along with it, suggesting that such brazenness cannot be conceptualized in non-Jewish terms. *Chutzpah* is not the only way critics code Trump as Jewish. Several commentators accuse him of behaving like a "Borscht Belt comic," referencing the Jewish comedians who performed in Catskill resorts frequented by Jews, and invoking bluster and boorishness as Jewish performance.[6] Peggy Noonan of the *Wall Street Journal* described Trump as "Woody Allen without the Humor," claiming the president's real problem is what she interprets as his failed masculinity. Noonan's analogy with Woody Allen codes Trump's inability to fulfill her masculine ideals as Jewish.[7] The sexist and antisemitic implications of her article provide a stunning example of why inferential antisemitism is a useful concept and why gender, sexuality, class, and Jewish difference demand intersectional analysis. By the way, I haven't seen comparisons made between Trump and non-Jewish comedians. After all, it is Trump's "Jewishness" and not his humor that these articles malign. Trump's New York origins and his bombast, wealth, greed, audacity, mendacity, and lechery—among other features—license antisemitic innuendo and inference.

Overt antisemitism is no longer socially acceptable in many circles, and particularly not in the same circles that decry the racism of white supremacist "deplorables" and criticize Trump. Nevertheless, the language, conceptual frameworks, and inferential patterns available to us in the United States today—and, for that matter, in many other parts of the world—still license antisemitic inferences based on codes similar to those deployed in Nazi Germany. It is troubling that even liberals' and progressives' expressions of contempt for President Trump are laced with Jewish coding. More than the outrages committed by the despicable white supremacist fringe, such coding indicates how deeply and pervasively antisemitism is woven into contemporary language and cultural norms. My study of Third Reich film comedies provides a set of critical tools for analyzing naturalized, implicitly antisemitic frameworks and other manifestations of inferential racism.[8]

Third Reich film comedy functioned in an auxiliary manner to the Nazi regime's genocidal antisemitism, mobilizing tropes of Jewish difference and reinforcing antisemitic hierarchies while imagining *Volksgemeinschaft*. Beyond *Nur nicht weich werden, Susanne!* and *Robert und Bertram*, which portray Jewish people as dishonest, profit-driven corrupters of German culture who seek to blend in with and seduce non-Jewish Germans, there is little overt antisemitism in Third Reich film comedy. Jewish characters and comedians disappeared soon after the Nazi takeover of the film industry and did not serve as objects of caricature, as one might expect. Instead, film comedy became, in Nazi terminology, *Judenrein*, and antisemitism took indirect, inferential forms, relying on codes of Jewish difference it had inherited from earlier eras. The Jewish remained visible primarily as a structuring absence: as omissions, vacancies, substitutes, and supplements that changed comedy's shape. Antisemitism had a strong impact on comic style not only because of the expulsion of Jewish film personnel, but also because of subtle pressure by officials and film critics to conform to what they deemed racially appropriate forms of German humor purged of Jewish wit and comicalness. "White Jews" stood in for Jewish characters in disciplinary narratives. Unlike "black Jews," or racial Jews, white Jews—Aryans who behaved in a Jewish-coded manner—could be taught to behave in a non-Jewish way and be integrated into the *Volksgemeinschaft* with a happy ending. Numerous *Verwechslungskomödien* played with boundaries and identities, managing some of the anxieties about modernity that the antisemitic construction of the masked Jew expressed more virulently. Comedy also confounded reality and illusion, truth and fiction, creating epistemic murk that helped blind audiences to Nazi atrocities.

Postwar Germans have treated the comedies of the 1930s and 1940s as classics, as a realm untouched by the unpleasantries of the Third Reich. Yet antisemitism's oblique effects on style and humor constitute its most durable legacy for German film comedy. The comedies made in the 1930s and 1940s established generic norms that persisted well into the 1950s and beyond, particularly in the Federal Republic of Germany (West Germany). The little-men comedians who made it big in the Third Reich dominated postwar comedy. From 1948 through 1980, Rühmann starred in several films yearly, appearing occasionally thereafter until his final feature film performance in *In weiter Ferne, so nah!* (Faraway, so close! Wim Wenders, 1992/93). Hans Moser performed in more than sixty films between the end of the war and his death in 1963. Theo Lingen made almost 100 postwar movies before passing away in 1978. Directors whose films were not overtly political, such as Paul Martin (*Glückskinder*), continued their careers uninterrupted. Even politicized directors like Veit Harlan (*Jud Süss*) made films after the war. Carl Froelich (*Engel*), winner of numerous Nazi honors and head of the *Reichsfilmkammer*, did not retire until 1951. His final film, *Stips*, was a comedy. Many Third Reich comedies have since been remade, including some of the films discussed in this book: not only *Die Blume von Hawaii* (Géza von Cziffra, FRG, 1953) and *Viktor und Viktoria* (see chapter 3), but also *Wenn wir alle Engel wären* (Günther Lüders, FRG, 1956), *Die Feuerzangenbowle* (Helmut Käutner, FRG, 1970), and *Die Abenteuer des Baron von Münchhausen* (The Adventures of Baron Münchhausen, Terry Gilliam, UK/FRG/Italy, 1988). There even seems to have been a loose adaptation of *Robert und Bertram* (Hans Deppe, FRG, 1961)—or an unfortunate recycling of a title with a fraught history—which preserved the 1939 film's central premise of two rogues gone wandering but not its overt antisemitism. Of course comedy evolved as time passed, and there were differences between

West and East German film. Nevertheless, just as Weimar left its mark on Nazi cinema, Nazi cinema had its own postwar "afterlife," as Rentschler has argued.[9] Because Third Reich comedy was perceived to have been apolitical, changes in filmmaking habits and audience preferences were particularly slow.

Insofar as they are also characterized by absences, displacements, and substitutions, expressions of Jewish difference in the broader postwar German cultural arena share structural features with Third Reich film comedy. Many codes of Jewish difference remained in place after the war, including but not limited to stereotypes about physical appearance; assumptions about behavior; contrasts between urban/rural and global/local; and presumptions about gender, sexuality, and social class. At the same time, however, Nazi antisemitism, its culmination in the Holocaust, and the international response to German war crimes permanently altered how non-Jewish Germans think about their relationships with Jewish people, how they understand Jewish difference, and how they perceive their own right and ability to speak about it. German postwar discourses of Jewish difference have both noteworthy continuities with older texts and performances and historically distinct causes and functions specific to post-Holocaust Central Europe. There are multiple reasons why Jews are absent from German postwar productions, including but not limited to their extermination and exile in the Nazi period. Bernd Marin describes a "post-Fascist anti-Semitism" in Central Europe, exemplified by Austria (which from 1938 on was part of the Nazi Reich), where few Jews are present and antisemitism is publicly disavowed yet flourishes on unacknowledged, unconscious levels.[10] The Holocaust and its public condemnation led to the "(re)privatization" of antisemitism in Austria because its articulation would threaten the legitimacy of those in power.[11] Through a process of "cultural sedimentation," stereotypes about Jews, symbolic coding of negative traits as Jewish, and linguistic shifts made in the Nazi period, antisemitism has persisted in Austria, marked by post-Holocaust repression and shame.[12] Marin describes this "Anti-Semitism without Anti-Semites" as a "paradoxical state of coexistence of the crystallization of prejudice and 'official' repression, where many Austrians 'must not' express any more the prejudices they want to articulate, or else 'cannot' perceive the prejudice they express despite their intentions."[13] Thus, silence about Jews in the postwar era results from attempts to expel antisemitism rather than from desires to expunge the Jewish. Nancy Laukner traces a resulting literary phenomenon structurally similar to but functionally different from the white Jews of Third Reich disciplinary humor. Laukner argues that surrogate Jews in postwar literature mostly do not camouflage or propagate antisemitic sentiments but rather tend to attack Nazi antisemitism indirectly or frame it as part of a larger, universal phenomenon.[14] Scholars have interpreted various other postwar articulations of Jewish difference through gaps, substitutions, and displacements as symptomatic of repression, guilt, shame, and denial and as incomplete or indirect attempts to negotiate meaning in wake of the Holocaust.[15]

Readers with strong affection for classical German film comedy or with approaches to film different from my own might challenge my argument on multiple grounds. To conclude, I would like to address several of their potential concerns:

1. **These films don't look antisemitic to me! Where are you getting this from?**
   Antisemitism in Nazi film is more widespread and more complex than the overt propagation of hateful stereotypes. *Antisemitism in Film Comedy in Nazi Germany* conceives of antisemitism as a subtle process of defining and excluding the Jewish. Humor, coded hints and traces, absences, and substitutes in Third Reich film comedy helped spectators imagine an abstract Jewishness and a German identity and community free from it. Film comedy's process of identifying and excising the Jewish was parallel and complementary to the mass murder of Jewish people in the Holocaust.

   Recognizing historical antisemitism is a challenge because films do not have transparent, stable meanings that are readily visible under any and all circumstances. Rather, films have multiple layers of potential meanings and ideological effects, which are activated and understood differently by individual viewers in different historical contexts. Put another way, films mean different things at different times to different people. The failure of antisemitic undercurrents to resonate with all audiences does not negate their presence. The inferential antisemitism I highlight in Third Reich comedies coexists with many other potential meanings. My interpretations are a product of the films themselves, of what I can reconstruct about their context using historical sources, and of my position as a Jewish-American intersectional feminist film scholar in the twenty-first century. Although the inferential antisemitism I describe supplements more obvious themes and messages in most Third Reich film comedies, the historical evidence, especially published film criticism, indicates that these supplemental meanings, or similar ones, were legible to audience members at the time. Noting potentially antisemitic meanings in any one of these films is interesting. Recognizing a pattern of antisemitic traces and inferences across half the films made in Nazi Germany, films understood to be innocent, and films that heavily influenced the development of postwar German cinema, makes their supplemental potential meanings more significant, both for German film history and for the study of racism and antisemitism in film. The analysis offered in this book, though focused in specific time and cultural confines, has broader implications for the study of race and generalized mechanisms of power and articulations of difference that reach well beyond the scope of this argument.

2. **Douglas Sirk (or Reinhold Schünzel, or [insert favorite artist or film of your choice]) was not an antisemite!**
With the exception of self-proclaimed Nazi antisemites, I am not accusing any individual of intentionally supporting antisemitism or the Holocaust. I uncover antisemitic resonances in common comic tropes and highlight particular films that exemplify them. The individuals involved in the production of these films did not necessarily mean to create antisemitic undercurrents, and they might not even have been aware of them. The Nazis wove antisemitism into the fabric of German society and institutions. My analyses of its indirect expressions illustrate how structural and institutional racism can permeate and affect society, even where it is difficult to see, and even in films made by people without racist intentions. Primo Levi has argued that during the Holocaust, institutional structures, power, and the weakness and ambiguity of human nature drew both perpetrators and victims into a moral "gray zone" that we who did not experience it should be hesitant to judge.[16] The German film industry was not a site of horror comparable to the ghettos, concentration camps, and death camps. Nor are the comedies I focus on in this book commensurate to or responsible for the atrocities and murders committed there. Nevertheless, insofar as Nazism and its social and institutional reforms encouraged ideological conformity, cinema too operated in a "gray zone" in which we can and should recognize shades of dark and light in the different films, and different degrees of consent and complicity among the different participants.

3. **You're paranoid!**
Some skeptics could accuse my readings of being hallucinatory (see point one). Others might challenge my focus for being both too negative and not activist enough. Eve Kosofsky Sedgwick, of *Epistemology of the Closet* fame, calls the uncovering of oppressive subtexts, as I do here, "paranoid reading," and criticizes such work for being all-encompassing, mired in negative affect, finding only what it is looking for, placing undue faith in exposure, and precluding other lines of thought and inquiry.[17] Sedgwick's polemical essay promotes "reparative reading," reading that adds value to texts, cultures, and communities, a form of reading she believed at the time to be all too scarce in LGBTQ studies.[18] Given Sedgwick's important work on literary expressions of the closet, one must assume that her 2003 polemic aimed to create

balance, not to eliminate scholarship on sexism, homophobia, transphobia, and other oppressive discourses altogether. Nevertheless, Sedgwick's criticism of paranoid reading and her desire that scholars stop obsessing about the negative fits in with a broader shift in the humanities around the turn of the twenty-first century, when the critical pendulum swung back toward topics like aesthetics and narratology, and murmurs about the death of ideology critique and cultural studies got louder.

Yet at the risk of sounding old-fashioned, whether or not we choose to examine them, those ideological subtexts are still there. So too are the damaging effects of structural and inferential racism, which today are very much in the public eye. I analyze the antisemitic subtexts of Third Reich film comedies neither to prove that Nazis were antisemites (they were) nor to accuse all Germans who love these films of being Nazis (they aren't). I do not get more pleasure from wallowing in the negativity around the Holocaust than I would from taking an affirmative approach to German film's artistic or technological innovation. Rather, I offer a study of inferential antisemitism in film that digs deeply into the mechanics of such representations and how to recognize them. In doing so, I aim to provide a concrete example of and methods and language for writing about antisemitism that hovers beneath the surface of texts. We are fools if we believe that politicized inferential antisemitism is no longer there.

Despite my emphasis on Nazi antisemitism, I offer my conclusions to a larger intellectual coalition. In a historical and political moment in which scholars and activists struggle to understand and combat structural and institutional racism and implicit bias, my book examines film comedy in Nazi Germany to illustrate specific ways of thinking and writing about how racism can be at work even when on the surface it does not appear to be. Dismantling racism requires broad alliances and a large array of tools. In a compelling essay, "Why I Went to Auschwitz," Ray Allen, retired NBA shooting guard, Olympic gold medalist, and actor, describes his longtime fascination with the Holocaust, his repeated visits to the United States Holocaust Memorial Museum in Washington, DC, and his trip to Poland, where he visited Auschwitz and spent time with a descendant of rescuers. Allen writes, "When I returned home to America, I got some very disheartening messages on social media regarding my trip. Some people didn't like the fact that I was going to Poland to raise awareness for the issues that happened there and not using that time or energy to support people in the black community. I was told my ancestors would be ashamed of me." Countering such criticism, Allen argues that learning about the Holocaust offers insights into what human beings are capable of. The lessons taught by its horrors and heroes can help people "to do a better job breaking through ignorance and the close mindedness and the divisions that are plaguing our society."[19]

I too believe that the lessons of the Holocaust have relevance beyond the communities touched most directly by it. My methods and conclusions both fill in gaps in the writing on German film and suggest ways to analyze other media and periods. I hope that the fruits of my scholarly labor not only augment understandings of Nazi cinema but also contribute to broader conversations about race and racism, conversations that currently are proceeding with renewed vigor. *Antisemitism in Film Comedy in Nazi Germany* shows that it is productive to study how films' seemingly innocuous formal and structural features and their explicit content deploy difference, license potentially unintended inferences, and create exclusive communities based on the pleasures of humor, even where racism, antisemitism, sexism, and all other "-isms" seem to have been wiped from the surface.

Notes

1. Cf. Spitzer, *Lives*.
2. Rappeport, "Donald Trump Deletes Tweet."
3. Kampeas, "When Ted Cruz slams Trump."
4. Just a few of many examples: Cooper, "What Trump Can Teach." "Republican Chutzpah." Cohen, "Trump's Handling."
5. Goebbels, "Mimicry."
6. Wilson, "The Trump Scampaign." Simon, "Trump Fails to Bully." Axelrod, "Hillary Clinton's Final Exam." Axelrod also accuses Trump of chutzpah.
7. Noonan, "Trump is Woody Allen."
8. Cf. Hall, "Whites of their Eyes."
9. See Rentschler, *Ministry*.
10. Marin, "Anti-Semitism," 57–74.
11. Marin, "Anti-Semitism," 60.
12. Marin, "Anti-Semitism," 69.
13. Marin, "Anti-Semitism," 59.
14. Lauckner, "The Surrogate Jew," 134.
15. See, for example: Adelson, "Touching Tales of Turks," 93–124; Sieg, *Ethnic Drag*, especially chapters 2 and 3.
16. Levi, "The Gray Zone," in *The Drowned and the Saved*, 36–69.
17. Sedgwick, "Paranoid Reading," 124–51.
18. Sedgwick, "Paranoid Reading," 149–51.
19. Allen, "Why I Went to Auschwitz."

WORKS CITED

Most of the DVDs listed below can be purchased from one or more of the following sources (listed alphabetically):
http://www.amazon.de
http://www.germanvideo.com/
http://www.ihffilm.com
http://www.rarefilmsandmore.com

Films Cited

Alles für Geld. Directed by Reinhold Schünzel. 1923. *Fortune's Fool*, US release, 1928. Accessed January 12, 2018. https://www.youtube.com/watch?v=Fe8HIcyd51E.
Allotria. Directed by Willi Forst. 1936. DVD. Leipzig: Kinowelt, 2007.
Der alte und der junge König. Directed by Hans Steinhoff. 1935. DVD. Berlin: Studiocanal, 2014.
Amphitryon. Directed by Reinhold Schünzel. 1935. DVD. Avondale: germanwarfilms.com, n.d.
Anders als die Andern. Directed by Richard Oswald. 1919. DVD. Munich: Edition Filmmuseum, 2006.
April! April! Directed by Detlef Sierck. 1935. DVD. Avondale: germanwarfilms.com, n.d.
Die Austernprinzessin. Directed by Ernst Lubitsch. 1919. *Lubitsch in Berlin: The Oyster Princess and I Don't Want to Be a Man*. DVD. New York: Kino International, 2006.
Die Blume von Hawaii. Directed by Géza von Cziffra. 1953.
Die Blume von Hawaii. Directed by Richard Oswald. 1932/33. DVD. Avondale: germanwarfilms.com, n.d.
Capriccio. Directed by Karl Ritter. 1938. DVD. Avondale: germanwarfilms.com, n.d.
Carl Peters. Directed by Herbert Selpin. 1941. DVD. Avondale: germanwarfilms.com, n.d.
Charleys Tante. Directed by Robert Stemmle. 1934. DVD. Avondale: rarefilmsandmore.com, n.d.
Dreyfus. Directed by Richard Oswald. 1930. DVD. Hamburg: Studio Hamburg Enterprises, 2011.
Donogoo Tonka. Directed by Reinhold Schünzel. 1935/36. DVD. Avondale: germanwarfilms.com, n.d.
Dr. Mabuse the Gambler. Directed by Fritz Lang. 1922. DVD. New York: Kino, 2006.
Ein Blonder Traum. Directed by Paul Martin. 1932. Avondale: germanwarfilms.com, n.d.
Einmal der liebe Herrgott sein. Directed by Hans Zerlett. 1942. Avondale: rarefilmsandmore.com, n.d.
Der ewige Jude. Directed by Fritz Hippler. 1940. DVD. Avondale: germanwarfilms.com, n.d.
Familientag im Hause Prellstein. Directed by Hans Steinhoff, 1927.
Die Feuerzangenbowle. Directed by Helmut Weiss. 1943/44. DVD. Berlin: Studiocanal, 2009.
First a Girl. Directed by Victor Saville. 1935. DVD. Tulsa: VCI Entertainment, 2012.

Die Frau meiner Träume. Directed by Georg Jacoby. 1943/44. DVD. Munich: Koch Media, 2009.
Glückskinder. Directed by Paul Martin. 1936. DVD. Avondale: germanwarfilms.com, n.d.
Die Gräfin von Monte Cristo. Directed by Karl Hartl. 1932. DVD. Avondale: rarefilmsand more.com, n.d.
The Great Dictator. Directed by Charles Chaplin. 1940. DVD. New York: Criterion Collection, 2011.
Hans Westmar. Directed by Franz Wenzler. 1933. DVD. Avondale: rarefilmsandmore.com, n.d.
Das hässliche Mädchen. Directed by Henry Koster. 1933. DVD. Avondale: germanwarfilms.com, n.d.
Hitlerjunge Quex. Directed by Hans Steinhoff. 1936. DVD. Chicago: International Historic Films, 2007.
It Happened One Night. Directed by Frank Capra. 1934. DVD. Culver City: Sony Pictures Home Entertainment, 2006.
In weiter Ferne, so nah! Directed by Wim Wenders. 1992/93. DVD. Paris, France: Studiocanal, 2006.
The Jazz Singer. Directed by Alan Crosland. 1927. DVD. Burbank: Warner Home Video, 2007.
Jud Süss. Directed by Veit Harlan. 1940. DVD. Chicago: International Historic Films, 2008.
Juden ohne Maske. 1938. Accessed January 2, 2018. https://archive.org/details/1937-Juden-ohne-Maske.
Der Kaiser von Kalifornien. Directed by Luis Trenker, 1935/36. DVD. Avondale: germanwarfilms.com, n.d.
Keine Feier ohne Meyer. Directed by Carl Boese. 1931. DVD. Avondale: rarefilmsandmore.com, n.d.
Kleider machen Leute. Directed by Helmut Käutner. 1940. DVD. Hamburg: Warner Home Video, 2008.
Die Koffer des Herrn O.F. Directed by Alexis Granowsky. 1931. DVD. Avondale: germanwarfilms.com, n.d.
Krach um Jolanthe. Directed by Carl Froelich. 1934. DVD. Avondale: germanwarfilms.com, n.d.
Lauter Lügen. Directed by Heinz Rühmann. 1938. DVD. Avondale: rarefilmsandmore.com, n.d.
Leinen aus Irland. Directed by Heinz Helbig. 1939. DVD. Chicago: International Historic Films, 2011.
The Life of Emile Zola. Directed by William Dieterle. 1937. DVD. Burbank: Warner Home Video, 2008.
Das Mädchen Irene. Directed by Reinhold Schünzel. 1936.
Der Maulkorb. Directed by Erich Engel. 1938. Avondale: rarefilmsandmore.com, n.d.
Metropolis. Directed by Fritz Lang. 1925/26. DVD. New York: Kino on Video, 2004.
Münchhausen. Directed by Josef von Báky. 1942/43. DVD. New York: Kino on Video, 2004.
Die Mysterien eines Frisiersalons. Directed by Erich Engel and Bertolt Brecht. 1922/23. DVD. *Bertolt Brecht Edition.* Berlin: Studiocanal, 2008.
Napoleon ist an allem Schuld. Directed by Curt Goetz. 1938. DVD. Avondale: germanwarfilms.com, n.d.
Nur nicht weich werden, Susanne! Directed by Arsen von Cserépy. 1934/35. DVD. Avondale: germanwarfilms.com, n.d.
Ohm Krüger. Directed by Hans Steinhoff. 1941. DVD. Avondale: germanwarfilms.com, n.d.
Petterson and Bendel. Directed by Per-Axel Branner. 1933. DVD. No further publication information available.

The Producers. Directed by Mel Brooks. 1968. DVD. Los Angeles: 20ᵗʰ Century Fox, 2010.
Quax in Afrika. Directed by Helmut Weiss. 1945. DVD. Hamburg: Ufa, 2006.
Robert und Bertram. Directed by Hans Deppe. 1961. DVD. Riegelsberg: Pidax Film Media, 2013.
Robert und Bertram. Directed by Hans Zerlett. 1939. DVD. Chicago: International Historic Films, 2011.
The Rocky Horror Picture Show. Directed by Jim Sharman. 1975. DVD. Los Angeles: 20ᵗʰ Century Fox, 2015.
Die Rothschilds. Aktien auf Waterloo. Directed by Erich Waschneck. 1940. DVD. Chicago: International Historic Films, 2007.
SA-Mann Brand. Directed by Franz Seitz Sr. 1933. DVD. Avondale: rarefilmsandmore.com, n.d.
Schuhpalast Pinkus. Directed by Ernst Lubitsch. 1916. Accessed January 12, 2018. https://www.youtube.com/watch?v=XIAPIDAZU_4.
Der Schuß im Tonfilmatelier. Directed by Alfred Zeisler. 1930. DVD. Avondale: rarefilmsandmore.com, n.d.
Sieben Jahre Pech. Directed by Ernst Marischka. 1940. DVD. Köln: Alive, 2007.
The Singing Fool. Directed by Lloyd Bacon. 1928. DVD. Burbank: Warner Home Video, 2009.
So ein Flegel. Directed by Robert Stemmle. 1934. VHS. Hamburg: Ufa/Atlas, 1996.
Die Stadt ohne Juden. Directed by H. K. Breslauer. 1924. DVD. Vienna: Filmarchiv Austria, 2008.
Stips. Directed by Carl Froelich. 1951.
The Adventures of Baron Munchausen. Directed by Terry Gilliam. 1988. DVD. Culver City: Sony Pictures, 2008.
The Testament of Dr. Mabuse. Directed by Fritz Lang. 1933. DVD. New York: Criterion, 2004.
The Wizard of Oz. Directed by Victor Fleming. 1939. DVD. Burbank: Warner Brothers, 2013.
The Thief of Bagdad. Directed by Alexander Korda. 1940. DVD. New York: Criterion, 2008.
The Thousand Eyes of Dr. Mabuse. Directed by Fritz Lang. 1960. DVD. Medford, OR: Sinister Cinema, 2009.
They Won't Forget. Directed by Mervyn LeRoy. 1937.
To Be or Not to Be. Directed by Ernst Lubitsch. 1942. DVD. New York: Criterion Collection, 2013.
Traumulus. Directed by Carl Froelich. 1936. Avondale: rarefilmsandmore.com, n.d.
Die Umwege des schönen Karl. Directed by Carl Froelich. 1937/38. DVD. Avondale: germanwarfilms.com, n.d.
Verräter. Directed by Karl Ritter. 1936. DVD. Avondale: germanwarfilms.com, n.d.
Victor/Victoria. Directed by Blake Edwards. 1982. DVD. Burbank: Warner Archive, 2012.
Viktor und Viktoria. Directed by Karl Anton. 1957.
Viktor und Viktoria. Directed by Reinhold Schünzel. 1933. DVD. Hamburg: Warner Home Video Germany, n.d.
Viktoria und ihr Husar. Directed by Richard Oswald. 1931. DVD. Avondale: germanwarfilms.com, n.d.
Weiberregiment. Directed by Karl Ritter. 1936. DVD. Avondale: germanwarfilms.com, n.d.
Die Welt ohne Maske. Directed by Harry Piel. 1933/34. DVD. Avondale: germanwarfilms.com, n.d.
Wenn wir alle Engel wären. Directed by Carl Froelich. 1936. DVD. Avondale: germanwarfilms.com, n.d.
Wenn wir alle Engel wären. Directed by Günther Lüders. 1956. Accessed January 12, 2018. https://www.youtube.com/watch?v=cu5E-MWbYE8.
Der zerbrochene Krug. Directed by Gustav Ucicky. 1937. DVD. Hamburg: Ufa, 2005.

Print Sources through 1945

Advertisement for *Petterson and Bendel*. *Der Film*, November 19, 1938.
Advertisement for *Schuhpalast Pinkus*. *Der Kinematograph*, June 21, 1916.
Advertisement for *Schuhpalast Pinkus*. *Lichtbild-Bühne*, August 12, 1916.
Amery, L. S. *The German Colonial Claim*. London: W&R Chambers, 1939.
Beierle, Alfred. "Der Weg zum deutschen Filmlustspiel." *Film Kurier*, July 6, 1933.
Benjamin, Walter. *Das Kunstwerk im Zeitalter seiner technischen Reproduzierbarkeit*. Reprint, Frankfurt/M.: Suhrkamp, 1994.
"Beseitigung der Kunstkritik: statt dessen Kunstbericht, Mindestalter für Kunstschriftleiter 30 Jahre, ein Erlaß des Propagandaministers." *Film Kurier*, November 28, 1936.
Betz, Hans-Walther. Review of *So ein Flegel*. *Der Film*, February 17, 1934.
Bormann, Martin. "The Relation Between National Socialism and Christianity." In *The Nazi Years: A Documentary History*, edited by Joachim Remak, 103. Long Grove: Waveland, 1990.
Bubendey, Friedrich. *Nur nicht weich werden, Susanne! Eine Komödie in fünf Aufzügen nach dem gleichnamigen Roman von Peter Hagen*. Berlin: Paul Steegeman Verlag, 1934.
D[emandowsky], [Ewald] v[on]. "Ein neuer Froelich-Film 'Wenn wir alle Engel wären': Eröffnungsvorstellung im Tauentzien-Palast." *Völkischer Beobachter*, October 11, 1936.
"Der deutsche Film." *Lichtbild-Bühne*, March 2, 1936.
"'Deutsche' Filme?" *Deutsches Wollen: Die Wochenzeitung für das junge Reich*, October 18, 1936.
"Die deutsche Filmpresse: ihre Resonanz und filmpublizistische Bedeutung im Spiegel ihres Umfangs." *Der Film*, July 19, 1935.
"Deutschland kann lachen – weil es lachen kann! Dem guten Filmhumor die höchste Auszeichnung." *Lichtbild-Bühne*, October 19, 1936.
"Dr. Goebbels sprach vor den deutschen Kritikern." *Lichtbild-Bühne*, December 17, 1935.
Dr. Joh. [pseud.]. Review of *So ein Flegel*. *Film Kurier*, February 14, 1934.
———. Review of *Viktor und Viktoria*. *Film Kurier*, December 27, 1933.
Dr. N. [pseud.]. "Forderungen an den deutschen Film." *Film Kurier*, April 8, 1933.
Dr. W. M. [pseud.]. "Steigendes Interesse für ernste Filme." *Film Kurier*, August 22, 1944.
E. K. [pseud.]. Review of *April! April! Deutsche Filmzeitung*, June 28, 1936.
Eckert, Gerd. "Filmkomik." *Das deutsche Volkstum* 19, no. 12 (December 1937): 890–91.
Eisler, Rudolf. *Handwörterbuch der Philosophie*. 2nd ed. Edited by Richard Müller-Freienfels. Berlin: E.S. Mittler, 1922.
Feder, Gottfried. *Die Juden*. 2nd ed. Munich: Franz. Eher Nachf., 1933.
"Film im Dritten Reich: Ans Reden und Artikeln der neuen Männer." *Deutsche Filmzeitung*, April 7, 1933.
"Filmbetrachtung als Erziehungsaufgabe." *Lichtbild-Bühne*, June 30, 1937.
Film-Prüfstelle, Berlin. Zulassungskarte, Prüfung-Nummer 52680. November 14, 1939. Bundesarchiv-Filmarchiv, Berlin.
"Das Filmtheater der Zukunft: Volksunterhaltungsstätte mit kultureller Geltung." *Film Kurier*, November 25, 1933.
Fischer, Hans Erasmus. "Wenn wir alle Engel wären: Carl Froelichs fröhlicher erfolg im Tauentzien-Palast." *Berliner Lokal-Anzeiger*, October 11, 1936.
Fritzsche, Hans. "Dr. Goebbels und sein Ministerium." In *Deutsche Führer Deutsches Schicksal: Das Buch der Künder und Führer des dritten Reiches*, edited by Hans Heinz Mantau-Sadlia, 330–42. Munich: Verlag Max Steinebach, 1934.

"Des Führers Aufruf an die deutschen Künstler: Auch dem deutschen Film ins Gewissen." *Film Kurier*, September 2, 1933.
"Für klare Scheidung: Die Judenfrage im neuen Deutschland." *Blick in die Zeit*, July 26, 1935.
G[eßner], A[lexander]. "Freiheit für den Schöpfer! Neuer Geist und Selbstverantwortlichkeit als Fundamente von dem neuen Filmgesetz." *Film Kurier*, May 13, 1933.
———. "'Volk' statt 'Publikum': Volkskunst muß fruchtbares Wirkungsfeld finden. Zähe Aufbauarbeit notwendig." *Film Kurier*, May 29, 1933.
———. "Schluß mit der Einförmigkeit! Der kommende Film muß den Weg zur Volksgemeinschaft bereiten: Filmstoffe und Startum." *Film Kurier*, June 29, 1933.
Goebbels, Joseph. "Mimicry." Translated by Randall Bytwerk. Originally published as "Mimikry" in *Das Reich*, July 20, 1941. Accessed June 29, 2017. http://research.calvin.edu/german-propaganda-archive/goeb18.htm.
Goebbels, Joseph, and Mjölnir [Hans Schweitzer]. *Die verfluchten Hakenkreuzler. Etwas zum Nachdenken*. Munich: Verlag Frz. Eher, 1932.
Graff, Sigmund. "Was ist komisch?" *Film Kurier*, February 25, 1938.
Hagen, Peter [pseud. for Willi Krause]. *Nur nicht weich werden, Susanne! Ein lustiger Roman*. Serialized in *Der Angriff*, April 19, 1933–May 31, 1933.
Hammer Tonfilm Verleih. *Verleih Programm 1935–1936*. Berlin: Erasmusdruck, 1935.
"Heiterkeit und Spannung aus zwei neuen Tobis-Filmen." *Der Film*, March 11, 1939.
Henseleit, Felix. "Heitere Filme mit ernstem Hintergrund." *Film Kurier*, December 2, 1941.
Herrmann, Hilde. "Humor der Völker im Film." *Literatur: Monatsschrift für Literaturfreunde* 41 (1938): 364.
Herzberg, Georg. "Robert und Bertram/Ufa-Palast am Zoo." *Film-Kurier*, July 15, 1939, 3.
———. [as G. H.] "Wortwitz im Film." *Film Kurier*, January 22, 1943.
Hippler, Fritz. *Betrachtungen zum Filmschaffen*. Berlin: Max Hesses Verlag, 1942.
Ho. [pseud.]. Review of *Nur nicht weich werden, Susanne! Kreuz Zeitung* 87, no. 21 [no date on clipping]. *Bundesarchiv-Filmarchiv*, File Folder Nr. 12313 I.
Holz, Karl. "Jüdische Jazzmusik verboten: Reichssendeleiter Hadamovsky macht ein Ende mit jüdischer Unkultur." *Der Stürmer* 13, no. 45 (November 1935): 6.
Hundt-Radowsky, Hartwig. *Die Judenschule, oder, Gründliche Anleitung in kurzer Zeit ein vollkommener schwarzer oder weisser Jude zu werden*. 3 vols. Jerusalem: in der neuen Buchhandlung, [1822–23].
"Ich wollt', ich wär' ein Huhn." *Das schwarze Korps*, November 26, 1936.
J. v. B. [pseud.]. "Die Aufgaben des volkhaften Films: Statt oberflächlicher Zerstreuung – neue Kraftquellen für das Volk. Vorbild gegenüber der Welt." *Film Kurier*, August 21, 1933.
Jerosch, Ernst. "Aufnahmebeginn bei 'Robert und Bertram.' Der Lohn der guten Tat. Unterhaltung mit Hans H. Zerlett/Zum ersten Mal: eine Filmposse. Humor mit und ohne Moral." *Der Film*, January 21, 1939.
———. "Der Schritt zur Filmposse: Robert und Bertram/Ufa-Palast am Zoo." *Der Film*, July 15 1939.
Jockisch, Hermann. "Vagabunden seit 83 Jahren!" *Mein Film in Wien*, February 10, 1939.
Johannsen, G. Kurt and H. H. Kraft. *Germany's Colonial Problem*. 1937. Reprint, Port Washington, NY: Kennikat Press, 1970.
K. [pseud.]. "Ist die Kritik als Erzieherin nötig? Das Recht auf Kritik." *Lichtbild-Bühne*, October 3, 1935.
K. R. [pseud.]. Review of *Nur nicht weich werden, Susanne! Völkischer Beobachter*, Berlin. January 26, 1935. *Bundesarchiv-Filmarchiv*, File Folder Nr. 12313 I.

Kadner, Siegfried. *Rasse und Humor*. Munich: J.F. Lehmanns, 1930.
———. *Rasse und Humor*, 2nd ed. Munich: J.F. Lehmanns, 1939.
Keller, Josef, and Hanns Andersen. *Der Jude als Verbrecher*. Berlin: Niebelungen Verlag, 1937.
Kracauer, Siegfried. "Das Ornament der Masse." *Das Ornament der Masse: Essays*, 50–63. Frankfurt/Main: Suhrkamp, 1963.
———. "Little Shop Girls Go to the Movies," 1927. Translated by Thomas Y. Levin. In *German Essays on Film*, edited by Richard W. McCormick and Alison Guenther-Pal, 99–111. New York: Continuum, 2004.
L. [pseud.]. Review of *April! April! Der Film*, October 26, 1935.
"Landstreicher im Himmel: Gespräch mit Hans H. Zerlett über den Film 'Robert und Bertram.'" *Film-Kurier*, January 17, 1939.
Macht, Karl. "Amerikanischer und deutscher Humor." Review of *Ritter ohne Furcht und Tadel*. *Der Angriff*, October 23, 1937.
Martini, Wolfgang. "Robert und Bertram." *Deutsche Filmzeitung*, July 23, 1939.
"Maßhalten auch im Heiteren. Komik und Humor: Ein Kapitel beherzigenswerter Filmdramaturgie." *Film Kurier*, August 5, 1940.
"Mehr Humor in Film." *Lichtbild-Bühne*, August 21, 1936.
"Nazis Determined to Make the Reich 'Entirely *Judenrein*' by April, Berlin Reports." *Jewish Telegraphic Agency*, November 7, 1941. Accessed July 13, 2017. https://www.jta.org/1941/11/07/archive/nazis-determined-to-make-the-reich-entirely-judenrein-by-april-berlin-reports.
"Der Neuaufbau des deutschen Films." *Kinematograph*, June 2, 1933.
Neumann, Carl, Curt Belling, and Hans-Walther Betz. *Film "Kunst," Film Kohn, Film Korruption*. Berlin: Verlag Hermann Scherping, 1937.
"Niveau auch im Unterhaltungsfilm: 'Geschäftserfolg' keine Entschuldigung mehr für mangelnden Geschmack. Der überlebte Schlager-Film." *Film Kurier*, August 25, 1933.
Olimsky, Fritz. "Palmen und Frauenträume: Sommer im Filmatelier." Clipping at *Stiftung Deutsche Kinemathek/Filmmuseum Berlin*, probably from the *Berliner Börsen-Zeitung*. January 29, 1933.
———. "Ungarische Version." Clipping at *Stiftung Deutsche Kinemathek/Filmmuseum Berlin*, probably from the *Berliner Börsen-Zeitung*. March 4, 1933.
R. [pseud.]. "Forderungen an den heiteren Film der Zeit." *Film Kurier*, October 28, 1933.
———. Review of *Nur nicht weich werden, Susanne! Film Kurier* 17.21 [no date on clipping]. *Bundesarchiv-Filmarchiv*, File Folder Nr. 12313 I.
"Rassenlehre und Filmproduktion." *Deutsche Filmzeitung*, May 20, 1934.
"Das Recht auf Humor: um das 'Heitere' des deutschen Films." *Film Kurier*, May 23, 1936.
Review of *Die Blume von Hawaii*. *Kinematograph*, April 7, 1933.
Review of *Donogoo Tonka*. *Deutsche Filmzeitung*, February 2, 1936.
Review of *Glückskinder*. *Film Kurier*, September 9, 1936.
Review of *Nur nicht weich werden, Susanne! Die Lupe*, Berlin. February 1, 1935. *Bundesarchiv-Filmarchiv*, File Folder Nr. 12313 I.
Review of *Schuhpalast Pinkus*. *Der Film*, June 17, 1916.
Review of *Viktor und Viktoria* from the *Nachtausgabe* cited in an Ufa advertisement for *Viktor und Viktoria*. *Film Kurier*, January 12, 1934.
Rmstr. [pseud.]. Review of *Nur nicht weich werden, Susanne! Deutsche Allgemeine Zeitung*, Berlin. January 26, 1935. *Bundesarchiv-Filmarchiv*, File Folder Nr. 12313 I.

"Robert und Bertram." *Paimann's Filmlisten: Wochenschrift für Lichtbild-Betrachtung,* July 14, 1939.
Roemisch, Bruno. "Was ist ein Volksfilm?" *Film Kurier,* April 19, 1933.
R[öhl], F. [pseud.]. Review of *Donogoo Tonka. Der Film,* January 25, 1936.
———. Review of *Glückskinder. Der Film,* September 19, 1936.
S. [pseud.]. "Blindbuchen." *Deutsche Filmzeitung,* April 14, 1935.
S. [pseud.]. Review of *Nur nicht weich werden, Susanne! B.Z. am Mittag,* nr. 22, 1935 [no date on clipping]. *Bundesarchiv-Filmarchiv,* File Folder Nr. 12313 I.
Sattig, Ewald. *Die deutsche Filmpresse.* Breslau: Brehmer and Minuth, 1937.
Schneider, [Albert]. [as A. S.] "Dr. Goebbels vor den Filmschaffenden: Ein neues Bekenntnis zum Film." *Lichtbild-Bühne,* December 16, 1935.
———. [as A. S.] Review of *April! April! Lichtbild-Bühne,* October 25, 1935.
———. [as A. S.] Review of *Donogoo Tonka. Lichtbild-Bühne,* January 25, 1936.
———. Review of *Glückskinder. Lichtbild-Bühne,* September 19, 1936.
———. Review of *Robert und Bertram. Lichtbild-Bühne,* July 15, 1939.
———. Review of *Wenn wir alle Engel wären. Lichtbild-Bühne,* October 10, 1936.
"Schünzel macht fröhlich and Froelich macht...?" *Deutsches Wollen: Die Wochenzeitung für das junge Reich,* October 18, 1936.
S[chwar]k, [Günther]. "Angst vor Humor? Wir brauchen nach wie vor Lustspiele, Schwänke und Unterhaltungsfilme." *Film Kurier,* May 22, 1937.
———. "Unterhaltungsfilm gleichberechtigt: im Dienste freudespendender Kraft auch staatspolitisch wertvoll." *Film Kurier,* October 19, 1936.
———. Review of *April! April! Film Kurier,* October 25, 1935.
———. Review of *Donogoo Tonka. Film Kurier,* January 25, 1936.
Siska, Heinz W., ed. *Wunderwelt Film: Künstler und Werkleute einer Weltmacht.* Heidelberg: Verlagsanstalt Hüdig & Co., [1943].
Sp[ielhofer], H[ans]. "Der neue Geschmack." *Deutsche Filmzeitung,* April 28, 1933.
Spoerl, Heinrich. "Die Angst vor dem Witz." In *Man kann ruhig darüber sprechen,* 7–8. Berlin: Paul Neff Verlag, 1937.
———. *Die Feuerzangenbowle: Eine Lausbüberei in der Kleinstadt.* Düsseldorf: Droste, n.d. [originally published 1933].
Stark, Johannes. "'Weisse Juden' in der Wissenschaft." *Das Schwarze Korps,* July 15, 1937.
"Streiflichter." *Völkischer Beobachter,* March 13, 1931.
Urgiß, Julius. "Künstlerprofil: Ernst Lubitsch." *Der Kinematograph,* Düsseldorf, August 30, 1916. Reprinted in *Lubitsch,* edited by Hans Helmut Prinzler and Enno Patalas, 89–90. Munich: C.J. Bucher, 1984.
Utermann, Wilhelm. "Der deutsche Lustspielfilm im jetzigen Kriege: der Humor soll Herz haben, soll redlich und aufrichtig sein!" *Film Kurier,* September 24, 1940.
"Verjudung und Geschäftemacherei im 'deutschen' Film." *Der Angriff,* March 1, 1933.
Volz, Robert. "Eine zeitgemäße Frage: Muß der heitere Film niveaulos sein? Frohsinn ist nicht Stumpfsinn! Zur Ethik im Filmlustspiel." *Der deutsche Film* 5, no. 1 (July 1940): 2–4.
———. "Krisis des Lustspielfilms?" Reprinted from the *Berliner Börsen Zeitung* in *Lichtbild-Bühne,* June 11, 1937.
W. P. [pseud.]. Review of *Viktor und Viktoria. Deutsche Filmzeitung,* January 21, 1934.
"Was ist Kulturschande?" *Der Stürmer* 13, no. 29 (July 1935): 6.

"Wie ist sowas nur möglich? Juden wollten Mädchen 'zum Film bringen'!" *Film-Kurier*, January 4, 1939.

Wortig, Kurt. *Der Film in der deutschen Tageszeitung*. Limburg an der Lahn: Limburger Vereinsdruckerei, 1940.

"Worüber lachen wir eigentlich?" *Film Kurier*, September 14, 1937.

Z. [pseud.]. "Erscheinungsformen des Spielfilms." *Lichtbild-Bühne*, March 25, 1936.

Zweig, Stephan. "Die Monotonisierung der Welt." *Berliner Börsen-Courier* 53, February 1, 1925. Reprinted in *Weimarer Republik: Manifeste und Dokumente zur deutschen Literatur 1918–1933*, edited by Anton Kaes, 268–73. Stuttgart: Metzler, 1983.

Post-1945 Secondary Sources

Adelson, Leslie. "Touching Tales of Turks, Germans, and Jews: Cultural Alterity, Historical Narrative, and Literary Riddles for the 1990s." *New German Critique* 80 (Spring–Summer 2000): 93–124.

Adorno, Theodor. *The Stars Down to Earth and Other Essays on the Irrational in Culture*. Edited by Stephen Crook. London: Routledge, 1994.

Albrecht, Gerd. *Nationalsozialistische Filmpolitik: Eine soziologische Untersuchung über die Spielfilme des Dritten Reichs*. Stuttgart: Ferdinand Enke Verlag, 1969.

Allen, Ray. "Why I Went to Auschwitz." *The Players' Tribune*, August 3, 2017. https://www.theplayerstribune.com/ray-allen-why-i-went-to-auschwitz/.

Ameskamp, Simone. "Fanning the Flames: Cremation in Late Imperial and Weimar Germany." In *Between Mass Death and Individual Loss: The Place of the Dead in Twentieth-Century Germany*, edited by Alon Confino, Paul Betts, and Dirk Schumann, 93–112. New York: Berghahn, 2008.

Anderson, Benedict. *Imagined Communities: Reflections on the Origin and Spread of Nationalism*. New York: Verso, 1983.

Ascheid, Antje. *Hitler's Heroines: Stardom and Womanhood in Nazi Cinema*. Philadelphia: Temple University Press, 2003.

———. "Nazi Stardom and the 'Modern Girl': The Case of Lilian Harvey." *New German Critique* 74 (Spring/Summer 1998): 57–89.

Ashkenazi, Ofer. *Weimar Film and Modern Jewish Identity*. New York: Palgrave Macmillan, 2012.

Atluri, Tara. "Lighten Up?! Humour, Race, and Da Off Colour Joke of Ali G." *Media, Culture & Society* 31, no. 2 (2009): 197–214.

Axelrod, David. "Hillary Clinton's Final Exam." *The New York Times*, September 24, 2016. https://www.nytimes.com/2016/09/25/opinion/campaign-stops/hillary-clintons-final-exam.html?_r=0.

Bailey, Constance. "Fight the Power: African American Humor as a Discourse of Resistance." *Western Journal of Black Studies* 36, no. 4 (2012): 253–63.

Baranowski, Shelley. *Nazi Empire: German Colonialism and Imperialism from Bismarck to Hitler*. Cambridge: Cambridge University Press, 2011.

Bartov, Omer. *The "Jew" in Cinema: From* The Golem *to* Don't Touch My Holocaust. Bloomington: Indiana University Press, 2005.

Bauman, Zygmunt. "Allosemitism: Premodern, Modern, Postmodern." In *Modernity, Culture and 'the Jew'*, edited by Bryan Cheyette and Laura Marcus, 143–56. Stanford: Stanford University Press, 1998.

"Beilstein." Accessed January 2, 2018. http://www.beilstein-mosel.de.
"Beilstein in vergangener Zeit." Accessed January 2, 2018. http://www.beilstein-stadtfueh rung.de/historisch_2.htm.
Bel, Germá. "Against the Mainstream: Nazi Privatization in 1930s Germany." *Economic History Review* 63, no. 1 (February 2010): 34–55.
Beller, Steven. "The Right Mélange: Viennese Operetta as a Stage for Jewish Humor." In *Studies in Contemporary Jewry*, vol. 25, *A Club of Their Own: Jewish Humorists and the Contemporary World*, edited by Eli Lederhendler, 3–23. Oxford: Oxford University Press, 2016.
Ben-Amos, Dan. "The 'Myth' of Jewish Humor." *Western Folklore* 32, no. 2 (April 1973): 112–31.
Benz, Wolfgang. *Bilder vom Juden: Studien zum alltäglichen Antisemitismus*. Munich: C.H. Beck, 2001.
Bergman, David, ed. *Camp Grounds: Style and Homosexuality*. Amherst: University of Massachusetts Press, 1993.
Bhabha, Homi. "Of Mimicry and Man: The Ambivalence of Colonial Discourse." In *The Location of Culture*, 85–92. London: Routledge, 1994.
Bial, Henry. *Acting Jewish: Negotiating Ethnicity on the American Stage and Screen*. Ann Arbor: University of Michigan Press, 2005.
Billig, Michael. *Laughter and Ridicule: Towards a Social Critique of Humour*. London: Sage Publications, 2005.
Bini, Andrea. *Male Anxiety and Psychopathology in Film: Comedy Italian Style*. New York: Palgrave Macmillian, 2015.
Boerger, Angelina. "Kultveranstaltung 'Die Feuerzangenbowle': Stilgerecht mit Frack, Zylinder und Stock." *Aachener Zeitung*, November 22, 2015. http://www.aachener-zeitung .de/lokales/aachen/kultveranstaltung-die-feuerzangenbowle-stilgerecht-mit-frack -zylinder-und-stock-1.1231250.
Bonilla-Silva, Eduardo. *Racism without Racists: Color-Blind Racism and the Persistence of Racial Inequality in America*. 4th ed. Lanham, MD: Roman and Littlefield, 2014.
Brandom, Robert. *Making it Explicit*. Cambridge, MA: Harvard University Press, 1994.
Bratton, Susan Power. *The Natural Aryan and the Unnatural Jew: Environmental Racism in Weimar and Nazi Film*. PhD diss., University of Texas at Dallas, 1997.
Brown, Timothy S. *Weimar Radicals: Nazis and Communists between Authenticity and Performance*. New York: Berghahn Books, 2009.
Browning, Christopher. "One Day in Jozefow: Initiation to Mass Murder." In *Lessons and Legacies: The Meaning of the Holocaust in a Changing World*, edited by Peter Hays, 196–209. Evanston: Northwestern UP, 1991.
——. *Ordinary Men: Reserve Police Battalion 101 and the Final Solution in Poland*. New York: HarperCollins, 1992.
Buerkle, Darcy. "Caught in the Act. Norbert Elias, Emotion and *The Ancient Law*." *Journal of Modern Jewish Studies* 8, no. 1 (March 2009): 83–102.
——. "Gendered Spectatorship, Jewish Women and Psychological Advertising in Weimar Germany." *Women's History Review* 15, no. 4 (September 2006): 625–36.
——. *Nothing Happened: Charlotte Salomon and an Archive of Suicide*. Ann Arbor: University of Michigan Press, 2013.
Butler, Judith. *Bodies That Matter: On the Discursive Limits of "Sex."* New York: Routledge, 1993.

———. *Gender Trouble.* New York: Routledge, 1990.
Campbell, Joan. *Joy in Work, German Work: The National Debate, 1800–1945.* Princeton: Princeton University Press, 1989.
Carter, Erica. *Dietrich's Ghosts: The Sublime and the Beautiful in Third Reich Film.* London: British Film Institute, 2004.
———. "Marlene Dietrich: The Prodigal Daughter." In *Dietrich Icon*, edited by Gerd Gemünden and Mary R. Desjardins, 186–207. Durham: Duke University Press, 2007.
Cleto, Fabio, ed. *Camp: Queer Aesthetics and the Performing Subject.* Ann Arbor: University of Michigan Press, 1999.
Cohen, Richard. "Why Trump's Handling of a Deutsche Bank Loan is so Foreboding." *The Washington Post*, July 20, 2017. https://www.washingtonpost.com/blogs/post-partisan/wp/2017/07/20/why-trumps-handling-of-a-deutsche-bank-loan-is-so-foreboding/?utm_term=.3d636be89ada.
Conrad, Sebastian. *German Colonialism: A Short History.* Cambridge: Cambridge University Press, 2012.
Cooper, Ryan. "What Trump Can Teach the Democrats about Chutzpah." *The Week*, January 24, 2017. http://theweek.com/articles/675151/what-trump-teach-democrats-about-chutzpah.
Courtade, Francis, and Pierre Cadars. *Geschichte des Films im Dritten Reich.* Translated by Florian Hopf. Munich: Carl Hanser Verlag, 1975.
Critchley, Simon. *On Humor.* London: Routledge, 2002.
Cuomo, Glenn R., ed. *National Socialist Cultural Policy.* New York: St. Martin's Press, 1995.
Dammeyer, Manfred, ed. *Der Spielfilm im Dritten Reich.* Oberhausen: Arbeitsseminar der Westdeutschen Kurzfilmtage Oberhausen, 1966.
Davis, Christian. *Colonialism, Antisemitism, and Germans of Jewish Descent in Imperial Germany.* Ann Arbor: University of Michigan Press, 2012.
Dennis, David B. *Inhumanities: Nazi Interpretations of Western Culture.* Cambridge: Cambridge University Press, 2012.
Distelmeyer, Jan, ed. *Spaß beiseite, Film ab. Jüdischer Humor und verdrängendes Lachen in der Filmkomödie bis 1945.* Munich: Edition Text + Kritik, 2006.
Doherty, Thomas. *Hollywood and Hitler, 1933–1939.* New York: Columbia University Press, 2013.
Dopp, Werner. *125 Jahre Berliner Konfektion.* Berlin: Ernst Staneck, 1962.
Dyer, Richard. *The Matter of Images: Essays on Representations.* New York: Routledge, 2002.
Egea, Juan F. *Dark Laughter: Spanish Film, Comedy, and the Nation.* Madison: University of Wisconsin Press, 2013.
Ehlers, Klaas-Hinrich. "Der deutsche Gruß in Briefen: zur historischen Soziallinguistik und Pragmatik eines verordneten Sprachgebrauchs." *Linguistik Online* 55, no. 5 (2012). http://www.linguistik-online.de/55_12/ehlers.html.
Eisner, Lotte. *The Haunted Screen.* Berkeley: University of California Press, 1994.
Elsaesser, Thomas. "Moderne und Modernisierug: Der deutsche Film der dreißiger Jahre." *Montage/av* 3, no. 2 (1994): 23–40.
Fisher, Jaimey, ed. *Generic Histories of German Cinema: Genre and its Deviations.* Rochester, NY: Camden House, 2013.
Fox, Jo. *Filming Women in the Third Reich.* New York: Berg, 2000.
Friedländer, Saul. *Nazi Germany and the Jews.* Vol. 1, *The Years of Persecution, 1933–1939.* New York: Harper Collins, 1997.

———. *Nazi Germany and the Jews*. Vol. 2: *The Years of Extermination, 1939–1945*. New York: Harper Collins, 2007.
Friedman, Régine Mihal. *L'image et son Juif*. Paris: Payot: 1983.
———. "Male Gaze and Female Reaction: Veit Harlan's *Jew Süss* (1940)." In *Gender and German Cinema*, vol. 2, edited by Sandra Frieden, Richard McCormick, Vibeke Petersen, and Laurie Melissa Vogelsang, 117–33. Providence, RI: Berg, 1993.
Friedman, Sam and Giselinde Kuipers. "The Divisive Power of Humour: Comedy, Taste and Symbolic Boundaries." *Cultural Sociology* 7, no. 2 (2013): 179–95.
Führer, Karl Christian. "Two-Fold Admiration: American Movies as Popular Entertainment and Artistic Model in Nazi Germany 1933–1945." In *Mass Media, Culture and Society in Twentieth-Century Germany*, edited by Karl Christian Führer and Corey Ross, 97–112. London: Palgrave MacMillan, 2006.
Ganeva, Mila. *Women in Weimar Fashion: Discourses and Displays in German Culture, 1918–1933*. Rochester, NY: Camden House, 2008.
Georgakas, Dan. "Ethnic Humor in American Film: The Greek Americans." In *A Companion to Film Comedy*, edited by Andrew Horton and Joanna E. Rapf, 387–406. Chichester, UK: Wiley-Blackwell, 2013.
Gillota, David. *Ethnic Humor in Multiethnic America*. New Brunswick, NJ: Rutgers University Press, 2013.
Gilman, Sander L. *Difference and Pathology: Stereotypes of Sexuality, Race, and Madness*. Ithaca, NY: Cornell University Press, 1985.
———. *Jewish Self-Hatred: Anti-Semitism and the Hidden Language of the Jews*. Baltimore: Johns Hopkins University Press, 1990.
———. *The Jew's Body*. New York: Routledge, 1991.
Göktürk, Deniz. "Strangers in Disguise: Role-Play beyond Identity Politics in Anarchic Comedy." *New German Critique* 92 (Spring–Summer 2004): 100–22.
Goldhagen, Daniel. *Hitler's Willing Executioners: Ordinary Germans and the Holocaust*. New York: Vintage Books, 1997.
Görtz, Franz Josef, and Hans Sarkowicz. *Heinz Rühmann 1902–1994: Der Schauspieler und sein Jahrhundert*. Munich: C.H. Beck, 2001.
Grange, William. *Hitler Laughing: Comedy in the Third Reich*. Lanham, MD: University Press of America, 2006.
Gunning, Tom. "The Cinema of Attractions: Early Film, its Spectator, and the Avant Garde." In *Early Cinema: Space, Frame, Narrative*, edited by Thomas Elsaesser and Adam Barker, 56–62. London: British Film Institute, 1990.
Habich, Christiane. *Lilian Harvey*. Berlin: Haude und Spener, 1990.
Haehnel, Birgit. "'The Black Jew' An Afterimage of German Colonialism." In *German Colonialism, Visual Culture, and Modern Memory*, edited by Volker M. Langbehn, 238–259. New York: Routledge, 2010.
Hake, Sabine. *German National Cinema*. London: Routledge, 2002.
———. *Popular Cinema of the Third Reich*. Austin: University of Texas Press, 2001.
Hales, Barbara, Mihaela Petrescu, and Valerie Weinstein, eds. *Continuity and Crisis in German Cinema 1928–1936*. Rochester, NY: Camden House, 2016.
Hall, Stuart. "The Whites of their Eyes: Racist Ideologies and the Media." In *Silver Linings: Some Strategies for the Eighties. Contributions to the Communist University of London*, edited by George Bridges and Rosalind Brunt, 28–52. London: Lawrence and Wishart, 1981.

Hans, Jan. "Musik- und Revuefilm." In *Mediale Mobilmachung I: Das Dritte Reich und der Film*, Mediengeschichte des Films Band 4, edited by Harro Segeberg, 203–28. Munich: Wilhelm Fink Verlag, 2004.
Harrod, Mary. *From France with Love: Gender and Identity in French Romantic Comedy*. London: I.B. Tauris, 2015.
Harten, Hans-Christian, Uwe Neirich, and Matthias Schwerendt. *Rassenhygiene als Erziehungsideologie des dritten Reichs: Bio-bibliographisches Handbuch*. Berlin: Akademie, 2006.
Heinig, Herbert Louis. *The "Black Jew," Germans, Nazis and Nature's Other Creatures*. Bloomington, IN: Author House, 2004.
Heins, Laura. *Nazi Film Melodrama*. Chicago: University of Illinois Press, 2013.
Hennefeld, Maggie. "Destructive Metamorphosis: The Comedy of Female Catastrophe and Feminist Film Historiography." *Discourse* 36, no. 2 (Spring 2014): 176–206.
Herf, Jeffrey. *The Jewish Enemy*. Cambridge: The Belknap Press of Harvard University Press, 2006.
——. *Reactionary Modernism*. Cambridge: Cambridge UP, 1984.
Herzog, Dagmar. "How 'Jewish' is German Sexuality? Sex and Antisemitism in the Third Reich." In *German History from the Margins*, edited by Neil Gregor, Nils Roemer, and Mark Roseman, 185–203. Bloomington: Indiana University Press, 2006.
Hickethier, Knut. "Der Ernst der Filmkomödie." In *Mediale Mobilmachung I: Das Dritte Reich und der Film*, Mediengeschichte des Films Band 4, edited by Harro Segeberg, 229–46. Munich: Wilhelm Fink Verlag, 2004.
Hill, Murray. "Humour in Nazi Germany and its Post-War Rehabilitation." *Forum for Modern Language Studies* 20, no. 1 (January 1984): 4.
Hirte, Ronald. "Vom Antlitz zur Maske: Eine Ausstellung in Weimar und das Menschenbild der Naturwissenschaftlichen Anthropologie." *Historische Anthropologie* 8, no. 2 (August 2000): 272–90.
Hollstein, Dorothea. *Jud Süss und die Deutschen: Antisemitische Vorurteile im nationalsozialistischen Spielfilm*. Frankfurt/Main: Ullstein, 1983.
Horton, Andrew, and Joanna E. Rapf. *A Companion to Film Comedy*. Chichester, UK: Wiley-Blackwell, 2013.
Hull, David Stewart. *Film in the Third Reich: A Study of the German Cinema 1933–1945*. Berkeley: University of California Press, 1969.
John, Catherine A. "Black Film Comedy as Vital Edge: A Reassessment of the Genre." In *A Companion to Film Comedy*, edited by Andrew Horton and Joanna E. Rapf, 343–64. Chichester, UK: Wiley-Blackwell, 2013.
Joseph, Ralina L. "Imagining Obama: Reading Overtly and Inferentially Racist Images of our 44th President, 2007–2008." *Communication Studies* 62, no. 4 (2011): 389–405.
Kaes, Anton. *From Hitler to Heimat: The Return of History as Film*. Cambridge, MA: Harvard University Press, 1989.
Kampeas, Ron. "When Ted Cruz slams Trump for 'chutzpah,' should Jews be offended?" *The Times of Israel*, February 7, 2016. https://www.timesofisrael.com/when-ted-cruz-slams-trump-for-chutzpah-should-jews-be-offended.
Kanzog, Klaus. *"Staatspolitisch besonders wertvoll": ein Handbuch zu 30 deutschen Spielfilmen der Jahre 1934 bis 1945*. Munich: Diskurs Film, 1994.
Kaplan, Marion A. *The Making of the Jewish Middle Class: Women, Family, and Identity in Imperial Germany*. New York: Oxford UP, 1991.

Kasten, Jürgen, and Armin Loacker, eds. *Richard Oswald: Kino zwischen Spektakel, Aufklärung und Unterhaltung.* Vienna: Verlag Filmarchiv Austria, 2005.
Kater, Michael H. *Different Drummers: Jazz in the Culture of Nazi Germany.* New York: Oxford University Press, 1992.
Kessel, Martina. "Race and Humor in Nazi Germany." In *Beyond the Racial State: Rethinking Nazi Germany*, edited by Devin O. Pendas, Mark Roseman, and Richard F. Wetzell, 380–401. Cambridge: Cambridge University Press, 2017.
King, Geoff. *Film Comedy.* London: Wallflower Press, 2002.
Kleinhans, Bernd. *Ein Volk, ein Reich, ein Kino: Lichtspiel in der braunen Provinz.* Cologne: PapyRossa Verlag, 2003.
Klemperer, Viktor. *I Will Bear Witness: A Diary of The Nazi Years.* 2 vols. New York: Modern Library, 1999.
Klotz, Marcia. "Epistemological Ambiguity and the Fascist Text: *Jew Süss, Carl Peters*, and *Ohm Krüger*." *New German Critique* 74 (1998): 91–124.
Klüger, Ruth. *Still Alive: A Holocaust Girlhood Remembered.* New York: The Feminist Press, 2003.
Koonz, Claudia. *The Nazi Conscience.* Cambridge, MA: Belknap Press, 2003.
Koop, Volker. *Warum Hitler King Kong Liebte, aber den Deutschen Micky Maus verbot: Die geheimen Lieblingsfilme der Nazi-Elite.* Berlin: be.bra verlag, 2015.
Körner, Torsten. *Ein guter Freund: Heinz Rühmann. Biographie.* Berlin: Aufbau, 2001.
Kreimeier, Klaus. "Antisemitismus im nationalsozialistischen Film." In *Jüdische Figuren in Film und Karikatur: Die Rothschilds und Joseph Süß Oppenheimer*, edited by Cilly Kugelmann und Fritz Backhaus, 135–57. Frankfurt/Main: Jüdisches Museum, 1996.
———. "Von Henny Porten zu Zarah Leander. Filmgenres und Genrefilm in der Weimarer Republik und im Nationalsozialismus." *Montage/av* 3, no. 2 (1994): 41–54.
———. *Die Ufa-Story: Geschichte eines Filmkonzerns.* Frankfurt/Main: Fischer Taschenbuch Verlag, 2002.
———. *The Ufa Story.* New York: Hill & Wang, 1996.
Kruse, Joseph A. "'Man kann ruhig darüber sprechen. Heitere Geschichten und Plaudereien': Heinrich Spoerls kleinste Formate." In *Heinrich Spoerl: Buch- Bühne-Leinwand*, edited by Joseph A. Kruse, 35–44. Düsseldorf: Droste Verlag, 2004.
Krutnik, Frank, ed. *Hollywood Comedians: The Film Reader.* London: Routledge, 2003.
Kuzniar, Alice. *The Queer German Cinema.* Stanford, CT: Stanford University Press, 2000.
Langbehn, Volker M., ed. *German Colonialism, Visual Culture, and Modern Memory.* New York: Routledge, 2010.
Lange, Matthew. *Antisemitic Elements in the Critique of Capitalism in German Culture, 1850–1933.* Bern: Peter Lang, 2007.
Lauckner, Nancy A. "The Surrogate Jew in the Postwar German Novel," *Monatshefte* 66, no. 2 (Summer 1974): 133–44.
Leiser, Erwin. *"Deutschland, erwache!" Propaganda im Film des Dritten Reiches.* Reinbek bei Hamburg: Rowohlt, 1968.
Lendvai, Paul. *Anti-Semitism in Eastern Europe.* London: MacDonald, 1971.
Levi, Primo. *The Drowned and the Saved.* New York: Simon & Schuster, 1989.
Levitt, Laura. "Redressing Jewish Difference in Tania Modelski's 'Cinema and the Dark Continent.'" *Journal of Religion and Film* 1, no. 2 (October 1997): article 5 (n.p.).
Lionis, Chrisoula. *Laughter in Occupied Palestine: Comedy and Identity in Art and Film.* London: I.B. Tauris, 2016.

Lipiner, Michael. "American Jews: The True Hollywood Story." *Haaretz*, February 27, 2014. https://www.haaretz.com/israel-news/culture/leisure/.premium-1.576635.
Loentz, Elizabeth. "The Literary Double Life of Clementine Krämer: German-Jewish Activist and Bavarian 'Heimat' and Dialect Writer." *Nexus: Essays in German-Jewish Studies* 1 (2011): 109–36.
Longerich, Peter. *Goebbels: A Biography.* New York: Random House, 2010.
Lowry, Stephen, and Helmut Korte. *Der Filmstar: Brigitte Bardot, James Dean, Götz George, Heinz Rühmann, Romy Schneider, Hanna Schygulla und neuere Stars.* Stuttgart: J.B. Metzler, 2000.
Lowry, Stephen. "Heinz Rühmann – The Archetypal German." In *The German Cinema Book*, edited by Tim Bergfelder, Erica Carter, and Deniz Göktürk, 81–89. London: BFI, 2002.
———. *Pathos und Politik: Ideologie in Spielfilmen des Nationalsozialismus.* Tübingen: Niemeyer, 1991.
Makela, Maria. "The Rise and Fall of the Flapper Dress: Nationalism and Anti-Semitism in Early-Twentieth-Century Discourses on German Fashion." *Journal of Popular Culture* 34, no. 3 (Winter 2000): 183–208.
Marin, Bernd. "'Anti-Semitism without Anti-Semites'? Austria as a Case in Point." *Political Psychology* 2, no. 2 (Summer 1980): 57–74.
Martin, Benjamin G. *The Nazi-Fascist New Order for European Culture.* Cambridge, MA: Harvard University Press, 2016.
Matthews, Nicole. *Comic Politics: Gender in Hollywood Comedy After the New Right.* Manchester: Manchester University Press, 2000.
Medhurst, Andy. *A National Joke: Popular Comedy and English Cultural Identities.* London: Routledge, 2007.
Mersch, Britta. "Uni-Kultfilm 'Feuerzangenbowle': Jeder nor einen wönzigen Schlock." *Spiegel Online*, December 18, 2006. http://www.spiegel.de/unispiegel/wunderbar/uni-kultfilm-feuerzangenbowle-jeder-nor-einen-woenzigen-schlock-a-454719.html.
Merzinger, Patrick. *Nationalsozialistische Satire und "Deutscher Humor": Politische Bedeutung und Öffentlichkeit populärer Unterhaltung 1931–1945.* Stuttgart: Franz Steiner Verlag, 2010.
Meyer-Sickendiek, Burkhard, and Gunnar Och, eds. *Der jüdische Witz: Zur unabgegoltenen Problematik einer alten Kategorie.* Paderborn: Wilhelm Fink, 2015.
Moeller, Felix. *Der Filmminister: Goebbels und der Film im Dritten Reich.* Berlin: Henschel, 1998.
Moltke, Johannes von. "Camping in the Art Closet: The Politics of Camp and Nation in German Film." *New German Critique* 63 (Fall 1994): 76–106.
Morreall, John. "Philosophy of Humor." *The Stanford Encyclopedia of Philosophy*, December 21, 2016. http://plato.stanford.edu/archives/spr2013/entries/humor/.
Motadel, David. *Islam and Nazi Germany's War.* Cambridge, MA: Harvard University Press, 2014.
Neubauer, Hans-Joachim. *Judenfiguren: Drama und Theater im frühen 19. Jahrhundert.* Frankfurt/Main: Campus-Verlag, 1994.
Newton, Esther. *Mother Camp: Female Impersonators in America.* Englewood Cliffs: Prentice-Hall, 1972.
Nicosia, Francis R. *Nazi Germany and the Arab World.* Cambridge: Cambridge University Press, 2014.

Noack, Frank. "Retrospektive Laurel und Hardy im Berliner Babylon." *Der Tagespiegel,* June 13, 2015. http://www.tagesspiegel.de/kultur/retrospektive-laurel-und-hardy-im-berliner-babylon-suesser-matsch-ernster-quatsch/11912890.html.

Noonan, Peggy. "Trump is Woody Allen without the Humor." *The Wall Street Journal,* July 27, 2017. https://www.wsj.com/articles/trump-is-woody-allen-without-the-humor-1501193193.

O'Brien, Mary-Elizabeth. *Nazi Cinema as Enchantment: The Politics of Entertainment in the Third Reich.* Rochester, NY: Camden House, 2004.

Osten, Ulrich von der. *NS-Filme im Kontext sehen! "staatspolitisch besonders wertvolle" Filme der Jahre 1934–1938.* Munich: Diskurs-Film-Verlag Schaudig und Ledig, 1998.

Otte, Marline. *Jewish Identities in German Popular Entertainment, 1890–1933.* New York: Cambridge University Press, 2006.

Overy, R. J. *The Nazi Economic Recovery 1932–1938.* Cambridge: Cambridge University Press, 1996.

Pearse, Holly A. "Charlie Chaplin: Jewish or Goyish?" *Jewish Quarterly: Contemporary Politics, Writing, and Culture,* November 26, 2010. http://jewishquarterly.org/2010/11/charlie-chaplin-jewish-or-goyish/.

Peregrin, Jaroslav. *Inferentialism: Why Rules Matter.* London: Palgrave Macmillan, 2014.

Phillips, M. S. "Nazi Control of the German Film Industry." *Journal of European Studies* 1, no. 1 (1971): 37–68.

Poblete, Juan, and Juana Suárez, eds. *Humor in Latin American Cinema.* New York: Palgrave Macmillan, 2016.

Prawer, S. S. *Between Two Worlds: The Jewish Presence in German and Austrian Film, 1910–1933.* New York: Berghahn Books, 2005.

Prazan, Michaël. *L'écriture génocidaire: l'antisémitisme en style et en discours, de l'affaire Dreyfus au 11 septembre 2001.* Paris: Calmann-Lévy, 2005.

Quaresima, Leonardo. "Der Film im Dritten Reich. Moderne, Amerikanismus, Unterhaltungsfilm." *Montage/av* 3, no. 2 (1994): 5–22.

Rappeport, Alan. "Donald Trump Deletes Tweet Showing Hillary Clinton and Star of David Shape." *The New York Times,* July 2, 2016. https://www.nytimes.com/2016/07/03/us/politics/trump-clinton-star-of-david.html.

Reid, Mark A. *Redefining Black Film.* Berkeley: University of California Press, 1993.

Reimer, Robert C., ed. *Cultural History through a National Socialist Lens: Essays on the Cinema of the Third Reich.* Rochester: Camden House, 2000.

Reisaus, Joachim. "Die Wiederkehr der 'Blume von Hawai' [sic]: Paul Abrahams Operette in Leipzig wiederentdeckt." *LeipzigAlmanach: das Online-Feuilleton,* April 5, 2004. http://www.leipzig-almanach.de/cgi-bin/vm/vio.matrix?kd=2679aa66a707cea&el=654331919.

Rentschler, Eric. *The Ministry of Illusion: Nazi Cinema and Its Afterlife.* Cambridge: Harvard UP, 1996.

"Republican Chutzpah, from Donald Trump to Mitch McConnell." *New York Daily News,* February 8, 2017. http://www.nydailynews.com/opinion/republican-chutzpah-donald-trump-mitch-mcconnell-article-1.2967666.

Reskin, Barbara. "2002 Presidential Address: Including Mechanisms in our Models of Ascriptive Inequality." *American Sociological Review* 68 (February 2003): 1–21.

Reuveni, Gideon, and Sarah Wobick-Segev, eds. *The Economy in Jewish History: New Perspectives on the Interrelationship between Ethnicity and Economic Life.* New York: Berghahn Books, 2011.

Robertson, Pamela. *Guilty Pleasures: Feminist Camp from Mae West to Madonna*. Durham: Duke UP, 1996.
Robinson, Amy. "It Takes One to Know One: Passing and Communities of Common Interest." *Critical Inquiry* 20 (Summer 1994): 715–36.
Rogin, Michael. *Blackface, White Noise: Jewish Immigrants in the Hollywood Melting Pot*. Berkeley: University of California Press, 1996.
Rosenberg, Roberta. "Jewish 'Diasporic Humor' and Contemporary Jewish-American Identity." *Shofar* 33, no. 3 (2015): 110–38.
Rupnow, Dirk. *Judenforschung im Dritten Reich: Wissenschaft zwischen Politik, Propaganda und Ideologie*. Baden-Baden: Nomos, 2011.
Salt, Barry. "Dissolved Away." *The Velvet Light Trap* 64 (Fall 2009): 79.
Salys, Rimgaila. *The Musical Comedy Films of Grigorii Aleksandrov: Laughing Matters*. Chicago: Intellect, 2009.
Schäfer, Julia. *Vermessen, gezeichnet, verlacht: Judenbilder in populären Zeitschriften 1918–1933*. Frankfurt: Campus Verlag, 2005.
Schlör, Joachim. *Das Ich der Stadt: Debatten über Judentum und Urbanität 1822–1938*. Göttingen: Vandenhoeck and Ruprecht, 2005.
Schmokel, Wolfe W. *Dream of Empire: German Colonialism, 1919–1945*. New Haven: Yale University Press, 1964.
Schöning, Jörg, and Erika Wottrich, eds. *Reinhold Schünzel: Schauspieler und Regisseur (revisited)*. Munich: edition text + kritik, 2009.
Schulte-Sasse, Linda. *Entertaining the Third Reich: Illusions of Wholeness in Nazi Cinema*. Durham: Duke UP, 1996.
Sedgwick, Eve Kosofsky. "Paranoid Reading and Reparative Reading, or, You're So Paranoid, You Probably Think this Essay is About You." In *Touching Feeling: Affect, Pedagogy, Performativity*, 124–51. Durham, NC: Duke University Press, 2003.
———. *Epistemology of the Closet*. Berkeley: University of California Press, 1990.
Seeßlen, Georg. *Klassiker der Filmkomik: Geschichte und Mythologie des komischen Films*. Reinbek bei Hamburg: Rowohlt, 1982.
Segeberg, Harro. "Erlebnisraum Kino: Das Dritte Reich als Kultur- und Mediengesellschaft." In *Mediale Mobilmachung I: Das Dritte Reich und der Film*, Mediengeschichte des Films Band 4, edited by Harro Segeberg, 11–42. Munich: Wilhelm Fink Verlag, 2004.
Serventi, Silvan, and Françoise Saban. *Pasta: The Story of a Universal Food*. Translated by Antony Suggar. New York: Columbia University Press, 2002.
Shohat, Ella. "Ethnicities-in-Relation: Toward a Multicultural Reading of American Cinema." In *Unspeakable Images: Ethnicity and the American Cinema*, edited by Lester D. Friedman, 215–50. Urbana: University of Illinois Press, 1991.
Sieg, Katrin. *Ethnic Drag: Performing Race, Nation, Sexuality in West Germany*. Ann Arbor: University of Michigan Press, 2002.
Silverman, Kaja. *The Subject of Semiotics*. New York: Oxford UP, 1983.
Silverman, Lisa. *Becoming Austrians: Jews and Culture Between the World Wars*. Oxford: Oxford University Press, 2012.
———. "Beyond Antisemitism: A Critical Approach to German Jewish Cultural History." In *Nexus 1: Essays in German Jewish Studies*, 27–45. Rochester, NY: Camden House, 2011.
———. "Reconsidering the Margins: Jewishness as an Analytical Framework." *Journal of Modern Jewish Studies* 8, no. 1 (March 2009): 103–20.

Simon, Roger. "Trump Fails to Bully, Loses Bluster." *Politico*, September 17, 2015. https://www.politico.com/story/2015/09/simon-says-gop-debate-trump-213764.
Sontag, Susan. "Fascinating Fascism." In *Under the Sign of Saturn*, 73–105. New York: Farrar, Straus, & Giroux, 1980.
Spector, Scott. "Modernism without Jews: A Counter-Historical Argument." *Modernism/Modernity* 13, no. 4 (November 2006): 615–33.
Spitzer, Leo. *Lives in Between: Assimilation and Marginality in Austria, Brazil, and West Africa, 1780–1945*. Cambridge: Cambridge University Press, 1989.
Stahr, Gerhard. *Volksgemeinschaft vor der Leinwand? Der nationalsozialistische Film und sein Publikum*. Berlin: Verlag Hans Thiessen, 2001.
Stargardt, Nicholas. *The German War: A Nation Under Arms, 1939–1945*. London: Bodley Head, 2015.
Steber, Martina, and Bernhard Gotto, eds. *Visions of Community in Nazi Germany: Social Engineering and Private Lives*. Oxford: Oxford University Press, 2014.
Steinberg, Michael. *Judaism Musical and Unmusical*. Chicago: University of Chicago Press, 2007.
Steinweis, Alan E. "Cultural Eugenics: Social Policy, Economic Reform, and the Purge of Jews from German Cultural Life." In *National Socialist Cultural Policy*, edited by Glenn R. Cuomo, 23–38. New York: St. Martin's Press, 1995.
Stratenwerth, Irene. "Vorspiel auf dem Theater: vom Possenspiel der Brüder Herrnfeld zu den Lubitsch-Komödien im Kino." In *Pioniere in Celluloid: Juden in der frühen Filmwelt*, edited by Irene Stratenwerth and Hermann Simon, 147–65. Berlin: Henschel, 2004.
Szobar, Patricia. "Telling Sexual Stories in the Nazi Courts of Law: Race Defilement in Germany, 1933–1945." *Journal of the History of Sexuality* 2, nos. 1–2 (2002): 131–63.
Taschwer, Klaus. "'Lösung der Judenfrage': Zu einigen anthropologischen Ausstellungen im Naturhistorischen Museum Wien." In *Wie ein Monster entsteht: Zur Konstruktion des Anderen in Rassismus und Antisemitismus*, edited by Kirstin Breitenfellner and Charlotte Kohn-Ley, 153–80. Bodenheim: Philo, 1998.
Taussig, Michael. *Shamanism, Colonialism, and the Wild Man: a Study in Terror and Healing*. Chicago: University of Chicago Press, 1987.
Tegel, Susan. *Nazis and the Cinema*. London: Hambledon Continuum, 2007.
Thüna, Ulrich von. "Die deutsche Filmkomödie der Depressionsjahre 1930–1933." In *Photokina 1980 Katalog*, 317–25. Köln: Messe- und Ausstellungsgesellschaft, 1980.
Tirrell, Lynne. "Derogatory Terms: Racism, Sexism, and the Inferential Role Theory of Meaning." In *Language and Liberation: Feminism, Philosophy, and Language*, edited by Christina Hendricks and Kelly Oliver, 41–78. Albany: SUNY University Press, 1999.
Tooze, Adam. *The Wages of Destruction: The Making and Breaking of the Nazi Economy*. New York: Viking 2006.
Trumpener, Katie. "The René Clair Moment and the Overlap Films of the Early 1930s: Detlef Sierck's *April! April!*" *Film Criticism* 23, nos. 2–3 (Winter/Spring 1999): 33–45.
Urwand, Ben. *The Collaboration: Hollywood's Pact with Hitler*. Cambridge: Belknap Press of Harvard University Press, 2013.
Volkov, Shulamit. "Antisemitism as a Cultural Code – Reflections on the History and Historiography of Antisemitism in Imperial Germany." *Leo Baeck Yearbook* 23 (1978): 25–46.
Volkov, Shulamit. *Germans, Jews, and Antisemites: Trials in Emancipation*. New York: Cambridge University Press, 2006.

Waidenschlager, Christine, and Christa Gustavus, eds. *Mode der 20er Jahre*. Berlin: Berlin Museum and Wasmuth, 1993.

Wallach, Kerry. *Passing Illusions: Jewish Visibility in Weimar Cinema*. Ann Arbor: University of Michigan Press, 2017.

Wedel, Michael. "Die entfesselte Stimme: Marta Eggerth und die Tradition der Operette im Musikfilm der 30er Jahre." In *Zauber der Bohème: Marta Eggerth, Jan Kiepura und der deutschsprachige Musikfilm*, edited by Günter Krenn and Armin Loacker, 197–237. Vienna: Filmarchiv Austria, 2002.

Weinstein, Valerie. "Anti-Semitism or Jewish 'Camp'? Ernst Lubitsch's *Shoe Palace Pinkus* (1916) and *Meyer from Berlin* (1918)." *German Life and Letters* 59, no. 1 (January 2006): 101–21.

———. "Dissolving Boundaries: Assimilation and Allosemitism in E. A. Dupont's *Das alte Gesetz* (1923) and Veit Harlan's *Jud Süss* (1940)." *German Quarterly* 78, no. 4 (Fall 2005): 496–516.

———. *Mistaken Identity in Wilhelmine, Weimar, and Nazi Film*. PhD diss., Cornell University, 2000.

———. "Third Reich Film Comedy as a Place of Politics: Masculinity, Marriage, and Mayhem in Karl Ritter's *Capriccio* (1938)." *The Place of Politics in German Film*, edited by Martin Blumenthal-Barby, 85–104. Bielefeld, Germany: Aisthesis, 2014.

———. "(Un)Fashioning Identities: Ernst Lubitsch's Early Comedies of Mistaken Identity." In *Visual Culture in Twentieth-Century Germany: Text as Spectacle*, edited by Gail Finney, 120–33. Bloomington: Indiana UP, 2006.

———. "'White Jews' and Dark Continents: Capitalist Critique and its Racial Undercurrents in Detlef Sierck's *April! April!* (1935)." In *Continuity and Crisis in German Cinema 1928-1936*, edited by Barbara Hales, Mihaela Petrescu, and Valerie Weinstein, 132–48. Rochester, NY: Camden House, 2016.

———. "Working Weimar Women into the National Socialist Community: Carl Froelich's Women's Labor Service Film, *Ich für Dich -- Du für mich* (1934), and *Mädchen in Uniform* (1931)." *Women in German Yearbook* 25 (2009): 28–49.

Welch, David. *Propaganda and the German Cinema 1933-1945*. Oxford: Clarendon Press, 1983.

Westphal, Uwe. *Berliner Konfektion und Mode: Die Zerstörung einer Tradition 1836–1939*. 2nd ed. Berlin: Hentrich, 1992.

Wilson, Rick. "The Trump Scampaign's Only Chance Now is if Hillary Gets Mauled by a Bear." *Heat Street*, June 24, 2016. http://heatst.com/politics/rick-wilson-the-trump-scampaigns-only-chance-now-is-if-hillary-is-mauled-by-a-bear/.

Winokur, Mark. *American Laughter: Immigrants, Ethnicity, and 1930s Hollywood Film Comedy*. New York: St. Martin's Press, 1996.

Witte, Karsten. "Film im Nationalsozialismus: Blendung und Überblendung." In *Geschichte des deutschen Films*, 2nd ed., edited by Wolfgang Jacobsen, Anton Kaes, and Hans Helmut Prinzler, 117–66. Stuttgart: Metzler, 2004.

———. "Die Filmkomödie im Dritten Reich." In *Die deutsche Literatur im Dritten Reich*, edited by Horst Denkler and Karl Prümm, 347–63. Stuttgart: Reclam, 1976.

———. "How Fascist is *The Punch Bowl*?" Translated by Michael Richardson. *New German Critique* 74 (Spring/Summer 1998): 31–35.

———. "The Indivisible Legacy of Nazi Cinema." *New German Critique* 74 (Spring/Summer 1998): 23–30.

———. *Lachende Erben, Toller Tag: Filmkomödie im Dritten Reich*. Berlin: Vorwerk 8, 1995.
———. "Too Beautiful to be True: Lilian Harvey." Translated by Eric Rentschler. *New German Critique* 74 (Spring/Summer 1998): 37–39.
Woods Peiró, Eva. *White Gypsies: Race and Stardom in Spanish Musicals*. Minneapolis: University of Minnesota Press, 2012.
Wright, Rochelle. *The Visible Wall: Jews and Other Ethnic Outsiders in Swedish Film*. Carbondale: Southern Illinois University Press, 1998.

INDEX

Die Abenteuer des Baron von Münchhausen (Gilliam), 249
Abraham, Paul, 68, 69, 71, 82
Adorno, Theodor W., 37
Albers, Hans, 44, 219, 220, 223, 226
Albrecht, Gerd, 187
Allen, Ray, 253–54
Allen, Woody, 103, 247
Alles für Geld (Schünzel), 169
Allotria (Forst), 99, 112, 122, 130, 132
Der alte und der junge König (Steinhoff), 128
American films: alleged Jewish control of, 41; banning of, 7, 112, 216; blackface minstrelsy in, 76–77; German rivalry with, 11, 32n59, 54, 83–84, 97, 100, 112, 122; Jewish difference in, 22–23; Nazi appeasement in, 21–22; percentage of shown in Germany, 97; screwball comedies, 98, 112–13
Americanness, German ideas of, 77, 94n85, 112–14, 120
Ameskamp, Simone, 228
Amphitryon (Schünzel), 101–2, 130
Anders als die Andern (Oswald), 69, 101
Anderson, Benedict, 10–11, 22
Andrews, Julie, 100
antisemitism: in Austria, 48, 222, 250; contemporary, 247–48, 253–54; economics and, 62; Hitler and, 62, 184, 216; inferential, 2, 11, 14–16, 24, 25–27, 36–38, 45–57, 99, 127–28, 141, 149, 154–56, 168, 248, 251–53; "new anti-Semitism" of Wilhelmine era, 12; overt, 2, 3–4, 7, 10, 14–17, 27, 36–45, 51, 55–56, 63, 68, 141, 163, 168, 184; racial, 2–3, 12, 26, 69, 71, 72–73, 80, 141, 161, 192; roots of, 12–14, 39; tropes of, 9–10, 16, 37. *See also* Jewish difference; propaganda
April! April! (Sierck), 29, 130, 155–57, 161, 163–72, 174, 179–80, 188, 190, 199, 209, 234; critical reception of, 163–64, 168–69, 171
Arno, Siegfried, 19, 50, 55, 137

Ashkenazi, Ofer, 20, 23, 79, 109
Die Austernprinzessin (Lubitsch), 165, 168
"authorial passing," 24

Baranowski, Shelley, 186
Beierle, Alfred, 49, 52, 106–7, 140
Beller, Steven, 69, 79
Benny, Jack, 137
Bettauer, Hugo, 199
Betz, Hans-Walther, 70, 233; with Neumann and Belling, 40–42, 47, 57n17, 61, 62
Bewegungsfilme, 90–91
Bhabha, Homi, 78
Bial, Henry, 22–23
Biedermeier period, 203
Biegel, Erwin, 197
Bildt, Paul, 174
Billig, Michael, 9, 21
blackface (and brownface), 73, 74, 76–78, 102, 221
blackness and Jewishness, 72–73, 77, 78, 81, 94n39, 167, 182n52, 249
blind (and block) booking, 86
Die Blume von Hawaii (Oswald), 27, 62, 68–82, 91–92, 102, 141, 180, 188, 190, 209; remake of, 249
Blut und Boden concept, 42, 51
Bois, Curt, 19, 137
Bormann, Martin, 229
Börne, Ludwig, 45, 58n45
Bressart, Felix, 208
Breuer, Siegfried, 194
Brown, Timothy S., 159
Bubendey, Friedrich, 63, 93n17
Buerkle, Darcy, 23
Burns, George, 137
Butler, Judith, 22

Cagliostro, Alessandro, 222
Cantor, Eddie, 137

275

capitalism and Jews, 41, 49–51, 157–58, 203; in *April! April!*, 164, 171; in *Donogoo Tonka*, 173, 175, 179–80; stock capitalist characters, 64–66, 154–55, 164–65, 168, 174, 179
Capriccio (Ritter), 188, 209
Carl Peters (Selpin), 217
Carstens, Lina, 165
Carter, Erica, 7, 136, 146
censorship, 3, 5, 6–7, 19, 22, 134; *Die Blume von Hawaii* and, 68, 78; Krause and, 63
Chamisso, Adelbert von, 233
Chaplin, Charles, 22, 137, 207–8
Charleys Tante (Stemmle), 188
chutzpah, 175, 247
cinema attendance and viewing policies, 6–8, 31n21, 32n38, 216
Clinton, Hillary, 247
Colbert, Claudette, 112–13
colonialism, 29, 72–74, 78, 80, 119, 155, 157, 158, 159–60, 172, 176–80; colonial whiteness, 62, 69, 72, 78–80, 172, 178, 180
"comedian comedies," 136–40
cosmopolitanism, 13, 51, 77; in *Die Blume von Hawaii*, 71–72; in *Viktor und Viktoria*, 104, 105, 106, 107, 110
Coward, Noel, 53
cremation, 228–30, 232, 243
Cruz, Ted, 247
Cserépy, Arsen von, 63, 86. See also *Nur nicht weich werden, Susanne!*
Czeruchin, Thomas, 121

Dachorganisation der Filmschaffenden Deutschlands, 111
Daudert, Charlott, 165–66
Delschaft, Maly, 82, 84, 85
Demandowsky, Ewald von, 145
Dietrich, Marlene, 138
dissolve technique, 225–26, 229, 235–36, 238, 240, 244n2
Doherty, Thomas, 22
Dohm, Will, 147
Donogoo Tonka (Schünzel), 29, 130, 155–57, 161, 173–80, 223; reception of, 173–74, 175, 178–79
Doppelgänger figure, 223, 224, 233, 234
double coding, 22–24, 109

Dr. Mabuse, der Spieler (Lang), 175, 183n72
Dreyfus (Oswald), 69
Dreyfus affair, 22, 34n115, 69
Dyer, Richard, 19–20

Egea, Juan, 10
Eckert, Gerd, 145
Eggerth, Marta, 69, 79–80, 81
Ein blonder Traum (Martin), 67–68, 84
Einmal der liebe Herrgott sein (Zerlett), 138
Einstein, Albert, 61, 228
"epistemic murk," 30, 217–18, 220, 232, 235–43
Erlebnis aesthetic, 7
Ersatz. See substitution
"ethnic drag," 73–74, 80
Der ewige Jude (Hippler), 4, 17, 137, 141, 184, 192–93, 226, 244n2
exhibitions on Jews, 16–18, 33n99, 137, 162, 192
exoticism, 71–72, 82

Familientag im Hause Prellstein (Steinhoff), 169
Feder, Gottfried, 159, 160, 176
Die Feuerzangenbowle (Weiss), 29–30, 133, 213–14, 217–18, 220, 232–44, 244n2; current popularity of, 1; dissolve in, 226; epistemic murk in, 30, 232, 235–43; fascism in, 214, 243, 244n2; Jewish absence in, 30, 232–34; mistaken identity in, 188, 190; remake of, 249
Fidesser, Hans, 74, 75
Filmkreditbank, 5, 50
Filmprüfstelle, 5
film star role in Nazi Germany, 138
Finck, Werner, 165–66
First a Girl (Saville), 100
Fischer, Fritz, 74, 76
Ford, Henry, 114
Frank, Harry, 82
Die Frau meiner Träume (Jacoby), 188
Frenchness, German ideas of: comedy and wit, 49, 55, 145, 148; language, 47, 54, 175, 195; modernity and cosmopolitanism, 47–48, 80, 199–200
Freud, Sigmund, 37, 44, 174
Friedländer, Saul, 39
Friedmann, Semmy, 88

Fritsch, Willi, 113
Froelich, Carl, 130–31, 135–36, 141, 146, 150n19, 154; later career of, 249

Gable, Clark, 112–13
garment industry, Jews and, 16, 33n96, 48, 52, 70, 118, 169–70
gender representations, 64, 79, 91, 167; in *Viktor und Viktoria*, 101, 102–10; in *Wenn wir alle Engel wären*, 129
German comedies: characteristics and functions of, 3, 6, 8–12, 21, 50, 98–99; discrepancy in, 52–53; dominance of, 1–2, 98, 216; drunkenness in, 115–16, 144–45, 170–71, 236; escapist function of, 3, 29, 61, 83, 118, 163, 213–14, 216–17, 235, 241–43; gender shifts in, 102–3, 128; "little men" in, 103, 138–39, 152n69, 249; pedagogical and disciplinary purposes of, 9–10, 21, 55, 63–64, 67, 81–82, 154, 197, 199; persistence of Nazi-era norms, 249–50; varieties of, 98–99, 105
German film industry: alleged Jewish dominance of, 40–42, 47–48, 66, 91; Nazi structure of, 5–6, 40, 49, 97–98, 216
German film journalism, 45–56, 61, 98, 110–11, 122–23
German humor, 21, 27, 28, 41, 48–49, 51, 55, 99, 119, 134, 149–50, 233; dogs and, 105–7; Herrmann on, 53; Kadner on, 43–45, 49, 51–52, 103–4, 140, 141–42, 189, 205, 223; Schwark on, 52; *Viktor und Viktoria* and, 100–101, 103; *Wenn wir alle Engel wären* and, 130, 132, 135, 140–41, 145–46, 148–49
Gerron, Kurt, 137
Gilman, Sander, 94n39, 182n52, 182n65, 198
Gleichschaltung, 5–6, 31n21, 52, 127
Glückskinder (Martin), 28, 54, 99–100, 112–23, 128, 129, 130, 141–42, 188, 209, 234; ersatz function of, 112–13, 119–21; "I Wish I Were a Chicken" number in, 117–19; reception of, 113, 118–19, 122–23, 132
Godden, Rudi, 195
Goebbels, Joseph, 5, 6–7, 39–40, 42, 46, 47, 49, 50, 67, 86, 91, 100, 122, 130, 216–17; on American tolerance, 77; on capitalism and Jews, 158, 160; on *chutzpah*, 175, 247; on film criticism, 52, 54, 98; on Goetz, 54; Krause and, 63; *Münchhausen* and, 218–19; propaganda orchestration by, 216, 232; Schünzel and, 101, 174; Ufa and, 216, 218–19; *Die verfluchten Hakenkreuzler*, 190–91; on white Jews, 162
Goethe, Johann Wolfgang von, 165
Goetz, Curt, 53–54, 115, 123, 139
Goldberg, Heinz, 69
Gotto, Bernhard, 8
Graff, Sigmund, 188–89, 205
Die Gräfin von Monte Christo (Hartl), 94
Gray, Baby, 80
Great Depression, 5, 22, 157
Great Dictator, The (Chaplin), 22, 207–8
Grimm Brothers, 45
grotesque genre, 90, 91
Grünbaum, Fritz, 137
Gunning, Tom, 136

Haehnel, Birgit, 94n39
Hake, Sabine, 3, 79, 102, 139, 182n65
Hall, Stuart, 14–15, 16
Hans Westmar (Wenzler), 90–91
Harlan, Veit, 135, 249
Hart, Ferdinand, 74, 76, 81
Harvey, Lilian, 105, 106, 112, 113, 120–21
Heine, Heinrich, 45, 58n45
Henckels, Paul, 237
Herf, Jeffrey, 215, 217
Herrmann, Hilde, 53, 54–55, 60n103, 123, 140
Herzberg, Georg, 199, 200, 202
Herzog, Dagmar, 187
Hippler, Fritz, 9–10, 21, 55, 162
History Channel, 26
Hitler, Adolf, 62, 77, 111, 138, 159–60; colonialism and, 160, 179; film mockery of, 207, 208; goal to exterminate Jews, 184, 216; *Mein Kampf*, 133
Hitlerjunge Quex (Steinhoff), 90–91
Hitler Youth, 6
Höhn, Carola, 163
Hollywood. *See* American films
Holocaust, 2, 4, 26, 186, 211n52, 228, 229, 250–54; escapist comedies and, 213–18, 231, 240–41; film treatments of, 29–30
homosexuality, 69, 101–3, 182n65

Hörbiger, Paul, 49, 53, 139
Hübner, Herbert, 195
Hull, David Stewart, 86
humor. *See* comedies; German humor; Jewish humor
Hundt-Radowsky, Hartwig, 160

Imhoff, Fritz, 194
individualism, 9, 80, 104, 229
inferences, 15–16, 36–38
innuendo, 37–38
internationalism. *See* cosmopolitanism
In weiter Ferne, so nah! (Wenders), 249
Irmen-Tschet, Konstantin, 221
Islam, 174
It Happened One Night (Capra), 112–13, 122

Jäger, Malte, 193
Jahr, Adolf, 88
jazz, 71–72, 77, 118–19
Jazz Singer, The (Crosland), 76–77, 78
Jerosch, Ernst, 202–3
Jew farce genre, 194–95, 197
Jewish assimilation, 23, 109, 111, 141–42, 165, 190–91; in *Die Blume von Hawaii*, 62, 73, 77, 79–81; in *Jud Süss*, 129, 141; in *Robert und Bertram*, 29, 195–96, 199–200; in other films, 94n60
Jewish conspiracy theories, 159, 160, 173–74, 186
Jewish difference (and Jewishness), 9–25, 38, 42–43, 248; disease metaphors and, 12, 38, 42, 161–62, 178; disguise and, 190–96, 204, 209, 201n22; Germanness vs., 11, 14, 19; kleptomania and, 204; language and, 50, 64, 66, 193–94 (*see also* Yiddish); masculinity and, 102–3, 106, 137, 182n65, 247–48 (*see also* gender representations); as Other, 78, 200, 234; sexuality and, 37, 38, 44, 56, 67, 91, 102, 109–10, 129, 187, 191–92, 196, 200, 201; in *Viktor und Viktoria*, 102–3. *See also* blackness and Jewishness; capitalism and Jews; double coding; "white Jews"
Jewish film personnel, purge of, 4, 5, 19–20, 27, 38–40, 42, 97–98, 125n35, 219, 248–49; *Viktor und Viktoria* and, 101–2

Jewish humor (and comic techniques), 4, 11, 19, 20–21, 27, 28, 45–46, 49, 51, 55–56, 137; Goetz and, 53–54; Herrmann on, 53, 54–55; Kadner on, 43–45, 53, 70; noteworthy comedians, 19, 137
Jewish question, 13, 18, 199, 202
Jewish scriptures, 38, 57n7
Jolson, Al, 76, 77, 78–79
Juden ohne Maske (documentary), 192
Jud Süss (Harlan), 4, 8, 128, 129, 141, 168, 184, 193–94, 197, 205, 217, 222, 226
Junkermann, Hans, 80

Kadner, Siegfried: on German humor, 43–45, 49, 51–52, 103–4, 140, 141–42, 189, 205, 223; on Jewish humor, 43–45, 53, 70
Kaes, Anton, 25
Der Kaiser von Kalifornien (Trenker), 160
Kampers, Fritz, 206
Kästner, Erich, 219
Keine Feier ohne Meyer (Boese), 55
Keller, Josef, and Hanns Andersen, 38, 48
Kemp, Paul, 74, 115, 138–39
Kessel, Martina, 10
Kestin, Erich, 115
Kleider machen Leute (Käutner), 188, 209
Kleist, Heinrich von, 54
Klitzsch, Ludwig, 219
Klotz, Marcia, 30, 217
Die Koffer des Herrn O.F. (Granowsky), 67–68
Kracauer, Siegfried, 163–64
Krach um Jolanthe (Froelich), 44, 99, 128, 130
Kraus, Karl, 45
Krause, Willi, 63, 67, 87
Kreimeier, Klaus, 19, 169, 211n52, 219
Kriminalkomödien, 84
Kulturfilme, 7, 220
Kulturschande, 39
Kuzniar, Alice, 109

Laukner, Nancy, 250–51
Laurel and Hardy, 74, 94n45
Lauter Lügen (Rühmann), 53
Leander, Zarah, 138, 156
Leibelt, Hans, 236

Leinen aus Irland (Helbig), 4, 21, 155, 184–85, 194
Levitt, Laura, 78
Lieck, Walter, 197
Life of Emile Zola, The (Dieterle), 22
Lingen, Theo, 20, 138–39, 249
Lipiner, Michael, 22
Loentz, Elizabeth, 24
Loewy, Ronny, 20
Lubitsch, Ernst, 19, 20–21, 48, 50, 110, 137, 199, 234

Maack, Alfred, 201
Das Mädchen Irene (Schünzel), 112, 130–31
Marenbach, Leni, 142, 147–48
Marian, Ferdinand, 160, 193, 197; in *Münchhausen*, 222–23, 226
Marin, Bernd, 250
Marr, Wilhelm, 12
Martin, Paul, 112, 249. *See also Glückskinder*
Martini, Wolfgang, 200, 202
Marx Brothers, 22, 137
Marxism, 159
Matthews, Nicole, 9
Der Maulkorb (Engel), 133
Méliès, Georges, 226
Melzer, Karl, 52
Merzinger, Patrick, 134
Messter, Oskar, 136
Metropolis (Lang), 221
Meyerinck, Hubert von, 170
Mickey Mouse, 113, 119, 121
mimesis vs. masquerade, 73–74, 81, 199, 206
mistaken-identity comedies, 21, 29, 50, 98, 101, 141, 165, 186–90, 207–9, 233, 249; *Doppelgänger* in, 234. *See also Robert und Bertram*
Mjölnir (Hans Schweizer), 190–91
Moser, Hans, 20, 53, 138–39, 249
Mostel, Zero, 175
Müller, Renate, 102, 104
Münchhausen (Baky), 29–30, 44, 214, 217–32, 234, 242–43; historical sources of, 219, 221; Jewish difference in, 222–28, 231
Die Mysterien eines Frisiersalons (Engel and Brecht), 90

Napoleon ist an allem Schuld (Goetz), 53, 54–55
Nazi economic views, 157–60, 178
Neumann, Carl, Curt Belling, and Hans-Walther Betz, 40–42, 47, 57n17, 61, 62
newsreels, 7, 8, 220
New Woman, 103, 108
Noonan, Peggy, 247–48
Nuremberg Laws, 12, 101, 159, 192, 210n27
Nur nicht weich werden, Susanne! (Cserépy), 4, 8, 21, 27, 62–69, 71, 90–92, 127, 155, 168, 248; *Lieb mich mal in Honolulu* parody within, 66–67, 81–85; reception of, 84, 86–88, 90, 92, 95n71

O'Brien, Mary-Elizabeth, 196, 204–5
Ohm Krüger (Steinhoff), 160, 217
Olimsky, Fritz, 74
Ondra, Anny, 174
operettas, 1, 61, 69, 79, 82
Oswald, Richard, 32n64, 69–71. *See also Die Blume von Hawaii*

Patalas, Enno, 211n52
Paulsen, Harald, 142
Penslar, Derek, 154
Petrovich, Iván, 79
Petterson and Bendel (Branner), 88–90, 95nn84–85, 155
Ponto, Erich, 236, 238
Producers, The (Brooks), 175–76
propaganda, 3, 186, 192; Goebbels's view of, 6; propaganda films, 4, 21, 62–92, 184–86, 192–94
Propaganda Ministry (Reichsministerium für Volksaufklärung und Propaganda), 1, 4–8, 16, 19–20, 24, 61, 91–92, 97–98, 232; the press and, 16, 46; Ufa and, 156

Quax in Afrika (Weiss), 178, 183n75

Raeder, Gustav, 194
Raether, Arnold, 111
Rassenschande, 192, 203
Reichsfilmdramaturg, 5, 63
Reichsfilmkammer, 5, 52, 135

Reichsministerium für Volksaufklärung und Propaganda. *See* Propaganda Ministry
Reichspropagandaleitung, 192
Reisaus, Joachim, 71
Rentschler, Eric, 3, 113, 223, 250
Reskin, Barbara, 26–27
Rex, Eugen, 67, 74, 76, 81
Robert und Bertram (Zerlett), 4, 165, 184, 194–206, 209, 248; Biedermeyer in, 200–204, 212n69; capitalists in, 155, 203–4; mistaken-identity theme in, 21, 29, 141, 186, 194, 204, 205; parvenus in, 165, 169, 196; reception of, 195, 198–200, 202; remake of, 249; Yiddish in, 168, 195, 196–97
Robinson, Amy, 34n129
Rocky Horror Picture Show, The (Shaman), 1
Röhl, F., 122
Röhm, Ernst, 158
Die Rothschilds: Aktien auf Waterloo (Waschneck), 184
Rühmann, Heinz, 20, 49, 53–54, 55, 103, 178; career of, 150n19, 249; in *Die Feuerzangenbowle*, 1, 232–33, 236, 240–41; in *Wenn wir alle Engel wären*, 128, 132, 136, 138–41, 147–48
Rust, Carla, 200

Sais, Tatiana, 199
Salfner, Heinz, 174
SA-Mann Brand (Seitz), 90
Saphir, Moritz Gottlieb, 45
"Schlemihl" character, 233
Schmonzetten, 47–48, 52
Schneider, Albert, 120, 122, 143, 178, 200, 202
Schönhals, Albrecht, 163, 173
Schorlemmer, Heinz, 201
Schröder, Arthur, 200
Schuhpalast Pinkus (Lubitsch), 234
Schulte-Sasse, Linda, 3, 134, 205, 223
Schünzel, Reinhold, 32n64, 101, 105, 110–11, 123, 130–31, 156, 174. *See also Donogoo Tonka*; *Viktor und Viktoria*
Schur, Willi, 66, 67
Der Schuß im Tonfilmatelier (Zeisler), 84
Schutzstaffel (SS), 43, 119
Schwark, Günther, 52, 175
Schweikart, Hans, 53, 54

Sedgwick, Eve Kosofsky, 252–53
Seifert, Kurt, 195
Shakespeare, William, 187, 208, 239
Shaw, George Bernard, 53
Shohat, Ella, 4, 22
Sicherheitsdienst (SD), 7–8
Siedel, Erhard, 166, 168
Sieg, Katrin, 73–74, 80, 206
Siemens, Friedrich, 228
Sierck, Detlef (Douglas Sirk), 156, 252. *See also April! April!*
Silverman, Lisa, 13, 59n77
Sima, Oskar, 74, 115, 175
Singing Fool, The (Bacon), 76
slapstick, 21, 108, 139, 141
social mobility, 81, 163–64
Söderbaum, Kristina, 193
So ein Flegel (Stemmle), 233–35
Spanish films, 10–11
Speelmans, Hermann, 221, 230
Spielhofer, Hans, 61
Spoerl, Heinrich, 128, 132–33, 135, 139, 141, 246n70; *Man kann ruhig darüber sprechen*, 133–34
Staal, Viktor, 174
Die Stadt ohne Juden (Breslauer), 48, 199
Stargardt, Nicholas, 215–16, 217
Stark, Johannes, 160–63
Straaten, Inge van der, 197–98
Steber, Martina, 8
Stips (Froehlich), 249
Streicher, Julius, 38
"structuring absence," 19–20, 24, 99, 218, 219, 232–234
substitution, 2, 4–5, 11, 20–21, 24–25, 27–30, 74, 99–100; *Glückskinder* and, 112–17, 119–22, 141–43

Taussig, Michael, 217, 224
Taylor, Frederick, 114–15
They Won't Forget (LeRoy), 22
Thief of Baghdad, The (Powell et al.), 218
Thimig, Hermann, 102
Three Stooges, 137
Thüna, Ulrich von, 163
Tiedke, Jakob, 49
To Be or Not to Be (Lubitsch), 22, 207–8

Tonfilmoperetten, 69–70, 83, 84
Tooze, Adam, 157
Tran and Helle comic shorts, 7, 216
Traumulus (Froelich), 136
Trump, Donald, 247–48
Trumpener, Katie, 61, 164

Ufa (Universum-Film AG), 101, 110, 131, 156, 216, 218–19, 223–24; *Münchhausen* and, 218–19, 223–24
Die Umwege des schönen Karl (Froelich), 154, 174, 188, 209
Urgiß, Julius, 20
Urwand, Ben, 21–22

Verebes, Ernö, 80
Verordnung zur Ausschaltung der Juden aus dem deutschen Wirtschaftsleben, 7
Verräter (Ritter), 129
Verwechslungskomödien. See mistaken-identity comedies
Victor/Victoria (Edwards), 100, 249
Vihrog, Jessie, 64
Viktoria und ihr Husar (Oswald), 70
Viktor und Viktoria (Schünzel), 28, 99–111, 128, 129, 137, 141–43, 182n65, 188, 190, 209
Volk concept, 7, 42, 70, 80, 111, 158, 204; humor tastes of, 49, 52, 119; movie tastes of, 40, 49–50
Volkov, Shulamith, 12
Volksgemeinschaft ideal, 5, 6, 8–12, 14, 19, 21, 28–30, 37, 56, 77, 138, 154, 158–59, 209, 213; *April! April!* and, 168, 171–72, 178, 179, 234; imperialism and, 172; as "Jewish-free" (*Judenrein*), 215, 248–49; the press and, 46, 47; *Susanne* and, 63–64, 82, 92
Volksstücke, 98

Waldau, Gustav, 49
Wallach, Kerry, 23

Warnecke, Peter, 95n71
Wäscher, Aribert, 108, 175
Weiberreigiment (Ritter), 44
Weimar Republic cinema, 3, 7, 11, 19–20, 51, 61, 62, 83–84, 97, 99; agitprop, 91; commercialism of, 67–68; *Die Blume von Hawaii* and, 68–70; double coding in, 23–24; Jewish presence in, 40–41, 48, 70, 83, 100, 219; *Susanne* and, 63–64, 66; *Viktor und Viktoria* and, 100, 109–10
Weiß, Bernhard, 93n14
Die Welt ohne Maske (Piel), 155, 174
Wenn wir alle Engel wären (Froelich), 21, 28, 105, 128–36, 140–50; drunkenness in, 145; Goebbels on, 129; rating honor for, 28, 105, 123, 128–30, 132, 135, 141, 149; reception of, 123, 130–31, 150n13; remake of, 249; stylistic choices in, 129, 136, 145–48
Westermeier, Paul, 167
"white Jews," 21, 29, 155, 160–63, 168, 203, 204, 249, 251; in *Donogoo Tonka*, 173–74, 176–79
Wilde, Oscar, 53
Witte, Karsten, 3, 112, 114, 122, 163–64, 187, 204, 211n52; on *Die Feuerzangenbowle*, 213, 241, 244n2
Wizard of Oz, The (Fleming), 218
Wohlbrück, Adolf, 108
Woods Peiró, Eva, 11
Wortig, Kurt, 46

Yiddish, 47, 48, 50, 64, 66, 168, 175, 194, 233; contemporary uses of, 247; in *Robert und Bertram*, 168, 195, 196–97

Zantop, Suzanne, 178
Der zerbrochene Krug (Ucicky), 54
Zerlett, Hans, 200, 202. See also *Robert und Bertram*

VALERIE WEINSTEIN is Associate Professor and Graduate Program Director in the Department of Women's, Gender, and Sexuality Studies and affiliate faculty in German Studies, Judaic Studies, and Film and Media Studies at the University of Cincinnati. She is coeditor (with Barbara Hales and Mihaela Petrescu) of *Continuity and Crisis in German Cinema, 1928–1936*.

www.ingramcontent.com/pod-product-compliance
Lightning Source LLC
Chambersburg PA
CBHW050338230426
43663CB00010B/1910